44 0537616 7

D1338630

Loneliness in Childhood and Adolescence

In the early 1960s and 1970s, some authorities in the field of psychology did not believe that children experienced loneliness. This book ushers in a new wave of thinking about loneliness and demonstrates that loneliness is a common, if not universal phenomenon experienced by children as well as adolescents and adults. The book represents a thorough examination of current theory and research on loneliness among children and adolescents, including consideration of definitional and assessment issues, with loneliness viewed as an emotion and as one outcome of social information processing. Other chapters consider children's own understanding of loneliness, distinctions between loneliness and being alone, and the correlates of loneliness in very young children. Both parental and peer contributions to childhood and adolescent loneliness are examined. During the adolescent period, a primary focus is on links between loneliness and various aspects of the development of self, as well as gender differences in the relation between loneliness and maladjustment. In addition to providing extensive coverage, *Loneliness in Childhood and Adolescence* seeks to provide a balanced view of the topic of loneliness by considering some of its positive outcomes. This landmark volume will be valuable for researchers and practitioners in psychology and related fields such as education and it should stimulate research on loneliness in childhood and adolescence for many years to come.

Ken J. Rotenberg is Associate Professor of Psychology at Lakehead University. He is also author of *Disclosure Processes in Children and Adolescents*.

Shelley Hymel is Professor of Psychology in the Department of Educational Psychology and Special Education at University of British Columbia.

Loneliness in Childhood and Adolescence

Edited by

KEN J. ROTENBERG
Lakehead University

SHELLEY HYMEL
University of British Columbia

CAMBRIDGE
UNIVERSITY PRESS

PUBLISHED BY THE PRESS SYNDICATE OF THE UNIVERSITY OF CAMBRIDGE
The Pitt Building, Trumpington Street, Cambridge, United Kingdom

CAMBRIDGE UNIVERSITY PRESS
The Edinburgh Building, Cambridge CB2 2RU, UK   http://www.cup.cam.ac.uk
40 West 20th Street, New York, NY 10011-4211, USA   http://www.cup.org
10 Stamford Road, Oakleigh, Melbourne 3166, Australia

First published 1999

Printed in the United States of America

Typeset in 9.75/12.5 Palatino and Optima in LATEX 2_ε [TB]

A catalog record for this book is available from the British Library

Library of Congress Cataloging-in-Publication Data
Loneliness in childhood and adolescence / edited by Ken J. Rotenberg,
    Shelley Hymel.
        p.   cm.
    ISBN 0-521-56135-3 (hardcover)
    1. Loneliness in children.   2. Loneliness in adolescence.
    I. Rotenberg. Ken J.   II. Hymel, Shelley.
    BF723.L64L64   1999
    155.4′18 – dc21   98-45621
                                                                              CIP

ISBN 0 521 56135 3 hardback

Contents

Contributors

ROBIN F. ABRAMS, Department of Psychology, Emory University, 532 Kilgo Circle, Atlanta, GA 30322.

STEVEN R. ASHER, Bureau of Educational Research, University of Illinois, 1310 S. Sixth Street, Champaign, IL 61820.

JAY BELSKY, Department of Human Development, Pennsylvania State University, University Park, PA 16802.

LISA J. BERLIN, Center for the Study of Young Children and Families, Teacher's College, U-525 W. 120th-Box 39, New York, NY 10027.

SONDRA H. BIRCH, Educational Psychology Department, University of Illinois, 1310 S. 6th Street, Champaign, IL 61820-3952.

WILLIAM M. BUKOWSKI, Department of Psychology, Concordia University, Montreal, Quebec, H3G 1M8, Canada.

KIM B. BURGESS, 183 Children's Research Center, University of Illinois, 51 Gerty Drive, Champaign, IL 61820.

JUDE CASSIDY, Department of Psychology, University of Maryland, College Park, MD 20742-4411.

NICKI R. CRICK, Institute of Child Development, University of Minnesota, 51 E. River Road, Minneapolis, MN 55455.

LUC GOOSSENS, Catholic University of Leuven, Center for Developmental Psychology, Tiensestraat 102, B-300 Leuven, Belgium.

JENNIFER K. GROTPETER, Institute of Behavioral Science #9, University of Colorado, Campus Box 442, Boulder, CO, 80309.

LAURA HAYDEN THOMSON, Children's Assessment and Treatment Centre, 255 Ontario Street South, Milton, Ontario, L9T 2M5, Canada.

ANDREA HOPMEYER, Department of Psychology, University of Illinois, 403 E. Daniel Street, Champaign, IL 61821.

SHELLEY HYMEL, Department of Educational Psychology and Special Education, Faculty of Education, University of British Columbia, 2125 Main Mall, Vancouver, British Columbia, V6T 1Z4, Canada.

LINDA J. KOENIG, Centers for Disease Control and Prevention National Center for HIV/STD/TB Prevention Division of HIV/AIDS Prevention Epidemiology Branch, 1600 Clifton Road, N.E. MS-E45, Atlanta, GA 30333.

BECKY J. KOCHENDERFER, Educational Psychology Department, University of Illinois, 1310 S. 6th Street, Champaign, IL 61820-3952.

DONNA M. KOVACS, Department of Psychology, University of Michigan, 580 Union Drive, Ann Arbor, MI 48109.

JANIS B. KUPERSMIDT, Department of Psychology CB#3270, University of North Carolina, Chapel Hill, NC 27599-3270.

GARY W. LADD, Educational Psychology Department, University of Illinois, 1310 S. 6th Street, Champaign, IL 61820-3952.

SHARON F. LAMBERT, Educational Psychology Department, University of Illinois, 1310 S. 6th Street, Champaign, IL 61820-3952.

MONICA A. LANDOLT, School of Family and Nutritional Sciences, University of British Columbia, Vancouver, British Columbia, V6T 1Z4, Canada.

REED W. LARSON, Department of Human and Community Development, University of Illinois, 1105 W. Nevada Street, Urbana, IL 61801.

ALFONS MARCOEN, Catholic University of Leuven, Center for Developmental Psychology, Tiensestraat 102, B-300 Leuven, Belgium.

JEFFREY G. PARKER, Department of Psychology, Pennsylvania State University, 521 Moore Building, University Park, PA 16802.

JENNIFER T. PARKHURST, 2762 Bella Vista Lane, Boulder, CO 80302.

DANIEL PERLMAN, School of Family and Nutritional Sciences, University of British Columbia, 2205 East Mall, Vancouver, British Columbia, V6T 1Z4, Canada.

CAROL M. ROCKHILL, Department of Human Development and Family Studies, University of Illinois, 1310 S. 6th Street, Champaign, IL 61801.

KEN J. ROTENBERG, Department of Psychology, Lakehead University, 955 Oliver Road, Thunder Bay, Ontario, P7B 5E1 Canada.

JILL L. SAXON, Bureau of Educational Research, University of Illinois at Urbana – Champaign, Champaign, IL 61820.

CONSTANTINE SEDIKIDES, Department of Psychology CB#3270, University of North Carolina, Chapel Hill, NC 27599-3270.

KATHY B. SIGDA, Department of Psychology CB#3270, University of North Carolina, Chapel Hill, NC 27599-3270.

LORRIE K. SIPPOLA, Department of Psychology, University of Saskatchewan, 9 Campus Drive, Saskatoon, Saskatchewan, S7N 5A5, Canada.

DONATO TARULLI, Department of Psychology, University of Waterloo, Waterloo, Ontario, N2L 3G1, Canada.

BEVERLEY TERRELL-DEUTSCH, Psychology Department, Peel Board of Education, North Field Office, 9 West Drive, Brampton, Ontario, L4T 4T2, Canada.

MARY ELLEN VOEGLER, Department of Psychology CB#3270, University of North Carolina, Chapel Hill, NC 27599-3270.

LISE M. YOUNGBLADE, Psychology Department, University of Colorado at Colorado Springs, 1420 Austin Bluffs Parkway, Colorado Springs, CO, 80933-7150.

INTRODUCTION

1 | Childhood and Adolescent Loneliness: An Introduction

KEN J. ROTENBERG

After reviewing the literature, both academic and nonacademic (e.g., popular media), it has become obvious to me that loneliness is an inherent part of the human condition. Most likely, every person experiences loneliness at some time during the course of his or her life, at least in a transient form. Moreover, loneliness appears to be a cross-cultural phenomena, one identified and examined in an array of countries: Australia (e.g., Renshaw & Brown, 1992), Canada (e.g., Boivin, Hymel, & Bukowski, 1995), Belgium (e.g., Marcoen & Brumagne, 1985), Israel (Margalit & Ben-Dov, in press), and the United States (Cassidy & Asher, 1992). The universality of loneliness may well arise, as Baumeister and Leary's (1995) theory implies, from the universal need for belongingness – the need to establish stable social bonds with others who care. In that context, loneliness is the cognitive and affective reaction to the threat to social bonds. Indeed, loneliness has been regarded in the literature as comprising two related components: (a) a cognitive component, comprising the discrepancy between desired social relationships and actual social relationships, either quantitatively or qualitatively, and (b) an affective component, comprising the negative emotional experiences of disorientation, lostness, and loneliness (see Peplau & Perlman, 1982; Rotenberg, 1994). The chapters in this book are guided by this conceptualization of loneliness, although they vary considerably in the emphasis placed on the two components.

Research supports the conclusion that a stable pattern of loneliness poses a serious threat to an individual's mental health and psychosocial functioning (see McWhirter, 1990). This is exemplified by the link between psychosocial maladjustment and loneliness when it is assessed by conventional scales, such as the revised UCLA Loneliness Scale and Asher, Hymel, and Renshaw's (1984) Loneliness and Social Dissatisfaction Scale. For example, loneliness has been found to be associated with depression, alcoholism, obesity, and suicide in adults (Anderson & Harvey, 1988; Peplau & Perlman, 1982; Sadava & Thompson, 1987; Schumaker,

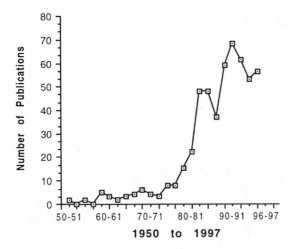

Figure 1.1. Number of publications on loneliness during childhood and adolescence from 1950 to 1997.

Krejci, Small, & Sargent, 1985; Wenz, 1977). Loneliness in children has been found to be associated with being rejected by peers, being victimized, aggression, shyness, and disruptive behavior (Asher et al., 1984; Asher & Wheeler, 1985; Boivin et al., 1995; Cassidy & Asher, 1992).

Given the apparent universality of loneliness and its link to psychosocial maladjustment, it is truly surprising that research on loneliness has emerged rather recently in the history of psychology. Although interest in loneliness dates back several decades (see Perlman & Landolt's chapter, this volume), loneliness in adulthood was examined by researchers in psychology primarily within the past 25 years, and researchers have only made a concerted effort to investigate loneliness in childhood and adolescence within the past 15 years. Figure 1.1 displays the publication rates of research on loneliness during childhood and adolescence (excluding college samples) from 1950–1951 to present day. As the figure displays, there is a scarcity of research on that phenomenon prior to the 1980s. By the mid-1980s, particularly after Asher et al. (1984) published their influential article and scale, there was a dramatic increase in research on loneliness during childhood and adolescence. As shown in Figure 1.1, the research on this topic has progressed at a rapid pace. As is often the case in emerging domains of inquiry, however, the research has been guided by varied theories and by divergent methods and measures; all of which have been published across a wide array of journals. The purpose of this book is to bring these varied theories and lines of research "together" to provide a source for future investigators. To that end, the book includes chapters that cover the prevailing theoretical and conceptual frameworks, new theories, integrations of research findings, and novel findings on the topic. This book is published with the hope that it will help make loneliness in childhood and adolescence a premier topic in the discipline of developmental psychology.

Popular misconceptions have sometimes served to impede research during the course of history. For example, the great psychologist William James in 1980, and various psychologists and physicians during the 1950s and 1960s, viewed infants as passive nonperceivers whose world was one characterized by confusion. Such beliefs delayed the discovery of what researchers now know today: Infants possess an amazing array of perceptual and cognitive abilities (see Mandler, 1990). Beliefs regarding the absence of loneliness in children may have similarly delayed the investigation of loneliness for that period in development. Sullivan (1953) proposed that loneliness first emerged during preadolescence and arose when adolescents failed to establish chumships – close relationships with same-sex peers. Similarly, Weiss (1973) advanced the notion that loneliness was only possible in adolescence; the point in development when individuals strived to achieve attachment to others besides their parents. As a counterpoint to this presentation, let me emphasize that both Sullivan and Weiss have made significant contributions to the understanding of loneliness and social functioning.

One major difficulty typically encountered in emerging lines of inquiry is how to conceptualize and measure the phenomenon under consideration. Not surprisingly, this is one of the challenges faced by researchers examining loneliness during childhood and adolescence. The problem is exacerbated by the fact that whatever theoretical framework authors adopt, loneliness is regarded as a subjective experience. By necessity, researchers assess loneliness from individuals' self-reports of their perceptions, affective states, or both. Furthermore, this task is particularly difficult because the self-reports are provided by children and adolescents. Children have limited linguistic ability and they, as well as adolescents, may express themselves in ways that do not coincide with adult expression and interpretation. In recognition of these issues, the book begins with a chapter by Terrell-Deutsch (Chapter 2) that is dedicated to examining the ways that loneliness in children and adolescents have been conceptualized and measured in the literature. In the next chapter (Chapter 3), Cassidy and Berlin outline the application of attachment theory to loneliness. According to this theory, when children develop an insecure attachment to the adult caregiver, they form internal working models of child and adult that, through generalization, increase the likelihood that they will experience loneliness in peer interactions.

The book includes chapters that present new theories to account for loneliness in childhood and adolescence. In Chapter 4, Parkhurst and Hopmeyer focus on loneliness as an emotion. On the basis of normative patterns of social and cognitive development, these authors propose a model of how loneliness changes with age and of the skill deficit, and other emotions which are associated with loneliness at different ages. In contrast to that orientation, Crick, Grotpeter, and Rockhill describe in Chapter 8 the cognitive, social-information-processing approach to loneliness. These authors propose that children's experience of loneliness is determined, in part, by their establishment of social databases that are compiled from their experiences with peers. As a result of those experiences–database, children develop patterns of making attributions to peers, developing goals, and generating responses to peer interaction. Crick and her colleagues present research indicating that there are links between those cognitive components and children's loneliness. In addition to attachment theory, Cassidy and Berlin draw on transactional principles in their chapter (Chapter 3) to explain how parents affect their children's loneliness. In yet another chapter (Chapter 5), Hymel, Tarulli, Hayden Thomson, and Terrell-Deutsch adopt a phenomenological approach to the study of loneliness in children and examine children's naive concepts and experiences of loneliness. These researchers found that children describe loneliness as affective and cognitive in nature and as associated with a variety of contexts or causes including loss, conflict, broken loyalties, rejection, exclusion, temporary absence, being ignored, and dislocation. It is interesting to note that there were a number of similarities but also some important differences between the ways that children conceptualize loneliness and the ways that researchers in the field conceptualize loneliness in children.

There is a growing interest in the nature and causes of loneliness in young children, and this interest is evident in a number of chapters. This line of investigation may be truly regarded as a new frontier because, as mentioned, loneliness was believed to emerge only by adolescence. Burgess, Ladd, Kochenderfer, Lambert, and Birch (Chapter 6) describe the theory and research pertaining to loneliness in children when they enter school, specifically during kindergarten. These authors review recent research indicating that loneliness in kindergarten children is linked to friendship, peer-group acceptance, victimization, aggression, withdrawal, teacher–child relationships, parent characteristics, and parenting styles. In Chapter 7, Youngblade, Berlin, and Belsky describe their research on the relation between 5- to 7-year-old children's loneliness and their social functioning earlier in development. Similar to research on adolescents and adults, these authors distinguished between loneliness and being alone; they found that the children's loneliness was not significantly correlated with the aversion to being alone nor the ability to be alone. These researchers found, however, that the children's loneliness was significantly correlated with classroom behavior, time in peer settings, perceived peer acceptance, and specific quality of friendship interactions with peers. In some cases though, the direction of the correlations was contrary to expectation.

In Chapter 9, I outline the fundamental theories and hypotheses advanced to account for the parental antecedents of children's loneliness; this refers to the parental behavior and emotional states that affect children's loneliness. I found that the antecedents of children's loneliness during adolescence were different from those in middle childhood. Adolescents' loneliness was linked to their mothers' loneliness, perceived lack of warmth by their mothers and fathers, and lack of their mothers' tendency to promote peer relationships positively. By contrast, children's loneliness was linked to greater warmth and involvement by mothers. The different pattern of findings were interpreted with respect to compensatory parenting practices by mothers.

In Chapter 10, Parker, Saxon, Asher, and Kovacs clarify the distinction between friendship and peer acceptance as factors contributing to loneliness in children and adolescents. Parker and his colleagues complete their chapter by summarizing their research indicating that loneliness in children and adolescents is linked to the qualities of friendship.

The chapters on loneliness during adolescence exclusively deal primarily with three themes: (a) the distinction between being alone and loneliness, (b) the identity development, and (c) the implication of loneliness for mental health and academic achievement. In Chapter 11, Goossens and Marcoen conceptualize loneliness as a multidimensional phenomena and address the issue of whether loneliness in adolescents is linked to ego-identity development. In Chapter 12, Larson considers adolescence as a time when, in western culture, adolescents are pulled between an imperative for social connection and an imperative for individualism. Larson used his well-known method of having adolescents report their emotional state during their daily living to examine naturally occurring instances of loneliness. The research revealed that psychological maladjustment in adolescents is consistently correlated with experiencing loneliness in social contexts but not reliably correlated with experiencing loneliness when they were alone at home. Larson proposes that being home alone serves a positive function for adolescents by providing them with the opportunity for emotional regulation and exploration of their self-identity. Both the chapters by Goossens and Marcoen and by Larson provide some intriguing data on the positive outcomes associated with loneliness and solitute as an opportunity for emotional regulation and exploration of self-identity. Kupersmidt, Sigda, Sedikides, and Voegler report research in Chapter 13 that was guided by an integration of self-discrepancy theory and contemporary findings on the social facets of loneliness. Kupersmidt and her colleagues report finding that loneliness in adolescents was associated with the frequency with which they experienced discrepancies between their ideal self and their actual self, with respect to such domains as having a best friend and being accepted by the peer group. Sippola and Bukowski (Chapter 14) take the approach that loneliness during adolescence is linked to divided self, comprising an individual's experience of being phony and not expressing what he or she really thinks and feels. In support of this hypothesis, Sippola and Bukowski report two studies showing that divided self was significantly associated with loneliness in adolescents and mediated the relation between loneliness and self-disclosure. In Chapter 15, Koenig and Abrams review the research bearing on sex differences in loneliness and report that sex differences appear to emerge by adolescence, with girls demonstrating lower loneliness than boys. In addition, these authors report a $2^1/_2$-year longitudinal study that examined the links between loneliness and subsequent psychopathology and academic performance. Koenig and Abrams report that chronic (consistent) loneliness in girls was associated primarily with psychopathology, whereas chronic loneliness in boys was associated primarily with poor academic performance.

In the final chapter (Chapter 16), Perlman and Landolt describe the links between the theory and research on loneliness during childhood and adolescence (as covered in this book) and the large body of theory and research on loneliness in adults. In so doing, these authors place the theory and research covered in this book within a broad developmental scheme.

Let me conclude by saying that this edited book is truly a collective effort. It represents the convergence of a myriad of theories, approaches, and studies – all designed to reveal the nature of loneliness during childhood and adolescence. The grand hope is that the light that has been shed on that topic will serve to guide research for years to come.

II

THEORETICAL AND ASSESSMENT ISSUES

2 The Conceptualization and Measurement of Childhood Loneliness

BEVERLEY TERRELL-DEUTSCH

Work on childhood loneliness has been fairly late in coming to the field, partly because, until recently, it has been a commonly held view that children are not susceptible to feelings of loneliness. However, recent work (see Rotenberg, this volume) has demonstrated that these assumptions are incorrect and that even young children can, and do, experience loneliness. Given this recognition, it becomes important to consider how children's feelings of loneliness can best be assessed. The present chapter examines three of the currently available childhood loneliness measures in terms of their utility, the psychometric properties of each, and the interrelationships among them. However, because measurement approaches are derived from theory, it is first appropriate to begin with a brief overview of theoretical arguments regarding loneliness and then turn to how these conceptual notions have been operationalized in terms of efforts to assess loneliness in childhood.

Theories of Loneliness in the Adult Literature

Within the adult literature, two major theories of loneliness have gained prominence over the past 25 years: the social needs theory and the cognitive processes approach.

Social Needs Theory

The social needs theory (Bowlby, 1973; Sullivan, 1953; Weiss, 1973, 1974) suggests that loneliness is a response to a relational deficit that gives rise to a yearning for the insufficient relationship. "The longing for interpersonal intimacy stays with every human being from infancy throughout life; and there is no human being who is not threatened by its loss.... The human being is born with the need for contact and tenderness" (Fromm-Reichmann, 1980, p. 342). The social needs perspective suggests that unless one's interpersonal relationships satisfy this inherent set of social needs, loneliness will result. The social needs approach, thus, emphasizes the affective, or feeling, aspects of loneliness yet also proposes that sometimes people may experience loneliness without recognizing the true nature of their distress.

Weiss's (1973) typology, perhaps the best known among those advocating the social needs approach, suggests a fundamental distinction between social loneliness and emotional loneliness. He described social loneliness as a perceived deficit in social integration; that is, failing to feel part of an interconnected group of friends that shares common interests and activities. He described this type of loneliness to be like that of the small child whose friends are all away; feelings of exclusion, marginality, boredom, and restlessness are key. The person suffering social loneliness is driven to "find the kinds of activities he or she can participate in, the network or group that will accept him or her as a member" (Weiss, 1973, p. 22). Questionnaire items designed to assess social loneliness might be "I feel like nobody wants to play with me" or "I always get left out of things."

Emotional loneliness, on the other hand, was described by Weiss (1973) as being the perceived lack of a truly intimate tie, the absence of a close, emotional relationship in which one feels accepted, secure, cared about, and understood. Weiss compared the loneliness of emotional isolation to that of a small child who fears his or her parents have abandoned him or her. Feelings of anxiety, emptiness, and utter aloneness (e.g., "I'm the only one left on the planet") are key. Weiss (1973) described emotionally lonely people as "forever appraising others for their potential as providers of the needed relationship" (p. 21). Questionnaire items designed to tap emotional loneliness might be "I have a friend I can talk to about anything" or "Somebody in my family loves me no matter what."

Weiss (1973) suggested that the state of social loneliness is qualitatively distinct from that of emotional loneliness and, thus, what may be a successful treatment for one will not necessarily treat the other. Social loneliness, he argued, can be remedied only by the development of a supportive, accepting social network and emotional loneliness by the development of a close, intimate relationship. However, Weiss also suggested that people might "change their standards for appraising their situations and their feelings, and, in particular, that standards might shrink to conform more closely to the shape of a bleak reality" (p. 228). Thus, over time, he suggested that loneliness might be ameliorated to some degree (though not eliminated) without the specific relationship deficit, be it social or emotional, having been satisfied.

It should be noted that the distinction made between social and emotional forms of loneliness as described by social needs theorists does not imply that there is no overlap between the two. For example, Russell, Peplau, and Cutrona (1980) found a high degree of common variance shared between emotional and social loneliness. Although conceptually distinct, these two forms of loneliness may be likely to co-occur.

Cognitive Processes Theory

Cognitive processes theory (Peplau, Miceli, & Morasch, 1982; Peplau & Perlman, 1979), in contrast to the social needs theory, suggests that loneliness results not from unmet inherent social needs but from dissatisfaction with one's perceived social relationships. In other words, loneliness results when one experiences and recognizes a discrepancy between what one wants or hopes for in one's social relationships and what one actually achieves. For this reason, the cognitive processes approach has been described as the "discrepancy view" of loneliness that examines loneliness from the "insider's perspective, focusing on how the lonely person perceives and evaluates her or his social life, not on how outside observers might assess it" (Peplau et al., 1982, p. 137). The cognitive processes approach emphasizes, not the affective component of loneliness, but the cognitive, intellectual aspects of the experience of loneliness. People, thus, judge themselves against a variety of standards and when they observe a discrepancy between this standard and what they experience, then loneliness will result.

According to cognitive processes theorists, loneliness results from two broadly defined categories of events; first, changes in a person's actual social relationships (e.g., loss of a loved one), and, second, changes in a person's desired or expected social relationships (e.g., a child moving to a new neighborhood may inappropriately expect to make friends easily). To assess loneliness, as defined by cognitive process theory, one might, therefore, develop such questionnaire items as "There is someone I miss a lot" or "Sometimes other kids won't let me play with them when I want to."

Proponents of this discrepancy view of loneliness suggest that the cognitive appraisals and evaluations people make about their relationships are influenced by their previous history of social relationships as well as their observations of the relationships of others. However, exactly how these two factors influence the selection of the standard against which people compare themselves is yet unknown. Thus, two people with objectively identical or very similar social situations may experience them entirely differently. One individual may be quite happy and content, whereas the other may experience loneliness as a result of a discrepancy he or she perceives between what he or she has in their relationships and what is desired. In Townsend's (1973) words, "Loneliness cannot be regarded as the simple direct result of social circumstances, but is rather an individual response to an external situation to which other people may react quite differently" (p. 183). Hence, one person might be quite contented working in a solitary outpost for weeks on end, whereas another might be lonely in the middle of a crowd.

In summary, in spite of the conceptual differences outlined here, there are three important points of overlap found in the way that scholars in general, and the social needs and cognitive processes theorists in particular, view loneliness. First, it is agreed that loneliness results from a deficiency in one's social relationships. Second, loneliness is a subjective experience and can only be judged from the individual's own perspective. Third, the experience of loneliness is unpleasant and distressing. Although current theories of loneliness have been derived from work with adults and adolescents, recent research suggests that these theories apply equally well to child populations (see Rotenberg, this volume).

Measurement of Childhood Loneliness

Considerable research effort in the area of childhood loneliness has taken the form of scale development. Thus, there are currently at least three very different self-report measures available for assessing loneliness in elementary school-age children. These include the Illinois Loneliness Questionnaire (ILQ; Asher et al., 1984), the Louvain Loneliness Scale for Children and Adolescents (LLCA; Marcoen, Goossens, & Caes, 1987), and the Relational Provision Loneliness Questionnaire (RPLQ), developed by Hayden (1989). See the Appendix for items of all three scales.

The Illinois Loneliness Questionnaire

The most frequently used and cited measure is the ILQ (Asher et al., 1984). This self-report 24-item questionnaire contains 16 primary items that focus on feelings of loneliness and social dissatisfaction and 8 filler items that investigate hobbies and interests (e.g., "I like to read"). Children respond by indicating on a 5-point scale how much each statement is a true description of themselves. Children's responses to the 16 nonfiller items are then summed to create a single loneliness score.

Much of the work in the development of the ILQ was inspired by the work of the team who developed the adult UCLA (University of

California, Los Angeles) Loneliness Scale (Russell et al., 1980; S. Hymel, 1996, and S. R. Asher, 1996, personal communications). Originally, Asher et al. had set out in the development of the ILQ to assess four different dimensions of loneliness: (a) children's feelings of loneliness (e.g., "I'm lonely"), (b) children's perceptions of the degree to which certain important relationship provisions were being met (e.g., "There's nobody I can go to when I need help"), (c) children's perceptions of their social competence (e.g., "I'm good at working with other kids"), and (d) children's appraisals of their current peer relationships (e.g., "I have lots of friends"). However, a subsequent factor analysis suggested one factor only, with the loneliness items loading with the highest values. Because of the diverse content, the authors ended up referring to the ILQ as a measure of "loneliness and social dissatisfaction."

Previous research (see Asher, Parkhurst, Hymel, & Williams, 1990, for a review) has shown that the ILQ has excellent psychometric properties, consistent factor structure across samples, high internal consistency, and good test–retest reliability (Hymel et al., 1983, as cited in Hymel & Franke, 1985).

Examination of the individual items of the ILQ reveals that although the content is variable, most focus on peer relationships exclusively, though a few are worded in such a way as to be interpretable in either a peer or a family context (e.g., "I feel alone" or "I feel left out of things"). The scale includes items representing cognitive appraisals and perceptions (i.e., the cognitive processes approach) and items representing both emotional (e.g., "I have nobody to talk to") and social (e.g., "I am well liked by the kids in my class") forms of loneliness (i.e., the social needs approach). However, because there was no effort to make specific the distinction between these forms of loneliness or the contexts in which loneliness occurs, a single global score indicating whether the child is lonely or not on a continuum is derived. In presenting this unidimensional concept of loneliness, the scale, thus, assumes that there is a fundamental commonality in the experience of loneliness (which varies only in intensity) regardless of cause.

The Louvain Loneliness Scale for Children and Adolescents

The second scale, the LLCA, created in Belgium by Marcoen et al. (1987), is a multidimensional scale in which the authors have attempted to identify variations in the loneliness experience by differentiating among types of loneliness. The LLCA includes four subscales: one tapping peer-related loneliness (Loneliness–Peer); one tapping parent-related loneliness

(Loneliness–Parent); and two subscales that are quite novel, being affective measures indicating how much a child likes or dislikes being alone, the Affinity for Being Alone (Alone–Positive), and the Aversion to Being Alone (Alone–Negative) subscales. Each subscale has 12 items, for a total of 48 items. Children answer on a 4-point scale to what degree each item is true or not true for them. Scores are then totaled for each subscale. Research conducted by Marcoen et al. has demonstrated the psychometric integrity of the LLCA with its high internal consistency and excellent factor structure. In addition, validity data were collected for each subscale, including a set of social, ecological, and intrapersonal variables that successfully predicted variance in children's loneliness scores.

Examination of the individual items reveals that within the peer and parent subscales, there are items tapping affect associated with loneliness ("I feel sad because nobody wants to join in with me") and items tapping both emotional ("I think there is no single friend to whom I can tell everything") and social ("I feel left out by my parents") forms of loneliness. The scale is, thus, consistent with the concepts of the social needs theory. Some aspects of the cognitive processes approach are also tapped by the peer and parent subscales. For example, judging oneself according to an external standard, and finding a discrepancy between what one wants socially and what one has achieved, is evident in the items "I think I have fewer friends than others" and "I want to be better integrated in the class group." Furthermore, self-evaluation (of social competence) and cognitive discrepancies identified between what the individual wants and what they have achieved are tapped by the items "Making friends is hard for me" and "I find it hard to talk to my parents." There are also items that tap children's appraisals of their relationships (e.g., "I feel I have very strong ties with my parents") and items tapping the degree to which children perceive that their important relational needs are being met (e.g., "I find consolation with my parents"). However, neither the form of loneliness nor the nature of the judgments children make about their social relationships is examined separately within the peer and parent subscales, and single scores representing whether the child feels lonely in relation to peers and to parents only are derived.

The affective subscales of the LLCA (Aversion to Being Alone and Affinity for Being Alone) reflect aspects of the social needs approach in that there is considerable emphasis on personal feelings ("When I am alone, I feel bad" and "When I feel bored, I am unhappy"); indeed these subscales are described as affective in nature. However, one of the most interesting things about these two subscales is that in addition to measuring aversion to and affinity for being alone, they assess children's coping mechanisms; that is, how they cope with being alone when it is not desired (e.g., "When I am lonely I go to see other people myself") and what kinds of situations cause them to seek solitude ("When I have an argument with someone, I want to be alone to think it over").

In summary, although Marcoen et al. (1987) have incorporated separate peer and parent subscales to differentiate between the sources of loneliness in children, they have not evaluated social and emotional forms of loneliness or the cognitive processes associated with loneliness within both of these contexts as separate entities. The two affective scales, Aversion to Being Alone and Affinity for Being Alone, tap aspects of the loneliness experience (or, more correctly, the "being alone" experience) through assessment of feelings, cognitive evaluations, and self-appraisals not addressed in any of the other instruments.

The Relational Provision Loneliness Questionnaire

The RPLQ, developed by Hayden (1989), is unique in the field of childhood loneliness research because it was specifically developed to be consistent with Weiss's (1973) social needs theory and the distinction he made between social and emotional forms of loneliness. The RPLQ is, thus, also a multidimensional scale and attempts to assess loneliness by examining children's satisfaction with both peer and family relationships, but within each of these domains, the scale in addition looks at social and emotional forms of loneliness separately.

The RPLQ has four subscales: Peer-Group-Integration (How much does the child feel a part of and accepted by his or her peer group?), Peer Personal – Intimacy (Does the child have a friend he or she can share personal thoughts and feelings with, a friend he or she can count on and trust?), Family Group – Integration (How much does the child feel a part of and integrated with his or her family?), and Family Personal – Intimacy (Is there a family member the child can share personal thoughts and feelings with, a family member he or she can count on and trust?).

There are 7 items for each subscale, with a total of 28 items. The children answer each item on a 5-point scale. The psychometric properties of the RPLQ are documented (Hayden, 1989) with considerable support for its construct validity and high internal and test–retest reliability shown. Item analysis reveals that the RPLQ uses the wording "I feel" in 10 of the 14 integration items and in 2 of the intimacy items ("I feel part of a group of friends that does things together" or "I feel that I usually fit in with my family"), perhaps in an effort to emphasize the affective aspects of loneliness or social dissatisfaction, as social needs theory requires.

However, closer examination suggests that there is no real evaluation of how children feel, no items regarding sadness, depression, anxiety, and so forth. Rather, the RPLQ items tap cognitions and children's appraisals and evaluations of their social situations and, thus, also incorporate aspects of the cognitive processes approach.

However, the assumption underlying this scale appears to be that to the degree that relational provisions are insufficient (from the child's point of view), the child will suffer loneliness. That is, the RPLQ indirectly assesses children's loneliness by assessing their perceived lack of social support. Thus, the RPLQ could, perhaps, be described as much a measure of social support as it is a measure of loneliness. Indeed, the title of the instrument suggests its dual nature. Furthermore, the fact that none of the items mentions the term *loneliness* or *lonely* suggests that the RPLQ might best be viewed as an indirect measure of loneliness through its direct assessment of children's social support and satisfaction.

Comparison of the Three Childhood Loneliness Measures

To date, no study has considered all three loneliness scales in the same sample. This type of comparison is important because it gives insight into how the three different measures work and whether their inter-relationships are what, intuitively, would have been expected. Further-more, as with any other comparison, the relative merits and weaknesses of each measure will be revealed. Finally, such comparisons may give further insight into the nature of childhood loneliness.

The present study, comprising a comparison of the three scales, addressed the following questions: Does each measure work with the present sample? What are the underlying dimensions in each scale? Are they redundant or do they provide for an assessment of distinct aspects of the loneliness experience in childhood? How do these three children's loneliness scales and their subscales interrelate? Is any new information about the nature of loneliness revealed?

To evaluate and compare the utility and psychometric adequacy of these three different approaches to the assessment of childhood loneliness, Terrell-Deutsch (1991) asked children from 24 fourth- to sixth-grade classes ($n = 278$ girls and $n = 216$ boys) to complete each of the three scales as part of a larger research project on childhood loneliness. Initial analyses were conducted that confirmed the psychometric integrity and factor structure of each of the loneliness scales. Intercorrelations among the various scales, as obtained for the present sample, are presented in Table 2.1.

First to be considered are the relationships among those subscales of the different measures that would be expected to be highly related. For example, loneliness as measured by the ILQ would be expected to be strongly related to Peer-Related Loneliness on the LLCA and to Peer-Group-Integration and Peer Personal – Intimacy as measured by the RPLQ because all of these scales tap peer-related loneliness. That is, children who express loneliness with peers on the Asher et al. (1984) scale would also be expected to report loneliness on the peer subscale of the Marcoen et al. (1987) measure and the two peer subscales of the Hayden (1989) measure.

More specifically, we would expect loneliness as measured by the ILQ to be most strongly related to the Peer-Related Loneliness subscale of the LLCA because both scales provide a global estimate of overall feelings of social dissatisfaction with regard to one's peer relations (with items tapping both social and emotional forms of loneliness). Weaker, though still powerful, correlations between the ILQ and the two peer subscales of the RPLQ might also be expected because the Hayden scales differentiate between social and emotional forms of peer-related loneliness and, as such, would not be expected to relate as strongly to the more global estimates of peer-related loneliness provided by the ILQ. Moreover, although both the ILQ and the LLCA Peer subscale include both intimacy and peer-group-integration items, there are fewer intimacy than peer-group-integration items in both cases. Thus, one might expect that the relationship of the ILQ and the LLCA to the Peer-Group-Integration subscale of the RPLQ would be stronger than the relationship of these two scales to the Peer – Intimacy subscale.

Not surprisingly, as noted in Table 2.1, these five correlations are among the highest found in the entire matrix. The highest correlation obtained (with one intrascale exception) was, indeed, between the ILQ and the Peer Loneliness subscale of the LLCA. Both the ILQ and the Peer Loneliness subscale of the LLCA were also significantly correlated with perceptions of available peer support, as assessed by both peer subscales of the RPLQ, but, again, as expected, with somewhat weaker correlations. Also, as expected in both cases, these correlations were stronger for perceptions of peer-group integration than for perceptions of peer intimacy. Although this finding may well simply reflect the similar content tapped by the ILQ, the LLCA peer scale, and the RPLQ Peer-Group-Integration subscale, it also suggests that lonelier children (at least 10- to 12-year-old children) tended to report more dissatisfaction with being accepted by the peer group (as measured by the RPLQ) than they did with insufficient emotional intimacy with peers. This suggests that lonelier children distinguish between peer integration and peer intimacy difficulties as separate forms

Table 2.1. Intercorrelations of Childhood Loneliness Measures

	Illinois Loneliness Questionnaire (ILQ) (Asher et al., 1984)	Louvain Loneliness Scale for Children and Adolescents (LLCA) (Marcoen et al., 1987)				Relational Provisions Loneliness Questionnaire (RPLQ) (Hayden, 1989)		
	Illinois Loneliness Questionnaire	Loneliness – Peer	Loneliness – Parent	Aversion to Being Alone	Affinity for Being Alone	Lack Of Peer Personal – Intimacy	Lack Of Family Group – Integration	Lack Of Family Personal – Intimacy
Illinois Loneliness Questionnaire (Asher et al., 1984)	—	.75***	.36***	.06	.22***	.56***	.43***	.33***
Relational Provisions Loneliness Questionnaire (Hayden, 1989)								
Group – Integration	.67***	.57***	.32***	.03	.13**	—	.43***	.33***
Peer Personal – Intimacy	.46***	.39***	.27***	−.09	.02	—	.39***	.34***
Family Group – Integration	.39***	.25***	.69***	.01	−.05	—	—	.80***
Family Personal – Intimacy	.33***	.19***	.64***	−.02	−.03	—	—	—

Louvain Loneliness Scale for Children and Adolescents (Marcoen et al., 1987)

Loneliness – Peer	—	.28***	.23***	.35***
Loneliness – Parent	—	—	.01	.05
Aversion to Being Alone	—	—	—	.10*

Note. Ns = 466–481.
*p < .05. **p < .01. ***p < .001.

of suffering and tend to report greater distress with the former. Perhaps lack of peer integration is overall more painful than lack of peer intimacy because of its more public nature. Furthermore, it may be that children who lack peer intimacy can find substitutes for it in close relationships with siblings, parents, or other family or community members, but there is no substitute for more broad-based peer acceptance. Thus, the Peer Personal–Intimacy subscale of the RPLQ, although it does overlap to some degree with the Peer-Group-Integration subscale, tends to be a rather unique instrument with its concentrated focus on peer intimacy differentiated from peer-group integration.

Of additional interest in analyzing the interrelationships of the various loneliness scales and subscales was the finding that the family or parent subscale of the LLCA and the two RPLQ family-related subscales were highly correlated. This would be as expected because all three subscales tap parent-related loneliness. That is, children who reported loneliness in their family relationships on the LLCA Parent-Related Loneliness subscale also reported loneliness in their families on the RPLQ. It is interesting to note, however, that there is not a distinction in the family domain between integration and intimacy, as is found in the peer realm. It appears, as Hayden (1989) has suggested, that children do not make the distinction between integration and intimacy at a family level as they do with their peers, or perhaps that, in families, intimacy and integration tend to co-occur. With these results and these explanations, it is not surprising that a very strong correlation, indeed the most powerful in the entire matrix, was found between the two RPLQ family-related subscales (see column 8 in Table 2.1.).

In considering the relationships among the various scales and subscales examined in this study, it was interesting to note that there was some relation observed between the family and peer subscales across the measures. That is, there were not zero-order correlations across the family and peer dimensions of the various measures. Specifically, there was a moderately strong relationship between peer-related loneliness as measured by the ILQ and the parent-related loneliness as measured by the LLCA. Similarly, there were moderately strong correlations between the two peer subscales of the RPLQ and the parent-related loneliness scale of the LLCA. Furthermore, there were also modest correlations found between the peer-related loneliness subscale of the LLCA and the two family-related subscales of the RPLQ. Finally, there were also modest correlations found between peer loneliness as measured by the ILQ and family-related loneliness as measured by the two family subscales of the RPLQ.

Moreover, when examining intrascale correlations, we found the same pattern. Notably, within the LLCA, there was a modest but significant correlation found between the Peer-Related and the Parent-Related Loneliness subscales. Furthermore, within the RPLQ, too, moderate correlations were found among all four of the Peer Group – Integration, Peer Personal – Intimacy, Family Group – Integration, and Family Personal – Intimacy subscales (see columns 7 and 8 in Table 2.1).

On one hand this pattern of findings may suggest that there was some co-occurrence of loneliness across family and peer contexts. That is, children who are lonely at home may also tend to experience peer-related loneliness. On the other hand, it may be that there is some degree of overlap between loneliness, as measured across family and peer subscales, indicating that perhaps these scales are, to some extent, measuring the same thing. Alternatively, the significant relationships found among family and peer subscales may represent a bias in how children responded to the scales. In any case, the correlations obtained between family and peer subscales of the different measures were sufficiently low (ranging from .19 to .43) as to suggest that these are not identical measures; there are real differences between peer- and family-related loneliness as tapped by these questionnaires.

Of additional interest was whether loneliness as measured by these instruments was related to the affective scales of the LLCA that looked at aversion to being alone (Alone–Negative) and affinity for being alone (Alone–Positive). Relevant data are presented in columns 4 and 5 of Table 2.1. As can be seen, children's aversion to being alone seems to be a unique assessment that was not powerfully correlated with any of the other loneliness scales in the present sample. It was correlated at a significant but weak level with the peer scale of the LLCA, indicating a slight tendency for children reporting higher peer-related loneliness to also report a greater aversion to being alone, but this relationship was not a strong one and did not hold for correlations between this subscale and any of the other peer measures. This finding is, therefore, difficult to interpret. Moreover, further examination of the intercorrelations among the LLCA subscales reveals that children's aversion to being alone is not similar to their affinity for being alone, with a near-zero correlation noted between the two (see column 5). The relationship between aversion to being alone and other indexes of loneliness, then, remains somewhat perplexing.

Finally, with the Affinity for Being Alone subscale of the LLCA, results indicate significant, although modest, relationships with loneliness within the peer group as measured by the ILQ, the RPLQ Peer-Group-Integration subscale, and the LLCA's own Peer-Related Loneliness subscale. This suggests that children who reported greater peer-related loneliness also tended to report a slight affinity for being alone. That is, some children may learn that they like being alone by having loneliness experiences thrust on them, or children who are lonelier with respect to peers may tend to adopt a defensive attitude in order to cope with their loneliness. The relationship found between peer loneliness and affinity for being alone does not, however, hold for parent-related indices of loneliness with near-zero correlations found between these measures. Thus, the relationship between affinity for being alone and other indices of loneliness also remains puzzling and is open to further investigation.

Problems in the Measurement of Childhood Loneliness

There is no doubt that these three scales, the ILQ, the LLCA, and the RPLQ, have been, and continue to be, valuable and useful tools in the field of childhood loneliness research. Between them they address key concepts proposed by the theoretical approaches available at this time. Furthermore, they are attractive research tools because they are easy to use, have been standardized with respect to administration and evaluation techniques, and take little time to administer. Moreover, because of the subjective nature of the loneliness experience, it is unlikely that self-reports could ever be completely usurped by other measurement techniques. However, most researchers will also acknowledge that the scales discussed here, and all self-reports, have inherent flaws that detract from their usefulness and measurement accuracy.

First is a validity issue involving the threat to all self-reports of individuals responding to items in socially acceptable (or defensive) ways; that is, in ways that people recognize as not being an accurate reflection of their feelings and experiences but in ways that reflect more positively on the self. In the field of childhood loneliness research, this would lead to underreporting of feelings of loneliness. Affective–cognitive factors can also cause underreporting of loneliness in that certain children may be less aware of, or less able to recognize, their feelings of loneliness and so fail to report it accurately. For these two reasons, the validity of low loneliness scores may always be suspect. However, as Kagan, Hans, Markowitz, and Lopez (1982) have pointed out, though low scores may be suspect, children who do report feelings of loneliness usually do so accurately. Thus, more confidence can be placed in the self-reports of children who confirm their loneliness than in the self-reports of children who do not.

A second major difficulty in the field of childhood loneliness research is the fact that there is not yet available a loneliness scale that clearly differentiates between loneliness and self-concept of social competency with peers. Item analysis of the three measures described here has shown that the bulk of the items relate more to children's beliefs about their social competency with peers and their satisfaction with available forms of relational support than they do to loneliness per se, with only a few items on the ILQ and the LLCA (and none on the RPLQ) relating directly to loneliness. In fact, Terrell-Deutsch (1991) found that virtually every item of the ILQ was reflected, either word for word or conceptually, in the Relationship with Peers subscale of the Self-Description Questionnaire (SDQ; Marsh, Smith, & Barnes, 1983, 1985) – a scale developed to measure self-concept. Naturally, the statistical relationship between the ILQ and the Relationship with Peers subscale of the SDQ was extremely high ($r = .80$, $p = .001$). This redundancy of content on two measures purporting to measure different things is troubling.

A third problem in childhood loneliness research is that certain key aspects of the loneliness experience remain untapped by any of the presently available measures of loneliness. For example, variations in the duration of loneliness and specific environmental–situational antecedents of loneliness (e.g., death of a parent, family breakup, loss of a friend, or moving to a new community) have largely been ignored in currently available measures. Fourth, some fundamental theoretical issues remain untouched. For example, although there has been some effort to do so in the adult research, in the childhood loneliness literature, there has been a failure to differentiate between the emotional "state" of loneliness and the "trait" of loneliness. If theory is to drive the development of assessment and treatment techniques, then the state–trait distinction is an area worthy of future research efforts.

Finally, loneliness measurement techniques may also be criticized for their general failure to address the issue of validity in any convincing way. For example, although the present study certainly indicates that there is convergence among the various assessments of loneliness during childhood (in the sense that the tests are intercorrelated in meaningful and expected ways), it does not examine divergence among the scales. The one exception would be the near-zero correlation found between the Affinity for Being Alone and the Aversion to Being Alone subscales. Because these scales purport to measure completely different things, their failure to correlate may be taken as evidence of divergent validity. Although a few studies use this convergent–divergent approach in the examination of the validity of instruments (see Schmidt, 1976, and Russell et al., 1980), this approach is rare in the literature and provides a possible direction for future research.

Can Researchers Find More Satisfactory Ways to Measure Loneliness?

Although research looking at issues of the dynamics, characteristics, underlying dimensions, causes, and treatments for childhood loneliness has made impressive gains in this relatively young field, there continues to be a desire, if not a need, for the development of more satisfactory ways to measure loneliness. Some research effort has been directed at developing different assessment methods that omit self-report entirely. Other researchers have suggested adjuncts to self-report methods that, they believe, could improve the overall usefulness of self-reports.

For example, Kagan et al. (1982) have stressed that because children may be reluctant to verbalize or admit to feelings of loneliness, researchers need to consider more indirect indicators of such self-evaluations. Specifically, Kagan et al. have made two suggestions: triad sorting of self and peers and coding of empathic involvement from film data. In the triad-sorting method, children are asked to repeatedly sort all possible (or a representative number of) groups of three classroom peers (including themselves for some groupings) into the pair that is the most alike on the basis of each child's general behavior. A similarity index (the number of times a particular pair of children is put together) is calculated for each child, after which each child is asked to explain individually what the different arrangements of children might mean. Children could, thus, be described by peers as belonging to a lonely category or as falling somewhere along a lonely continuum, with the construct coming from how the child judges him- or herself. The second suggestion of these researchers involves the coding of empathic involvement from film data. Specifically, Kagan et al. have suggested showing children a video of children who epitomize the qualities (or lack thereof) of interest and observing the degree to which the viewer exhibits differential empathic behavior toward the video models (e.g., leaning toward the TV screen, smiling, and verbalizing when the character with whom the viewer identifies appears). Kagan et al. illustrated this procedure with a video about children who did or did not have problems learning to read, but a similar approach could be considered using a video of children who are or are not lonely.

Still, for both of these suggestions (peer assessments and empathic identification), one wonders whether loneliness could ever be clearly and definitively illustrated behaviorally. In addition, there are some who may always question the validity and accuracy of external informants on such an internal state as loneliness. Furthermore, with the proposed coding of empathic involvement technique, the difficulties with establishing reliability and validity on what would essentially constitute a projective test would be enormous.

Weiss (1982) brings us back to the individual's own perspective with his suggestion that new ways to measure loneliness might include his own preferred method that involves holding unstructured in-depth interviews with respondents, asking them to "Tell us about their lives, about times when they are with others and how they feel, about times when they are alone and how they feel. We might then infer from what they say whether they are lonely" (pp. 72–73). He also suggested presenting respondents with potentially loneliness-evoking pictures and asking them to describe what might be happening in the picture, what the person might be feeling, and whether they had ever felt that way, and, if so, how recently and how frequently (p. 73). Responses could then be coded in some systematic way, though, again, establishing reliability and validity for such a projective type of approach would be very difficult. It is with these suggestions, however, that Weiss emphasized the individual as the primary and, some would argue, the only appropriate source of information for such a subjective experience as loneliness.

It is due to this very subjectivity of the loneliness experience that it is unlikely that self-reports, notwithstanding their several problems, will ever be completely replaced by other assessment methods. However, there may be ways that the validity and utility of self-report measures can be improved to help overcome some of their deficiencies. Russell (1982) has suggested, for example, that supplementing self-reports with a wide variety of criterion variables could help to overcome the shortcomings of individual measures. Criterion variables could include such things as external sources of validation from peers, parents, or teacher ratings of children's loneliness or observed manifestations of loneliness, such as peer detachment. Efforts to address issues of divergent validity could also be implemented in the selection of criterion variables, such as was done with the development of the revised UCLA Loneliness Scale (Russell et al., 1980) when it was determined that loneliness scores were unrelated to feelings that are conceptually distinct from loneliness, such as "feeling hard working" or "having wide interests" (Russell, 1982, p. 91).

Alternatively, Epstein (1980) has described how the aggregation of scores significantly reduces measurement error and is, therefore, more predictive than the use of any single measure. He described several different types of aggregation, but the method involving averaging of children's scores over several different measures appears to be the most appropriate application for self-report loneliness research.

Finally, Parkhurst and Hopmeyer (this volume) have suggested that self-report loneliness instruments should be designed with the developmental nature of loneliness in mind so that different measures asking directly about children's experiences of loneliness (e.g., "I'm lonely") are used in conjunction with items tapping the changing social needs, cognitions, and feelings of children at different ages.

Summary

Examination of the ILQ, the LLCA, and the RPLQ together has yielded interesting and important information about the qualities, strengths, and weaknesses of each of the scales and has provided some new insights into the nature of childhood loneliness. Furthermore, some of the problematic aspects of the use of self-reports in general, and their use in loneliness research in particular, have been discussed and some suggestions for the possible improvement of such measurements provided.

Appendix

Illinois Loneliness Questionnaire
Asher, Hymel, and Renshaw (1984)

1. It's easy for me to make new friends at school.
2. I like to read.[a]
3. I have nobody to talk to.
4. I'm good at working with other kids.
5. I watch TV a lot.[a]
6. It's hard for me to make friends.
7. I like school.[a]
8. I have lots of friends.
9. I feel alone.
10. I can find a friend when I need one.
11. I play sports a lot.[a]
12. It's hard to get other kids to like me.
13. I like science.[a]
14. I don't have anyone to play with.
15. I like music.[a]
16. I get along with other kids.
17. I feel left out of things.
18. There's nobody I can go to when I need help.
19. I like to paint and draw.[a]
20. I don't get along with other children.
21. I'm lonely.
22. I am well liked by the kids in my class.
23. I like playing board games a lot.[a]
24. I don't have any friends.

---

[a] Indicate hobby or interest filler items.

Appendix (*Continued*)

The Louvain Loneliness Scale for Children and Adolescents

Marcoen, Goossens, and Caes (1987)

Loneliness – Peer Scale

4. I think I have fewer friends than others.
5. I feel isolated from other people.
7. I feel excluded by my classmates.
9. I want to be better integrated in the class group.
15. Making friends is hard for me.
17. I am afraid the others won't let me join in.
23. I feel alone at school.
27. I think there is no single friend to whom I can tell everything.
33. I feel abandoned by my friends.
35. I feel left out by my friends.
41. I feel sad because nobody wants to join in with me.
47. I feel sad because I have no friends.

Loneliness – Parent Scale

1. I feel I have very strong ties with my parents.
3. My parents make time to pay attention to me.
11. I feel left out by my parents.
16. I find consolation with my parents.
18. I find it hard to talk to my parents.
25. I can get along with my parents very well.
30. My parents are ready to listen to me or to help me.
37. I have the feeling that my parents and I belong together.
38. My parents share my interests.
43. My parents show real interest in me.
45. I doubt whether my parents love me after all.
48. At home I feel at ease.

Aversion to Being Alone (Alone–Negative) Scale

8. When I am lonely, I feel bored.
10. When I am alone, I feel bad.
12. When I feel lonesome, I've got to see some friends.
14. When I feel bored, I am unhappy.
20. When I am lonely, I don't know what to do.
22. To really have a good time I have to be with my friends.

(*Continued*)

Appendix (*Continued*)

---

24. When I am lonely time lasts long and no single activity seems attractive.
29. When I am alone, I would like to have other people around.
32. When I am bored I go to see a friend.
34. I feel unhappy when I have to do things on my own.
39. When I am lonely I go to see other people myself.
42. When I am bored, I feel lonesome.

Affinity for Being Alone (Alone–Positive) Scale
2. I retire from others to do things that can hardly be done with a large number of people.
6. I want to be alone.
13. I am looking for a moment to be on my own.
19. When I am lonely, I want to be alone to think it over.
21. When I have an argument with someone, I want to be alone to think it over.
26. When I am alone, I quiet down.
28. To think something over without uproar, I want to be alone.
31. I am happy when I am the only one at home for once, because I can do some quiet thinking then.
36. I want to be alone to do some things.
40. I retire from others because they disturb me with their noise.
44. Being alone makes me take up my courage again.
46. At home I am looking for moments to be alone, so that I can do things on my own.

Appendix (*Continued*)

Relational Provision Loneliness Questionnaire

Hayden (1989)

Peer Scale

Group – Integration

1. I feel part of a group of friends that does things together.
3. I have a lot in common with other children.
5. I feel in tune with other children.
7. I feel like other children want to be with me.
9. I feel that I usually fit in with other children around me.
11. When I want to do something for fun, I can usually find friends to join me.
13. When I am with other children, I feel like I belong.

Personal – Intimacy

2. There is someone my age I can turn to.
4. There is someone my age I could go to if I were feeling down.
6. I have at least one really good friend I can talk to when something is bothering me.
8. I have a friend who is really interested in hearing about my private thoughts and feelings.
10. I have a friend I can tell everything to.
12. There is somebody my age who really understands me.
14. There is a friend I feel close to.

Family Scale

Group – Integration

1. In my family, I feel part of a group of people that does things together.
3. I have a lot in common with people in my family.
5. I feel in tune with the people in my family.
7. I feel like people in my family want to be with me.
9. I feel that I usually fit in with my family.
11. When I want to do something for fun, I can usually find people in my family to join me.
13. When I am with my family, I feel like I belong.

Personal – Intimacy

2. There is someone in my family I can turn to.
4. There is someone in my family I could go to if I were feeling down.

(*Continued*)

Appendix (*Continued*)

6. I have at least one person in my family I can talk to when something is bothering me.
8. I have someone in my family who is really interested in hearing about my private thoughts and feelings.
10. I have someone in my family I can tell everything to.
12. There is someone in my family who really understands me.
14. There is someone in my family I feel close to.

3 | Understanding the Origins of Childhood Loneliness: Contributions of Attachment Theory

JUDE CASSIDY AND LISA J. BERLIN

Loneliness is a negative feeling, resulting from a belief that others are unavailable when desired. According to Bowlby's (1969/1982, 1973, 1980) attachment theory, children's early attachments to their parents contribute in important ways to children's beliefs about the availability of others. In this chapter, we consider the contributions of attachment theory and research to the understanding of early childhood loneliness. We begin by proposing ways in which attachment theory can contribute to the debate on the existence of loneliness in childhood. We then present a theoretical model of the connections between attachment and loneliness. We describe the ways in which children's attachment-related cognitive representations – of parents, of the self, of peers – may contribute directly to children's loneliness. Next, we describe more indirect pathways between attachment and loneliness: Attachment is viewed as contributing to loneliness through its influence on children's peer relations, and we review the empirical literature showing connections between attachment and peer relations. Finally, within a transactional framework, we consider the ways in which attachment and peer relations interact with a variety of additional factors to contribute to children's loneliness.

The Existence of Loneliness in Childhood

Any discussion of loneliness in childhood of necessity considers whether children experience loneliness. Earlier theorists suggested that it is not until adolescence that individuals experience loneliness. Sullivan (1953), for instance, described loneliness as a "phenomenon ordinarily encountered in preadolescence and afterward" (p. 261) when the need for intimacy in the context of a close friendship develops. Weiss (1973), similarly, argued that "loneliness proper becomes a possible experience only when in adolescence, parents are relinquished as attachment figures" and the individual can identify "unsatisfactory friendly acquaintances" (p. 90). Yet, the very existence of this volume, *Loneliness in Childhood and Adolescence*, indicates consensual thinking that loneliness not only exists in childhood but also that it is an important phenomenon related to child and adolescent functioning. In this section, we first review research that challenges the notion that childhood loneliness does not exist by indicating that children can experience loneliness and by defining the social and psychological experiences of lonely children. We then discuss ways in which attachment theory contributes to an understanding of the existence of loneliness in children.

Empirical Studies of Children's Loneliness

The past decade has witnessed an explosion of research addressing loneliness in children (see Asher et al., 1990, for a review). This research has demonstrated not only the feasibility but also the importance of investigating childhood loneliness. A growing body of studies has illustrated that many children – including those as young as 5 – can demonstrate a sophisticated understanding of loneliness, that childhood loneliness can reliably be measured, and that individual differences in child loneliness relate in theoretically predictable ways to several components of peer relationships including peer group behavior and acceptance, quality and quantity of friendships, and representations of self and peers. Virtually all childhood loneliness research has been conducted in schools, a method that has facilitated studying large cohorts of children, and thus has strengthened the generalizability of findings.

Several studies have provided evidence that children understand the meaning of loneliness. Cassidy and Asher (1992, 1993) reported that 93% of kindergarten and first-grade children could generate pertinent responses when asked about the meaning of loneliness, defining loneliness as a predominantly negative state resulting not only from being in particular situations but also from one's interpretations. The degree of complexity in children's understanding also related to their sociometric status, with greater understanding characterizing popular children (Cassidy & Asher, 1993; see also Hymel, Tarulli, Hayden Thomson, & Terrell-Deutsch, this volume, and Williams & Asher, 1992).

The measurement of individual differences in childhood loneliness has relied largely on some version of the Loneliness and Social Dissatisfaction Scale for Children (Asher et al., 1984) – a 24-item self-report assessment. This questionnaire has proved a sound index of children's loneliness and social dissatisfaction in the peer context (Asher & Wheeler, 1985; see also Terrell-Deutsch, this volume). Evidence of this measure's validity has come from numerous studies linking childhood loneliness to a host of early social troubles, including negative self-perceptions, withdrawal, submissiveness, low sociometric status, and fewer and lower quality friendships.

With regard to children's behavior and acceptance within the peer group, for example, assessments made by classmates, teachers, and independent observers are strikingly consistent in portraying lonely children as less well adjusted and less well liked than their peers. Concurrent and longitudinal relations have emerged between loneliness and isolation/withdrawal (Hymel, Rubin, Rowden, & LeMare, 1990; K. H. Rubin & Mills, 1988; Renshaw & Brown, 1993; K. H. Rubin, Hymel, & Mills, 1989). Studies of childhood loneliness have also revealed connections to sociometric status. Although measures of sociometric status have varied, children who report more loneliness have consistently been depicted as less accepted, less popular, or more likely to be classified as rejected by peers (Asher et al., 1984; Asher & Wheeler, 1985; Cassidy & Asher, 1992; Crick & Ladd, 1993; Hymel et al., 1990; Renshaw & Brown, 1993; K. H. Rubin & Mills, 1988; Rubin et al., 1989). Finally, loneliness has been associated with less harmonious interactions with a best friend (Youngblade, Berlin, & Belsky, this volume; Parker et al., this volume).

The study of childhood loneliness is becoming increasingly multidimensional as researchers have been considering simultaneously several aspects of peer relationships and their relation(s) to loneliness. For example, building on findings of studies indicating that it is the combination of withdrawal/submissiveness and peer rejection that distinguishes lonely children (e.g., Parkhurst & Asher, 1992; Williams & Asher, 1987), Boivin and Hymel (1997) developed and found support for a model, whereby peer status and treatment received from peers mediate associations between social behavior and loneliness (see also Boivin et al., 1995). Additionally, two studies have found that peer acceptance and quantity or quality of friendships contribute independently to child loneliness (Parker & Asher, 1993b; Renshaw & Brown, 1993; see also Parker & Seal, 1996). Finally, links between children's loneliness and children's representations of themselves and others have emerged from several inquiries. These studies have revealed both concurrent and longitudinal associations between loneliness and low perceived self-competence and self-worth (Hymel et al., 1990; K. H. Rubin & Mills, 1988; Rubin et al., 1989), as well as self-blaming attributional styles (Hymel, Franke, & Freigang, 1985; Renshaw & Brown, 1993; see also Crick & Ladd, 1993).

In summary, the research on childhood loneliness has offered compelling evidence of its place in early social development and, accordingly, its importance to developmentalists and educators. Consistent with the propositions of Hymel et al. (1990) and Rubin and Lollis (1988), childhood loneliness appears to be part of a complex constellation of "internalizing" social difficulties that include not only troubled peer relationships but also negative self-perceptions and withdrawal.

Contributions of Attachment Theory

Given empirical evidence of the existence of loneliness in childhood, the question of why it is that children are capable of experiencing loneliness remains. In this section, we discuss the contributions that attachment theory can make to understanding this phenomenon. One problem with previous perspectives on the nature of childhood loneliness is that the proposition that loneliness emerges "only when in adolescence, parents are relinquished as attachment figures" (Weiss, 1973, p. 90) is based on the faulty assumption that adolescents relinquish their parents as attachment figures. Ainsworth (1989) and Bowlby (1988) stated that adolescents and adults remain attached to their parents throughout their lives, even though the nature and behavioral manifestations of these attachments change dramatically. Ainsworth (1990), for instance, proposed that formation of an attachment to a peer in adolescence does not mean "the cessation of attachments to parents, although it does imply change in such attachments in that they no longer penetrate as many aspects of the person's life as they did before" (p. 467). Several studies have shown that most adolescents describe their relationships with their parents in ways that indicate that they still serve as important attachment figures for them. For instance, most adolescents love their parents and feel loved and supported by their parents in return (Offer, Ostrov, & Howard, 1981). In fact, adolescents tend to value their parents' advice more than that of peers and to be more likely to share values with their parents than with peers (Conger, 1977; Curtis, 1975). One study revealed that college students felt as close to their parents as fourth-graders did (Hunter & Youniss, 1982). Another study revealed that 15- to 17-year-olds are more likely to protest separation from their parents than from peers and are more likely to use their parents as a secure base than to use their peers (Hazan & Zeifman, 1994). Thus, within the attachment perspective, it is proposed not that attachments to parents are replaced sequentially by attachments to peers but, rather, that relationships with parents and peers develop as parts of different "behavioral systems" from early infancy. This proposition has important implications for understanding the existence of loneliness in children.

Bowlby (1969/1982) borrowed the concept of the behavioral system from the ethologists to describe the organization of a species-specific set of behaviors that leads to certain predictable outcomes, at least one of which offers clear survival advantage to the individual. Because individuals with a biologically based predisposition to behave in certain ways are thought to be more likely to survive to contribute to the gene pool, the concept of the behavioral system involves inherent motivation and there is no need to search for a more fundamental process or "drive." Behavioral systems important to many species include those governing food gathering, mating, sociability, giving care to young, attachment to parents, wariness of the unfamiliar, and exploration. Bowlby was principally interested in the attachment behavioral system – the system that, when activated, increased the likelihood of the individual gaining or maintaining proximity to an attachment figure. Yet, to understand the attachment behavioral system fully, Bowlby recognized the importance of examining the complex interplay among behavioral systems, whereby activation of one system may reduce the likelihood of activation of another (activation of the wariness system, for instance, may contribute to an activation of the attachment system and a reduction of the exploratory system).

Several researchers have proposed the existence of a "sociable" (or "affiliative") behavioral system that is distinct from the attachment behavioral system.[1] According to Ainsworth (1989), it is "reasonable to believe that there is some basic behavioral system that has evolved in social species that leads individuals to seek to maintain proximity to conspecifics, even to those to whom they are not attached or otherwise bonded, and despite the fact that wariness is likely to be evoked by those who are unfamiliar" (p. 713). Harlow and Harlow (1965) described the "peer affectional system through which infants and children interrelate . . . and develop persisting affection for each other" as an "affectional system" distinct from those involving infant and parents. Similarly, Bowlby wrote

"Affiliation" was introduced by Murray (1938): "Under this heading are classed all manifestations of friendliness and goodwill, of the desire to do things in company with others." As such it is a much broader concept than attachment and is not intended to cover behavior that is directed towards one or a few particular figures, which is the hallmark of attachment behavior. (1969/82, p. 229)

Bronson (1972) referred to affiliation as an "adaptive system" present in infancy and separate from attachment. Bretherton and Ainsworth (1974) examined the interplay among several behavior systems in infants,

[1] Following Greenberg and Marvin, 1982 (see also Ainsworth, 1989), we use the term *sociable system* rather than *affiliative system* throughout this chapter.

including the sociable and the attachment systems, and Greenberg and Marvin (1982) examined this interplay among preschool children. Hinde (1974) described nonhuman primate play with peers, which he identified as different from mother–child interaction, as "consum[ing] so much time and energy that it must be of crucial adaptive importance" (p. 227).

The sociable system, thus, is defined as the organization of the biologically based, survival-promoting tendency to be sociable with others. An important predictable outcome of activation of this system is that the individual is likely to spend at least part of his or her time in the company of others. For humans, when the species was first evolving, survival advantage was likely to have resulted because individuals who are in the company of others are much less likely to be killed by predators (Eisenberg, 1966).[2] The sociable system is likely to contribute to the individual's survival in other ways: Primates biologically predisposed to be sociable with others increase their ability to gather food, build shelter, and create warmth; and they learn about the environment more efficiently; and they gain access to a group of others with whom they may eventually mate (see Huntingford, 1984, for a review). Strong evidence of the importance of the sociable system for the development of young nonhuman primates comes from several studies, most notably that of Harlow (1969) in which monkeys reared with their mothers but without peers were seriously hindered in their social development and could not mate or parent effectively (i.e., reproduce; see also Miller, Caul, & Mirsky, 1967). The sociable system is most likely to be activated when the attachment system is not activated. According to Bowlby (1969/82),

A child seeks his attachment-figure when he is tired, hungry, ill, or alarmed and also when he is uncertain of that figure's whereabouts; when the attachment figure is found he wants to remain in proximity to him or her and may want also to be held or cuddled. By contrast, a child seeks a playmate when he is in good spirits and confident of the whereabouts of his attachment figure; when the playmate is found, moreover, the child wants to engage in playful interaction with him or her. If this analysis is right, the roles of attachment-figure and playmate are distinct. (p. 307)

According to Bowlby (1979), activation of many behavioral systems is accompanied by powerful feelings. For instance, joy is associated with maintenance of an attachment bond, anxiety with a threat to it, and

[2] It seems likely that association with peers arising from activation of the sociable system serves a protective function, even in contemporary society. Ladd and his colleagues, for instance, have provided evidence to suggest that children who have friends or playmates to be with during school (e.g., during recess) are less at risk for victimization–bullying by peers (see Burgess & Ladd, this volume).

sadness with its loss. Similarly, positive emotions are likely to be present when individuals are engaged in sociable interaction. Indeed, studies of infants interacting with a friendly adult woman show that most infants will smile repeatedly within a few minutes (Bretherton, 1978; Bretherton & Ainsworth, 1974; see also Bretherton, Stolberg, & Kreye, 1981). Studies of unfamiliar infant peer dyads show that infants smile at peers as early as 6 months (Vandell, 1980). Given the survival advantage derived from sociable behavior, the association of sad feelings with the lack of opportunity for social interaction would be adaptive. Individuals who feel lonely when lacking a social companion may be motivated to seek out others, thus increasing their likelihood of survival.

The signal function of lonely feelings may also be adaptive (cf. a functionalist approach to emotions; Barrett & Campos, 1987). Lonely feelings may signal to the individual that behavior to change the situation is called for and may signal to others that social interaction is desired. Thus, when a child is faced with the lack of social interaction, loneliness may be an adaptive response, from an evolutionary viewpoint as well as from a psychological viewpoint, because it increases the individual's likelihood of interaction with others. Weiss (1973) described the function of loneliness in similar terms: "Loneliness is a reaction to the absence of significant others based on mechanisms which may once have contributed to the survival of the species and which still are critical to the well-being of individuals" (p. 36).

The debate over the existence of loneliness in children may hinge on how loneliness is defined. In his discussion of adult loneliness, Weiss (1973, 1987) distinguished between "emotional loneliness" and "social loneliness," a distinction also useful in understanding loneliness in children. Weiss identified emotional loneliness as the absence of an attachment figure and social loneliness as the absence of a community (e.g., of friends, kin, and coworkers). A person who lacks an attachment figure cannot fill the void by getting more friends; nor can having an attachment figure compensate for the lack of friends. Evidence for the existence of these distinct forms of loneliness in adults comes from a study by Russell, Cutrona, Rose, and Yurko (1984). Within a behavioral systems approach, emotional loneliness is related to activation of the attachment system, and social loneliness is related to activation of the sociable system. Although these two behavioral systems are fundamentally distinct, there is an interplay between them. For example, when a man's wife is out of town for several weeks, he may feel emotional loneliness; he misses his attachment figure. An evening with a bowling companion may satisfy his desires for social companionship and may also distract him from his longing for his attachment figure, but the two relationships are not interchangeable.[3] Weiss (1973), although perhaps not interpreting the behaviors as we do, described what we consider to be, within the theoretical framework presented here, emotional and social loneliness in childhood:

> The provisions of social integration are distinct from those of attachment in that neither can be substituted for the other. The small boy whose sniffles lead to his being kept in by his mother while the other boys are out sledding, or, even worse, who is told by older boys to go home and not bother them, will not find the presence of a maternal attachment figure to sustain his feelings of well-being. Nor can children be solaced for the protracted absence of parents by the attention of age mates. Children need both friends to play with and parents to care for them. Similarly, adolescents need both a social network to provide engagement and an attachment figure to provide security. (p. 148)

Weiss's (1973) claim that it is not until adolescence that loneliness is experienced seems more likely to be the case for emotional loneliness than for social loneliness. Little is known about changes in the attachment and sociable systems that occur during adolescence. Certainly adolescence is a transitional period and by early adulthood, most individuals view a sexual partner rather than a parent as their principal attachment figure. During this transition, when the adolescent is less satisfied with the parent as the principal attachment figure but has not yet established an attachment relationship with a new figure, he or she may be more vulnerable to feelings of emotional loneliness than previously. It is, however, important to remember that an adolescent with a steady dating partner serving as an attachment figure may nonetheless experience social loneliness if sociable relationships with other peers are lacking. Younger children too may feel social loneliness when lacking satisfying peer relations.

Furthermore, it is important to consider the quality of an individual's attachment when considering the existence of emotional loneliness. It is proposed here that it is not simply having a principal attachment figure that reduces the likelihood of emotional loneliness, but rather it is having a principal attachment figure to whom one is securely attached. It is worth noting that, for adults, simply having an attachment figure (e.g., being married) may not preclude emotional loneliness; the quality of the attachment relationship may play a role. Thus, adults with an insecure attachment (i.e., an unhappy marriage) may be more prone than happily

---

[3] For data and more extensive discussion related to the interplay of the sociable system with other behavior systems, see thoughtful discussions in Ainsworth et al. (1978), Bretherton (1978), Bretherton and Ainsworth (1974), and Greenberg and Marvin (1982).

married adults to experience emotional loneliness and may even be as lonely as unmarried people. Similarly, it seems likely that younger children who lack a secure attachment relationship may also be vulnerable to feelings of emotional loneliness. Given that in most American middle-class samples approximately one fourth of infants are classified as insecurely attached to the mother (van IJzendoorn & Kroonenberg, 1988), emotional loneliness in children may not be an infrequent occurrence.

Asher et al. (1990) have taken a somewhat different view of emotional and social loneliness in children, suggesting that emotional loneliness may be related to the lack of close friendships and that social loneliness may be related to the lack of peer-group acceptance. These authors pointed out that when children (third through eighth graders) talk about loneliness, they use terms related both to intimate friendship ("no one to share your thoughts with") and to group acceptance ("feeling left out"; Hayden, Tarulli, & Hymel, 1988). There is increasing evidence that friendship and group acceptance are distinct components of children's peer relations and that each makes independent contributions to children's loneliness (Parker & Asher, 1993b; Parker et al., this volume). Strict adherence to Weiss's (1973, 1987) definitions, however, means that children's close friendships are not relevant to emotional loneliness because, according to Bowlby (1969/1982) and Ainsworth (1989), these relationships are not attachments. From the perspective of attachment theory, children's relationships with friends and with the larger peer group both serve the sociable system, although in different ways.[4]

In summary, the attachment system and the sociable system are best considered as two parallel systems, both biologically based and developing on parallel tracks from infancy. Observations of both humans and other primates clearly show differences between these two systems in what activates behavior, in what terminates behavior, and in the way behaviors are organized (Bretherton & Ainsworth, 1974; Harlow, 1969; Vandell, 1980). Lewis, Young, Brooks, and Michalson (1975), for instance, interpreted their observations of pairs of one-year-olds as follows:

---

[4] Just because certain relationship provisions are met within a relationship does not mean that the relationship is defined in those terms. For example, because a 1-year-old distressed about separation from his or her mother will direct his or her attachment behaviors to a friendly stranger does not mean the relationship with the stranger is an attachment relationship. Similarly, even though a mother may be a frequent playmate for her 5-year-old, it does not negate the fact that this relationship is essentially characterized as an attachment relationship. Thus, even though a child may at times turn to friends for comfort (Hazan & Zeifman, 1994), these friendships need not be essentially attachment relationships.

"Mothers are good for protection, peers for watching and playing with" (p. 56). Despite these differences (or perhaps because of them), it is clear that both peers and parents are important to children's happiness and that one cannot substitute for the other. An evolutionary perspective based on the notion of behavioral systems provides a theoretical framework that suggests that it is biologically adaptive that this should be so. Children who lack a secure relationship with an attachment figure may be prone to feelings of emotional loneliness from an early age. Even securely attached children may become more prone to emotional loneliness during adolescence as they shift from using the parent as the principal attachment figure and search for a peer to fill that role. Social loneliness, a phenomenon distinct from emotional loneliness, whereby children feel lonely because they lack sociable peers with whom to play and (later) talk, is also likely to be experienced starting in childhood.

Attachment, Representations, and Loneliness

Attachment theory makes a series of propositions about the ways in which individual differences in children's early attachments to parents affect their later abilities to form close, satisfying relationships. Among these propositions are several that suggest the possibility of links from child–parent attachment to children's loneliness, and in prior work we documented a link between attachment quality and loneliness. Specifically, in a longitudinal study of infant–mother attachment and loneliness in young children, we found that 5- to 7-year-olds who had been insecure–ambivalent in infancy reported the most loneliness, insecure–avoidant children reported the least loneliness, and secure children reported an intermediate level of loneliness (Berlin, Cassidy, & Belsky, 1995). We now present a model describing the different pathways through which attachment is expected to contribute to loneliness. All pathways are noted in Figure 3.1. In this section, we describe a set of pathways related to representations. In the following section, we describe a set of pathways related to peer relations.

Key to understanding the representation-related pathways between attachment and loneliness is the idea of internal representational models. According to Bowlby (1979), the development of a representational model begins during infancy when the child forms a model of the workings, properties, and characteristics of the parent. This model is thought to be strongly influenced by the child's repeated daily experiences in relation to attachment, "in fact far more strongly determined by a child's actual experience throughout childhood than was formerly supposed" (Bowlby,

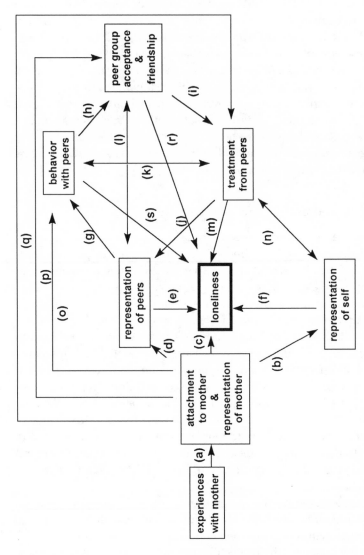

Figure 3.1. Contributions of child–mother attachment to children's loneliness. This figure, with a focus on child–mother attachment, describes only part of a more complex model needed to understand fully the connection of attachment to children's loneliness. The more complex model includes components of the child's attachment to the father and to other important people, as well as a variety of nonattachment-related individual, familial, and societal factors.

1979, p. 117). Particularly important aspects of these models concern the availability and responsiveness of the attachment figure. Thus, for instance, a child with a history of experiences in which the parent is generally responsive will form a representational model of the parent as behaving in such ways (see Figure 3.1, Path a).

Representational models can serve a useful purpose for the child, making unnecessary the construction of a new set of expectations for each situation involving the parent. For example, a child who has a representational model of his or her mother as available when needed may spend less time monitoring her movements than might a child unsure of his or her mother's availability. Representational models are important within social relationships not only because they guide behavior but also because they guide feelings and the processing of information (attention, perception, memory, and interpretation) within these relationships (Bowlby, 1980; Bretherton, 1990; Main, Kaplan, & Cassidy, 1985). These models are thought to become so deeply ingrained in the individual that the ways in which they influence behavior and feelings may become automatic. This situation carries with it both advantages and disadvantages. The automatic use of representational models can be highly efficient. This automatic nature may be a disadvantage, however, when models become inaccurate or outdated because it is difficult to update them if they are not conscious.

The notion of representational models (which Bowlby, 1969/1982, also called "working models") is similar to a variety of constructs within the developmental, social, clinical, and cognitive psychology literatures; for example, to constructs such as schema and relational models (see Baldwin, 1992, for a review; for review of literature suggesting that schemas influence behavior and information processing, see Fiske & Taylor, 1991). As Bowlby pointed out, the concept of these models is particularly similar to Piaget's (1937/1954) object concept, in that neither is a static image but rather a flexible and adaptable construction that permits successful navigation of the environment.

Representational models are thought to define security or insecurity of attachment: A secure child, for instance, is defined as one who has a representation of the parent as generally available and sensitively responsive when needed. Several recent studies have examined attachment and representations. Studies examining the doll-story narratives of preschool children found that secure children, compared with insecure children, were more likely to have coherent representations of the parents as protective and empathic (Bretherton, Ridgeway, & Cassidy, 1990), of the relationship with the mother as important, warm, and serving as a secure base in times of trouble (Cassidy, 1988), and of the child protagonist as having competent responses to separation (Main et al., 1985; Slough & Greenberg, 1990). The attachment-related representations of adults (their "current state of mind with regard to attachment") have been found in several studies to relate to parenting behavior (Crowell & Feldman, 1988, 1991; van IJzendoorn, Kranenburg, Zwart-Woudstra, van Busschbach, & Lambermon, 1991), to affect regulation (Kobak & Sceery, 1988), and to affect the behavior and attachment quality of the adult's child (Ainsworth & Eichberg, 1991; Benoit & Parker, 1994; Crowell & Feldman, 1988, 1991; Fonagy, Steele, & Steele, 1991; Main et al., 1985; van IJzendoorn et al., 1991). Furthermore, parents' attachment-related representations of their own children have also been found to relate to their children's representations of attachment and to the quality of their children's attachment to them (Benoit & Parker, 1994; Bretherton, Biringen, & Ridgeway, 1991; George & Solomon, 1996; Zeanah, Benoit, Hirschberg, Barton, & Regan, 1995).

For Bowlby (1973), the representational model of the attachment figure is inextricably intertwined with the representational model of the self (see also Sroufe, 1990). Over time, the child comes to believe that his or her parent will behave in certain predictable ways. On the basis of these experiences, the child simultaneously develops a complementary view of him- or herself. For example, if the child is loved and valued, he or she comes to feel lovable, valuable, and special. If, however, the child is neglected or rejected, he or she comes to feel worthless and of little value. According to Bowlby (1980),

[The secure child] is likely to possess a representational model of attachment figure(s) as being available, responsive and helpful and a complementary model of himself as at least a potentially lovable and valuable person. Those models will have been built up as a result of happy experiences during his childhood when his desires for love, comfort, and support will have been respected and met. (p. 242; Figure 3.1, Path b)

Empirical evidence of a connection between attachment and representations of the self has emerged from two studies. In the Minnesota Mother–Child Project (Sroufe, 1983), teachers rated the self-esteem of preschool children by using three measures and found that children who had been securely attached in infancy had higher self-esteem than children who had been insecurely attached in infancy. Cassidy (1988) reported a similar association between attachment and representations of the self in a sample of 6-year-olds.

Representational models of parents are thought to be closely linked not only to representational models of the self but also to representational models of at least some other people. This linkage is thought to occur through a process whereby representations of parents generalize to representations of others (Figure 3.1, Path d; Bowlby, 1973; Hazan & Shaver, 1987; Waters, Wippman, & Sroufe, 1979). It is, in fact, this process of generalization that is thought to account for the influence of early child–parent relationships on later relationships. According to Bowlby (1973),

An unwanted child is likely not only to feel unwanted by his parents but to believe that he is essentially unwantable, namely unwanted by anyone. Conversely, a much-loved child may grow up to be not only confident of his parents' affection but confident that everyone will find him lovable too. Though logically indefensible, these crude overgeneralizations are none the less the rule. Once adapted, moreover, and woven into the fabric of working models, they are apt hence forward never to be seriously questioned. (pp. 204–205)

To the extent that generalization of representations does occur, a number of issues are important to consider. What is the connection of representations of specific people to generalized representations? In their earliest relationships, children are thought to have specific representations about the likely availability and responsiveness of a few specific people. That children have specific representations of how people will behave is surmized from the fact that attachment to the mother is not necessarily related to attachment to the father (Belsky & Rovine, 1987; Main & Weston, 1981). According to Ainsworth (1989), once these initial representations are formed, they then contribute to the formation of new representations. Does the child's representation of attachment to the mother generalize to all other types of relationships with all other people? Are there parameters to this generalization? It may be that attachment representations generalize only to representations of other attachment relationships. If so, then, these representations would not be related to peer relationships, as these are generally not considered to be attachment relationships (Ainsworth, 1989). Yet because peer relationships are important relationships for young children and are associated with considerable intimacy and strong emotions (see Asher & Parker, 1989, for a review), attachment researchers have proposed that peer relations are the type of relationship likely to be related to attachment relationships (Sroufe & Fleeson, 1986). The extent to which representations about attachment relationships are carried over to people with whom one has sociable and important but nonattachment relationships needs to be considered and explored. It may be that generalization is more related to certain dimensions of peer relations (e.g., close friendships) than to others (e.g., popular status within a large group).

Despite the central importance of the notion of generalization, relatively little has been written about the nature of this generalization and about how it occurs (see, however, Bretherton, 1990; Main et al., 1985). The cognitive processes through which, according to Piaget (1937/1954), existing structures contribute to the development of new structures are likely to be relevant. Main et al. have described the role that such processes as attention and memory may play. Future research about the influence of experience on brain functioning and the development of neural pathways (Cicchetti & Tucker, 1994; Edelman, 1987; Schore, 1994) will undoubtedly contribute to understanding the process of generalization of representations.

Although there is no evidence that generalization is the process through which the link occurs, there are data suggesting a link between attachment and representations of peers. In a sample of German 5-year-olds, children were shown drawings of stories in which a peer caused a negative incident. The peer's intent was clearly intentional, clearly accidental, or ambiguous, and children were asked whether the peer intended for the negative event to occur. Children who had been securely attached to mother as infants tended to have "realistic or well-meaning" representations of peer intent, whereas children who had been insecurely attached had "unrealistic or negative" representations (Suess, Grossmann, & Sroufe, 1992). In a series of three studies, Cassidy, Kirsh, Scolton, and Parke (1996) provided children at ages 3, 6, and 9 with ambiguous stories (based on stories by Dodge & Frame, 1982) in which the children were to imagine that a peer caused a clearly negative event to happen to them but that the circumstances of the event and the peer's intent were ambiguous. As predicted, representations that the peer's intent was positive were positively correlated with secure attachment for the 6-year-olds and with parental acceptance (thought to be a central component of secure attachment; e.g., Ainsworth, Blehar, Waters, & Wall, 1978) for the 9-year-olds.

Children's representations – of the attachment figure, of the self, and of others – may all relate directly to children's loneliness. First, a representational model of the attachment figure(s) as unavailable as a source of comfort and affection may leave the child with such an emotional void that the child comes to experience a nearly perpetual state of longing for something missing, a state that may leave the child with a fundamental sense of loneliness within all social relationships (Figure 3.1, Path c). Second, representational models of the self as unappealing or unworthy of care might also contribute directly to children's feelings of loneliness. Children who have been unable to elicit comfort and care from their attachment figure(s) are likely to develop a sense of themselves as incompetent in eliciting caring from others as well (Waters & Sroufe, 1983). Ainsworth et al. (1978), having observed that the intense cries of some infants were ignored, proposed that these babies learned that their signals for care would not be responded to and learned that they were helpless in eliciting responses from others. A child with such a model may feel that he or she is not a person whom others (including peers) will like and will thus feel lonely (Figure 3.1, Path f). Finally, representational models characterizing others as more generally hostile, rejecting, or unavailable may contribute to a child's feelings that others are not likely to respond to his or her needs, one of which is for companionship (Figure 3.1, Path e). Bowlby (1988) has described extreme cases of attachment-related trauma as contributing to an increased likelihood that a child might "despair of ever having a secure or loving relationship with anyone" (p. 50). It is easy to imagine that such despair might contribute to pervasive feelings of loneliness. In summary, we propose that it is in part through children's representations of the attachment figure as unavailable, of the self as unworthy, or of others as rejecting that insecure attachment relates to children's loneliness.

Attachment, Peer Relations, and Loneliness

Starting with the initial studies of children's loneliness, researchers have proposed that the quality of children's peer relations would be associated with loneliness, and a sizable body of data has supported this proposition (Asher et al., 1984; Asher & Wheeler, 1985; Cassidy & Asher, 1992; Crick & Ladd, 1993; Hymel et al., 1990; Parker & Asher, 1993b; Renshaw & Brown, 1993; K. H. Rubin et al., 1989). Given these associations between peer relations and loneliness, any factors contributing to poor peer relations may also contribute to loneliness. In this section, we review evidence that children's attachments are associated with their peer relations and, thus indirectly, with children's loneliness.

In examining the connection between attachment and children's peer relations, we include in our model (see Figure 3.1) parts of models proposed by Dodge, Pettit, McClaskey, and Brown (1986) and by Boivin and Hymel (1997). The central components of this portion of the model are behavior with peers, peer-group acceptance and friendship, and treatment received from peers. According to Dodge et al., children's peer-related representations influence their behavior with peers, with more negative representations associated with more negative behavior (Path g; Dodge, Murphy, & Buchsbaum, 1984); negative behavior, in turn, contributes to being rejected by peers (Path h; Coie & Kupersmidt, 1983; Dodge, 1983); being rejected, in turn, increases the likelihood of receiving negative behavior from peers (Path i; Dodge & Frame, 1982; Gottman, Gonso, & Rasmussen, 1975); and finally, given evidence that even young children use knowledge of behavior to build representations (Gnepp, Klayman, & Trabasso, 1982; Heller & Berndt, 1981), it seems likely that experiences of being poorly treated will, in turn, contribute to the child's negative representations of peers (Path j). As Boivin and Hymel proposed (a proposition for which they found empirical support), direct paths from each of these components to children's loneliness also exist (Paths s, r, and m).

In this section, we examine the connection of attachment to three components of this model – behavior with peers, peer-group acceptance and friendship, and treatment from peers – all of which have been linked to children's loneliness. The research reviewed is extensive and multifaceted: There exist contemporaneous and longitudinal investigations of toddlers, preschoolers, and school-aged children. Investigators have examined children's interactions and relationships with unfamiliar peers, familiar peers, and close friends, with data provided by mothers, teachers, independent observers, and peers themselves. Although the findings are by no means uniform, they are strikingly consistent in their illustration of a relation between secure child–mother attachment and more harmonious peer relationships.

Attachment and Relations With Peers

Relations between attachment quality and behavior with peers (Figure 3.1, Path o) first emerged in a series of investigations from the Minnesota Mother–Child Study (see Elicker, Englund, & Sroufe, 1992, for a review). In one inquiry, toddlers who had been classified as insecurely attached 6 months prior were less sociable and less positively oriented toward a secure peer during laboratory free play than toddlers who had been securely attached (Pastor, 1981; see, however, Jacobson & Wille, 1986, for a failure to replicate). Another study of $3\frac{1}{2}$-year-olds reported greater peer competence in children who had been securely attached in infancy (Waters et al., 1979). In another preschool study, teachers rated 4- to 5-year-olds who had been securely attached as higher on ego-control and ego-resiliency than children who had been insecurely attached (Arend, Gove, & Sroufe, 1979). In still another preschool study, 4- to 5-year-olds who had been securely attached infants were rated by teachers as more socially competent than children who had been insecurely attached (LaFreniere & Sroufe, 1985).

Three additional preschool investigations were based on these same children. In one, securely attached children received higher empathy scores than insecure–avoidant children (Kestenbaum, Farber, & Sroufe, 1989). In another inquiry, securely attached children were less likely than insecure children to act as "victimizers" (Troy & Sroufe, 1987). Finally, securely attached children were viewed by both teachers and observers as exhibiting fewer behavior problems than avoidant and/or ambivalent children (Erickson, Sroufe, & Egeland, 1985; see also Fagot & Kavanagh, 1990, for both parallel and contradictory findings). Findings paralleling those of Sroufe and his colleagues have emerged from a longitudinal inquiry conducted in Southern Germany (Suess et al., 1992) and from an intervention study with temperamentally irritable Dutch infants followed up at 3.5 years (van den Boom, 1995). Two European studies in which both attachment quality and preschool behavior were examined concurrently at age 4 (Turner, 1991) and at age 6 (Wartner, Grossmann, Fremmer-Bombik, & Suess, 1994) also revealed similar findings. Contradictory findings, however, have emerged from a recent longitudinal investigation of attachment quality and behavior with peers (Howes, Matheson, & Hamilton, 1994).

In addition to the generally consistent findings of a connection between attachment quality and behavior toward peers in preschoolers, several studies have revealed this connection in school-aged children. In one study, insecurely attached 6-year-old boys were regarded less favorably by both teachers and classmates than securely attached boys; no attachment group differences emerged for girls (Cohn, 1990). In an investigation focusing on teacher-rated behavior problems, 18-month (but not 12-month) attachment group differences emerged for boys, with boys who had been insecurely attached more likely than boys who had been securely attached to be classified aggressive or passive–withdrawn (Renken, Egeland, Marvinney, Mangelsdorf, & Sroufe, 1989). In another study, 11-year-olds who had been securely attached infants were rated by their summer camp counselors as more socially competent than those who had been insecurely attached (Elicker et al., 1992).

Similar associations have emerged in several studies of close friendships. One investigation revealed that children classified as securely attached at age 2 were rated higher on "social responsiveness" during play with a "best playmate" at ages 2 and 5 (Pierrehumbert, Iannotti, Cummings, & Zahn-Waxler, 1989). Another study found that best friendships consisting of two securely attached 4-year-olds were more harmonious than those made up of one secure and one insecure child (Park & Waters, 1989). Additionally, in a recent longitudinal investigation of infant–parent attachment and 6-year best friendship, children who had been securely attached were less likely to engage in negative interactions than children who had been insecurely attached; however, there were no attachment group differences for positive interactions (Youngblade & Belsky, 1992). Finally, in Elicker et al.'s (1992) summer camp study, children who had been securely attached infants were more likely than other children to be judged by their counselors as having made at least one friend during camp (see also Lewis & Feiring, 1989).

Attachment, Peer Acceptance, and Treatment From Peers

In addition to illustrating associations between attachment quality and children's behavior with peers, research has documented links between attachment and two additional components of children's peer relationships that appear in our model: peer acceptance (Figure 3.1, Path p) and treatment received from peers (Figure 3.1, Path q). In LaFreniere and Sroufe's (1985) preschool study, securely attached children had higher sociometric status than insecurely attached children (see, however, Howes et al., 1994, for contradictory findings). In Cohn's (1990) investigation, secure 6-year-old boys were better liked by their classmates (see also Elicker et al., 1992). With regard to treatment received from peers, a study of unfamiliar toddler playmates found that children classified as securely attached were more positively responsive than playmates of children classified as insecurely attached (Jacobson & Wille, 1986). Similarly, in van den Boom's (1995) intervention follow-up, unfamiliar same-sex peers were more likely to make and maintain contact with a secure playmate than with an insecure playmate. Finally, in Troy and Sroufe's (1987) study of victimization, none of the preschoolers who had been classified secure in infancy was bullied.

Underlying Processes

What are the processes underlying the connection between attachment and these various components of peer relations? The role of cognitive representations was described in a previous section of this chapter. Several additional factors may be important. First, parents of secure children may provide their children with more opportunities to establish peer networks, which may in turn provide opportunities for practicing social skills and making friends. Some evidence for this supposition comes from a study of 3-year-olds: Attachment security was positively related to the quantity of these children's contacts with peers (Lieberman, 1977). Second, parents of securely attached children may teach their children to value relationships and may advise their children in such a way as to help them develop and maintain positive relationships. Third, secure children may be more likely to receive positive treatment from their parents and to observe their parents in harmonious interactions with their own adult peers. Then, secure children may model their parents' positive social behaviors. These processes are not mutually exclusive.

A Broader View of Childhood Loneliness: Attachment and Peer Relations Considered Within a Transactional Framework

Although there are many reasons why attachment theory would lead one to expect connections between insecure attachment and loneliness, the theory does not necessarily predict these connections to be strong. Indeed, in the only study examining children's loneliness and attachment, the connection between the two, though significant, accounted for a small proportion of the variance (Berlin, Cassidy & Belsky, 1995). Attachment is not linked to children's loneliness in a vacuum. The model linking attachment and children's loneliness that we have presented is best viewed as existing within a larger transactional framework (Sameroff & Chandler, 1975). The transactional perspective, like Bowlby's (1973) developmental pathways approach, suggests that it is the interaction of many factors – some stressors and some protective factors – that contributes to children's social and emotional development. To understand fully the connection of attachment and loneliness, it is important to examine this connection within the context of a complex interplay of additional factors. In this section, we use a transactional framework to consider a number of factors that may interact with child–mother attachment to contribute to children's loneliness. In doing so, we raise questions and make suggestions for future research.

When considering the role of attachment in children's loneliness, it is important to remember that the mother is not the only person to whom the child is attached (Bowlby, 1958). Starting in the first year, the child is likely to be attached to other important figures, particularly the father and other familiar caregivers (Goosen & van IJzendoorn, 1990), and these attachments are likely to contribute to the child's relationships with peers (Howes et al., 1994; Oppenheim, Sagi, & Lamb, 1988). Are these additional attachments as influential as the attachment to the mother? Do different attachments influence the child in different ways? What happens when one attachment figure suggests that the child is lovable and valuable and another suggests that the child is of little value? Do these conflicted views become integrated into one representational model of the self and others? If so, through what process and when does this occur? Can secure attachment to one parent serve as a buffer (i.e., decrease the likelihood of loneliness) in light of an insecure attachment to the other parent? Are same sex relationships (i.e., father–son or mother–daughter) particularly important?

Moreover, it is important to remember that the attachment component of the parent–child relationship is not the only component of that relationship likely to influence children's peer relations and loneliness. The connections between attachment and nonattachment components of child–parent relationships are important to consider. The attachment component of the relationship deals specifically with the parent's serving as a secure base for the child. Parents, however, are not only attachment figures for their children. They are also playmates, teachers, disciplinarians, and care providers, and they influence their children in these roles (Ladd, 1992; Putallaz & Heflin, 1990). A parent's ability in one of these roles is at least somewhat independent of his or her abilities in the other roles. One child may be securely attached to a parent who is also a clever, fun playmate, whereas another child may be securely attached to a parent who is a rather staid and unimaginative playmate. Yet another child may be insecurely attached to a parent who is a good playmate. What are the implications of these different types of parenting? Which of these components of parenting would have greater influence on children's peer relations and loneliness? Would different components have different influences on different areas of children's peer relations (e.g., group popularity vs. close friendship)? The extent to which parents support and encourage their children's peer relations is also likely to be important (see Rotenberg, this volume). In summary, we need to learn more about how much the child's attachment-related experiences, as compared to the child's other experiences with the parent, influence peer relations and loneliness. Furthermore, components of parental behavior unrelated to the child directly (e.g., parents' social relationships with adult peers) are likely to be important. Children may imitate their parents' interest in and behaviors with their own adult peers, and this may interact with attachment to influence children's loneliness.

It is also important to consider the interaction of attachment with children's wider social network of relationships outside the family. To what extent does having a large social network buffer an insecurely attached child from loneliness? Does a securely attached child living in an isolated single-parent family bring to school feelings of isolation that contribute to a longing for companionship and thus an increased opportunity for feeling disappointed and lonely?

Experiences with peers may interact with attachment to influence children's loneliness. For instance, experiences with peers may contribute to representations of peers and may, in fact, override the influence of representations generalized from attachment-related representations of the parent. Thus, if peers truly have hostile intent, if peers truly are an aggressive, dangerous group, even securely attached children are likely to have negative representations of them. Evidence that peer representations are influenced by relationships with peers comes from studies in which participants' representations varied as a function of beliefs about a specific peer (Rabiner & Coie, 1989; Waas, 1988). It may also be the case that insecure children with negative peer representations may develop more positive representations if they are well liked and well treated by peers. This scenario seems rather unlikely, however, given that children with negative representations may behave in ways that reduce the likelihood that they will become well treated and well liked. According to Main (1990), the likelihood of representations of peers separating from representations of parents – for instance, of the child realizing that the parent is rejecting but that not all others are – is more likely to occur with the coming of formal operations in adolescence than at younger ages.

Finally, attachment should be examined in conjunction with the child's individual biological characteristics (including temperament). A child may be temperamentally more aggressive or disruptive or withdrawn than others, and these behaviors might contribute to rejection and loneliness. A child's biologically based deficits may contribute to lower self-esteem that, in turn, may directly or indirectly effect his or her loneliness. Conversely, a child may become well liked for reasons that have nothing to do with attachment (e.g., if they are cute, smart, or athletic). A child, for instance, may be well liked for no reason other than the fact that he or she is a star baseball player. Because peers admire him or her and want to be around him or her, such a child may experience little loneliness, despite a relative lack of social skills. In fact, simply being with peers may increase the child's own social skills. Also, the positive treatment he or she receives from peers may serve to improve representations of peers and thus his or her own behavior toward them. There may also be temperamental differences in a child's proneness to feelings of loneliness when alone.

In summary, within a transactional framework, it is the interplay of a variety of individual, familial, social, and larger environmental factors that is important for understanding children's loneliness. Most empirical work examining children's loneliness has focused on a variety of aspects of peer relations, and findings that peer acceptance, friendship status, and friendship quality all make independent and additional contributions to children's loneliness (Parker & Asher, 1993b; Parker et al., this volume) underscore the likelihood of multiple influences on children's loneliness. We have outlined ways in which attachment may play a role, and we have suggested that the contribution of both attachment and peer relations to childhood loneliness must be considered within a broad context.

4 | Developmental Change in the Sources of Loneliness in Childhood and Adolescence: Constructing a Theoretical Model

JENNIFER T. PARKHURST AND
ANDREA HOPMEYER

Research on loneliness has demonstrated it to be a common experience during both childhood and adolescence. It is also an experience that varies both as a function of children's and adolescents' social lives and of their psychological characteristics (Asher et al., 1990; Hymel et al., 1983). However, the study of loneliness prior to adulthood has reached a point at which it could benefit from theoretical models regarding the factors and mechanisms contributing to loneliness at different ages. This chapter points to areas that need to be addressed by such theories, and it outlines a developmental theory of the sources of loneliness in childhood and adolescence.

In the course of developing a theoretical model, we address the following questions. First, because theories of loneliness have often been based on a particular understanding of what it refers to, we discuss a number of issues that affect the definition of loneliness. Second, several possible models of the relationship between social deficits and loneliness are considered. Third, the chapter discusses evidence regarding the emergence of loneliness, the cognitions and experiences associated with loneliness in childhood and adolescence, and the kinds of social relationships and relationship provisions that are valued at various ages. On the basis of these, a stage model is proposed. Fourth, these stages are used as a framework for suggestions regarding developmental changes in the skill deficits and the other emotions providing routes to loneliness. They are used to identify experiences at each stage that may produce lasting vulnerabilities to loneliness.

The Definition of Loneliness

Loneliness has been defined in a variety of ways by psychiatrists (e.g., Fromm-Reichmann, 1959; Zilboorg, 1938), psychologists (e.g., Perlman & Peplau, 1982; Rook, 1984), sociologists (e.g., Durkheim, 1951),

56

and philosophers (e.g., Mijuskovic, 1985). Among these definitions are repeated references to four elements. These include an affective tone described as painful, sad, or aching; a cognition of oneself as alone or isolated; a felt lack or deprivation of closeness, contact, or connection with others; and a variety of postulated causes or antecedents.

Many currently used definitions of loneliness are formulated primarily in terms of the conditions postulated to give rise to the emotion. For example, Perlman and Peplau (1981) defined loneliness as "the unpleasant experience that occurs when a person's network of social relationships is deficient in some way, either quantitatively or qualitatively" (p. 31). Such definitions are "mini theories" of the causes of loneliness rather than characterizations of the experience referred to as *loneliness*. They ignore the possibility that individuals might experience other emotions besides loneliness in those circumstances or that loneliness might sometimes be felt in different circumstances. Such definitions are also at odds with evidence that there is only a moderate relationship between the presence of deficiencies in individuals' social lives and their feelings of loneliness (Asher et al., 1984; Parkhurst & Asher, 1992; Shute & Howitt, 1990) or even between their degree of social dissatisfaction and their degree of loneliness (Rook, 1984). Finally, they give rise to measures that do not assess people's experience of loneliness directly but instead obtain information about perceived social deficits. If researchers use these to test the theories of loneliness upon which they are based, this results in the correlation of measures that have similar content, even if given different labels (see Nicholls, Licht, & Pearl, 1982). Most fundamentally, definitions based on conditions that might theoretically give rise to loneliness preempt validity for the underlying theory. With regard to this, Weiss (1982) made the point that "we should not prevent ourselves from testing our hypotheses by making them true by definition" (p. 72).

These difficulties are not remedied by attempts to recognize different types of loneliness arising from different causes. Three pairs of contrasting types have been widely adopted in the empirical literature. Mijuskovic (1985) distinguished types of loneliness in terms of the source of the sense of separateness involved. *Metaphysical* loneliness was defined as that deriving from the essential separateness of our existence and experience as selves, thus being a fundamental feature of the human condition. *Psychological* loneliness was defined as that resulting from actual or perceived social deficits. Beck and Young (1978) distinguished between loneliness emanating from an external cause and that with an internal cause. *Transient* loneliness is caused by a specific crisis or life transition that disrupts someone's social relationships; *chronic* loneliness is caused by a lack of social skills or the individual's cognitive style. Weiss's (1973) social–emotional loneliness distinction reflects the notion that different relationship deficits produce distinct subtypes of psychological loneliness associated with different secondary affects. *Social* loneliness results from lack of a network of social relationships that provide a sense of community. *Emotional* loneliness results from a lack of close personal attachments.

We believe a more generally useful approach is to treat loneliness as a unitary construct, defined in emotional terms. By emotion, we mean more than affect, following those researchers in the area of emotions (e.g., Lazarus, 1991) who define an emotion as something that comprises cognition and motivation as well as affect. Thus, the emotion called *guilt* includes a characteristic feeling of heaviness and anxiety but also includes an appraisal of personal responsibility for wrongdoing or harm, and a wish that the harm, wrongdoing, or responsibility for said harm or wrongdoing might be removed. Accordingly, we propose a definition of loneliness that includes the kind of cognitive appraisal of one's situation relative to one's goals and interests, the kind of affect, and the kinds of felt desires and longings that characterize the experience: Loneliness is a sad or aching sense of isolation; that is, of being alone, cutoff, or distanced from others. This is associated with a felt deprivation of, or longing for, association, contact, or closeness.

This generalized definition of loneliness draws on recurring elements in many previous definitions (e.g., Ferreira, 1962; Flanders, 1982; Woodward & Kalyan-Masih, 1990) and permits recognition of several kinds of variations in the nature and sources of people's experience of loneliness. First, it allows loneliness to have both internal and external causes. Second, it allows loneliness to be a response to a wide range of situations, perceptions, and ideas, including forms of isolation that are concrete and those that are figurative or abstract. This allows loneliness to be a response to somewhat different things at different ages, as there are changes in the levels of cognitive analysis that people are capable of (Harris, 1989) and in their social needs. Third, it permits loneliness to be only one of a number of emotional reactions to social deficits. Other emotional reactions, such as fear or boredom, are not subsumed as part of the loneliness experience, or of some particular variety of loneliness (e.g., social loneliness), and thus are left unexamined as variables.

The proposed definition of loneliness points to its motivational component by including the felt needs or longings that are part of the experience, but it does not specify characteristic lonely behaviors. There are several reasons why behavior should not be included in a definition of loneliness. First, though research has shown that emotions tend to be expressed in characteristic facial expressions, stances, and movements, and to promote specific behavioral tendencies (e.g., Lazarus, 1991; Roseman, Wiest, & Swartz, 1994), thus far no consistent pattern of expressive behavior or of action tendencies has been found to be specifically associated with loneliness. In fact, research suggests that people's response tendencies when lonely include both seeking human contact and spending time in solitude (Jones, 1982; van Buskirk & Duke, 1991). Second, the relationship between emotions and both expressive and motivated behavior is complicated, especially after early childhood, by individuals' increasing ability to disguise what they feel by inhibiting or modifying the expressions and behavioral tendencies produced by their emotions. Children are motivated to develop and exercise such ability as they become aware of the social conventions regarding expression of emotions and appropriate behavior and of the social consequences that result from their violation (Fine, 1981; Gottman & Parker, 1986; Saarni, 1988, 1989). Finally, leaving behavior out of the definition of loneliness makes it possible to study children's and adolescents' behavior when they are lonely as a function of their feelings of loneliness and their knowledge of strategies for overcoming loneliness or relieving its pain.

One implication of this discussion is that, except in the case of children so small that they cannot label their internal experience, assessments of loneliness should focus on individuals' experience of that emotion, as is true in direct measures of loneliness (e.g., "I feel lonely"). Most research on loneliness has not used direct measures. The majority of items on both the Revised UCLA Loneliness Scale (Russell et al., 1980) and the Loneliness and Social Dissatisfaction Questionnaire (Asher et al., 1984; Asher & Wheeler, 1985), the instruments used most widely to assess loneliness among adults and among children, respectively, ask individuals about social deficits and dissatisfaction with their social relationships (see Terrell-Deutsch, this volume). Beyond the problems pointed out earlier in using such scales to study the relationship between social deficits and loneliness, there are also problems with using them to diagnose loneliness. Although assessments of individuals' social dissatisfaction and perceived social deficits have been found to be correlated ($r = .40$ to $r = .60$) with pure measures of loneliness (de Jong-Gierveld, 1978; Hayden, 1989; Schmidt & Sermat, 1983), a high score on a scale made up primarily of social deficit and social dissatisfaction items need not represent loneliness. Individuals may obtain high scores on such a scale without endorsing descriptions of themselves as lonely. Many individuals who are dissatisfied with their social lives, may not, in fact, be lonely, as becomes apparent in the following section.

The Relationship Between Social Deficits and Loneliness

Before discussing developmental changes in the bases of loneliness during childhood and adolescence, consideration needs to be given to the nature of the relationship between social deficits and loneliness. We discuss two widely influential theoretical perspectives concerned with proximal and concurrent causes of loneliness prior to presenting our own perspective.

The Social Needs Perspective

Weiss (1974) theorized that an individual has six inherent social needs that are met in the context of specific social relationships: (a) attachment (relationships that provide a sense of safety and security), (b) social integration, (c) nurturance (the opportunity to care for another person), (d) reassurance of worth (evidence that the individual is skillful and able), (e) reliable alliance (assistance when needed), and (f) guidance (sage and honest advice). He proposed that if any of these needs are not adequately met, or a particular relationship is lost, then the individual will experience feelings of loneliness. The nature of the loneliness feelings experienced depends on the particular deficit that the individual experiences.

As an account of the sources of loneliness, Weiss's (1974) theory is limited in part by failure to identify the full range of provisions obtained from social relationships. Other important provisions include intimacy and affection; enjoyable stimulation; companionship; social comparison; evidence of one's power, influence, and importance; and a sense of purpose and meaning (Frankl, 1962; Ginsberg, Gottman, & Parker, 1986; Larson, 1990; McClelland, 1985). Lacks in some of these areas, such as intimacy and companionship, are strongly associated with loneliness.

A more fundamental problem, noted previously, is the lack of correspondence between loneliness and objective social deficits (for a detailed review, see Maragoni & Ickes, 1989). Consistent relationships between objective social deficits and loneliness have only been found among children (Asher et al., 1990; Parker & Asher, 1993b) and those found have not been strong. Subjective evaluation of relationships appears to be more important than the objective characteristics of those relationships. This finding has led to interest in a more cognitive perspective on the relationship between social deficits and loneliness.

The Cognitive Perspective

The most influential cognitive theory of loneliness still treats it as the emotional response that people experience in response to social deficits (Maragoni & Ickes, 1989). However, it proposes that people's personal standards for, and their subjective perceptions of, their personal relationships are more directly relevant to their feelings of loneliness than the objective features of individuals' lives. Thus, loneliness can be heightened or reduced by changing a person's subjective standards for relationships. Shaver, Furman, and Buhrmester (1985) have, in fact, found that chronically lonely individuals hold very high expectations for interpersonal relationships compared with nonlonely individuals and with whose loneliness is more transient. This theory also proposes that individuals' attributions or explanations regarding the causes of their relationship problems modulate their experience of loneliness. Individuals who suffer from chronic loneliness are more likely than others to explain their social failures as due to their own unchangeable personality traits and abilities (see Peplau et al., 1982, for a review of this literature).

Critiques of this theory (Rook, 1984, 1988; Shute & Howitt, 1990; Wood, 1986) have questioned its assumption that social dissatisfaction invariably leads to feelings of loneliness. Studies both of loneliness and of other social emotions point to a wide range of negative emotional reactions associated with social deficits and social dissatisfaction besides loneliness, including shame, humiliation, emptiness, boredom, grief, envy, jealousy, frustration, anger, hostility, anxiety, fear, and depression (Cassidy & Asher, 1993; Lewis, 1992; Mathes, Adams, & Davies, 1985; R. S. Miller, 1992; Nathanson, 1992; Paloutzian & Ellison, 1979; Parrott & Smith, 1993; Rubenstein & Shaver, 1982; Salovey, 1991; Scalise, Gintner, & Gerstein, 1984; Young, 1982). Rook (1984) has urged the development of theory to "predict when loneliness rather than some other emotion will be evoked by a dissatisfying interpersonal situation" (p. 1390). She argued that loneliness is only felt in situations in which the individual (a) feels estranged, rejected, or misunderstood or (b) must forego an activity because he or she lacks a companion. Wood, going even further, suggested that failure of a relationship to meet expectations only results in loneliness when a lack of understanding is involved.

Rook (1984) and Wood (1986) have suggested specific circumstances in which dissatisfaction with one's social relationships will be associated with loneliness. However, while estrangement, rejection, lack of companionship, and lack of understanding may all be especially likely to produce ideas of being alone, cutoff, or distanced in ways which one does not like, it is possible to imagine some of these perceptions leading at times to different emotional reactions. Lack of understanding might instead produce feelings of frustration. Rejection might produce feelings of humiliation or of shame. At the same time, reflection suggests that other circumstances besides these often induce feelings of loneliness. Having been let down or betrayed by a friend, for example, may induce a perception of oneself as being abandoned and alone, so that feelings of loneliness result.

The Perspective of Appraisal Theories of Emotions

Because of the problems with the ideas underlying the cognitive perspective as currently conceived, we suggest a different kind of cognitive understanding of loneliness that is more consistent with appraisal theories of emotions, such as that of Lazarus (1991). On the basis of this perspective, people's emotions in a given situation are determined not only by the nature of the situation (e.g., rejection by a friend) but also by the specific kinds of goals and interests that people bring to the situation and by people's appraisal of the situation relative to those goals and interests. In this way, rejection by a friend may represent loss of wanted closeness to someone loved and produce loneliness. However, rejection may also represent an insult to oneself or evidence of one's social impotence and produce humiliation (Klein, 1991; S. B. Miller, 1988). Or it may represent evidence of one's lack of worth as a person and produce shame (Lewis, 1992; Schneider, 1977; Tangney, Burgraf & Wagner, 1995). Additionally, rejection might represent the loss of that meaning which the friendship gave to one's life and produce feelings of emptiness (Frankl, 1962; Klinger, 1977). The likelihood of each kind of appraisal should be influenced not only by features of the particular situation but also by people's strongest concerns, by their beliefs, and by the availability to them of various possible interpretations of events (Klinger, 1977; Parkhurst & Asher, 1985). It should also be influenced by what people want from their relationships.

Along with this, we see value in returning to Weiss's (1974) proposal that social relationships serve several different kinds of fundamental goals and functions. However, perceived deficits in the various functions should differ in their likelihood of producing loneliness; perceived deficits in some functions should be more likely to produce other emotions. Lack of intimacy, concerned with people's need for closeness and connection to other people, should often produce loneliness. Lack of nurturance, concerned with connection to meaningful goals and purposes, should be more likely to produce emptiness. Lack of validation or reassurance of worth, concerned with people's need to feel of value, should often produce shame. Lack of dominance, concerned with people's need for control, power, respect, and social standing, should tend to produce humiliation.

Toward a Developmental Theory of Loneliness

None of the theories of loneliness discussed so far proposes differences in what produces this emotion at various stages during childhood and adolescence. On the basis of the previous discussion, two areas in which differences should have a particularly direct bearing on the basis of loneliness are developmental changes in (a) the kinds of contact, closeness, and association which are meaningful and (b) the kinds of relationships, social activities, and relationship provisions valued by children. Additionally, attention needs to be given to the stage of development when children first experience loneliness.

The Age When Children First Experience Loneliness

Children are able to define loneliness by kindergarten age (Cassidy & Asher, 1992, 1993). Anecdotal evidence indicates that even preschool children use loneliness as a label for their feelings. This does not mean that loneliness is not experienced even earlier. Babies and small children experience specific emotions before they are able to label them and long before they have the metacognitions necessary to define them. However, small children's and babies' inability to talk about their feelings makes it hard to study their internal experiences.

The difficulty of identifying specific emotions in babies and small children can be remedied in instances where there has been identification of a distinctive pattern of expression, goals, and action tendencies as being associated with a particular emotion. Research on the emergence of emotions in infancy has used such patterns to arrive at inferences about babies' emotional experience. A common approach that has been taken involves observation of babies' or young children's facial expressions, stance, and movements in a number of situations, including situations designed to elicit a specific emotional reaction. Studies using this approach have provided evidence that shame, humiliation, and envy are experienced by children as early as their third year (e.g., Frankel & Sherick, 1977; Lewis, Alessandri, & Sullivan, 1992), and empathy and embarrassment as early as 18 months (Lewis, 1992). It was noted previously that no clear pattern of expressive behavior has been identified for loneliness. Determination of whether there is a such a pattern is a matter that calls for study.

Currently the most suggestive evidence regarding the beginnings of loneliness comes from the attachment literature (see Cassidy & Berlin, this volume). During the second half of their first year babies begin to show distress when left alone in a strange situation without someone nearby to whom the child is attached and to whom the child can go for contact and reassurance (Ainsworth & Bell, 1970; Bowlby, 1973). Babies' and small children's responses to this situation have been characterized as anxiety or fear. However, this is a situation in which a baby or small child might represent him- or herself as physically alone, cutoff, or distanced from someone to whom the child wishes to be close to or with whom the child wants contact. If such a cognition is experienced in association with painful affect, and a strongly felt need for association, proximity, or contact, then the child's emotional experience when left alone in a strange place may also comprise loneliness. The behavior shown by babies and small children in this situation (e.g., trying to leave and follow the parent who has left them) shows motivation to reestablish contact. Small children in similar circumstances sometimes say that they feel lonely. It seems likely, then, that loneliness is an emotion first experienced no later than early childhood, and perhaps earlier. Our proposals for a developmental sequence in the bases and sources of loneliness begins with very young children.

Change in the Forms of Closeness, Contact, and Association Which are Longed for

Earlier it was suggested that loneliness can result from a range of experiences inducing representation of oneself as alone, cutoff, or distanced from others, along with a wish for association, contact, or closeness. A small child whose teddy bear is in the washing machine when she needs to cuddle him may feel lonely. A kindergarten child may feel lonely if he has no one to play with. A fourth grader may feel lonely if his friend has let him down, or if he is burdened by a terrible family secret that he must not tell others. A high school student may feel lonely because she imagines herself to be the only lesbian at school (NY Times, Feb. 28, 1996). That is, loneliness may result from representations of varying degrees of concreteness or abstractness.

There is a shift during the course of childhood and adolescence from the capacity to form representations of specific and concrete situations to the capacity to formulate abstract concepts (Fischer, 1980; Inhelder & Piaget, 1958). This is paralleled in the emotional realm by an increasing tendency to think about oneself and to conceptualize one's situation in terms of more abstract concepts (Harris, 1989). Harris has proposed that many emotions undergo systematic developmental transformations in what they are a response to, as a function of such cognitive developmental changes.

Along these lines, one would expect a progression, as in the examples provided earlier, from loneliness due to physical isolation and lack of physical contact toward loneliness resulting from increasingly abstract ways of being cutoff, distanced, and alone. Support for this progression can be seen in several existing studies. Cassidy and Asher (1992, 1993) reported that kindergarten and first-grade children described loneliness in terms of being literally alone and without a companion. Most children this age did not think that someone could feel lonely when playing with another person. However, Hayden et al. (1988; see Hymel, Tarulli, Hayden Thomson, & Terrell-Deutsch, this volume) found that many third- through eighth-grade students described loneliness as resulting from more psychological forms of distancing, such as conflicts, broken loyalties, violations of friendship expectations, threats to one's sense of inclusion in the group, and being ignored. Most children in this age range said that it was possible to feel lonely even when not alone. Van Buskirk and Duke (1991) quoted descriptions by young adolescents of loneliness resulting primarily from social isolation and by older adolescents of loneliness resulting of psychological isolation: not being understood by others or having no one to talk to. Similarly, Larson (1990) reported an increase in adolescence of loneliness related to awareness of a psychological breach or a lack of rapport or understanding.

Changes in the Value of Relationships, Social Activities, and Relationship Provisions

Children have little desire to be alone. With development, individuals show less need to be with others, and greater tolerance, or even desire for physical solitude. So adolescents, who are aware of their self-presentation when with others and who are developing an identity, value time by themselves as a chance for privacy and escape from being on stage, for autonomy from adults, and for self-definition (see Goossens & Marcoen, this volume; Larson, this volume). On the other hand, compared with adults, adolescents still experience time alone as more lonely relative to their other experiences (Larson, 1990).

At the same time, individuals show developmental changes both in those with whom they want association, closeness, and contact and in the kinds, amounts, and sources of association, proximity, or contact wanted. These could be expected to influence the sources of loneliness at various stages in children's development.

Sullivan (1953) theorized that younger children value attention from their parents, whereas preadolescents value relationships with "chums." He proposed a subsequent shift in adolescence to placing importance on peer-group acceptance. Research regarding developmental changes in the kinds of peer associations valued at various ages confirms this sequence but demonstrates that dyadic friendships and peer-group relationships are valued at much earlier ages than those Sullivan proposed.

Research has shown that even very young children often share strong mutual attachments with close friends (Gottman & Parkhurst, 1981; Gottman & Parker, 1986) that are important to them. However, there is little evidence that children prior to middle childhood consider it important to belong to a peer group as part of their social lives. Indeed, young children playing with a friend in a preschool setting commonly try to exclude interlopers (Corsaro, 1981).

In middle childhood, during primary or elementary school, groups of peers, or cliques become important in providing children with allies and associates with whom to engage in group activities. In early adolescence, cliques also provide a sense of belonging, and crowds become important as a source of a sense of identity (Brown, 1989). Along with the increased importance of cliques and crowds, young adolescents become increasingly preoccupied with their acceptance, dominance, and prestige among their peers (Butcher, 1986; Eder, 1985; Eder & Kinney, 1995; Humphreys & Smith, 1987; Weisfeld, Bloch, & Ivers, 1983). At this age, having a girlfriend or boyfriend becomes important, not as a source of intimacy, but as a means to social prestige.

During high school, there is a shift back toward emphasis on dyadic relationships. Adolescents pull away from the constraints on individualism exerted by crowds (B. Brown, 1989). Both friendships and romantic relationships become important as sources of intimacy, whereas a more individual identity is forged in the course of discussion and mutual comparison of philosophies, goals, and values with close friends.

Accompanying these shifts are changes in what children need from their parents and peers. The attachment literature reports that the periods of time over which children tolerate separation from attachment figures in strange places become longer and longer. The kinds of contact sought also change and become less physical (Main et al., 1985). Other literature points to still greater independence from parents in adolescence. Simultaneously, the importance of peer relationships increases, producing shifts between childhood and adolescence in the relative contributions of parental and peer relationships to individuals' experience of loneliness (Larson, this volume; Marcoen & Brumagne, 1985; Marcoen &

Goossens, 1993). Children and adolescents also indicate changes in the relationships from which they obtain various social provisions (Buhrmester, 1992; Buhrmester & Furman, 1987; Hunter & Youniss, 1982). Parents continue to be important to their adolescent children, but friends take on an increasing role as a source of intimacy.

Parallel to these changes, the friendship literature (e.g., Damon, 1979; Gottman & Parker, 1986) has proposed developmental changes in what children want from their friends. Preschool and early elementary school children want friends as stimulating companions with whom to engage in coordinated play and other collaborative activities. Shared fantasy, shared deviance, and shared glee and jokes are important; through these and other activities, friends create a strong sense of "we-ness" from which others are excluded. Older children gossip with their friends about other children in their social milieu and want allies to provide help and backing, as they navigate the wider social world. Adolescents want confidants with whom to talk about their social and personal lives and problems and, to an increasing extent, fellow-explorers in the search for identity (Larson, 1990).[1] This indicates shifts in the provisions that children and adolescents seek from their friends from an emphasis on companionship and fun, to reliable alliance, and then emotional support, advice, and discussion of philosophical issues as well. This predicts that peer-related loneliness should be related primarily to a lack of people to play with in late preschool and early elementary school, but also to a lack of people to go to for help in later elementary school and to a lack of people to talk to in adolescence.

A Developmental Framework for Understanding Age Changes in the Peer Relationships and the Cognitions Associated With Loneliness

Many of the changes in children's social relationships, in the social activities and provisions important to children at different ages and in the nature of the cognitions associated with loneliness, can be explained in terms of Fischer's (1980) proposals regarding cognitive changes during childhood and adolescence. Fischer's theory outlines a series of transformations in an individual's thinking within any given domain. The central

---

[1] We are not proposing that these activities begin at the ages when they are becoming important. Even very young pairs of friends gossip with each another, defend each other's interests, and engage with each other in self-disclosure and discussion of personal matters (Gottman & Parker, 1986). However, there is little that suggests that these activities are among those activities and functions that children value highly before the stages indicated or miss if they are not provided by their friendships.

ideas of the theory can be summarized as follows. In the course of development, the individual becomes capable of integrating increasing amounts
of information. At each successive stage, the individual is able to coordinate and summarize a number of pieces of information at that level
of complexity mastered at the previous stage. The child moves through
this process from an understanding of situations in physical, concrete
terms toward understandings of situations in increasingly abstract terms.
Cognitive development passes through a series of 10 steps. There are four
stages of sensorimotor development in infancy. The fourth of these, which
normally comes at the transition from infancy to childhood, is simultaneously the first of four steps in conceptualization and reasoning at the level
of representations during childhood. The fourth of these, usually around
the time of transition from childhood to adolescence, is also the first in
four steps in conceptualization and reasoning at the level of abstractions
that take place during adolescence and adulthood. (For a detailed account of this theory see Fischer, 1980.) Lamborn, Fischer, and Pipp (1994)
illustrated how the theory applies to developmental change in children's
understanding of social concepts.

Drawing on those stages that Fischer (1980) identified as normally occurring during childhood and adolescence, we propose five steps in children's and adolescents' abilities to think about relationships that influence
both what they want in their relationships with others and what makes
them feel lonely. In very early childhood (at the level labeled by Fischer as
single representations), the child is able to reflect on the concrete situation
of one individual. Examples of this would include representation of the
fact that one is physically alone or that the person one is attached to is
not present. At the second step (corresponding to Fischer's *mappings of
representations*) the child is able to reflect on and represent simple, concrete relationships between specific individuals. Examples of such relationships are physical similarities between oneself and a friend, one's joint
engagement with a friend in the same activity, or one is sharing understanding and enjoyment with a friend of a private joke (see Gottman, 1983;
Gottman & Parker, 1986). At the third stage (Fischer's *systems of representations*), the child can reflect on complex, concrete relationships between or
among specific individuals. Examples of such complex relationships are
thinking about one's treatment relative to specific others in a particular
group or about the reciprocal help-giving that takes place between oneself and a friend. At the fourth step (*systems of systems of representations* or
single abstractions), the child, now usually moving into early adolescence,
can think across a number of such complex relationships to develop an
understanding of relationships with others in terms of simple abstractions

that summarize these relationships. Examples of these are such constructs as friendship, popularity, and prestige. At the fifth step (*mappings of abstractions*), the older adolescent can coordinate abstractions. So the adolescent should be able to think about similarities or differences between his or her own moral values and those of his or her friend or discuss with a friend the distinction between prestige and popularity. Paralleling this cognitive sequence, we have proposed a series of five steps in the development both of children's and adolescents' peer relationships and of their peer-related loneliness. These are presented in Table 4.1.

Interestingly, the new bases and causes of loneliness associated with each stage that we have proposed largely parallel the bases for loneliness cited by children assigned by Spores (1995) to each of Selman's (1980) stages of social reasoning on the basis of their thinking about loneliness. On the basis of his findings, Spores has proposed an independently derived developmental sequence in which children and adolescents explain loneliness in terms of (a) temporary physical separation or isolation; (b) activity-deprived boredom; (c) equity-deprived interpersonal interaction; (d) an intimacy–deprivation state or trait; and (e) distinct societal, interpersonal, and intrapsychic subtypes of loneliness. Intrapsychic loneliness refers to loneliness caused by lack of a personal identity.

Spores's (1994, 1995) stages are concerned with changes in children's *understanding* of loneliness and its causes and remedies. His stages are not intended as a developmental account of the basis or causes of loneliness at different ages. Indeed, Spores appears to assume that the causes of loneliness at different ages are much the same (Spores, 1995). Nonetheless, Spores (1994) found a very strong positive correlation ($r = .70$) between the development of children's and adolescents' thinking about loneliness and their scores on the Asher et al. (1984) Loneliness and Social Dissatisfaction Scale.

We are theorizing, given that loneliness is a function of ideas of aloneness, separation, and distance, that it is not simply children's understanding of loneliness which changes. Rather than describing developmental changes in children's understanding of loneliness, we have proposed a sequence of developmental stages in the expanding *cognitive bases and causes* of loneliness. Such a theory appears to offer a better explanation of increases in loneliness with cognitive development. If developmental changes in the cognitions associated with loneliness result in an expanding range of ideas capable of eliciting loneliness, such changes should readily produce increases in loneliness.

The stages we have proposed in the bases and causes of loneliness would be expected to have a bearing on children's and adolescents'

Table 4.1. Developmental Change in the Sources of Loneliness

Age Range	New Peer Relationships	New Valued Functions and Activities Provided by Peers	New Cognitions Producing Loneliness	New Routes to Lonely Feelings Through Other Emotions
Toddler and early preschool	Attachments to peers	Reassurance, affection, attention, and companionship	Alone in strange place, want affection, no attention from others, and miss friend	Fear and distress
Preschool, kindergarten, and early primary school	Dyadic friendships	Fun of coordinated play, shared fantasy, deviance and humor, and sense of "we-ness"	No one to play with and no one will be your friend	Boredom
Primary school and elementary school	Cliques	Helpers, allies, defenders, gossips, and people to play group games and sports with	Conflict with friend; ostracism; rebuff; left out, let down, slighted, ignored, or disregarded by group; no one to go to for help; and treated meanly or unfairly by friends	Social anxiety; humiliation from slights, insults, unfair treatment, ridicule, or abuse and shame over lack of competence in areas valued by peers

Upper elementary grades, middle school, and junior high school	Crowds, prestige, acceptance, romantic flirtations, and crushes	Confidants, banter, sense of belonging, models, sense standing, sense of worth, meaning, and identity based on association with group	Breach of confidence, friendship betrayed, no one to confide in, feel socially distanced, don't belong, lack group to identify with, despised, nobody in others' eyes, not valued or important, and not likeable or attractive	Shame because unattractive, unlikeable, unacceptable, and unpopular and humiliation of felt damage to social standing or loss of face
High school and college	Romantic relationships	Fellow-explorers in search for identity based on self-understanding, ideology, values, goals, social roles, etc. and intimacy	Feel psychological distance, no rapport with others, no one to talk to about philosophical issues, not understood, feel like a social misfit, lack or loss of intimate relationship, and feel that will never find anyone to share intimate relationship with	Emptiness and alienation

understanding of loneliness. However, changes in their understanding of
loneliness should also reflect such cognitive changes as the ability of individuals at Fischer's (1980) mappings-of-abstractions stage (or Selman's
[1980] Stage 4) to make distinctions between and compare different bases
for loneliness. This is a major part of thinking about loneliness in Spores's
(1994, 1995) Stage 5.

Extending the Proposed Model

The proposed model can be used as a framework for thinking about other
aspects of the relation between developmental change and loneliness.
A major purpose of this chapter is to point to areas that would benefit
from theory regarding the relation between development and loneliness.
Accordingly, suggestions will be sketched regarding changes in several
areas, without any pretense at providing an exhaustive review of relevant
literature.

Changes in the Skill Deficits Contributing to Loneliness

At any given age, negative traits and skill deficits should predict loneliness
to the extent that they interfere with the establishment or maintenance of
relationships of the kinds important at that age. They may also predict
loneliness if they make it difficult for relationships to serve the functions
that children want them to serve.

In the developmental theory of loneliness that has been outlined, loneliness at the first stage, during very early childhood, is primarily a function of lack of physical contact or proximity. The main skills that predict
loneliness at this stage should be those that affect the child's ability to approach or to elicit proximity or contact from individuals who could serve
as a source of comfort and reassurance, such as means of locomotion and
verbal skills.

At the second stage described, during the late preschool, kindergarten,
and early elementary school period, skills predictive of children's degree
of loneliness might be expected to include those that help children to
initiate and engage in mutually enjoyable dyadic play with peers, to establish friendships based on such play, and to engage in activities that
make children aware of what they share with their friends. A few examples drawn from the literature on processes and skills found to be
important to these in the late preschool, kindergarten, and early elementary school years (Gottman, 1983; Gottman & Parker, 1986; Gottman &
Parkhurst, 1981; Parkhurst & Gottman, 1986; Putallaz & Gottman, 1981)

include adapting to the ongoing activities of those one is joining, communicating clearly, adjusting the politeness of one's requests appropriately, managing conflict within a dyad, reciprocating humor and expressions of affection, and engaging in social comparison that emphasizes similarities rather than differences.

During middle childhood, children need to be able to engage successfully in group activities such as sports and games (Asher & Wheeler, 1985; Page, Frey, Talbert, & Falk, 1992). Examples of other social skills that should be important for children to develop are the ability to form and carry out complex strategies involving a number of individuals, to judge when it is socially appropriate to pursue various strategies, to coordinate rules, to engage in productive negotiations over plans and rules within a group, and to apportion responsibilities and rewards within a group in ways that will avoid charges of unfairness and conflict (Fine, 1981; Gerson & Damon, 1978; Hopmeyer & Asher, 1997; Piaget, 1965; Spetter, La Greca, Hogan, & Vaughn, 1992).

Young adolescents are concerned with their social dominance and prestige as well as with their popularity in the group at an age when these have become more strongly related to one another (Wright, Zakriski, & Fisher, 1996). They need to demonstrate the simultaneous capacity to hold their own and avoid open expressions of vulnerability and to behave in ways that will promote liking and acceptance. Skills that have been identified as important at this age include the abilities to engage in the banter and playful sparring characteristic of this age without inflicting humiliation; to suppress expressions of sadness, embarrassment, and sentiment; and to use teasing and joking to convey attraction, affection, and compliments, talk about upsetting experiences, convey criticism, and brag about their achievements and abilities (Eder, 1987; Fine, 1981; Gottman & Parker, 1986).

As adolescents come to value intimate friendships in which they talk to one another about their personal lives, thinking about social and philosophical issues, and plans for the future, they need the skills to engage successfully and comfortably in intimate self-disclosure. This includes knowing how to move toward intimate self-disclosure at an appropriate rate, and at one that matches that of the other person (Rotenberg & Chase, 1992). Both failure to reciprocate self-disclosure by friends and a tendency to self-disclose at too intimate a level, or prematurely, are likely to result in damaged relationships. Inability to self-disclose is also likely to result in relationships that are unsatisfying. This is an area of functioning with which lonely college students have particular difficulties (Jones, 1982).

The implication is that different sets of social skills will be found to be correlated with loneliness at different ages. Changes should reflect both the importance of skills to satisfactory social relationships and the range of variation in children's mastery of these. Greatest variation in important skills may often exist during the period when they first become important. For example, Page et al. (1992) found that, compared with other age groups, a lack of the skills needed to engage in group sports and games was most strongly correlated with loneliness in the fourth and fifth grades.

Changes in Other Emotions Contributing to Loneliness

Another source of loneliness in which there is likely to be developmental change is the other emotions that provide routes to feelings of loneliness. Other emotions may lead to increased loneliness in several ways.

First, negative emotions may change individuals' criteria for closeness, contact, or association with others. So, for example, boredom may increase one's felt need for companionship. Experiencing shame may increase one's need for friends as a means to reassure oneself of one's worth in others' eyes. Humiliation that is due to perceived damage to one's social standing is likely to increase individuals' felt need for allies and influence with others. If these increased needs for companionship, validation, or alliance are not met, the result could be expected to be loneliness.

Second, emotions can produce behaviors that damage individuals' social relationships. So shame interferes with people's capacity for effective social interaction, inducing social paralysis, submissiveness, withdrawal, and avoidance (Bruch & Heimberg, 1994; Kahlbaugh & Haviland, 1994; Lewis, 1992; Nathanson, 1992; Roseman et al., 1994; Schneider, 1977; Tangney, Burgraf, & Wagner, 1995; Wicker, Payne, & Morgan, 1983). Humiliation may also result in withdrawal or in anger and revenge-taking (Cohen & Nisbett, 1994; Erdley & Asher, in press).

Finally, some emotions involve cognitions which promote a sense of being cutoff and distanced from others. Shame over one's lack of social poise, lack of emotional self-control, physical unattractiveness, puniness, or ineptitude can readily induce the belief that one is cutoff from others by virtue of being the kind of person one is. While piloting an instrument concerned with cognitions associated distinctively with humiliation, shame, guilt, and embarrassment among undergraduate students, the largest number of people associated shame with feeling isolated from those they wanted to feel close to (Parkhurst & Troop, 1999). When humiliation means a felt drop in social standing compared to those one has aspired to, or has become accustomed to being associated with, humiliation can also produce a sense of being cutoff, distanced, and lonely (W. Schwartz, 1979).

Examination of the stages outlined in Table 4.1 suggests additional routes to loneliness associated with each set of emotions, which have been included in the table.

Very young children rely on physical contact and physical proximity with parents and peers (Bowlby, 1969/1982; Lewis & Rosenblum, 1975) as sources of comfort and reassurance. Distress or fear is likely to increase children's felt need for closeness or contact with others; if unavailable, this may lead to feelings of loneliness. Cassidy and Asher (1993) reported that many 5- and 6-year-olds mentioned fear as a feeling associated with loneliness.

During the preschool and early primary school years, friends are also valued because they are those with whom children engage in the fun of coordinated play or of shared humor. Boredom may now provide an additional major route to longing for the company of peers and to loneliness if it is not available. Cassidy and Asher (1993) indicated that boredom was the main other emotion associated with feeling lonely among 5- and 6-year-olds.

During middle childhood, when group interaction becomes important, humiliation and social anxiety resulting from being teased, bullied, excluded, and treated unfairly by the group could be expected to increase children's isolation, their felt need for allies, who may be unavailable, and their experience of loneliness. Shame from perceiving oneself as socially incompetent may also produce a sense of isolation.

In contrast to children, young adolescents define themselves in terms of their social relationships (Damon & Hart, 1988; Fine, 1981; Kegan, 1982). Early adolescence is also a time of increased role-taking abilities, self-consciousness, and awareness of and concerns about one's social standing, value, and self-presentation. These changes in early adolescence result in increased experience of the self-evaluative emotions, including shame and humiliation (Bennett, 1989; Bruch & Heimberg, 1994; Crozier & Russel, 1992; Edelmann, 1990; Kahlbaugh & Haviland, 1994; R. S. Miller, 1992; Shields, Mallory, & Simon, 1990; Smith & Greenberg, 1981). During this period, feelings of shame that are due to negative perceptions of one's social worth, and of humiliation resulting from perceived deficits in one's social standing, could be expected to increase loneliness. In fact, much of the variance in loneliness among young adolescents is related to their concerns about being humiliated and victimized and to their self-reported vulnerability to humiliation and shame in response to hypothetical social mishaps (Hopmeyer, Parkhurst, & Asher, 1995; Parkhurst, Roedel, Bendixen, & Potenza, 1991).

Finally, during later adolescence and early adulthood, individuals are at the stage of establishing a coherent identity based on personal values, ideological stances, goals in life, vocation, and social roles. Many feel a sense of emptiness if unable to identify satisfying roles, goals, or incentives among those they see to be available to them in the social world they know. This may increase reliance on relationships with others as a source of meaning. Additionally, the cognitions associated with such emptiness can themselves contribute to a sense of estrangement or psychological distance from others (Klinger, 1977; Spores, 1995).

Processes Contributing to Vulnerability to Loneliness

Prior theorizing regarding the relation between developmental processes and loneliness has mostly sought to explain individual differences in individuals' vulnerability to loneliness. Two traditions of existent theory and research have addressed this question.

One group of theories, based on psychoanalytic theory and on attachment theory, has focused on processes in infancy and early childhood contributing to individual differences in vulnerability to loneliness in adulthood. Fromm-Reichmann (1959) and researchers influenced by attachment theory (e.g., Berlin et al., 1995; Cassidy & Berlin, this volume; Hecht & Baum, 1984) have proposed that a predisposition to loneliness emerges from a mother–child relationship that is lacking in intimacy, warmth, and supportiveness. This type of parenting style makes individuals fearful of rejection or wary of intimacy. Sullivan (1953) identified the same kind of mother–child relationship as problematic but saw the child as failing to learn the fundamental skills needed to form and maintain an intimate relationship.

Zilboorg (1938) suggested, in contrast, that a predisposition to loneliness resulted from a mother–child relationship that is overinvolved, overindulgent, and overprotective. This style would produce narcissistic individuals who considered the main goal of life to be loved and admired by others, had unrealistic expectations of their relationships with others, and had an exaggerated sense of self that interfered with their ability to bond emotionally with others. Andersson (1990) has suggested that the same parenting style interferes with development of ability to initiate relationships.

There is evidence that both parent–child styles are problematic. Loneliness is associated on the one hand with an insecure attachment style, particularly of the ambivalent variety (Berlin et al., 1995; Hecht & Baum, 1984), and with recollection of one's early relationship with parents as lacking in warmth and supportiveness (Goswick & Jones, 1982; Hojat, 1982; Lobdell & Perlman, 1986; Paloutzian & Ellison, 1982; Shaver & Rubenstein, 1980) and on the other hand with recollection of a family characterized by parental warmth, combined with parental overinvolvement and seclusion of the child (Andersson, 1990). Among lonely adults, cases can be found that are consistent with each of the four proposed routes to vulnerability to loneliness (Young, 1982).

A second theoretical tradition has identified processes during late childhood and early adolescence that contribute to the development of vulnerability to loneliness in sensitive children. A pattern of social anxiety, submissiveness (lack of dominance), and social withdrawal in middle childhood has been proposed to lead to rejection by peers, to negative self-perceptions, and to a variety of internalizing problems, including loneliness (see K. H. Rubin, 1985; K. H. Rubin, LeMare, & Lollis, 1990; K. H. Rubin & Mills, 1991). An increasingly strong relationship has been demonstrated between withdrawn behavioral style and low status in the dominance hierarchy and between both submissiveness and withdrawn behavioral style on the one hand and negative peer status, and loneliness on the other (e.g., Boivin, Thomassin, & Alain, 1989; Cassidy & Asher, 1992; Parkhurst & Asher, 1992; Rockhill & Asher, 1992; Williams & Asher, 1987; Wright et al., 1996). The relationship between withdrawn behavior and loneliness in late childhood and early adolescence has been shown to be mediated by negative peer status, victimization, and concerns about being teased and victimized (Boivin & Hymel, 1995; Boivin et al., 1997; Parkhurst et al., 1991).

There is also evidence that the internalizing problems and maladaptive behaviors of withdrawn and submissive children or young adolescents are influenced by a negative, shame-inducing attributional style. Such an attributional style is probably exacerbated by preadolescents' and young adolescents' particular readiness to respond to others' teasing by internalizing a lasting negative self-image (Cash, 1995; J. K. Thompson & Heinberg, 1993). It is when children attribute negative social experiences to their own incompetence, and young adolescents attribute such experiences either to their incompetence or to their lack of social standing and acceptability to others, that social withdrawal and bullying predict depression and lasting vulnerability to internalizing problems (Alsaker, 1989;

Olweus, 1993b; K. H. Rubin & Mills, 1991). A negative, shame-inducing attributional style is also associated during middle childhood and early adolescence with persistent loneliness (Hymel et al., 1983; Renshaw & Brown, 1993). Furthermore, shame produces social paralysis, submissive behavior, and withdrawal (e.g., Lewis, 1992; Schneider, 1977). Along these lines, we have found submissiveness among young adolescents to be associated with self-reported vulnerability to shame in response to social mishaps and teasing.

Comparison of the developmental sequence described earlier with K. H. Rubin and Mills's (1991) integration of the two literatures just described, the social tasks of each age (Erikson, 1950), and the patterns of behavior and emotions associated with loneliness among adults (Young, 1982) reveals many common themes. These suggest that there are experiences at each stage of development that contribute to vulnerability to loneliness.

Problems in the parent–child relationship in infancy promote vulnerability to loneliness by promoting either insecurity or narcissism and overly exacting standards for relationships. During early childhood and during the preschool to early elementary school period, parents who provide poor models and who fail to socialize interactional skills produce children with a poor ability to approach others and to form and maintain dyadic relationships. Additionally, parents who are overinvolved, intrusive, and overprotective, and who seclude the child from self-initiated and self-regulated interaction with peers, produce children who lack social self-confidence, independence, and initiative. Their children also have difficulty amusing themselves and are overdependent on others for stimulation.

During middle childhood, persistent subjection of sensitive, fearful children to ridicule, or to mean, unfair, or exclusionary treatment by peers, promotes social anxiety, avoidance, and children's perception of themselves as socially incompetent, especially if they are unable to defend themselves effectively and are without allies willing to defend them (Gottman & Parker, 1986; Parkhurst & Asher, 1992; K. H. Rubin & Mills, 1991). Social rejection, domination, and teasing in early adolescence promote loneliness by encouraging sensitive individuals to see themselves as unacceptable and lacking social worth and standing, resulting in an enduring sense of social isolation.

Finally, older adolescents who lack the vocational skills, the self-confidence, or the sense of vocation or commitment to life goals that are needed to establish an identity may remain overreliant on intimate relationships as a source of meaning and be especially vulnerable to loneliness when such relationships are not available. Alienation at this age from roles, values, and institutions that are available or approved in their social context may also lead individuals to perceive themselves as having little in common with others, thus forming a lasting sense of psychological isolation.

Conclusion

We have pointed to the need to develop theory regarding developmental changes in the sources of loneliness and regarding the developmental processes that contribute to lasting vulnerability to loneliness. Evidence suggests that, with development, the cognitions associated with loneliness have less to do with lack of physical contact and proximity, as in infancy and early childhood, and more to do with social and psychological isolation. The affiliative needs of children also undergo systematic changes. On the basis of these changes, it was proposed that the relationship deficits and social skill deficits producing loneliness change across development. With development, an expanding number of other emotions provide routes to loneliness, by increasing people's needs of others, by interfering with their relationships, or by producing a sense of social or psychological isolation. Finally, it was theorized that at each stage of social and emotional development, there are experiences capable of contributing to lasting susceptibility to loneliness.

Some of the other emotions proposed to increase loneliness, specifically humiliation, shame, and emptiness, represent damage, along with loneliness, to goals that figure prominently in the literatures on social motivation and on the needs of the self. This points to the usefulness of looking to these literatures (e.g., Atkinson, 1966; P. Brown & Levinson, 1978; Deci & Ryan, 1991; Frankl, 1962; McClelland, 1985) to develop not simply a developmental theory of loneliness but a more general developmental theory of emotional responses to social relationship deficits (Parkhurst & Cain, 1999).

5 | Loneliness Through the Eyes of Children

SHELLEY HYMEL, DONATO TARULLI, LAURA
HAYDEN THOMSON, AND BEVERLEY
TERRELL-DEUTSCH

In the 1970s and 1980s, a great deal of social psychological research was directed toward the study of loneliness in adults. Among the issues addressed in this literature were the perceived causes of loneliness, the nature of the interpersonal deficits implicated in the experience of loneliness, the measurement of loneliness, and the strategies used to cope with loneliness (e.g., see Peplau & Perlman, 1982a; Perlman & Landolt, this volume; Rook, 1984, for reviews). Investigators appear to have converged on the idea that the rather common experience of loneliness was in fact a very differentiated phenomenon because the nature and expression of loneliness could vary according to its duration, the type of the relational deficits involved, and its motivational and behavioral correlates (Rook, 1984). In short, a consensus had emerged that loneliness is a multidimensional phenomenon, at least among adults.

Inspired by efforts in the area of adult loneliness, developmental and clinical psychologists have shown an increasing concern for children's experience of loneliness (e.g., Asher et al., 1990; Margalit, 1994). Though it had been suggested (Sullivan, 1953; Weiss, 1973) that true loneliness cannot be experienced until preadolescence or adolescence, more recent analyses (e.g., Burgess, Ladd, Kochenderfer, Lambert, & Birch, this volume; Cassidy & Asher, 1992; Youngblade, Berlin, & Belsky, this volume) have shown that even younger children, no less often and perhaps no less deeply than adults, are well acquainted with the experience of loneliness. Unlike psychological accounts of loneliness in adult populations, however, research in the area of children's loneliness, with few exceptions (e.g., Marcoen et al., 1987), has yet to appreciate fully the multidimensional nature of the phenomenon as it takes shape in children's lives. Most fundamentally, research on childhood loneliness has often proceeded without adequate or sustained consideration of the varied contexts and interpersonally significant events in children's lives within which the experience of loneliness unfolds.

Much of the research on children's loneliness has emerged as an off-shoot of the literature concerning peer relationships and peer rejection. The tendency to frame children's loneliness largely in terms of the characteristics of children's peer relations is evident in some of the earliest writings in the area. For example, on the basis of observational studies of preschool children and logs about friendship from older children, Z. Rubin (1980) stressed the absence of companionship from friends as the dominant theme underlying children's loneliness. Even earlier, Sullivan (1953) conceived of loneliness as the absence of a close one-to-one relationship with a peer.

In more recent research, we found a similar tendency to conceive of children's loneliness largely in terms of difficulties experienced within the peer system. For example, although some of the more frequently used self-report measures of children's loneliness also include consideration of relationships with parents (Marcoen & Brumagne, 1985; Marcoen et al., 1987), all children's loneliness measures contain items that ask children to reflect on and evaluate their social status within the peer group (see Terrell-Deutsch, this volume), with some focusing exclusively on the peer system (Asher et al., 1984). The often implicit assumption underlying the construction of such measures is that children's loneliness is best conceived in terms of perceived deficiencies in peer relations – an assumption that is perpetuated by the subsequent adoption and widespread use of such measures by other investigators. Indeed, much of the current research on childhood loneliness examines how various aspects of children's interpersonal relations with peers, especially classmates, predict feelings of loneliness (e.g., Asher et al., 1990; Boivin & Hymel, 1997; Boivin et al., 1995; Burgess et al., this volume; Ladd, Kochenderfer, & Coleman, in press; Parker & Asher, 1993; Parkhurst & Asher, 1992; Youngblade, Berlin, & Belsky, this volume). Although such research has been valuable in helping researchers to understand how particular aspects of childhood peer relations contribute to children's feelings of loneliness, the propriety of this assumption is questionable, especially in view of the rather mundane if often overlooked fact that children's social lives span a diversity of interpersonal contexts. Although there have been some efforts to consider relationships with both parents and peers in exploring childhood loneliness (e.g., Marcoen & Brumagne, 1985), especially in recent years (e.g., see Cassidy & Berlin, this volume; Rotenberg, this volume), the primary emphasis remains on links between loneliness and peer affiliations.

That real or perceived difficulties with peers have emerged as a primary source of children's loneliness strikes us, in many respects, as an indisputable fact, consistent with what both empirical research and common sense tell us about the value that children – and adults, too – attach to acceptance by peers. Relationships with parents are also an obvious focus, given that parents constitute the initial and primary relationship in most children's lives (see Cassidy & Berlin, this volume). Nevertheless, it is well recognized that the child's social world consists of a rich network of relationships including peers, parents, siblings, relatives, teachers, and even pets (Furman & Buhrmester, 1985; Hartup, 1980). Furthermore, we would point out that the companionship and intimacy provisions emphasized by Z. Rubin (1980) and Sullivan (1953), respectively, are not unique to the peer group but are received, for example, from family members as well (Furman & Buhrmester, 1985). Accordingly, any attempt to describe children's loneliness would do well to consider the child's wider social world, including both nuclear and extended family, school and neighborhood peers, friends, as well as acquaintances, and so on.

In this chapter, we argue for the need to consider children's loneliness as it emerges across the diverse relational contexts that children inhabit. In developing a more differentiated portrayal of children's loneliness, one of our basic concerns was that such a descriptive framework be informed by what children themselves had to say about loneliness and the situations in their lives that give rise to it. Generally, we have found that most efforts to conceptualize children's loneliness do not adequately accommodate children's own voices but instead rely largely on conceptual categories imposed in advance by adult investigators. For example, efforts to develop childhood loneliness scales (e.g., Asher et al., 1984; Marcoen & Brumagne, 1985) have been guided in large part by the concerns and presuppositions of the investigators or are patterned after previous research with adult populations, this at the expense of children's own understanding of loneliness. Although this tendency is certainly common, and perfectly reasonable in light of the theoretical concerns (e.g., social competence and sociometric status) that frequently underlie such efforts at scale construction, we think it equally important to broaden the range of sources for our developmental analyses and to incorporate children's own voices in our conceptualizations of what, after all, is children's experience of loneliness.

Children Talk About Loneliness

Accordingly, several years ago we took a step back, returned to the source, and simply talked with children about their experiences with loneliness (Hayden et al., 1988). In doing so, we sought to elaborate a more variegated, differentiated picture of children's loneliness – one that adequately reflected the diverse interpersonal contexts and events that children encounter in the course of their lives. Two of the present authors, Laura Hayden Thomson and Donato Tarulli, began by interviewing third-through eighth-grade children ($N = 132$) with a view to understanding how they defined and experienced loneliness. Our concerns about incorporating children's own descriptions of loneliness were reflected in our decision to draw on the responses children gave to open-ended questions about their understanding and experience of loneliness. Equally important was our decision to utilize a qualitative data-analytic strategy that we felt would help us to remain faithful to what children themselves had to say about loneliness. In effect, we endeavored to enlist children as co-collaborators, relying heavily in our analysis on their own personal accounts of loneliness, allowing these to inform, to the fullest extent possible, the descriptions at which we arrived in the course of our investigation.

The participants (74 girls and 58 boys) came from 11 different classrooms in a single school in a moderate-sized southern Ontario, Canada, community, with approximately equal numbers of children at each grade level. The children ranged from 8 to 13 years of age, were predominantly Caucasian, and were primarily from middle-class backgrounds. The interview, that lasted about one-half hour, proceeded in such a manner that questions of a more general nature preceded those that required children to disclose more personally relevant information. Specifically, we asked children to define loneliness and to indicate what the term meant to them ("What does loneliness mean?") and to tell us about situations that precipitate loneliness ("What kinds of things make a person feel lonely?"). We also asked children to relate their personal experiences with loneliness ("What kinds of things have made you feel lonely?" and "Tell me about a time when you felt lonely."). Probes were used primarily to elicit further information about children's personal loneliness experiences (e.g., why the event happened and why it made them lonely). The open-ended format allowed children to express, in a relatively unconstrained manner, their views on loneliness and their accounts of loneliness experiences. Children appeared comfortable and displayed no apparent difficulty in disclosing their thoughts about loneliness in this context. Furthermore, we found that children frequently offered their ideas about loneliness in the form of stories or narratives; that is, in the form of accounts that depicted the unfolding of a concrete series of experienced or hypothetical events. This occurred even when children were not asked explicitly to recount a loneliness episode. Children's responses to the interview were recorded verbatim for subsequent analyses.

Our task was to develop a descriptive, conceptual framework that could account for the full range of children's responses to our questions about loneliness. To this end, children's responses were analyzed qualitatively, our primary goal being the identification of recurrent themes in the textual data at hand. The data-analytic strategy we adopted was inspired by the concept-indicator model on which the grounded theory analysis is based (Strauss, 1987). According to this model, data – in this case children's verbal descriptions and accounts of loneliness – are taken as empirical indicators of a concept derived from the data at hand. The model involves a constant comparison among indicators, a process that requires the investigator to note similarities and differences in the data. Perceived uniformities in the data are translated into categories that express conceptually similar classes of events. In the next procedural step, the emergent categories undergo further refinement, elaboration, and differentiation as they are compared with additional indicators. The process continues until the identified categories achieve the best possible fit to the available data. In this regard, we may say that the concepts that emerge from the analysis are grounded in the data.

In keeping with the guidelines of this analytic strategy, we began our analysis with a close reading of children's responses to the interview questions. As we confronted similarities and differences among children's descriptions, we derived labels to reflect the emergent categories. The propriety and inclusiveness of the themes we identified were constantly questioned by referring back to children's actual responses. Eventually, we moved to increasingly higher levels of abstraction as we sought to describe the similarity of the events and situations that children described. In the end, we derived a number of thematic categories that we agreed reflected the diversity in children's responses and that could account for all the responses at hand. In essence, the analysis involved a dialogical interplay between the text of children's responses and emerging descriptive themes. A no less important part of this process, however, was the dialogue between the investigators, an extended and sometimes exhausting discursive process over the course of which proposed thematic categories were challenged, redescribed, renamed, and refined, and during which we sought, as much as possible, to keep our own interpretations in check, testing them constantly against childrens own understandings and descriptions.

The results of our qualitative analysis supported our hypothesis that children's loneliness is a multidimensional phenomenon. Specifically, children's responses suggested to us that they perceive and experience loneliness in terms of three distinct features or components, as depicted in Figure 5.1: an *affective dimension* reflecting the emotional character of loneliness, a *cognitive dimension* entailing children's appraisals of the availability of various relational provisions, and a *set of interpersonal situations or contexts* giving rise to loneliness. Although these are depicted as three conceptually distinct aspects of loneliness in Figure 5.1, they are clearly interrelated and in fact tended to co-occur in any given child's description of loneliness. Thus, the three conceptual components identified here are reflected in and derived from children's own descriptions of loneliness, but they do not necessarily represent distinctions explicitly made by the children themselves. Nevertheless, these distinctions are useful in providing us with a framework for understanding children's perspectives on loneliness.

Affective Dimension

Children's expressions of the affective dimension of loneliness was observed in two ways: in the explicit emotional or affective terms used to describe the experience and in the use of metaphorical terms or expressions. With regard to the former, children typically offered descriptions of loneliness that included specific references to emotion terms, most notably sadness and boredom (e.g., "It means being sad" and "You're bored and you have no one to play with"). Children also frequently used the locution "feel" or "feeling" in their definitions (e.g., "*feeling* unneeded," "*feeling* left out," "you *feel* like an outsider," "no one *feels* like playing with you and you *feel* like you don't have any friends," "you're by yourself and *feel* like there's nobody there for you," and "you *feel* like everyone is against you and you have no one to turn to" [italics ours]). Such responses reflect children's awareness of the felt or affective dimension of loneliness or at least their implicit acknowledgment that loneliness is emotional in nature. (For a discussion of loneliness as an emotional experience, see Parkhurst & Hopmeyer, this volume.)

Children also communicated the felt aspect of loneliness through the use of explicit metaphorical terms or expressions (e.g., "a blank feeling," "it's just like nothing," "they feel they're in a corner," "to be left alone, kept in a cage or something," and "like you're the only one on the moon"). Loneliness does not appear to have any unique or commonly experienced identifying internal–physiological correlates, yet it presents one with an undeniable felt dimension, a dimension that may not be readily conceptualized in terms of its inherent properties and that, consequently, can be best understood or described by appealing to other clearer concepts; hence, the need for metaphorical definition.

AFFECTIVE DIMENSION

EMOTION TERMS

METAPHORICAL EXPRESSIONS

COGNITIVE DIMENSION

RELATIONAL PROVISIONS

    Companionship

    Inclusion

    Emotional Support

    Affection

    Reliable Alliance

    Enhancement of Worth

    Opportunities for Nurturance

LONELINESS VS. BEING ALONE

ABSENCE OF (SPECIFIC) RELATIONSHIPS

INTERPERSONAL CONTEXTS

PHYSICAL SEPARATION

    Loss

    Dislocation

    Temporary Absence

PSYCHOLOGICAL DISTANCING

    Conflict

    Rejection

    Broken Loyalties

    Exclusion

    Being Ignored

Figure 5.1. A framework for understanding children's experience of loneliness.

Cognitive Dimension

The second component of our framework reflects a cognitive dimension, with particular emphasis on children's appraisals of relational provisions. Central to children's definitions and personal accounts of loneliness was the perception that the provisions one expects to receive from relationships were being threatened or were not forthcoming. Children interpreted and assessed interpersonal relationships in terms of their implications regarding the availability of various forms of support. The relational provisions described by the children in our sample were not unlike those that have been identified in previous work in the area of social support (e.g., Furman & Robbins, 1985) and are not inconsistent with cognitive deficit theories of adult loneliness (e.g., Maragoni & Ickes, 1989; Peplau, Miceli, & Morasch, 1982; Peplau & Perlman, 1979; for reviews see Parkhurst & Hopmeyer, this volume; Terrell-Deutsch, this volume). However, it is important to underscore that these relational provisions did not appear to be uniquely associated with any particular affective reaction, nor with particular interpersonal contexts that children mentioned, but rather were associated with a variety of interpersonal events and emotional correlates. Moreover, although relations with other children (classmates, friends, acquaintances, neighborhood peers, teammates, etc.) were a major focus in children's loneliness accounts, there was also frequent reference to other interpersonal relationships, including those with parents, extended family members, siblings, other adults, and even pets. Seven different types of support or themes were evident in children's descriptions of relational provisions: companionship, inclusion, emotional support, affection, reliable alliance, enhancement of worth, and opportunities for nurturance.

Companionship

Very commonly, children defined loneliness in terms of the absence of a companion with whom to share activities or talk. This lack of companionship was frequently accompanied by references to boredom. For example, children defined loneliness as "not being able to play with or talk to anyone" or as arising when there is "no one around that you can do things with."

Inclusion

When the absence of companionship was interpreted as the result of the negative actions of a peer or family member, children questioned their membership in the larger group. In this regard, children's accounts reflected their concerns over the need for a sense of inclusion; that is, a sense of belonging to and being accepted by the larger group. For example, children spoke of "wanting to be in the crowd but they won't accept you," "not being part of the group," "feeling left out," and "trying to be part of the new group of kids."

Emotional Support

Another relational provision, which we labeled *emotional support*, was reflected in statements such as the following: "If you have a problem, there's no one there to talk to about it" and "Thinking that you really don't have someone that you can turn to or a close friend." The central theme here was the unavailability of an intimate other with whom to share personal problems and on whom one can rely for supportive understanding.

Affection

Affection, construed in terms of "being liked or loved" was another relational provision that children mentioned. In defining loneliness, children implicated this provision in statements such as the following: "Like you have no one that really likes you and you're all alone" and "Without anybody to love you."

Reliable Alliance

Reliable alliance concerns friendship expectations of loyalty, trust, and continued availability. For example, children would describe situations in which a close friend would abandon them for another group, or would fail to be "on my side."

Enhancement of Worth

With enhancement of worth, the concern is with others' affirmation of one's value. For example, one child described the situation in which, "You have something exciting, and no one wants to hear it."

Opportunities for Nurturance

In some cases, children suggested that relationships offer opportunities for nurturance, such as those provided in the acts of caring for a younger sibling or a pet.

There were also less direct means by which children expressed concerns over relational provisions. Indeed, a dominant theme in children's loneliness talk was that of "being alone," implying the absence of all relational provisions, at least temporarily. However, a frequently reiterated definitional point in the loneliness literature concerns the distinction between loneliness and being alone. Strictly speaking, the two terms are not synonymous: To be alone is to be "separated, apart, or isolated from others," whereas to be lonely implies the experience of "a sad or disquieting feeling of isolation" – at least according to one dictionary's definitions. Of interest then is whether children are able to recognize the distinction between loneliness and the state of being alone, a distinction considered essential to an adultlike understanding of the phenomenon of loneliness. When the children in our study were asked if one has to be alone to be lonely, the overwhelming response (regardless of age) was no; children's justifications for this response certainly demonstrated that they understood that one can be lonely in the presence of others. In short, despite frequent reference to "being alone" in their accounts of loneliness, it seemed clear that children could express the formal definitional distinction between loneliness and being alone. It is in light of this demonstrated understanding that we must consider some of the responses children provided to questions about the meaning of loneliness. As we intimated earlier, children very frequently responded "being by yourself" or "when you're all alone" to such questions. It should be evident by now, however, that in using such expressions, children were not implying their strict literal meanings; rather, children were suggesting a particular kind of being alone, namely, that which one associates with being destitute of friendly companionship or interpersonal support more generally. Responses in which children provided elaborations of the more general descriptor "alone" bear this out: "You wouldn't have anyone to play with and you would be all by yourself," "You don't have that many friends," and "You're sort of all alone all the time and unhappy."

Lastly, a less abstract expression of the absence of relational provisions or of concern over their availability came in the form of statements in which loneliness was defined as the absence of specific relationships, typically friends and to a lesser extent family. The following definitions of loneliness are exemplary in this regard: "having no friends," "having no brothers or sisters," and "being the only kid in the family." As with statements about being alone, children who offered such responses elaborated by making explicit reference to relational provisions (e.g., "When you don't have any friends and there's no one to play with and you're bored" and "They have no friends and there isn't anyone they can turn to").

Interpersonal Contexts

Finally, our qualitative analysis of children's talk about loneliness led to the identification of eight different contexts for children's loneliness, each describing a particular interpersonal situation that children associated with feeling lonely: loss, dislocation, temporary absence, conflict, rejection, broken loyalties, exclusion, and being ignored. These were subsumed under two more superordinate headings, physical separation and psychological distancing. The eight context categories, however, should not be considered independent or mutually exclusive. In effect, each category directs our attention to particular features of situations that children mentioned in talking about loneliness and to potential differences in the way in which loneliness is experienced. It is also important to note that within each of these categories, children's accounts of loneliness could involve individuals from the peer or family social networks or the broader community. Although a few of the categories tended to involve primarily peer networks (as in the case of broken loyalties) or primarily family networks (as in the case of loss because of death or divorce), it is clear that both family and peer networks are important considerations in virtually every context. As well, reference to both affective and cognitive dimensions of loneliness were described within the specific interpersonal contexts distinguished later.

The superordinate category of physical separation comprises three descriptive contexts: loss, dislocation, and temporary absence. The thematic element that unifies these descriptive classifications is the emphasis on limitations or reduction in the child's access to important others (e.g., friends, parents, siblings, or pets). These limitations arise as a consequence of situational circumstances that impose a spatio-temporal barrier between these important others and the child.

Loss

Children frequently mentioned loss of proximity to important others (in this case, to those with whom they had developed secure, positive relationships) as a source of loneliness. Specifically, children talked about situations that rendered access to others as irrecoverable (as in the case of the death of an important other) or as seriously curtailed (as in the case of parents' divorce or separation or a friend moving away). In either case, children are subjected to relatively enduring structural changes to their interpersonal network that seriously constrain the availability of the relational provisions derived from important other(s) (e.g., affection from a parent, companionship from a friend, or the opportunity for nurturance provided by a pet).

Examples: (a) "When my dog died I was lonely 'cause I always played with him." (b) "When my parents separated and I didn't understand it that much. Dad was my favorite. He always listened to my problems. He always understood it."

Dislocation

Children also provided descriptions of situations in which they emphasized being displaced or dislocated from a familiar interpersonal setting to one in which they were newcomers. As newcomers, they often faced the task of integrating themselves into the new social group, most typically the peer group (e.g., going to camp or moving to a new neighborhood). In such contexts, the child must confront the prospect of making new friends or entering into a pre-established social group. There is a recognition that a period of accommodating oneself to new physical and interpersonal surroundings will precede one's social integration and that during this period one may be without companionship and consequently susceptible to bouts of loneliness.

The idea of dislocation might also be applied, in a somewhat more abstract sense, to children's "movement" through life, to settings where one faces increased expectations regarding relationships (e.g., high school). Indeed, in the context of a question that asked children to indicate what it might be like for them "a year or two from now," some children, typically the oldest, mentioned that they might feel lonelier because of the greater concerns in high school about making friends or, as one girl put it, about "boys and dances and stuff" that require one to decide "what to do and not to do." Children identified such situations as potential sources of loneliness in much the same way that they described being uprooted and immersed into a new neighborhood, perhaps one with an alternative code of behavior.

Dislocation can certainly entail the loss of an important other, as was made clear by a number of children who, in relating their accounts of moving to a new neighborhood, for example, spoke of "losing friends." Although both themes, loss and dislocation, could co-occur in children's narratives, our differentiation of the two themes is based on the notion that although the theme of loss focuses on the loss of an important other, the theme of dislocation stresses children's current personal circumstances and the prospect of making new friends. More simply, and perhaps more important, the distinction preserves the orientational differences reflected in children's talk about those situations in which one experiences an altered interpersonal milieu.

Examples: (a) "When I moved here, I knew nobody here. I knew I'd feel lonely. I'm not good at making friends at first." (b) "Going to camp for the first time. No one would be there that you knew."

Temporary Absence

Children most frequently associated loneliness with common and transitory events in which they were temporarily separated from others on whom they relied to provide certain relational provisions, notably companionship. Children referred to such situations as parents being away, being at home alone, having friends leave for the cottage, and having a brother or sister away from home. The children expressed their sense of loneliness under such circumstances more generally in terms of not having anything to do, or anyone to play with or talk to. Understandably, children often referred to the boredom they felt under such circumstances. In situations described under the rubric of temporary absence, children are in familiar surroundings and often have recourse to other relationships but must cope with "not having anything to do" (e.g., looking for other friends or spending time with the dog).

Examples: (a) "All of your friends have gone to the cottage and you don't have anyone to play with." (b) "When your mom and dad work full time and you have to babysit yourself. You might have no one else to play with and your mom and dad can't entertain you."

The superordinate theme of *psychological distancing* includes those situations in which children identify or interpret interpersonal actions as the source of their loneliness. Here, loneliness is not precipitated simply by the absence of others, as in physical separation, but rather by perceived deficiencies in interpersonal relationships. The five thematic categories that make up this more general theme are conflict, broken loyalties, rejection, exclusion, and being ignored.

Conflict

The theme of conflict describes situations in which loneliness arises from fights or arguments with peers, siblings, or parents. Conflicts were viewed as bidirectional in the sense that there was an ongoing reciprocal interchange between the people involved. Conflicts were particularly distressing because they transpired between friends and often resulted in the disruption of a formerly positive relationship (e.g., "She used to be my friend; she was a good friend"). Often children described the potential for fights with a friend to escalate into conflicts between themselves and the larger peer group. This typically involved friends taking sides against each other. The common worry expressed by children was that "everyone was going to be turning against me." Threats to both companionship and intimacy were frequently mentioned as the reason conflict situations were associated with loneliness.

Examples: (a) "If you were disagreeing with your friend and have a fight and all the other friends go on her side." (b) "I had no one to play with...couldn't lean on anyone when I needed help." (c) "I have no friends...they are all ganging up."

Rejection

Rejection emerged as the most blatant form of psychological distancing. Rejection was expressed verbally (e.g., name calling or teasing), non-verbally (e.g., someone intentionally moving their lunch pail away from yours), and in the form of physical attacks or threats. Unlike conflict, rejection is unidirectional, all actions being directed against the targeted child. The negative intentions of the antagonist(s) are clear and indisputable, and there seems to be little opportunity for the child to rebut. Children primarily mentioned being rejected by similar-aged others (as opposed to adults), including best friends, siblings, acquaintances, and unfamiliar peers. Usually, the targeted child would spontaneously offer a reason for being rejected. Although specific personal qualities (e.g., being "megasmart" or a "nerd," wearing glasses, or being fat) were frequently mentioned as sources of rejection, more general reasons centered around peers or family members not wanting or liking them (e.g., "Maybe kids just don't want to play with me" or "My sister wouldn't want to play with me 'cause she's in grade eight"). Sometimes the reason for rejection would be obscure or unknown, as is apparent in one girl's comment that "I don't know what I had done and they didn't want to tell me." Children appraised rejection situations in terms of their implications for a range of relational provisions including companionship, intimacy, and a sense of inclusion.

Examples: (a) "Being bothered all the time by people, like when people go around calling you names and teasing you behind your back. That really hurts." (b) "When I sit beside them in lunch, they move my lunch pail away."

Broken Loyalties

The theme of broken loyalties described two types of situations. First and most frequently this theme was reflected in descriptions that referred to a friend being "taken away," the idea being that if someone "took away" a friend, by playing with or talking to that friend, this implied that the relationship was faltering or no longer a reliable one (e.g., "Seems like your friend doesn't want you around anymore"). Asked why they felt lonely when their friend was "taken away," children offered the following sorts of responses: "The person was my best friend, I had nobody to play with";

"Because she's the only one I can tell my problems to . . . when the other girl takes her away from me I can't really talk to anybody"; and "Because she was my friend and she didn't want to stay with me any longer." The common theme was that the departed friend is no longer able to provide the social or emotional support that the child has come to expect from that friend, thereby breaking his or her friendship loyalties.

In the second type of scenario that we included under the theme of broken loyalties, three children form a friendship group, and there is a tendency for the friends to periodically arrange themselves into pairs, leaving one person out of their activities or discussions. Children spoke of this triad situation as upsetting because it involved close friends – friends who violated the expectation that friends do not exclude one another from their activities.

Examples: (a) "When my best friend goes and plays with another and you feel left out." (b) "Last year, two of my friends, we'd pair off and leave the other out."

Exclusion

In the case of exclusion, loneliness was associated with situations in which the children perceived themselves to be left out or excluded from a desired group of people or from some desired activity. Children described instances of being excluded from both peer-group and family activities (e.g., not being invited to a party or being excluded from an older sibling's activities). It was not always clear that the other person intended to exclude the child, although the child certainly believed he or she was left out. In terms of relational provisions, the effect of such exclusion was often described as creating problems in the social arena, leading to a lack of companionship (e.g., "No one else around to play with") and threats to one's sense of inclusion (e.g., "Not being part of a group").

Examples: (a) "When they're standing in front of me and invite another friend for sleepover and not me, right in front of me." (b) "Playing a game only a certain amount of people can play and they say you can't play."

Being Ignored

This category includes situations in which children perceived that they were being ignored, not noticed or not attended to by others, especially people who are important to them (e.g., "If you like someone and they just ignore you"). Although it is not always clear that such ignoring behavior is purposeful or intentional, it is nevertheless interpreted in a negative light, suggesting that the children or their ideas, opinions, needs, and so on are not important enough to warrant attention. It seemed that as a result of being ignored, children felt lonely because they questioned their relations with others or believed simply that there was no receptive audience (e.g., "If you have something exciting and no one wants to hear it"). Underlying such descriptions is often the belief that one should not be ignored by people who are important to you (e.g., "When friends say they're really friends but ignore you"). Thus, others are primarily guilty of failing to act, reflected in what they do not do, rather than any direct, hostile, or negative behavior directed toward the children, as in rejection. In those cases in which children spoke of being ignored, they often mentioned threats to the relational provisions of enhancement of worth (e.g., feeling unimportant or forgotten about) and companionship.

Examples: (a) "When you're talking and they won't listen to you." (b) "When your friends say they're real friends but ignore you."

Generally, the results of our qualitative analysis indicated that children's loneliness is indeed a complex and multidimensional affair. Although the earlier cited work of Z. Rubin (1980) and Sullivan (1953) captures elements of this complexity, the present results suggest that an account of the differentiated character of children's loneliness needs to move beyond a specification of the companionship and intimacy provisions found in peer and parent relationships to a more complete elaboration of the variety of relational provisions and interpersonal contexts implicated in children's experience of loneliness. Our findings point to the need to consider loneliness within children's broader social network, including children's relationships with school and neighborhood peers, parents, siblings, relatives, other adults, and even pets, and in a wider variety of interpersonal contexts, and in reference to a more extensive set of relational provisions and affective states.

Generality of the Loneliness Experience

The richness of children's talk about loneliness provided us with considerable insight into the breadth and variety of children's loneliness experiences, but this also raised some very fundamental "next" questions. How generalizable are these particular themes across children? Is the experience of loneliness similar for boys and girls? Do popular and rejected children, the primary foci of previous research on childhood loneliness, experience loneliness in similar ways and in similar contexts? Several years later, we embarked on a second phase of this research to begin to address some of these questions. In particular, as part of a larger research project (Terrell-Deutsch, 1991), we considered whether these same categories or contexts of loneliness would apply to a different sample of children. In this research, we used quantitative analyses in an effort to verify our qualitative findings.

In a separate sample ($N = 455$), we assessed the frequency with which preadolescent children associated their experience of loneliness with the interpersonal situations previously identified (Hayden et al., 1988). We also examined whether the likelihood of children experiencing loneliness in any of these situations varied as a function of their gender or classroom social status. Specifically, fifth- and sixth-grade children (199 boys and 256 girls, 10–12 years of age) from 24 classrooms in 10 elementary schools within largely middle-class urban communities participated in this second study. The children were divided into popular, average, and unpopular groups on the basis of peer sociometric ratings provided by all classmates ("How much do you like to play with this person at school?") on a 5-point scale and that were standardized within classrooms (see Terrell-Deutsch, 1991, for details regarding methods and procedures). Popular children (85 girls and 59 boys) were those whose sociometric ratings were at least one-half standard deviation above the classroom mean; average status children (98 girls and 67 boys) were those whose ratings were within one-half standard deviation of the classroom mean; and unpopular children (73 girls and 73 boys) were those whose ratings were at least one-half standard deviation below the classroom mean.

In a group testing situation, the children were asked to respond to a Loneliness Anticipation Questionnaire (Terrell-Deutsch, 1991), which was developed on the basis of the qualitative results described previously. In this questionnaire, the children were presented with a series of eight different hypothetical situations that reflected each of the eight different interpersonal contexts that children had previously described as giving rise to loneliness (Hayden et al., 1988):

Temporary absence:	"Suppose you're home alone one day and no one else is around."
Loss:	"Suppose someone you really care about is moving away."
Dislocation:	"Suppose you are moving away."
Conflict:	"Suppose you have a fight with someone you really care about."
Broken loyalties:	"Suppose someone you really care about is 'taken away' by someone else."

Rejection: "Suppose someone you really care about calls you names or teases you or treats you like you are worthless."

Exclusion: "Suppose people you really care about leave you out of things."

Being ignored: "Suppose someone you really care about ignores you."

Effort was made to describe the "others" in global or general terms (e.g., "Someone you really care about") so that respondents could apply each example to anyone in their broader social network, including adults and peers, immediate and extended family, classroom as well as neighborhood peers, and so forth.

To evaluate the degree to which children viewed each context as one that might lead to loneliness, we asked the children to rate how lonely each situation would make them feel (5-point scale, *not at all lonely* to *very, very lonely*), with higher scores indicative of greater expectations for feeling lonely in that context. Internal consistency for these ratings, across contexts, was high ($\alpha = .82$). To evaluate the degree to which children themselves had experienced loneliness in each context, we asked the children to indicate if this situation had ever happened to them (yes–no response).

We later evaluated children's responses to these questions in terms of variations as a function of both gender and status by using chi-square analyses (to examine gender and status group differences in the number and percentage of children who reported experiences in each context) and Gender × Status multivariate analyses of variance (MANOVAs; to examine gender and status group differences in the degree to which children rated each context as loneliness engendering). Results of these analyses are presented in Tables 5.1 and 5.2 and are summarized briefly below.[1]

Overall, as can be seen in the first column of Table 5.1, nearly one third or more of the children reported that they had experienced loneliness in each of the eight different situations described, suggesting that these eight interpersonal contexts were indeed likely settings for feelings of loneliness. Children were most likely to have experienced loneliness in response to conflict and temporary absence, with 55% and 64% of the children reporting such experiences, respectively.

---

[1] Results of the Gender × Status MANOVA revealed a significant overall main effect for gender but no significant main effect for status and no Gender × Status interaction. Thus, for the sake of simplicity, results are presented separately for each of these two independent variables.

Table 5.1. Children's Experience of Loneliness Across Interpersonal Contexts: Variations as a Function of Gender

| Situational Context | Percentage of Children Indicating That This had Happened to Them[a] | | | | Mean Expected Loneliness Ratings for Each Context[b] | | |
	Overall ($Ns = 430–454$)	Boys ($ns = 176–191$)	Girls ($ns = 227–252$)	χ^2	Boys ($ns = 185–199$)	Girls ($ns = 241–255$)	Univariate F
Loss	41	35	45	4.04*	3.47	3.87	9.05**
Conflict	55	47	61	8.41**	2.47	3.47	65.68***
Broken loyalties	31	18	41	27.24***	3.33	3.84	14.64***
Rejection	34	28	39	5.33*	2.76	3.66	35.87***
Exclusion	31	24	36	6.99**	3.13	3.73	23.42***
Temporary absence	64	64	64	0.20	1.96	2.13	0.56
Being ignored	31	28	33	1.41	2.82	3.53	19.95***
Dislocation	48	44	50	1.33	3.32	3.77	8.37**

[a] Question asked of children: "Did this ever happen to you?"
[b] Question asked of children: "How lonely would this make you feel?" Responses ranged from 1 (*low loneliness*) to 5 (*high loneliness*).
* $p < .05$. ** $p < .01$. *** $p < .001$.

Table 5.2. Children's Experience of Loneliness Across Interpersonal Contexts: Variations as a Function of Social Status–Popularity

Situational Context	Percentage of Children Indicating That This had Happened to Them[a]			Mean Expected Loneliness Ratings for Each Context[b]		
	Popular (ns = 128–142)	Average (ns = 145–160)	Unpopular (ns = 128–140)	Popular (ns = 136–144)	Average (ns = 156–165)	Unpopular (ns = 137–145)
Loss	39	44	39	3.66	3.79	3.65
Conflict	55	58	52	3.11	3.07	2.91
Broken loyalties	31	30	32	3.62	3.74	3.48
Rejection	37	35	31	3.44	3.27	3.13
Exclusion	32	33	27	3.52	3.46	3.44
Temporary absence	63	64	64	2.03	1.97	2.20
Being ignored	36	29	28	3.27	3.28	3.15
Dislocation	44	48	51	3.86	3.48	3.47

Note. All comparisons across status groups were nonsignificant in both chi-square analyses (columns 1–3) and multivariate analyses of variance (columns 3–6). These data are presented for illustrative purposes.

[a] Question asked of children: "Did this ever happen to you?"

[b] Question asked of children: "How lonely would this make you feel?" Responses ranged from 1 (*low loneliness*) to 5 (*high loneliness*).

Gender Differences

With regard to gender, results of chi-square analyses indicated that a significantly larger proportion of girls reported experience with five of the eight contexts: loss, conflict, broken loyalties, rejection, and exclusion. Thus, although each of these contexts represents a potential source for childhood loneliness regardless of the gender of the child, more girls than boys appear to have experienced loneliness in terms of the loss of someone they really cared about who moves away (loss), the pain of a fight with someone they cared about (conflict), the betrayal of having someone they cared about "taken away" by someone else (broken loyalties), and the humiliation of being teased or left out by people they cared about (rejection and exclusion).

When we evaluated children's ratings of how lonely children would expect to feel in each of the eight loneliness contexts by using Gender × Status MANOVAs, we found only a significant overall effect of gender (Wilks = .829), $F(11, 439) = 8.20$, $p < .001$) and nonsignificant variations as a function of status or the interaction of status and gender. As shown in the last three columns of Table 5.1, girls anticipated feeling significantly more lonely than boys in seven of the eight contexts. Thus, it appears that, at least in the 10–12 year age range, more girls report experiencing loneliness in many of these contexts and girls generally expect to feel more lonely than boys across contexts.

Status Differences

Results of both chi-square analyses and MANOVAs failed to reveal any variations in reported loneliness experiences as a function of status groups (see Table 5.2). In other words, contrary to what one might expect, similar numbers of popular, average, and unpopular children reported having experienced each of the eight loneliness situations, with at least 25% of the children in each status group describing such a situation in their past. Moreover, popular, average, and unpopular children were similar in the degree to which they expected to feel lonely in each of these situations. Although rejected or unpopular children (relative to their more accepted peers) have consistently been found to report greater feelings of loneliness overall (see Asher et al., 1990 for a review), our results suggest that children of all status groups experience feelings of loneliness, and do so across similar contexts and with similar expectations regarding just how lonely they expect to feel in each. Perhaps rejected or unpopular children simply experience these contexts more frequently, although further research would be necessary to evaluate this speculation. Importantly, however, these data point to the fact that the contexts in which children experience loneliness are not unique or limited to low-status children but are familiar to children across the status hierarchy.

Consistent with results obtained for the sample as a whole, it would appear that children anticipated that being "home alone" would result in relatively less loneliness, this being true even before McCauley Caulkin provided them with a wealth of ideas for things to do when left home alone in the recent movie of the same name. In the other seven interpersonal contexts, children reported that they would generally expect to feel lonely, with anticipated loneliness ranging from moderate, especially in the context of conflict or being ignored, to quite high, with expected loneliness ratings consistently above the mean of the scale. The greatest anticipated loneliness was expected in response to loosing someone you really care about regardless of whether such a loss occurred as a result of moving (loss and dislocation) or being "taken away" by others (broken loyalties).

Conclusions

The descriptive framework we have presented suggests a number of important features of children's loneliness. First, our analysis of children's own spontaneous descriptions of loneliness serves to confirm and support extant conceptions of childhood loneliness. For example, children's persistent reference to the affective or felt component of loneliness supports arguments by Parkhurst and Hopmeyer (this volume) regarding loneliness as an emotional experience. Children's descriptions of the various relational provisions (or lack thereof) associated with loneliness lend credence to cognitive deficit models of loneliness (e.g., Maragoni & Ickes, 1989; Peplau et al., 1982; Peplau & Perlman, 1979; see Parkhurst & Hopmeyer, this volume, or Terrell-Deutsch, this volume, for overviews of such models). The fact that children focused primarily on interpersonal relations with age mates in their descriptions of loneliness supports such an emphasis in current self-report measures of loneliness (see Terrell-Deutsch, this volume, for a review). At the same time, the present results suggest that loneliness is certainly not confined to children's experiences with peers but instead reflects the broader social world in which children live, echoing previous research on the diversity of children's potential sources of social support (e.g., Furman & Robbins, 1985).

Second, the present results serve to qualify and expand on previous research on childhood loneliness. For example, results of our quantitative study indicate that loneliness experiences do not necessarily differ across children who are more vs. less popular among their peers. These findings may initially appear to counter previous research that has consistently demonstrated significant relations between poor social status among classmates and self-reports of loneliness (see Asher et al., 1990; Parker et al., this volume, for reviews). However, the correlations reported in previous research have typically been quite modest in magnitude (suggesting that children at all status levels are likely to experience loneliness to some extent) and typically address reported loneliness derived from particular situations and others, most notably, peer relations within school (given the content of the items included in the self-report instruments utilized). In our interviews, every child was readily able to describe situations in which he or she had felt lonely. Loneliness, then, appears to be a common experience, regardless of how well one is situated within a classroom peer group. Perhaps the experience of loneliness is both inevitable and necessary, if only to provide children with the striking contrast of how to cope with "me," despite some preference for "we."

Third, it is noteworthy that results of our initial qualitative analyses were supported by more quantitative data obtained from a different sample of children. Results of both types of analyses demonstrate the range and diversity of children's loneliness experiences. Not all children reported the experience of loneliness across all contexts, but a substantial number of children did report experiencing loneliness in each of the identified contexts. Although the degree of loneliness experienced varied across children as well as situations, each context has the potential to set the stage for interpersonal loneliness. Thus, children appear to have ample opportunities to experience loneliness across a variety of contexts and with regard to a number of different types of interpersonal relationships.

Despite the diversity of contexts in which loneliness is experienced by children, it is not clear from the present data whether the experience of loneliness, albeit affectively unpleasant, is in fact detrimental. Given the frequent reference to feelings of boredom, one might speculate that such experiences provide children with opportunities for discovering themselves and for finding out how to occupy their own time without the benefit of social company. We must not overlook the possibility that the experience of loneliness may provide children with opportunities for positive self-development (see Larson, this volume, and Goossens & Marcoen, this volume, for further discussions of this possibility). Indeed, within our own qualitiative data, children's descriptions of how they deal with loneliness often spoke to the positive possibilities emerging from the experience of loneliness. In response to our questions about how they coped with loneliness, children mentioned a range of activities and strategies, many of which carried the potential for self-discovery and self-growth. Although strategies like "watching television" and "listening to music" were certainly mentioned, children also "cope" with their loneliness in ways that appeared more obviously to promote self-development and the establishment of positive bonds with others. Representative examples of such responses include the following: "Just talk to my mom and tell her how I feel," "Called on friends that lived further away," "Read," "Play the piano," "Sometimes I go outside and ask if I can walk the neighbor's dog," "Go outside and ride my bike," "Tried to make friends again," "Hobbies or something," "Play with the computer," "Think about everything and sort everything out in my mind," "Sometimes I talk to a guidance counselor," "Make up stories," and "Write letters to friends."

In advocating the view that loneliness may be associated with positive self-development, we are simply echoing what strikes us as a persistent but often overlooked theme in the literature. In his early work on the subject of existential loneliness, for example, Moustakas (1961) asked that loneliness – in all its pain and inevitability – be regarded as a uniquely human experience that holds the potential for fostering a deeper sensitivity and awareness of one's self and one's world. According to Moustakas, it is in the recognition and acceptance of people's existential loneliness, rather than in their efforts to deny, overcome, or escape it, that they come to experience their lives – including bonds to others – in a more meaningful, growth-inducing way. In describing the situations that nearly every child faces at one time or another, situations very much like those mentioned by the children in our study, Moustakas (1961) further suggests that experiences of loneliness for children, as for adults, do not necessarily produce feelings of defeat and alienation, but rather "have potential value and are a way to learning and to a new life" (p. 43).

The view that the experience of loneliness may provide opportunities for learning and self-transformation also recalls the more general philosophical arguments put forth regarding the special nature of hermeneutic experience. In Gadamer's (1989) view, for example, hermeneutic experience has the character of disappointment: It is a process that consists of the disappointment or disconfirmation of some expectation, of some previously held assumption about one's self or one's world. By definition, such experience entails a change in self-understanding. More specifically, being experienced in this sense means being aware of the contingency and partiality of one's own views. Through such experience, people do not learn this or that specific thing, nor do they necessarily acquire the kind of knowledge that will allow them to "know better the next time." Rather, what they learn is to be more open to new experience, more willing to learn from what is "other." To the extent that the experience of loneliness gives rise to questions and doubts about people's own self-sufficiency and reminds them of their limits and need for others, it would appear that it shares at least some of the structural characteristics of the hermeneutic experience so conceived.

In summary, the present examination of children's own narratives and accounts of their own personal anecdotes provides clear evidence that loneliness is a common and familiar experience for children. Generally, we were struck by the complexity and inclusiveness of children's talk about loneliness. On the basis of our interpretation of children's definitions and stories, a picture of loneliness emerges that portrays the affective–cognitive nature of this experience. As we have shown, the affective side of loneliness was captured in children's reference to emotion terms (e.g., sadness, boredom, and feelings) and in their use of metaphorical expressions. The cognitive content of loneliness is reflected in children's appraisals of relationships (e.g., "no friends") and, in particular, their associated provisions. The third feature of children's loneliness suggested by children's talk concerns the variety of contexts with which loneliness was associated.

Our findings point to the need to consider loneliness within children's broader social networks, including a consideration of children's relationships with school and neighborhood peers, parents, siblings, relatives, other adults (e.g., coaches, teachers, and counselors), and even pets. Additionally, the results of our analysis suggest that each of these relationships can offer children a variety of interpersonal provisions. Children's loneliness stories were especially illuminating in this regard; these stories depicted the possible overlap between relationships and the provisions they offer. This complexity may be best appreciated by considering children's stories of loneliness experiences. Examples are provided in the Appendix. As we mentioned earlier, these stories can integrate the various aspects of children's loneliness from specific contextual cues to self-relevant relational appraisals.

We should emphasize that our proposed framework for conceptualizing both the nature of loneliness and the specific contexts in which it may be experienced should not be considered fixed. Indeed, we would encourage investigators to further examine the usefulness and applicability of this framework, especially developmentally. Furthermore, there is the issue of whether, for any one child, the situations associated with loneliness reflect isolated occurrences or more enduring interpersonal conditions. If the latter, how does this bear on the child's social adjustment?

Another important issue that has received little or no attention concerns the socialization of loneliness. It is our view that the relational provisions implicated in the experience of loneliness reflect not biological needs but rather cultural expectations regarding what relationships a person ought to have and what relationships should offer in terms of interpersonal support. If relational provisions are indeed socioculturally determined, then research aimed at identifying the everyday contexts in which children learn about loneliness and the conditions that surround its expression is warranted.

Acknowledgment

The first study described in this chapter was previously presented as a paper co-authored by Hayden, Tarulli, and Hymel at the Biennial University of Waterloo Conference on Child Development, Waterloo, Ontario, Canada, May, 1988. The data considered in the second study described in this chapter were collected as part of doctoral research conducted by Beverley Terrell-Deutsch.

Appendix: Examples of Children's Loneliness Narratives

Boy, Grade 5

"I was living in Greenvalley. It was a Sunday. All the stores were closed, I had no money. Jason, a friend, had to go to his aunts. I decided to call on Jamie, but no one was home. I went to turn on the TV and only church stuff was on. I went upstairs to play with my toys, but it was so boring. The dog was behind the couch so I didn't want to bother him. Mom was sleeping. My sister was baby-sitting. It wasn't my day." [Why did that make you feel lonely?] "There was no one to talk to or play with, nothing to listen to."

Girl, Grade 5

"When I first moved here, I missed my really good friend, Allison. We played a lot. Since she was not there, I had no really good friends. We didn't see each other for a long time. I saw her once in Grade 3, I haven't seen her since." [Why did that make you feel lonely?] " 'Cause I missed her'. Cause I wouldn't find another friend that was like her. We always shared stuff, talked on the phone. On P. D. days, we went places together. Always walked to school together when we could. I missed all my friends. I didn't like the new school. I always wanted to move back."

Girl, Grade 6

"Today everybody's going to Mary Ann's party in the group. I'm sort of the one that gets left behind. I'm not invited to the party so I won't do anything on the weekend. Anywhere the whole group goes, I don't." [Why did that make you feel lonely?] "I'm just the person that gets left back. Maybe they don't realize that I get left, that I'm there, but it happens all the time."

(Continued)

Appendix: (*Continued*)

Girl, Grade 7

"Two years ago when my dog Fred ran away. He never came back and I kept asking God to bring him back. This year my brother wrote a book on Fred and I started to cry." [Why did that make you feel lonely?] "I was mostly with him all the time and proud of him to be my dog because he was a hunting dog. He was getting older and I thought I needed to take care of him. I didn't get to see his sad eyes anymore."

Girl, Grade 8

"Last year, at the beginning of the year, I had a friend, Sandy. Then she went with another group of people who didn't like me. They would walk away when I'd go over to Sandy. They started spreading rumors about me to make everyone hate me. Sandy also didn't hang around me 'cause her other friends didn't like me." [Why did that make you feel lonely?] "I didn't have any friends. They didn't want to be near me."

Boy, Grade 6

"When I first moved to the school, we were outside playing at school [with my old friend from my other school]. And they started pushing me around and tried to beat me up and I tried to ignore them. They thought I was chicken since I wouldn't fight. They were making fun of my glasses and thinking I was stupid. They tried to push me down when I was skating on the ice. [It] happened for a while after I came; on and off it might happen now. A lot of lads were bugging me. I think I'm alright 'cause I can run faster than them."

Note.   The above-mentioned examples are children's stories about their own loneliness experiences and reflect the variety of contexts and relational provisions cited by children in describing loneliness.

III | LONELINESS IN CHILDHOOD

6 | Loneliness During Early Childhood: The Role of Interpersonal Behaviors and Relationships

KIM B. BURGESS, GARY W. LADD, BECKY
J. KOCHENDERFER, SHARON F. LAMBERT,
AND SONDRA H. BIRCH

Decades ago, prominent theorists assumed that loneliness could only be experienced in adolescence and adulthood when needs for social intimacy, beyond those which parents could provide, were thought to begin (e.g., Sullivan, 1953; Weiss, 1973). This reasoning is reminiscent of psychoanalytic theorists who likewise believed that children could not experience depression (see Rutter, 1986). Similar to theory and research on depression, such thinking may have stultified empirical work on loneliness in young children because very few studies have been conducted on loneliness at this stage of development. Recently, however, researchers have recognized that, along with the need to be physically and emotionally close to significant others, young children are able to discern their social situation and emotional state. An initial estimate that about 10% of 5- to 7-year-old children feel very lonely or dissatisfied with their social relationships at school (Cassidy & Asher, 1992) supports the notion that young children can actually feel sadness about solitude. Furthermore, children in kindergarten and first grade comprehend the concept of loneliness, reporting that loneliness is "a feeling of being sad and alone" (Cassidy & Asher, 1992).

Given the incidence of loneliness in early childhood and the importance of this phenomenon, the researchers in our lab have studied loneliness among young children in the school environment. Our starting point for investigation was the fall of kindergarten, a time when children have just entered grade school and are making a transition to a new setting and social situation. Hymel, Tarulli, Hayden Thomson, and Terrell-Deutsch (this volume) have reported that feeling lonely often accompanies the occurrence of major life events, such as loss of a significant other or moving to an unfamiliar place. Although starting school constitutes a normative transition because it is experienced by all children, this event can nevertheless bring forth unpleasant emotions as children attempt to adjust to new circumstances.

109

Consistent with young children's own conceptions of loneliness, we similarly define this construct as being alone and feeling sad. Consequently, our loneliness scale includes items referring to feeling sad and alone in school but does not include items referring to social dissatisfaction.[1] Central to the experience of loneliness is the subjective appraisal or feeling that one lacks a connection with others. Consistent with an interpersonal orientation, we view loneliness as occurring in the context of relationships, and thus we chose to examine the domains of children's peer, teacher–child, and parent–child relationships because these relational systems are central in young children's social ecologies and capture a large portion of their social contacts. Inherent in our examination of the social realm is the assumption that relationship processes between children and their peers, teachers, or parents are bidirectional or reciprocal in nature. We also assert that children's relationships, or their features, yield certain provisions and serve as supports or stressors.

The purpose of this chapter is to provide a preliminary description of relationship and social–behavioral factors associated with loneliness in early childhood. Toward this end, we review current knowledge about the empirical linkages between children's relationship systems, interpersonal behaviors, and loneliness. First, evidence that links forms of peer relationship, including friendship, peer-group acceptance, and peer victimization, with loneliness is examined; second, data pertaining to features of the teacher–child relationship including closeness, dependency, and conflict are considered; and third, findings relevant to the parent–child relationship including quality, parent characteristics, and parenting styles are reviewed. Also considered is the child's propensity to engage in specific modes of interaction with peers, especially aggressive and withdrawn behavioral styles. Not only are aggressive and withdrawn behaviors exhibited in the social context and partly reflect how children relate to others but these behaviors may be directly or indirectly linked to childhood loneliness via affective and cognitive processes (cf. Rubin et al., 1990).

---

[1] In our studies loneliness was defined as feeling sad and alone in school, and was measured with five items that directly referred to the concept of loneliness or to those feeling states (e.g., "Are you lonely at school?" and "Are you sad and alone at school?"). Included among these items are several from the Cassidy and Asher (1992) scale and others devised by Ladd and colleagues (e.g., Ladd et al., 1996). This loneliness scale is similar to the one that Parker and Asher (1993) call a "pure" loneliness scale because this scale does not contain additional items that are likely to tap aspects of children's dissatisfaction with their peer relationships. Therefore, our scale differs somewhat in item content from the Cassidy and Asher loneliness scale, which also contains items referring to children's perceptions of their peer relationships.

Consistent with our focus on young children's relationships and the environment, we draw on interpersonal theories to elucidate mechanisms that could account for the research findings in each relationship domain. Key themes and issues that have emerged in this literature are considered in the final section, along with future research directions. We begin this chapter by considering the relation between young children's peer relationships and loneliness – a domain in which the largest body of empirical evidence has accumulated.

Peer Relationships and Loneliness

Participation in peer relationships is an essential part of social life during childhood, and the experiences that children encounter in this context may have an important bearing on their emotional adjustment, including feelings of loneliness. Past research suggests that feelings of loneliness may stem from experiences in three relational contexts, including friendship, peer-group acceptance, and bullying–victimization (Asher et al., 1984; Olweus, 1993b; Parker & Asher, 1993b).

Friendship refers to a dyadic and mutually regulated relationship that exists between a child and another peer. Several indexes have evolved to represent aspects of this relational context, including the size of the child's friendship network (i.e., number of mutual friendships), participation in a "very best friendship," and quality of the friendships (see Bukowski & Hoza, 1989; Parker & Asher, 1993b). Peer-group acceptance refers to the quality of a child's relations with his or her social group as reflected by evidence of consensual liking or disliking by group members for individuals within the peer group (see Ladd & Kochenderfer, 1996). Victimization can be viewed as a relationship because it is marked by a unique and enduring pattern of interactions that occur between children and specific bullies or attackers (see Elicker et al., 1992; Troy & Sroufe, 1987). Peer victimization and peer rejection are not synonymous concepts, even though rejected children are often the recipient of negative overtures from peers (Coie & Kupersmidt, 1983; Gottman et al., 1975). Perry, Kusel, and Perry (1988) have shown that not all rejected children are victimized, and conversely, not all victimized children are rejected. Furthermore, Ladd, Kochenderfer, and Coleman (1997) found that peer acceptance and victimization were differentially associated with children's school adjustment.

Peer Relationship Processes and Provisions: Pathways Toward and Away From Loneliness

A prominent assumption in the peer relations literature is that children derive important benefits from peer interactions (see Berndt & Ladd, 1989;

Hartup & Sancilio, 1986). Unfortunately, the reverse may also be true; that is, children's peer experiences may not always be positive or contribute to their development and well-being (see Berndt, 1989; Hartup, 1996). In our research with young children (ages 5–7), we have conceptualized peer relationships as contexts in which children are exposed to specific experiences (e.g., interactional processes) that, in turn, foster both positive and negative psychological states within the individual (e.g., feelings of closeness vs. mistrust; see Weiss, 1974). Propositions about the "effects" of particular forms of relationship, or the processes and provisions that children likely derive from their participation in certain forms of relationship have, to some extent, been articulated in the literatures on friendship, peer-group acceptance, and peer victimization (see Asher & Coie, 1990; Berndt & Ladd, 1989; Bukowski, Newcomb, & Hartup, 1996).

Efforts to test propositions that might account for linkages between peer relationships and loneliness in young children are at an early stage compared with those undertaken with older children, adolescents, and adults. Young children's feelings of loneliness at school may be linked to forms of school maladjustment. Ladd and Coleman (1997), for example, found that loneliness is a moderately stable phenomenon in kindergarten-age children ($r = .41$ from fall to spring of kindergarten) and one that is positively correlated with negative perceptions of classmates and lower levels of school liking. More important, findings from recent investigations have begun to address the question of whether loneliness is associated with the types of relationships that young children form with peers, including friendship, peer acceptance, and victimization. Although preliminary, these findings provide an empirical basis for examining many of the propositions advanced about the contributions of early peer relationships to children's feelings of loneliness.

Friendship. Friendship implies the presence of an emotional tie between a child and a peer. This tie, and other forces (e.g., mutual attraction), provides a context for ongoing processes or interactions that, depending on their valence and content, influence not only the progression of the relationship (e.g., stability) but also the provisions that are likely to evolve for each partner. Friendships may differ in the processes that evolve over time (e.g., the balance of supportive vs. conflictual interactions) and, therefore, vary in the provisions children receive. A number of investigators have developed models of the processes and provisions (i.e., qualities) that may be present in children's friendships and have devised measures for assessing individual and developmental differences in these relationship properties (for a review, see Ladd & Kochenderfer, 1996). Among young children, investigators have tended to focus on friendship processes such as validation, aid, self-disclosure, and conflict (see Ladd, Kochenderfer, & Coleman, 1996; Parker & Gottman, 1989). These processes are seen as having the potential to confer on children provisions such as a sense of security, support, and self-affirmation that, in turn, may inhibit negative emotional states, such as loneliness. In contrast, conflict can be seen as a stressor that negatively affects the same provisions and ultimately undermines the friendship bond and precipitates negative affective states including loneliness.

Evidence linking aspects of young children's friendships with loneliness is emerging in the literature. Coleman (1993) obtained measures of kindergarteners' number of mutual friendships and participation in a "very best friendship" and found that both forms of friendship correlated negatively with loneliness at the beginning and end of the school year. Similarly, Ladd et al. (1997) interviewed 200 5-year-olds about the same friendship features and found that both were inversely related to loneliness. In this study, however, the number of friendships measure was more strongly and consistently related to loneliness ($r = -.27$ for fall, $-.33$ for spring; $ps < .01$) than was the very best friendship measure ($r = -.11$ for fall, $-.14$ for spring; $p < .05$ only for spring). Moreover, the quantity of children's friendships in the fall of the school year predicted changes in loneliness over time. Perhaps when negotiating the transition to grade school, children experience higher levels of support and lower levels of distress when they possess larger friendship networks in the classroom. Evidence indicating that the size of children's friendship network is an important predictor of early adjustment is consistent with evidence from other investigations (see Ladd, 1990; Vandell & Hembree, 1994).

The thesis that differences exist in the quality of children's friendships, and that loneliness may be pronounced in friendships that lack supportive or affirming resources, has only recently been examined with older children (e.g., see Bukowski & Hoza, 1989; Parker & Asher, 1993; see also Parker et al., this volume). Findings from these studies support the premise that friendships differ in quality and that those lacking in key provisions (e.g., support) or those having higher levels of difficulty (e.g., conflict) are less likely to remain intact (see Berndt, Hawkins, & Hoyle, 1986) and more likely to foster feelings of loneliness. Efforts to extend this line of investigation to young children have only recently been undertaken, but the results that have emerged thus far are, in many respects, consistent with those reported for older samples.

Ladd et al. (1996) developed a measure of perceived friendship quality and assessed each of five friendship processes (i.e., validation, aid, disclosure of negative affect, exclusivity, and conflict) for children who had a close friend in their classrooms. These scores were used to predict changes in loneliness over the school year and results showed that, for boys but not girls, higher levels of conflict in friendship were associated with gains in loneliness. Additionally, gains in loneliness over the school year were associated with higher levels of self-disclosure (i.e., talk about negative affect) in friendships. These findings were interpreted as evidence indicating that boys may be more adversely affected by conflict in their friendships than are girls. Boys' apparent vulnerability in this regard was attributed to several factors, including the tendency for young males to have fewer friends when faced with relationship difficulties and greater difficulty resolving conflicts with friends (see Berndt, 1981; Parker & Asher, 1993). The finding that talk with friends about negative affect predicted gains in loneliness suggested that when young children struggle with emotional difficulties (e.g., feeling lonely at school), they may rely on a close friend to seek solace or unburden themselves. Studies of the conversations that occur between young friends richly illustrate young children's use of friends as resources for coping with negative affect, such as fears (see Parker & Gottman, 1989).

Thus, although only a small corpus of evidence has been assembled on the relation between young children's friendships and loneliness, the findings are consistent with the proposition that early friendships, because of the largely supportive provisions they can offer, inhibit feelings of loneliness. It has also become apparent that friendships vary in quality and that, particularly for young boys, friendships that contain higher levels of conflict may foster feelings of loneliness in school.

Peer-Group Acceptance. Although there is no clear consensus as to the processes that high- versus low-accepted children experience in peer groups, current hypotheses stem from the premise that children's reputations among classmates determine the quality of their interactions and participation in peer activities. It has been hypothesized that, compared with well-accepted children, those who are poorly accepted are more often forced to occupy marginal roles in the peer group, subjected to various forms of mistreatment, and excluded from peer activities (Ladd, 1988; Ladd & Kochenderfer, 1996). Consistent with these premises, it has been shown that classmates direct positive behaviors toward liked children but treat disliked peers more punitively (Ladd, 1983; Masters & Furman, 1981). Also, rejected children are more likely to be avoided by peers, denied access to peer activities, and experience other forms of exclusion (Ladd, Price, & Hart, 1990). These experiences thwart basic needs that children have to "belong" or to engage in nonaversive interactions with members of their social group (see Baumeister & Leary, 1995; Furman & Robbins, 1985) and to feel some degree of "relatedness" with classmates at school (Connell & Welborn, 1991). Missing provisions, such as a reduced sense of belongingness in the peer group, may give rise to negative affective states such as feelings of alienation and loneliness.

Recent investigations with young children in school settings reveal a consistent pattern of results: Children who are not well accepted by classmates report higher levels of loneliness than do better accepted children. With 5- to 7-year-old children, Cassidy and Asher (1992) found that loneliness (as measured on a loneliness and social dissatisfaction scale) correlated −.23 with children's sociometric ratings in the spring of the school year. Similarly, Ladd and Coleman (1997) assessed children's peer acceptance in kindergarten and found that sociometric ratings correlated −.29 ($p < .01$) with loneliness during the second month of school. Using a larger sample, Ladd et al. (1997) found that early peer acceptance, in the fall of the school year, correlated negatively with loneliness in both the fall and spring of kindergarten ($r = -.29$ in the fall, −.17 from fall to spring; $ps < .05$), and fall peer acceptance predicted significant changes in loneliness over the school year. Fall loneliness, however, was not associated with changes in children's peer acceptance.

In summary, consistent with research on older samples, there is evidence to suggest that young children's social standing in classroom peer groups is a correlate of loneliness (see Asher et al., 1984; Parker & Asher, 1993b; Renshaw & Brown, 1993). Low peer acceptance, which may be experienced by children as exclusion from peer activities and, ultimately, as a lack of belongingness in the classroom, may be an important contributor to young children's feelings of alienation and loneliness at school.

Peer Victimization. Victimization implies that children are regularly exposed to abusive interactions (e.g., verbal, or physical aggression), and this form of relationship has been hypothesized to undermine children's feelings of trust (toward peers), security, and safety in the school environment (see Alsaker, 1993; Hoover & Hazler, 1991; Slee, 1993). In turn, feelings of mistrust, or fearfulness, toward classmates are hypothesized to cause victimized children to withdraw from peer interactions or to isolate themselves from social and scholastic activities in school. Over time, these feelings and the social isolation that may accompany them may lead children to feel alienated and lonely. Consistent with these propositions, researchers have shown that victimized children are more anxious and insecure and are more likely to dislike and avoid school, as compared with nonvictimized classmates (Boulton & Underwood, 1992; Kochenderfer & Ladd, 1996a; Olweus, 1993b). Given these findings, it is not surprising that victimized children report high levels of loneliness (Alsaker, 1993; Boulton & Underwood, 1992; Kochenderfer & Ladd, 1996a).

Unfortunately, most of the research on victimization is based on concurrent assessments (Alsaker, 1993; Boulton & Underwood, 1992); thus, it has been unclear whether victimization is a cause or a consequence of children's loneliness. Yet, Kochenderfer and Ladd (1996a) examined the causal priority of peer victimization and children's school adjustment by gathering data on the frequency of children's exposure to peers' aggression and their feelings of loneliness in the fall and spring of kindergarten. Results showed that changes in loneliness could be predicted from early (fall) peer victimization, but changes in victimization could not be predicted by early loneliness. Furthermore, based on the timing and extent of victimization, these investigators assembled four groups of children (e.g., fall only, spring only, stable, and nonvictimized) and found that spring-only victims did not become more lonely than the nonvictim group until spring when they were targeted for peers' aggression. Children in the stable victim group (i.e., abused both fall and spring) reported significantly higher levels of loneliness in both the fall and spring of the school year compared with the nonvictim group.

Another goal of the Kochenderfer and Ladd (1996a) study was to ascertain whether children's loneliness abated once they were no longer exposed to peers' aggression, or if it intensified when victimization continued throughout kindergarten. Children in the fall-only victim group were significantly lonelier than nonvictims in the fall, but they did not differ significantly from nonvictims in the spring of kindergarten. However, the decrease in loneliness from fall to spring for the fall-only group was not significant, suggesting that feelings of loneliness may persist even after victimization subsides. Furthermore, these investigators found that stable victimization experiences exacerbated feelings of loneliness.

In summary, peer victimization has consistently been linked with loneliness (Alsaker, 1993; Boulton & Underwood, 1992; Kochenderfer & Ladd, 1996b; Ladd et al., 1997), and abusive interactions appear to precipitate children's feelings of loneliness (Kochenderfer & Ladd, 1996a). These findings support the proposition that victimization and the negative "provisions" conferred by this relationship (e.g., mistrust and anxiety) are antecedents of loneliness among young children.

Relative Contributions of Peer Relationships to Loneliness in School.
To understand the impact of children's peer relations on adjustment, investigators have begun to gather data on multiple types of relationships. Empirical efforts to distinguish the contributions of different forms of relationships have focused on friendships and peer acceptance, and findings support the claim that these relationships contribute differentially to children's adjustment (see Bukowski & Hoza, 1990; Ladd, 1990; Ladd & Coleman, 1997; Parker & Asher, 1993).

In a recent longitudinal study with young children, Ladd et al. (1997) gathered data on several forms of peer relationships (i.e., number of friends, very best friendship, peer acceptance, and peer victimization) and found that number of mutual friendships and peer victimization emerged as unique predictors of children's loneliness during the fall and spring of kindergarten. In contrast, the contributions made by peer acceptance were largely redundant with the number of friends and peer victimization indices. On the basis of these findings, the authors suggested that the provisions conferred by peer acceptance, such as belongingness, may also be available to children through friendships. Because the number of mutual friendships did account for unique variation in loneliness, it was concluded that friendships may provide additional provisions that deter loneliness, such as emotional support. Similarly, peer victimization accounted for unique variation in children's loneliness, suggesting that the experiences encountered in abusive relationships are unique in their ability to promote loneliness. In addition to feelings of alienation and exclusion, overt maltreatment by peers may undermine children's trust in their classmates, thus interfering with the ability to form friendships that mitigate loneliness.

These findings are consistent with the hypothesis that different forms of relationship offer children provisions that are unique relative to the others. In other words, peer relational systems differ in the benefits or costs that children receive from participating in such relationships, and, in turn, those relationships differ in how they affect children's emotional adjustment. Next, aspects of children's social behaviors that might affect their relationships are considered.

Aggressive and Withdrawn Social Behaviors: Connection With Loneliness?

Although aggression and social withdrawal are not forms of relationship, these behavioral patterns do occur in the context of social interaction.

Childhood aggression, which signifies an externalizing or undercontrolled pattern of behavior, has typically been defined in terms of physical acts, such as hitting and kicking others and verbal acts, such as teasing, arguing, and interrupting (see H. C. Quay & Werry, 1986). Unlike aggression, social withdrawal reflects an overcontrolled pattern of behavior and has been variously labeled *shyness, behavioral inhibition,* and *social isolation.* Because of the heterogeneity of this construct (see K. H. Rubin & Asendorpf, 1993), conceptual and empirical distinctions have been drawn between active isolation, which originates from the peer group, and passive withdrawal, which originates within the individual (K. H. Rubin & Mills, 1988; Younger & Daniels, 1992). Individuals who are passively withdrawn tend to isolate themselves from the peer group as a result of physiological and/or social anxiety. Even though aggressive and withdrawn behaviors usually occur in an interpersonal context and are inherently connected to social–emotional functioning, the potential effects of such interaction styles on young children's feelings of loneliness have not been well researched.

The premise that aggressive or withdrawn children are at risk for social and emotional maladjustment has been clouded by the fact that these behavioral styles have often been confounded with indices such as peer-group rejection. Specifically, researchers have tended to categorize children into subgroups of aggressive-rejected and withdrawn-rejected children and then have studied differences among them. Thus, whether aggressive children or withdrawn children experience loneliness solely as a result of their behaviors is not yet understood. Answering this question would be a useful endeavor, especially because not all aggressive children are rejected, nor are all withdrawn children rejected (cf. Perry, 1995). Cassidy and Asher (1992) found that children who had high loneliness scores did differ on behavioral dimensions: They were more shy–withdrawn, more aggressive, more disruptive, and less prosocial than those who had low loneliness scores. Although these results suggest an association between shyness–withdrawal or aggression and loneliness, they do not demonstrate causal priority. In addition, the authors caution that once sociometric status (peer acceptance) has statistically been controlled, the link weakens or disappears.

It is reasonable to expect that some passively withdrawn children would experience feelings of loneliness, given their infrequent interaction with peers or lack of social involvement relative to age mates. Because of spending more time alone, their chances of feeling isolated and lonely might increase. It is also plausible that aggressive children incur negative affective outcomes, given their problematic relationships with peers. In a longitudinal study, however, Ladd and Burgess (1999) compared aggressive, withdrawn, and nonaggressive–nonwithdrawn children from the fall of kindergarten to Grade 2 and found that neither aggressive nor withdrawn children felt more lonely than their nonaggressive–nonwithdrawn counterparts. In other words, the evidence that exists on this point suggests that withdrawn children and aggressive children do not feel lonely during early childhood (see Youngblade et al., this volume).

Perhaps withdrawn children are not lonely until middle childhood because, as observational studies have shown, solitary or nonsocial activity among young children is not unusual (K. H. Rubin & Clark, 1983). As children progress into middle childhood, however, social withdrawal is viewed negatively by peers (Younger, Gentile, & Burgess, 1993) and may generate negative consequences such as peer rejection and loneliness. Even theorists like Piaget (1926) and Sullivan (1953) argued that peer interaction, or lack of it, would have the greatest impact on development toward late childhood because social involvement becomes increasingly important at those ages; indeed, some support for this premise exists. In a longitudinal study, passive withdrawal at age 7 predicted loneliness by Grade 5 (Hymel et al., 1990; see also K. H. Rubin et al., 1989; K. H. Rubin & Mills, 1988) but aggression did not. A concurrent study with fifth graders (K. H. Rubin et al., 1993) showed that highly withdrawn boys, but not girls, reported higher loneliness than did average and aggressive children. Again, aggressive children seemed to be happy with their social situation according to their own reports.

An interesting finding emerged when Ladd and Burgess (1999) identified children who were both aggressive and withdrawn in the fall of kindergarten and followed them to Grade 2. Relative to aggressive, withdrawn, or average children, aggressive–withdrawn (comorbid) children were consistently more lonely, dissatisfied, friendless, and victimized by peers during early grade school. Their higher level of loneliness may be attributed to the fact that these children manifest a more complex form of social maladjustment, and this places them at greater risk for socioemotional problems. In particular, both types of behaviors seem to increase the likelihood of social alienation and counteract a satisfying emotional connection: Aggressive behaviors repel peers and withdrawn behaviors reduce opportunities for interaction. Thus, children who exhibit the combined behavioral pattern may have difficulty generating friendships or emotional bonds and feel distressed or lonely.

It is also possible, however, that children's behavioral styles and relational difficulties (e.g., low peer acceptance and few friendships) account for the association with loneliness. Perhaps the reason why withdrawn children are not lonely in early childhood but become lonely in middle childhood is that classmates begin to reject them. Evidence consistent with this hypothesis has emerged in several studies in which researchers have formed subgroups – specifically, withdrawn-rejected children reported higher levels of loneliness compared with average status and aggressive-rejected children (e.g., Hymel, Bowker, & Woody, 1993; Parkhurst & Asher, 1992). Although it might be expected that aggressive-rejected children would report higher levels of loneliness because of rejection, aggressive children overestimate and misinterpret their own competencies relative to peers' evaluations (Hymel et al., 1993) and perceive themselves just as positively as average children view themselves (Burgess & Younger, 1996). Burgess and Younger suggested that aggressive children either lack self-awareness or tend to deny negative traits and, therefore, are unable or unwilling to acknowledge feeling lonely. Moreover, aggressive children could be unaware, at least at a young age, that their classmates are rejecting them. Another explanation for why aggressive-rejected children do not report being lonely is that they spend much time with their peers and have more friends than do withdrawn-rejected children; therefore, they are less likely to feel excluded (Asher et al., 1990).

To better address the issue of whether peer rejection could be a proximate cause of loneliness, instead of the behaviors themselves being solely responsible, researchers have begun to use different designs and analytical strategies. Results from two recent longitudinal studies conducted with children in middle-to-late childhood suggest that the effects of children's behaviors on loneliness are mediated by negative peer experiences. Boivin et al. (1995) found that being rejected and victimized by peers mediated the relation between social withdrawal and loneliness in fourth- and fifth-grade children 1 year later. In another school sample, Renshaw and Brown (1993) studied the relative contributions of aggression, withdrawal, and peer acceptance to later loneliness. Withdrawn behavior and low peer acceptance predicted self-reports of loneliness, but aggressive behavior did not. Notwithstanding the significance of these results, questions about behavioral styles and interactional processes in early childhood remain unresolved.

Prospective longitudinal studies that begin in kindergarten will undoubtedly help to illuminate the developmental trajectories faced by aggressive, withdrawn, and aggressive–withdrawn children. To continue examination of the relation between loneliness and social factors in the school environment, we turn our attention to the relationship that children form with their teachers.

Teacher–Child Relationships and Loneliness

In addition to children's peers, researchers have proposed that classroom teachers are a central part of children's support systems in the school environment (e.g., Cauce, Felner, & Primavera, 1982; Dubow & Tisak, 1989; Furman & Buhrmester, 1985); however, there has been little exploration of how teacher–child relationships are associated with young children's adjustment in school contexts. Furthermore, there have been even fewer studies of how the quality of children's relationships with their teachers is related to children's affective experience in school. The few studies that have addressed this issue yield evidence that certain aspects of the teacher–child relationship are indeed associated with children's loneliness in school (e.g., Birch & Ladd, 1996, 1997).

Among the features of the teacher–child relationship that may be associated with children's adaptation in school contexts are conflict, closeness, and dependency. Closeness in the teacher–child relationship could function as a support for a young child in the school environment because it reflects a warm, affective tie with a significant adult in the classroom. Teacher–child closeness encompasses the extent to which children approach the teacher, talk about their feelings and experiences, and utilize the teacher as a source of support or comfort when upset. In contrast, teacher–child conflict refers to the extent to which interactions between a child and a classroom teacher are characterized by discord and poor rapport. Conflictual teacher–child relationships may be emotionally upsetting to young children and may maintain or result in various negative affective states, including feelings of loneliness in school. Dependency in the teacher–child relationship indicates the extent to which a child exhibits an excessive reliance on the teacher and differs from closeness in its functions and developmental implications.

It is considered adaptive for closeness to increase and for dependency to decrease as children grow older; relationship theorists have also recognized these distinctions. Attachment theorists, for example, have differentiated between secure attachment and dependency (see Bowlby, 1982). Children who remain highly dependent on the classroom teacher may be reluctant to explore the school environment, including other social relationships (e.g., peer relationships). These children may be less engaged or involved in social or learning tasks in the classroom, which may foster feelings of loneliness and isolation. It is also plausible that children who are already feeling lonely in the classroom context may turn to the teacher as a source of support or that help-seeking may manifest itself as dependent behavior toward the teacher.

Consistent with this premise, Birch and Ladd (1997) found that teacher-rated dependency was positively associated with children's self-reported loneliness in kindergarten. Children who were rated as dependent on their classroom teacher reported feeling more lonely in school than did less dependent children. Other features, such as teacher–child conflict, have also been associated with loneliness. Birch and Ladd (1994) found that, after controlling for loneliness in the fall of kindergarten, children who had conflictual relationships with teachers continued to express higher levels of loneliness in the spring of kindergarten.

As children progress through school, they typically encounter a different classroom teacher at every grade level. The quality of the new teacher–child relationship may be similar to that of prior teacher–child relationships, or significant changes may occur; hence, the degree of continuity versus change that occurs in the teacher–child relationship may affect children's loneliness in school. Several authors have proposed that the loss of social support is a stressor or risk factor for maladjustment (e.g., Heller, 1979; Holmes & Rahe, 1967). Thus, children who are involved in a close relationship with their teacher one year, but who do not establish a close relationship with their teacher the following year, may feel more lonely in school than other children. Children who maintain dependent or conflictual ties with teachers may experience similar difficulties. Because it is considered adaptive for dependency to decrease over time, children who are highly dependent in kindergarten and who maintain this relationship feature with their first-grade teacher may be more at risk for loneliness. Chronic conflict with teachers may also cause children to feel lonely in school, and, conversely, reduced conflict from year to year may mitigate children's feelings of loneliness.

Guided by these hypotheses, Birch and Ladd (1996) explored the extent to which different patterns of relationship continuity and change from kindergarten to first grade were associated with children's loneliness in first grade. They found that children who were rated as dependent by both kindergarten and first-grade teachers felt more lonely in first grade than did children who were rated as low in dependency in first grade only. For the conflictual dimension of the teacher–child relationship, there was a nonsignificant trend in the expected direction. Children with consistent conflictual relationships tended to feel more lonely than did children with nonconflictual relationships across both years.

In summary, children's relationships with their classroom teachers have important implications for their affective experience in the school environment. Teacher–child relationships that are conflictual, dependent, or lacking in closeness are likely to be related to loneliness in school. To continue our focus on the main adult figures in young children's lives, we next consider the quality of relationships with parents.

Parent–Child Relationships and Loneliness

Although connections between parent–child relationships and children's social competence have been established (Baumrind, 1967; LaFreniere & Sroufe, 1985; Parke & Ladd, 1992), there has been relatively little empirical research on familial factors associated with loneliness in children. Much of the evidence in this domain has been gathered on adolescent samples (Lobdell & Perlman, 1986; Shaver & Rubenstein, 1980); yet researchers have begun to study younger samples and examine parent–child relationships as correlates of loneliness (Berlin et al., 1995; Henwood & Solano, 1994). Generally, researchers have focused on three aspects of the family – quality of the parent–child relationship, parent characteristics, and parenting style – as predictors of loneliness in early childhood.

Quality of the Parent–Child Relationship

Recent evidence links children's attachment to the primary caregiver with loneliness during early childhood (see Cassidy & Berlin, this volume). Five- to 7-year-old children who had been classified at age 12 months as insecure–ambivalent reported more loneliness than did secure or insecure–avoidant children (Berlin et al., 1995). The insecure–ambivalent attachment style is marked by trouble separating and reuniting with the caregiver and by inconsistent or low maternal responsiveness (Cassidy & Berlin, 1994). It has been proposed that children who fit the insecure–ambivalent classification have internal working models that lead them to display heightened emotionality or weakness, a strategy originally used to attract the attention of the attachment figure (Cassidy & Berlin, 1994). This strategy may generalize to other relationships, including those with peers.

Parent Characteristics

Psychological Adjustment. Parents' psychological adjustment has been associated with their parenting behaviors and children's socioemotional functioning (Downey & Coyne, 1990; Zahn-Waxler, Denham, Iannotti, & Cummings, 1992). Parents experiencing psychological difficulties appear to have a reduced ability to provide for their children's emotional and social needs (Zahn-Waxler et al., 1992). For instance, the children of depressed mothers are at greater risk of experiencing depressive symptoms, including loneliness (for reviews see Downey & Coyne,

1990; Gelfand & Teti, 1990), social difficulties (Hammen et al., 1987), and externalizing behaviors (Billings & Moos, 1983; Lee & Gotlib, 1989), although the exact mechanisms responsible for this heightened risk are not well understood. Furthermore, it is not clear whether the heightened risk is specific to depression or whether the risk is also evident in children whose parents suffer from other disorders (Downey & Coyne, 1990). Also, the heightened risk experienced by children of depressed parents may be the result of other stressors which affect parents and children (Crnic & Greenberg, 1990; Dodge, 1990; Rutter, 1990).

Links between parent and child loneliness have been examined, but the mechanisms responsible for such relations have not been established. Henwood and Solano (1994) found that mothers' reports of loneliness were positively associated with first-grade children's reports of loneliness ($r = .25$, $p < .05$), but there was no significant association between fathers' and children's reports of loneliness. Lobdell and Perlman (1986) found a positive association between female college-aged students' reports of loneliness and their mothers' reports of loneliness ($r = .26$, $p < .01$). These results suggest that loneliness may be transmitted from parents to their children; however, these correlational data only allow speculations about the direction of the association and the processes underlying the association.

Parent Interpersonal Style. Parents' style of interacting during social encounters has also been associated with child loneliness. Henwood and Solano (1994) found that both children's loneliness and mothers' loneliness were significantly correlated with relationship-enhancing strategies in hypothetical social situations – these children and their mothers were more likely to offer ineffective strategies for initiating or maintaining social interaction. Loneliness in mothers and children was also associated with having negative attitudes toward others. Lonely children rated other children as less friendly, fair, truthful, well behaved, and trustworthy, whereas lonely mothers rated others as less kind, truthful, trustworthy, and more self centered and exploitive. Thus, mothers' social strategies and orientation toward others may influence their children's loneliness through children's modeling of their mothers' relationship strategies and social orientation. Unfortunately, the association between children's loneliness, their social strategies and orientations and their mothers' relationship strategies and attitudes toward others was not examined by Henwood and Solano. This information would provide a better understanding of possible modes of transmission between parent to child and would illuminate potential mediators of childhood loneliness.

Parenting Style

Researchers who have contributed to the parenting styles literature have used two dimensions of parent behavior, parental warmth and parental control, to construct typologies of parenting behaviors (e.g., authoritative, authoritarian, indulgent, and neglectful; see Maccoby & Martin, 1983; see Rotenberg, this volume). More recently, Steinberg (1990) has suggested that the dimension of psychological autonomy granting is also important in adolescence. Although links between parenting style and children's behavior and competence have been documented in the literature (see Maccoby & Martin, 1983), the nature of association between parenting style and loneliness has only recently been examined.

Parental Warmth. Parental warmth has been associated with children's socioemotional outcomes (Maccoby & Martin, 1983), including loneliness. Stocker (1994) found that children in Grade 2 who perceived low warmth from mothers and friends reported more loneliness than children who perceived high maternal warmth and low warmth from friends. Warmth in the mother–child relationship may compensate for possible negative outcomes associated with low warmth in peer relationships, such as loneliness.

As part of a longitudinal study conducted in our lab (Lambert, 1997), aspects of the parent–child relationship were assessed by observations of interactions between kindergarten students and their primary caregiver. Preliminary analyses showed that boys whose parents displayed high levels of warmth and responsiveness during the interaction reported less loneliness than boys whose parents displayed lower levels of warmth and responsiveness, $t(1, 202) = 2.36$, $p < .05$; but this pattern did not hold for girls. This result suggests that parent behaviors may be more important for boys' affective outcomes than for girls'. Or, it may be necessary to consider other aspects of the home environment to understand loneliness in girls. Similarly, MacDonald and Parke (1984) found stronger associations between parent behaviors and social competence in boys, but not in girls. These results highlight the importance of considering possible sex differences in parents' socialization of their children and the consequences for children's social and affective outcomes.

Parent–Child Interaction Style. Parent–child interaction provides the children with the opportunity to learn rules of social interaction, including contingent responding and affective matching, which are likely to facilitate the formation and maintenance of relationships with others.

Parents' lack of positive involvement with their children has been associated with self-reported loneliness in college-aged students (Lobdell & Perlman, 1986). Similarly, analyses from our lab (Lambert, 1997) showed that girls whose interactions with their parents were characterized by high engagement (i.e., active and warm involvement during conversation) reported less loneliness than girls whose interactions with parents were less engaged, $F(1, 198) = 6.97$, $p < .01$. A similar trend was found for boys.

Overall, the available evidence suggests that children's relationships with parents have important implications for their social and emotional adjustment. Although different theoretical rationales have been offered for the association between parent–child relationships and children's affective outcomes, there is some consensus about the type of relationship that is beneficial for children. Relationships that feature warm, involved, and supportive parent behaviors and that provide children with responsiveness and emotional security are associated with positive outcomes (Baumrind, 1967; Bowlby, 1969/1982; Maccoby & Martin, 1983). In contrast, the absence of a secure parent–child relationship including low parental warmth, responsiveness, and behavioral control tends to be associated with poor psychological outcomes for children, including loneliness (e.g., Berlin et al., 1995; Downey & Coyne, 1990; Stocker, 1994).

Conclusion and Future Directions

To better understand the role that relationships play in early socioemotional adjustment, it has become increasingly important for investigators to examine the many forms of relationship that operate within young children's social ecologies. The evidence reviewed in this chapter points to a number of interpersonal correlates of loneliness in young children, many of which stem from specific features of their relationships with peers, teachers, and parents.

Relationships and Loneliness in Young Children: Evaluating the Fit Between Theory and Data

The evidence that has emerged thus far is consistent with the frequently cited proposition that relational deficits or stressors underlie feelings of loneliness in young children. Conversely, findings support the contention that relationship supports are negatively correlated with loneliness. In view of the fact that much of this evidence is correlational, inferences about causal priority are tentative; further research is needed to examine the direction of effect implied by this premise.

Several forms and features of children's peer relationships, particularly those formed with classmates, appear to be associated with loneliness in early school settings. Children reported higher levels of loneliness when they were participants in relationships that, most likely, exposed them to stressful processes. Peer rejection, a relational context in which children are excluded from peer activities and treated in a punitive manner, was associated with higher levels of loneliness. Similarly, peer victimization, a context in which children are exposed to threatening and abusive interactions, emerged as a significant correlate of loneliness.

Unlike certain forms of peer relationship such as friendship and victimization, a connection between socially withdrawn or aggressive behaviors and loneliness in early childhood was generally not demonstrated. However, young children who exhibit both aggressive and withdrawn behaviors may be at risk for loneliness. Although such findings are intriguing, further research is needed on a range of behavioral styles.

In both school and home environments, adult–child relationships appear to play a role in children's affective adjustment. Specifically, conflictual, dependent, and distant teacher–child relationships have emerged as predictors of loneliness; moreover, the degree to which these features are consistent from year to year seems to increase the likelihood of loneliness. Issues pertaining to continuity and change in relationships should therefore be considered in future studies.

In addition to the teacher–child relationship, aspects of the parent–child relationship are associated with child loneliness. The principal correlates to emerge in this literature were low maternal warmth and insecure–ambivalent attachment patterns. Such findings suggest that children become lonely when their mothers are emotionally unavailable. This interpretation is supported by evidence indicating that children reported less loneliness when their interactions with parents were characterized by active involvement. Finally, parents' self-reports of loneliness were associated with children's self-reports of loneliness. Overall, these findings suggest that behaviors, emotions, and needs in both members of the parent–child dyad may influence children's loneliness.

Future Directions: Investigating Loneliness Within and Across Young Children's Relationship Systems

Progress toward an understanding of the nature of the linkages that exist between loneliness and young children's relationships will require a detailed examination of both within-relationship and between-relationship factors. Such an approach will enable investigators to probe the internal dynamics of individual relationships that may contribute to affective

outcomes such as loneliness, as well as the interconnections among relationships that are part of a child's larger social ecology (e.g., multiple
pathways and independent or contingent patterns of influence).

Research is needed on individual relationships, such as those formed
with peers, teachers, and parents, to better understand the functions they
serve in children's affective development. In the context of peers, for
example, children form relationships that not only differ in type (e.g.,
friendship, group acceptance, and victimization) but that also differ in
the quality of the experiences and socialization inputs for participants.
What transpires within specific forms of relationships, or the central or
dominant socialization experiences imparted to children, is not yet well
understood. Ladd and Kochenderfer (1996), Ladd et al. (1996), and Ladd
et al. (1997) have argued that peer relationships differ in both the processes (e.g., observable interactions) that children are exposed to and in
the types of provisions (i.e., psychological benefits or costs) that accrue for
children as a result of their participation in specific processes. Thus, understanding how specific types of relationship affect loneliness, and how
each exerts an influence on this outcome (e.g., processes inherent within
particular forms of relationship and their associations with loneliness),
are important objectives for future investigations.

Also merited are investigations that examine a larger portion of young
children's social ecologies and the contributions that different relational
systems make to early affective development. As Parke (1992) and Ladd
(1991) have argued, individual relationships are embedded in larger social ecologies and may play unique or overlapping roles in the genesis
and maintenance of adjustment difficulties. Thus far, little effort has been
made to explore how different forms of relationship, and the processes or
provisions they make available to children, operate together to influence
outcomes such as loneliness.

Objectives that may help to guide research on within- and across-
relationship linkages are presented in the following sections. Conceptual–
theoretical issues and methodological approaches and problems are raised
for consideration.

Within Peer Relationships. Investigators in the peer relations field
have begun to draw clearer conceptual distinctions between the types of
relationships that children form with peers (see Bukowski & Hoza, 1989;
Parker & Asher, 1993), and there has been some progress at mapping
the associations between loneliness and children's participation in different types of peer relationships (e.g., friendship, peer acceptance, and
victimization). Much less is known about the properties of individual

relationships (e.g., processes and provisions) and the role that these dynamics play in the development of loneliness. Exceptions include studies of perceived friendship processes conducted with older children (e.g., see Berndt & Perry, 1986; Furman & Buhrmester, 1985; Parker & Asher, 1993), and some of which have been completed with samples of young children (e.g., Ladd et al., 1996). Far less is known about the relationship processes and provisions that have been hypothesized to operate within other forms of peer relationships (e.g., peer rejection and victimization) and their linkages with loneliness.

Thus, there is a need for more precise theories about the processes and provisions that are available to children in different types of peer relationships, and this work should be accompanied by studies that will enable investigators to evaluate such premises and to determine whether such features are related to loneliness. In expanding the conceptual maps in this domain, investigators should consider factors such as the types of peer relationships available to children at different periods of development; the processes and provisions existing within these relationships and their functions at different points in development; and the value of specific provisions in different social contexts or ecologies (e.g., schools versus home or neighborhoods). It will also be important to consider opposing directions of effect, including the possibility that children's adjustment status or trajectories partly determine their access to peer relationships and the types of provisions elicited.

Within Teacher–Child Relationships. Compared with research on peer relationships, investigation of the teacher–child relationship as a potential contributor to children's emotional well-being is at a much earlier stage, and more remains to be learned about the potential adaptive significance of this relationship. Important conceptual advances have been made toward identifying key features of the teacher–child relationship that may have an important bearing on children's socioemotional adjustment in school settings (Birch & Ladd, 1997; Howes & Phillipsen, 1996), and a modest corpus of evidence has begun to accumulate on the associations of particular features with loneliness.

Findings that link qualities of the teacher–child relationship and children's affective adjustment in school have tended to come from studies in which investigators have singled out particular relationship features (e.g., closeness, conflict, or dependency) and examined these features as independent correlates of child adjustment. However, as researchers in investigative domains such as the parenting styles area have learned, features that describe complex constructs, such as relationships, are often interrelated. This observation may also be true for the qualities that have been used to describe the teacher–child relationship (see Birch & Ladd, 1997).

An important next step in this area would be to articulate the relations that may exist among features of the teacher–child relationship, both theoretically and empirically. With this footing, it may be possible to construct typologies of the teacher–child relationship, as has been done with parenting styles, and to examine adjustment outcomes that are associated with particular typologies. It might be proposed, for example, that children whose relationships with teachers are conflictual and dependent but low in closeness are most at risk for loneliness in school. Howes and Phillipsen (1996) provide preliminary support for propositions of this nature: Children who had dependent but not conflictual relationships with teachers showed better school adjustment than did children who had both dependent and conflictual teacher–child relationships. Here again, it will be important to investigate linkages regarding the opposite direction of effect; that is, the possibility that the adjustment problems children exhibit in classrooms are responsible for the types of relationships they form with teachers.

Within Parent–Child Relationships. The existing research on the parent–child relationship and child reports of loneliness suggests that a range of parental and familial factors play a role in loneliness (see Cassidy & Berlin, this volume; see Rotenberg, this volume). Family processes, such as attachment styles, maternal–paternal depression, marital conflict, and parenting skills, warrant further research attention. Because research on the parent–child relationship and loneliness is correlational, it is not possible to draw firm conclusions about the direction of influence. Although it is tempting to assume that causality traverses from parent to child, a child's temperament or psychological adjustment may influence his or her ability to develop and sustain relationships, and thereby affect loneliness indirectly (Stocker, 1994). Thus, it is reasonable to suggest that associations between the parent–child relationship and child loneliness involve reciprocal influences between parents and children (Conrad & Hammen, 1989). Longitudinal data would provide essential information about the parental antecedents of loneliness in children, as well as clarify the direction of effect.

Across-Relationship Linkages. This approach to the study of loneliness is evident in the peer relations literature, in which investigators have attempted to determine whether different forms of peer relationship (e.g., friendship, peer acceptance, or victimization) operate as separate or combined influences on children's loneliness (e.g., Bukowski & Hoza, 1989; Ladd et al., 1997). Efforts to probe linkages by examining the relative contributions of adult versus peer relationships are far less common and pose many challenges. Just as the presence of a supportive peer relationship (e.g., a best friend; see Parker & Asher, 1993) may buffer low-accepted children from feelings of loneliness in school, qualities of the teacher–child relationship may buffer (or exacerbate) the negative feelings that often accompany poor peer relationships. Moreover, important gender differences may exist in the way children utilize or benefit from differing relational systems (see Koenig & Abrams, this volume).

Findings reported by Birch and Ladd (1994) support this avenue of investigation. Groups of boys and girls whose relationships differed in two relational systems – dependency in the teacher–child relationship and classroom peer acceptance – were compared on changes in loneliness from fall to spring of kindergarten. For boys, regardless of their level of dependency on the classroom teacher, fall peer-group acceptance was negatively associated with spring loneliness (controlling for fall loneliness). In contrast, girls who were accepted by classmates and who were low in dependency reported less loneliness in school than any other group of girls. Furthermore, among girls who were rated as highly dependent on their teachers, peer-group acceptance was not associated with self-reports of loneliness. Thus, it would appear that there are important gender differences in the provisions that children derive from teacher and peer relationships, and, within each gender, these provisions combine in different ways to influence loneliness.

Clearly, further investigations are needed to better understand how the inputs children receive from different relational systems combine to influence loneliness. Assumptions based on conceptual models that delineate alternate pathways of influence should also be examined. Children's temperaments, behavioral orientations, or psychological adjustment may, for example, influence their ability to develop and to sustain supportive relationships with both adults and peers.

Risk and Protective Factors

It is also possible to conceptualize the relative or contingent effects of multiple relationships (i.e., either within a single system, such as children's peer relations, or across systems) in terms of the developmental risks or benefits they pose for young children in school settings (see Ladd, 1996). In particular, the interplay between different relationships that operate simultaneously in children's lives, and the functions they serve (e.g., supports or stressors), can be construed in terms of compensatory and protective effects (see Garmezy, Masten, & Tellegen, 1984).

Within a compensatory model, the risks posed by one relationship or relational system may be partially offset by the benefits of another relationship or system (i.e., additive model). For researchers interested in early loneliness, a key question is whether the positive features of one relationship can compensate for negative experiences in another relationship domain. Just as Patterson, Cohn, and Kao (1989) found that maternal warmth compensated for behavioral problems experienced by children who were rejected by their classmates, it would also be interesting to test whether maternal warmth alleviates loneliness among rejected children (see Rotenberg, this volume).

In contrast, some types of relationships or relationship features may serve a protective function and thereby reduce the overall risk posed by children's participation in other more deleterious forms of relationship (i.e., contingent and moderated model). Children who form a supportive relationship with their classroom teacher, for example, may be more resistant to negative treatment by peers and, thus, are less vulnerable to loneliness. Hypotheses of this type deserve attention in future investigations.

Finally, it is also possible that the experiences children encounter across relationships or relational systems are uniformly negative and expose them to multiple forms of risk. A number of researchers have shown that, as children are exposed to larger numbers of negative experiences or stressors, their risk for maladjustment increases dramatically (see Patterson, Vaden, & Kupersmidt, 1991; Rutter, 1979; Sameroff & Seifer, 1983). Thus, perhaps children whose relational ecologies are fraught with negative experiences are especially at risk for emotional difficulties, such as loneliness. Another possibility is that difficulties that begin in one relationship generalize to others, thereby adversely affecting a large portion of the child's social system. Children who have difficulty interacting with parents, for example, may bring similar relationship expectations to school and may precipitate negative relationships with other adults, such as teachers. Furthermore, children who are upset about problems they encounter with peers at school and who are unable to communicate these feelings to parents may feel isolated and misunderstood in the home environment. Such possibilities warrant consideration in future studies.

Theoretical and Methodological Considerations

It is time for investigators to articulate frameworks within which to generate hypotheses, organize findings, and evaluate competing explanations. For those who study young children, it may be useful to formulate hypotheses about the determinants of loneliness that precede school entry, such as the parent–child relationship (see Cassidy & Berlin, this volume). K. H. Rubin et al. (1990) have speculated that early attachment status, particularly an insecure attachment to the primary caregiver, may place children at risk for social withdrawal in peer contexts and contribute to later internalizing problems. Of course, many other theoretical perspectives on children's temperament, behavioral styles, relationships, and so on might lend themselves to this purpose.

Developmentalists have long been aware of the importance of framing their research questions within a developmental perspective; that is, recognizing that a phenomenon such as loneliness can change as children grow older and that the factors underlying its expression can also change with age (see Parkhurst & Hopmeyer, this volume). This perspective still holds important lessons for those who investigate loneliness in the future. Even though loneliness occurs at all stages of development, the experience is not necessarily the same at all age levels. Furthermore, children of different ages may be lonely for different reasons or loneliness may have different origins at different ages. At various points in the life cycle, there may also be gender differences in the causes of loneliness and in girls' and boys' coping strategies (an issue addressed by Koenig & Abrams, this volume). Lastly, the stability of loneliness may change with age. Although loneliness appears to be a relatively stable experience in middle childhood, it may be less so during early childhood. Social difficulties that lead to *short-term* loneliness might be quantitatively and qualitatively different from those that predict *long-term* loneliness (Renshaw & Brown, 1993).

Understanding the etiology of loneliness and mapping the developmental pathways to and from loneliness could be incorporated into researchers' agendas. There may be several pathways to loneliness during childhood. It seems apparent that children who are disliked and excluded by peers on a frequent basis tend to feel lonely, but this form of sadness may well evolve from children's unsuccessful attempts at social contact. Hence, one way to think about the etiology of loneliness is that it is an affective state stemming from an unsatisfactory social life, especially children's unmet needs for emotional closeness (cf. Weiss, 1974). Another possibility is that loneliness is a manifestation of underlying internalizing problems, such as a symptom of depression, and this view presupposes a different etiology – one that does not necessarily hinge on the quality of children's social experiences.

To conclude, it is disheartening to learn that a significant number of young children currently experience, or are at risk for, moderate-to-severe levels of loneliness. Unfortunately, researchers have only begun to learn about where and why young children are vulnerable to loneliness, and they understand even less about how to curb or prevent this potentially debilitating experience. It is clear that, as early as kindergarten, a significant proportion of children feel lonely in school. However, it seems likely that school settings are not the only context in which children experience loneliness, nor are school-related events and processes the only potential determinants of this condition (see Hymel et al., this volume). Ultimately, loneliness should be investigated in a broader social milieu, both within and across children's relationship systems, and from a developmental perspective, both within and across age groups using cross-sectional as well as longitudinal designs. Because some socialization contexts have received more research attention than others (e.g., schools), investigators should expand their efforts to include relatively unexplored settings such as neighborhoods (Bryant, 1985) and playgrounds (see Hart, 1993), as well as a broader range of interpersonal ties including children's relationships with fathers, siblings, and extended family members (e.g., grandparents, aunts, and uncles). Cross-contextual and cross-relational linkages also deserve greater investigative attention, especially in light of the fact that children are typically members of multiple social ecologies and participants in many different types of relationships (see George & Hartmann, 1996; Ladd et al., 1997). As investigators explore these avenues and expand their knowledge base, it will be possible to design and implement interventions that can prevent or reduce loneliness during early childhood.

Acknowledgment

Preparation of this chapter was supported by National Institute of Mental Health Grant MH-49223 to Gary W. Ladd.

7 | Connections Among Loneliness, the Ability to Be Alone, and Peer Relationships in Young Children

LISE M. YOUNGBLADE, LISA J. BERLIN, AND
JAY BELSKY

Until recently, psychologists have neglected the issue of childhood loneliness, perhaps because, in part, of early theorists' assertions that loneliness does not become a viable experience until adolescence. Sullivan (1953), for example, described loneliness as a "phenomenon ordinarily encountered in preadolescence and afterward" (p. 261) when the need for intimacy in the context of a close friendship or "chumship" develops. Likewise, Weiss (1973) argued, "Loneliness proper becomes a possible experience only when, in adolescence, parents are relinquished as attachment figures" and the individual can identify "unsatisfactory friendly acquaintances" (p. 90).

Recent investigations of children's understanding of loneliness, however, clearly challenge these ideas (Hymel et al., this volume), as children as young as 5 have been identified who are lonely (Cassidy & Asher, 1992; 1993). In fact, all but 7% of a sample of kindergarten and first-grade children studied by Cassidy and Asher (1992) were able to define loneliness as a basically negative state and could produce relevant responses when asked about the meaning of loneliness. Moreover, this ability varied as a function of sociometric status, as more popular children evinced greater complexity in their understanding of loneliness (Cassidy & Asher, 1993). Similar findings regarding children's basic understanding of loneliness have also emerged from studies involving third- through eighth-grade children (Hymel et al., this volume) and third- through sixth-grade children with and without mild mental retardation (Williams & Asher, 1992). These investigations document the existence of loneliness considerably earlier than Sullivan (1953) and Weiss (1973) originally claimed (see also Burgess et al., this volume).

Beyond chronicling the existence of loneliness in childhood, and children's understanding of it, recent investigations have also begun to examine connections between childhood loneliness and key aspects of both family (e.g., Berlin et al., 1995; Cassidy & Berlin, this volume; Rotenberg, this volume) and peer relationships (see Asher et al., 1990; Burgess et al., this volume; Parker et al., this volume). Even though there have been tremendous strides in the understanding of childhood loneliness, several important issues remain to be addressed. In this chapter, we consider two of these. The first issue has to do with the ability to be alone. It is generally acknowledged that loneliness is a subjective state not equivalent to simply being alone (e.g., Peplau & Perlman, 1982b). At the same time, clinicians (e.g., Winnicott, 1965) have identified the ability to be alone as an important component of autonomous functioning. Conceivably, a child's ability to be alone may mitigate the experience of loneliness. An ability to tolerate and even enjoy being alone may protect a child from feeling lonely when alone. On the other hand, an inability to be alone or an aversion to aloneness may increase a child's vulnerability to feeling lonely when alone. Consideration of children's ability to be alone, therefore, actually raises two issues: that of its relation to childhood loneliness and that of its relation to children's social experiences. The relation between time alone and loneliness has been examined in college students (e.g., Russell, Peplau, & Cutrona, 1980) and adolescents (Larson, this volume), and the concepts of "affinity for" and "aversion to" aloneness have been explored in adolescents (Goossens & Marcoen, this volume). With one exception (Terrell-Deutsch, this volume), however, links between childhood loneliness and ability to be alone have not as yet been empirically addressed. Also, compared with the study of childhood loneliness, correlates of children's ability to be alone remain mostly unresearched.

The second isssue concerns the peer correlates of loneliness in young children. In general, extant studies of childhood loneliness have focused on older children, well entrenched in elementary school. This body of research has highlighted the relations of children's social withdrawal, peer-group status, social cognition, and friendship to loneliness. With the exception of research by Cassidy and Asher (1992, 1993) and Ladd and colleagues (see Burgess et al., this volume), however, little explicit attention has been devoted to links between loneliness and aspects of peer relationships in younger children.

In this chapter, we consider the connections among loneliness, the ability to be alone, and several aspects of peer relationships in a group of young children aged 5 to 7. In discussing these issues, we follow the common definition of loneliness used in the literature to refer to a sad subjective state resulting from dissatisfaction with one's social experiences (e.g., Peplau & Perlman, 1982b). In contrast to others (Goossens & Marcoen, this volume), who consider the ability to be alone an aspect of loneliness, we regard the ability to be alone as a personality characteristic that may moderate children's feelings of loneliness. Specifically, we address two principal questions in this chapter. First, to what extent are loneliness and the ability to be alone associated? Second, to what extent are individual differences in early childhood loneliness and the ability to be alone related to four aspects of peer relationships: (a) classroom behavior with peers, (b) general peer experience, (c) perceived peer acceptance, and (d) friendship quality?

To address these issues, we drew on longitudinal data from the Pennsylvania Child and Family Development Project (Belsky, Gilstrap, & Rovine, 1984; Belsky, Rovine, & Fish, 1989; Belsky, Youngblade, Rovine, & Volling, 1991). It should be noted at the outset that this research was not explicitly designed as a study of loneliness and we are therefore limited by the available data. In particular, the measures of peer correlates (of loneliness) used in this study are not strictly comparable to measures used in research with older children. However, data collected within this project at multiple time points during early childhood are available that have bearing on the study of loneliness and are representative of several aspects of peer relationships identified in the literature. The paucity of extant data about the correlates of early childhood loneliness and ability to be alone justifies such an effort, at least in the spirit of stimulating further research.

The data we consider in this chapter are based on 68 children (38 boys and 30 girls)[1] who were studied at 4, 5, and 5 to 7 years of age. Participants were White and came from middle- and working-class families living in central Pennsylvania. At 4 years of age, teachers evaluated children's classroom behavior with peers.[2] Within a month of the child's fifth birthday, laboratory observations of interactions between the target child and a close or best friend of the same age and sex were conducted (see Youngblade & Belsky, 1992, for details). In addition, at this visit, the child's perceptions of peer acceptance were assessed and mothers provided information about the child's general peer experiences. When the child was between 5 and 7 years of age, but always subsequent to the

---

[1] Because we found no evidence of sex differences in the outcome measures nor in the relations between outcome measures and independent variables, data for boys and girls were pooled for the analyses reported in this chapter.

[2] Not all of the children attended preschool or day care at 4 years; therefore, teacher ratings were only available for a subset of 49 children.

Table 7.1. Time Table of Peer Relationship and Loneliness and Ability to be Alone Assessments

---

Four-year probe
  Preschool Behavior Questionnaire (Behar & Stringfield, 1974)
  Classroom Behavior Inventory (Schaefer, Edgarton, & Aaronson, 1978)
Five-year probe
  Maternal Report of General Peer Experience
  Pictorial Scale of Perceived Competence and Social Acceptance in Young
    Children: Peer Acceptance Scale (Harter & Pike, 1984)
  Behavioral Observation of Friendship Interaction
Five- to seven-year probe
  Loneliness and Social Dissatisfaction Questionnaire for Young Children
    (Cassidy & Asher, 1992)
  Ability to Be Alone Questionnaire for Young Children (Berlin, 1990)

---

friendship phase of the project, loneliness and ability to be alone were measured (see Berlin, 1990, and Berlin et al., 1995, for details).[3] Table 7.1 presents the assessment time line.

Relations Between Early Childhood Loneliness and the Ability to Be Alone

The first issue that we examined was whether there was a relation between loneliness and the ability to be alone in early childhood. A number of studies have been carried out to explore aloneness or the ability to be alone in adolescents or adults. Unfortunately, few of these inquiries have directly examined the relation between loneliness and aloneness or the ability to be alone. In one relevant study, Russell et al. (1980) found that college students' loneliness was associated with the amount of time they spent alone each day, the number of times they had dined alone, and the number of weekend nights they had spent alone in the previous 2 weeks.

---

[3] It should be noted that although we aimed to assess loneliness and ability to be alone when children were 7 years of age ($n = 16$), because of project resource constraints, the loneliness and ability to be alone data had to be collected within a short period of time. This meant that some of the children were also assessed at 5 ($n = 27$) and 6 ($n = 25$) years of age. However, it should also be noted that there was, on average, a 15-month ($SD = 8.6$ months, range = 2–30 months) gap between the friendship and the loneliness phases of the project. Because of cell-size limitations, all loneliness data were collapsed across age for the analyses we report here.

Participants' perceptions of their time alone, however, were not assessed. In a more recent line of research, Larson (this volume) used an experience-sampling procedure to measure preteens' and adolescents' loneliness and time alone in daily experience. Larson found that more loneliness was correlated with more time spent alone for 5th and 6th graders but that there was no significant association between loneliness and time alone for adolescents. Larson suggests that adolescents use time alone in a deliberate way for self-reflection and identity work (see also Goossens & Marcoen, this volume); this does not appear to be the case for younger children. Connections between attitudes toward being alone and loneliness, however, were not specifically examined. In contrast to studies that use measures of time spent alone, Goossens and Marcoen (this volume) have used a multidimensional loneliness scale to study affinity for and aversion to aloneness in five different samples of Belgian 5th- through 12th-grade students. Although this scale includes subscales reflecting affinity for and aversion to aloneness, specific relations between affinity for and aversion to aloneness and loneliness were neither posited nor probed.

The only data concerning childhood loneliness, ability to be alone, and their relation, come from Terrell-Deutsch's (this volume) study of 494 fourth- to sixth-grade children. In this investigation, children's aversion to being alone was generally unrelated to loneliness. Affinity for being alone showed a perplexing relation to loneliness, as children who reported more loneliness also reported more affinity for being alone. Terrell-Deutsch suggests that perhaps some children learn that they like being alone by having lonely experiences thrust on them or, conversely, that some children say they like being alone as a way of coping with their loneliness. Given the puzzling nature of these results, replication is called for before any definitive conclusions are drawn. Moreover, to date, no study has examined these constructs in younger children.

In the current study, we directly explored the connection between loneliness and the ability to be alone in young children. To do so, we examined scores on two measures administered to the children when they were 5- to 7-years old: the Loneliness and Social Dissatisfaction Questionnaire for Young Children (Cassidy & Asher, 1992) and the Ability to Be Alone Questionnaire for Young Children (Berlin, 1990; Berlin et al., 1990; Berlin, Youngblade, & Belsky, 1991). Cassidy and Asher's loneliness scale consists of 16 principal items that assess children's feelings of loneliness and social dissatisfaction in the peer group at school. Responses were scored on a 3-point scale and summed to create a total loneliness score ($\alpha = .71$). Scores could range from 16 to 48, with higher scores indicating greater self-reported loneliness. In the current sample, loneliness scores ranged from 16 to 30 ($M = 20.45$, $SD = 3.68$). Thus, loneliness was present, although the range of scores was somewhat limited.

The Ability to Be Alone Questionnaire for Young Children (Berlin, 1990) includes 25 items, scored on a 3-point scale, that tap children's perceptions of being alone. Although this questionnaire's items and factors are similar to the Louvain Loneliness Scale for Children and Adolescents (Marcoen et al., 1987), the Ability to Be Alone Questionnaire was developed independently and from a somewhat different theoretical perspective. Specifically, within this perspective, children's capabilities and feelings about being alone are seen not as aspects of loneliness – which is viewed principally as an experience – but as personality characteristics that may mitigate loneliness.

Using the data from the current sample, we performed an exploratory factor analysis which revealed that this measure consists of two moderately correlated factors ($r = -.49$, $p < .001$): one reflecting an aversion to being alone ($\alpha = .87$) and one reflecting an ability to be alone ($\alpha = .71$; see Table 7.2). Scores could range from 7 to 21 ($M = 12.85$, $SD = 4.32$) on the aversion scale and from 4 to 12 ($M = 8.43$, $SD = 2.33$) on the ability scale; higher scores reflected greater aversion and ability, respectively.

Table 7.2. Factor Loadings for the Principal Items of the Ability to Be Alone Questionnaire for Young Children

Principal Items	Aversion Scale	Ability Scale
Do you feel lonely when others are too busy to be with you?	.78	
Do you like being by yourself for a short period of time?		.58
Do you miss being with others when you're all by yourself?	.66	
Do you feel happy when you're all by yourself?		.59
Do you like being by yourself?		.46
Are you bored when there's no one to play with?	.72	
When you're at home and everyone there is busy, do you miss having someone to be with?	.76	
Do you feel calm and relaxed when you're by yourself?		.63
Do you feel sad when you have to spend time on your own?	.72	
When no one is around, do you want someone to be with you?	.79	
When you're all by yourself, do you wish you had a friend to play with?	.60	

Note. For ease of interpretation, this table contains only items summed to create the composite and factor loadings greater than .45.

Correlational analyses indicated that children's scores on the loneliness scale were not significantly correlated with the aversion to being alone ($r = -.02$) nor the ability to be alone ($r = .03$) scales. The first correlation is consistent with Terrell-Deutsch (this volume), who similarly found no connection between loneliness and aversion to being alone in children who were at least 2 years older than the children in the current study. The second correlation, however, is not consistent with Terrell-Deutsch's finding that loneliness was significantly related to young children's ability to be alone.

Several possibilities may explain our null results. First, it is conceivable that children averse to being alone may arrange never to be alone and, thereby, may prevent their own loneliness (Berlin, 1990). Support for this interpretation comes from another finding in the present study, to be discussed later, that young children who were more averse to being alone spent more time in peer settings. Second, although the ability to be alone may mitigate children's loneliness when alone (or, perhaps, when socially withdrawn), the Loneliness and Social Dissatisfaction Questionnaire (Cassidy & Asher, 1992) focuses on social experiences in the school. A more complete understanding of the relation between childhood loneliness and ability to be alone may require a broader sampling of situations in which children experience loneliness, including time spent alone (Berlin, 1990).

Third, developmental differences may help to explain why Terrell-Deutsch (this volume) found a relation between loneliness and affinity for being alone, whereas we discerned no relation between loneliness and ability to be alone. As Terrell-Deutsch argues, perhaps at older ages, children understand and process the experiences of being lonely and being alone in ways that allow them insight into "using" an affinity for being alone as either a coping or a learning device. Younger children might not have the cognitive sophistication with which to make such connections. This suggests that, in future work, developmental changes in children's understanding of their ability to be alone and its subjective relation to their own experience with loneliness should be considered.

Connections Between Early Childhood Loneliness, Ability to Be Alone and Several Aspects of Peer Relationships

Our second focus in this chapter concerns the connections between early childhood loneliness, ability to be alone, and peer relationships. A burgeoning corpus of research has revealed childhood loneliness to relate to several different aspects of peer relationships, including children's social behavior, particularly social withdrawal (e.g., Hymel et al., 1990; K. H. Rubin et al., 1989); peer-group status (Asher et al., 1990); self-perceptions (e.g., Hymel et al., 1990; K. H. Rubin et al., 1989); and friendship quality (Parker & Asher, 1993b; Renshaw & Brown, 1993). Compared with the study of childhood loneliness, however, peer correlates of children's ability to be alone have been neglected. In fact, researchers have examined only the link between ability to be alone and friendship quality, with somewhat equivocal results (Marcoen & Goossens, 1989; Marcoen et al., 1987). In this section, we consider four aspects of peer relationships and their connections to loneliness and the ability to be alone. We first present a brief review of previous research and then discuss analyses from the current study relevant to that domain.

Connections With Social Behavior: Withdrawal and Aggression

A number of investigators have documented connections between childhood loneliness and social withdrawal. Rubin, Hymel, and their colleagues, for example, reported both contemporaneous and longitudinal associations showing that lonelier children were more withdrawn, in terms of observations of passive withdrawal and peer nominations of isolation–withdrawal, during the elementary school years (Hymel et al., 1990; K. H. Rubin & Mills, 1988; K. H. Rubin et al., 1989). In their study of 5- to 7-year-old children, Cassidy and Asher (1992) found connections between loneliness and peer ratings of shyness and withdrawal (see also Crick & Ladd, 1993, and Renshaw & Brown, 1993, for similar findings with older children). Although Cassidy and Asher found that the lonelier children were more shy and withdrawn, they also reported that teachers and peers rated the lonelier children as more disruptive–aggressive and less likely to engage in prosocial behavior than children who had reported less loneliness.

Research involving subtypes of peer rejection also highlights social withdrawal, particularly in combination with rejection, as a correlate of loneliness in the elementary- and middle-school years. Boivin, Poulin, and Vitaro (1994) found that aggressive-withdrawn-rejected children (but not aggressive-rejected children) were more lonely than their average-status peers. Comparing withdrawn-rejected children to aggressive-rejected children, Williams and Asher (1987; see also Asher & Williams, 1987) found that the former reported significantly more loneliness than the latter. Also, submissive-rejected students identified by their peers as "easily-pushed-around" reported more loneliness than their average-status classmates (Parkhurst & Asher, 1992; see also Boivin et al., 1989).

In summary, the data indicate not only that loneliness is related to social withdrawal but also that the combination of withdrawal and rejection appears to be a particularly potent correlate of loneliness. Links between loneliness and externalizing behaviors, such as aggression, have been found less often. Consequently, although there is some evidence to suggest that lonely children are aggressive (e.g., Boivin et al., 1994; Cassidy & Asher, 1992), most data would suggest that loneliness is part of an internalizing pattern of social problems, at least for older children (see Hymel et al., 1990, and K. H. Rubin & Lollis, 1988).

The picture is less clear for younger children. It is possible that social withdrawal may not be associated with loneliness (see also Burgess et al., this volume), whereas other behaviors may be. During the early childhood years, solitary or nonsocial activity is normative (Parten, 1932; K. H. Rubin, Fein, & Vandenberg, 1983). Thus, there is little reason to expect nonsocial children to be singled out by their peers as displaying behavior deviant from age-group play norms or for nonsocial children to feel more left out of group activity than many other peers. If so, social withdrawal may or may not be related to loneliness as it is with older children, when individuals who are behaviorally inhibited may become increasingly salient to their age mates, relegated to the periphery of the peer group, and feel badly about such experience (K. H. Rubin et al., 1990; Younger & Boyko, 1987). In any case, given the associations between loneliness and externalizing behavior, as well as the connections between loneliness and internalizing behavior reviewed earlier, it seems important to consider a broad spectrum of behavior in the case of the younger children from the current study.

Behavior With Peers

In our work, we explored this possibility by examining connections between early childhood loneliness, ability to be alone, and teachers' ratings of a broad range of behavior with peers. When children were 4, teachers provided ratings of classroom behavior using the Preschool Behavior Questionnaire (PBQ; Behar & Stringfield, 1974) and the Classroom Behavior Inventory (CBI; Schaefer, Edgarton, & Aaronson, 1978). To reduce the subject: variable ratio and to create more reliable composites (Rushton, Brainerd, & Pressley, 1983), a principal-components analysis was performed on the combined 3 PBQ and 10 CBI subscales.[4]

---

[4] Details of this analysis are available from Lise M. Youngblade.

Table 7.3. Correlations of Early Childhood Loneliness and Ability to Be Alone With Peer Relationships

| | 5- to 7-Years-Old | | |
| | Loneliness | Aversion Scale | Ability Scale |
Peer Relationships			
Four-years old: Classroom behavior with peers[a]			
Task orientation/autonomy	.00	−.32*	.48***
Hostility	−.01	.19	−.25‡
Anxiety/dependence	−.03	.29*	−.36**
Five-years old: Perceived peer acceptance[b]			
Perceived acceptance	−.25‡	−.07	−.02
Five-years old: Experience with peers[c]			
Time in peer settings	.24‡	.26*	−.23‡
Number of children in peer settings	.11	−.01	.07
Five-years old: Friendship quality[d]			
Target child positive	.26‡	.19	.00
Target child negative	.06	.05	−.02
Friend positive	.08	.10	.04
Friend negative	.29*	.05	−.02

[a] $ns = 45$–49.   [b] $ns = 55$–58.   [c] $ns = 58$–61.   [d] $ns = 55$–58.
‡ $p < .10$.   * $p < .05$.   ** $p < .01$.   *** $p < .001$.

Three factors emerged: Task Orientation/Autonomy ($\alpha = .92$), which reflects creativity, independence, verbal intelligence, and task orientation; Hostility ($\alpha = .87$), which reflects agression and hostility; and Anxiety/Dependence ($\alpha = .84$), which reflects introversion, dependence, anxiety, and fearfulness.

Unlike Cassidy and Asher (1992), we did not find that there were significant correlations between early childhood loneliness and children's behavior as rated by teachers (see Table 7.3). One account for the lack of significant correlations is that the teachers in the current study rated the children's behavior 1 to 3 years before the children competed the loneliness scale. Had we had contemporaneous teacher assessments, as did Cassidy and Asher, our results might have replicated theirs. Furthermore, knowing the degree of stability of loneliness as well as the stability of children's behavior in this sample may have clarified the relation between loneliness and classroom behavior with peers. The assessment context may also have obscured the relation between loneliness and classroom behavior. In our study, teachers rated children's behavior in the context of one group of classmates. Children's reports of loneliness were made later with, presumably, a different group of peers as referents.

The links between aversion to being alone, ability to be alone, and teachers' ratings, however, did indicate concordance between children's self-reported feelings about being alone and their classroom behavior (see Table 7.3). Children who were less averse to being alone and more able to be alone were observed by their teacher to be more autonomous and less dependent. There was also a trend for children who were less able to be alone to be more hostile.

Recall that the majority of published data support the notion that loneliness is part of an internalizing pattern of social problems (see Hymel et al., 1990, and K. H. Rubin & Lollis, 1988). Our data further imply that children's ability to be alone (i.e., the lack of) may be related to internalizing behaviors, such as anxiety and dependency, as well. Moreover, children's ability to be alone may also be related to externalizing behaviors, as we found a marginally significant negative association between children's ability to be alone and teacher-rated hostile and aggressive behavior. Children's preschool experiences with peers, thus, may contribute to the development of the ability to be alone. Conversely, perhaps children who are more tolerant of being alone seek out different kinds of social experiences with peers. Given the correlational nature of our data, the direction of effects is unclear. The results do suggest, however, that further attention to loneliness, ability to be alone, and children's behavioral profiles is needed.

Connections With Sociometric Status and Peer Experience

Studies of loneliness in children repeatedly have shown significant relations between loneliness and sociometric status. Although the sociometric method has varied, lonely children in elementary and middle school have consistently been shown to be less accepted or more rejected by their peers (see Asher et al., 1990). A recent study of kindergarten and first-grade children also documented an association between loneliness and peer rejection (Cassidy & Asher, 1992). Thus, the loneliness–peer rejection relation appears quite robust. To be considered, though, is that past investigations have usually considered group status within one particular classroom. However, children are often part of multiple groups of other children, including but not limited to the classroom. Therefore, consideration of more general peer experience (e.g., time spent with other children and number of other children) may be informative as well.

General Peer Experience

In the current study, although peer sociometrics were unavailable, assessments of more general peer experience were available. When the children were 5, mothers reported on two aspects of their child's peer experiences: (a) peer hours, a summary score of the number of hours spent in contexts (e.g., kindergarten, family day care, preschool, and swimming lessons) that involved peers and, thus, peer interaction; and (b) number of other children, the sum of the number of other children involved in each of the peer contexts.

The correlations between general peer experience and loneliness and the ability to be alone were somewhat equivocal (see Table 7.3). On one hand, the relations between aversion to being alone, ability to be alone, and time in peer settings made intuitive sense: Children who were more averse to being alone and less able to be alone spent more time in peer settings. Thus, children who have a hard time spending time by themselves may arrange – or have parents who arrange – to compensate for this by placing themselves in social situations.

On the other hand – and contrary to our expectations – a trend emerged for the lonelier children to spend more time in peer settings. It is possible that for young children, too much time spent with peers is overwhelming and leads to feelings of loneliness. It is also possible that this finding is the result of a methodological confound, because our measure of time in peer settings is confounded with the number of settings in which children are involved. The correlation between loneliness and time spent in peer settings may imply that children's participation in multiple settings prevents them from becoming part of any one peer group, which may, in turn, lead to loneliness.

Another interpretation of these results pertains to young children's understanding of loneliness. Common definitions of loneliness suggest that loneliness stems from a discrepancy between actual and desired contacts (Peplau & Perlman, 1979; Peplau et al., 1982). To experience loneliness, then, young children need to acquire a notion of desired social contact and be able to recognize sufficient discrepancy between actual and desired social contacts. This must happen when children spend time with peers, and it likely emerges after young children have had more extensive experience with peers. In other words, it would appear necessary for children to experience sufficient contact with peers to develop some sense of what is desirable versus achieved, which may explain why loneliness was correlated with the amount of time spent with peers. However, because the correlation was only marginally significant, this finding merits replication before any conclusions can be made with confidence.

Connections With Self Perceptions

Individual differences in childhood loneliness have been associated with children's perceptions of themselves. Research indicates that children who attribute social failure to internal and stable circumstances report higher levels of loneliness (Hymel et al., 1985; Renshaw & Brown, 1993; see also Crick & Ladd, 1993). Perhaps children who blame themselves for their social difficulties come to believe that they are socially inept and give up trying to establish successful relationships with peers. Over time, this may lead to increased social withdrawal and more extreme feelings of loneliness (Renshaw & Brown, 1993). It is also the case that lonely children feel badly about themselves. Hymel, Rubin, and their colleagues have found childhood loneliness to be associated with lower levels of perceived self-competence and self-worth in middle childhood (Hymel et al., 1990; K. H. Rubin & Mills, 1988; K. H. Rubin et al., 1989). Connections between loneliness and self-perception have not been examined with young children.

Perceived Peer Acceptance

In the current study, we explored the link between early childhood loneliness and children's perceptions of their own acceptance in the peer group. When children were 5, they completed the Peer Acceptance sub-scale ($\alpha = .60$) of the Pictorial Scale of Perceived Competence and Social Acceptance in Young Children (Harter & Pike, 1984). As seen in Table 7.3, there was a trend for more lonely children to perceive themselves as less accepted by their peers. There were no significant correlations between either scale of the Ability to Be Alone Questionnaire (Berlin, 1990) and children's perceived peer acceptance.

Before commenting on these findings, a caveat should be raised. There is some degree of overlap in terms of item content between the loneliness scale and the perceived peer acceptance scale. Consequently, the perceived peer acceptance scale may be viewed as "simply" validating the loneliness scale. However, despite some redundancy, the measures are also distinct. For example, the perceived peer acceptance scale refers to activities with peers in more global contexts (e.g., "Eats dinner at friends' houses") than the loneliness scale, on which the items only refer to activities at school (e.g., "Do you have lots of kids to talk to at school"). Nevertheless, the correlation between loneliness and perceived peer acceptance should be viewed cautiously because of the potential confound of method variance.

Renshaw and Brown (1993) argued that general acceptance by the peer group might promote perceptions of interpersonal competence (Bukowski

& Hoza, 1989) and feelings of belonging (Asher et al., 1984), which in turn enhance psychological well-being and enable children to allay or cope effectively with any feelings of loneliness. Although we do not have measures of peer-group sociometrics, our data do underscore the fact that children's interpretation of their peer experiences is relevant to their feelings of loneliness. Moreover, the current data are congruent with research documenting links between loneliness and perceived self-competence in middle childhood (Hymel et al., 1990; K. H. Rubin et al., 1990).

Connections With Friendship

The final aspect of peer relationships we address concerns connections between childhood loneliness, ability to be alone, and friendship. Two studies have investigated the links between loneliness and friendship in third- to sixth-grade children (see Parker et al., this volume, for review). In the first, Parker and Asher (1993b) found that children without best friends were more lonely than children with best friends, regardless of how well accepted they were. Moreover, in analyses using only those children with best friends, Parker and Asher found that six self-reported markers of friendship quality (e.g., validation and caring and conflict resolution) were strong predictors of loneliness, both before and after controlling for peer acceptance. In addition, acceptance made a substantial contribution to loneliness over and above the contribution of friendship quality. Thus, both acceptance and friendship quality appear to make significant independent contributions to childhood loneliness (Parker & Asher, 1993a). A second set of researchers also found acceptance and friendship quality to contribute approximately equally to the prediction of loneliness and that both aspects of peer adjustment appeared to have something unique to offer with respect to predicting loneliness (Renshaw & Brown, 1993). Thus, these studies indicate that friendship offers children, even those low in peer acceptance, some protection from feelings of loneliness. To date, however, no study has examined the link between loneliness and friendship in early childhood. Given Cassidy and Asher's (1992) work documenting links between loneliness and peer acceptance for this age group, similar consideration is needed regarding connections between loneliness and friendship in early childhood.

Associations between ability to be alone and friendship quality have been documented also. Marcoen and Goossens (1989) found that students who reported more affinity for aloneness had fewer intimate friends than students who reported less affinity, whereas aversion to aloneness related to having argued with a same-sex friend. The modest level of these correlations, as well as their rather equivocal nature, speaks to the need for further attention to links between ability to be alone and friendship.

The studies just reviewed used self-reports of dyadic friendships or sociometrically derived reciprocated best-friend scores. In the current research, we drew on observations of children's behavior with a close friend to examine associations between early childhood loneliness, ability to be alone, and friendship quality. Observational measures of friendship were used in the current investigation because 5-year-olds may not completely understand the concept of a close or best friend, despite the fact that they show behavior indicative of close friendship (Youngblade & Belsky, 1992).

Friendship Interaction

At 5 years, children were observed in the laboratory with a close or best friend. Each child's behavior during two free-play episodes was coded every 30 seconds along 14 dimensions (involvement, positive initiation, positive reaction, negative initiation, negative reaction, focused attention, dominance, submission, attention to camera, attention to rules, social strategies, positive affect, negative affect, and distress); kappas ranged from .60 to 1.00, with a mean of .75.[5] Principal-components analyses were conducted to reduce the number of variables (see Youngblade, 1990, for details). Two factors emerged from these analyses: positive and negative interaction. Each child then received a summary score on these factors (i.e., child positive, child negative, friend positive, and friend negative).

The correlations between early childhood loneliness, ability to be alone, and friendship interaction were somewhat perplexing (see Table 7.3). With respect to loneliness, we expected that more loneliness would be related to less harmonious relations between friends. We found, as expected, that more loneliness was related to more negative behavior from the children's friend. Unexpectedly, we also found a trend for lonelier children to display more positive behavior toward their friend. Because of the trend level, as well as the opposite direction of effect, this finding should be replicated before breathing too much meaning into it. Finally, there were no associations between ability to be alone and friendship interaction. Although admittedly speculative, several explanations for these findings come to mind.

The links between loneliness and friendship interaction may be understood by simultaneously considering links with peer relations. Parker and Asher (1993a) and Renshaw and Brown (1993) argued that both peer acceptance and friendship make important contributions to loneliness. In

---

[5] A coding manual is available on request from Lise M. Youngblade.

this study, loneliness was associated with both perceived peer acceptance and observed friendship behavior. It is possible that lonely children who feel unaccepted by their peers act more positively toward their friend than do other children as a way of finding solace from dissatisfying peer-group experiences. Taken together, the negative relation between loneliness and perceived peer acceptance and the positive association between loneliness and the friend's negative behavior raise the prospect that the loneliest children find support in neither of these places; that is, despite positive overtures, they still are treated negatively by their friend and feel unaccepted by their peers.

The lack of association between ability to be alone and friendship quality was somewhat surprising. In the case of the ability scale, it may be that children who are better able to be alone simply have less investment in friendship, and thus there is no relation to either positive or negative friendship interaction. In the case of the aversion scale, however, we expected children who disliked being alone would interact more positively with a friend, as a way of keeping the friend engaged and thereby preventing their own loneliness. Perhaps, however, for children who are averse to being alone, it is enough to have friends or peers with whom to interact, regardless of the quality of the interaction. In other words, the number of friendships may be related to aversion more than the quality of any one particular friendship.

Summary and Issues for Future Research

In this chapter, we considered loneliness and the ability to be alone in early childhood. We found that, in our sample of 5- to 7-year-olds, loneliness was not significantly related to either ability to be alone or aversion to being alone. However, more lonely children tended to perceive themselves as less accepted by peers and tended to spend more time with peers than less lonely children. These lonely children also tended to interact positively with a close friend, even though the friend was negative toward them. We also discerned that children who were more averse to being alone were less autonomous and more anxious and dependent; these children also spent more time with peers than children who were less averse to being alone. Finally, children who reported a higher ability to be alone were also more autonomous, less anxious, somewhat less hostile, and tended to spend less time with peers than their less able counterparts.

Our work, in addition to that by Parker and Asher (1993b) and by Renshaw and Brown (1993), suggests that peer-group relations and friendships are important correlates of loneliness in young children. What needs to be further clarified is the nature of these connections. Weiss (1973) distinguished between two types of loneliness: *social loneliness*, which stems from feeling left out of a group, and *emotional loneliness*, which comes from the lack of a close, intimate relationship with another person (Asher et al., 1990; Parker & Asher, 1993a; Terrell-Deutsch, this volume). Although several measures of loneliness have been developed that tap aspects of both social and emotional loneliness (see Terrell-Deutsch, this volume), further work is needed to investigate their relations to specific aspects of peer relationships (e.g., peer-group acceptance, behavior, perceptions, and friendship). Moreover, the role that the ability to be alone plays in these relations must also be addressed.

In addition, a thorough understanding of childhood loneliness and ability to be alone should take into account links among children's various relationships (peers, friends, families, etc.). Although comprehensive theoretical models of loneliness have been proposed (e.g., K. H. Rubin et al., 1990), extant empirical research on the correlates of loneliness has typically focused on either the peer world (e.g., Asher et al., 1990) or the family (e.g., Berlin et al., 1995); research combining family and peer precursors of loneliness in early childhood is rare (however, see Cassidy & Berlin, this volume, for a theoretical model of the development of childhood loneliness, which incorporates both family and peer relationships).

Finally, further attention to children's subjective interpretations of their experiences is needed. With the exception of Hymel et al.'s (this volume) and Cassidy and Asher's (1992, 1993) work, little data addressing children's understanding of loneliness are available, particularly as the data relate to social experience. No data regarding children's understanding of the ability to be alone have been reported.

Limitations of the Study

No study is without limitations, and several weaknesses of the present work need to be highlighted. First, the data reported here are from a longitudinal investigation not originally or specifically designed to study loneliness. Second, our measures are not directly comparable to those used by researchers who have explicitly investigated these phenomena. Third, it remains possible that the design of our research confounded our results as measures of different relations were taken at different ages. However, it should be noted that many theoretical frameworks of the development of children's social relationships, most notably those with peers and friends, do not propose substantial developmental changes within the age group (i.e., early childhood) used in the current work (Parker & Gottman, 1989; Yeates & Selman, 1989; Youniss, 1980).

A fourth concern is that our sample was relatively small and vulnerable to selection effects. It is possible that the most well-functioning children were in the families who continued to participate longitudinally. In addition, loneliness and the ability to be alone, while present in this sample, were limited, which may have restricted our ability to find significant correlates. Finally, the magnitude and the number of significant and marginally significant correlations were small. It is difficult to determine whether the hypothesized links, derived from previous research with older participants in many cases, failed to emerge, or were counterintuitive, because the sample size was too small, or because of problems with measurement or design, or because the hypothesized relations do not exist at this young age. Future studies that address the limitations in design and measurement that are problematic here will help to resolve this issue. In addition, longitudinal investigations initiated in early childhood may illuminate whether and to what extent the phenomenon of loneliness, ability to be alone, and their correlates change with age.

Conclusion

Our goal in this chapter was to explore connections among loneliness, ability to be alone, and various facets of peer relationships in early childhood. We found that loneliness and ability to be alone were not significantly related, but that each was related to different aspects of antecedent peer relationships. Although exploratory, these findings offer food for thought and suggest directions for future research. Work is needed to extend these findings as well as to incorporate them into the larger picture of the development of loneliness and the ability to be alone.

Acknowledgment

The work reported herein was supported by a grant from the National Institute of Child Health and Human Development (RO1HD15496) and by a National Institute of Mental Health Research Scientist Development Award (KO2MH00486) to Jay Belsky.

8 | A Social-Information-Processing Approach to Children's Loneliness

NICKI R. CRICK, JENNIFER K. GROTPETER,
AND CAROL M. ROCKHILL

What do most boys/girls do when they want to be mean to another boy/girl?

They try to beat them up if they're mad ... Stop being that person's friend ....
They don't speak to them anymore .... Fight and act unkind .... They cuss at
them usually .... They roll their eyes and talk about them .... Try to kick their
butts .... Thumb their nose and walk away .... Tell lies about that person.

What do most boys/girls do when they want to be nice to another boy/girl?

They ask them to hang out with them .... They talk to them or loan them
stuff .... They say nice things .... Suck up .... Let them go bike riding and
let them play games .... Play with them at recess .... Cheer them up and help
them .... Say they are sorry and pat them .... Stand in front of them if they are
getting bullied.[1]

As the earlier responses illustrate, children are likely to experience a
variety of events in the course of their day-to-day interactions with peers,
both positive and negative. For example, on any given school day, a child
may receive support from a friend when she scores poorly on an exam,
she may be teased by the class bully when he notices a small tear in her
dress, or she may be simply ignored by her classmates most of the day.
What do these kinds of peer experiences mean to children, and how do
they affect the conclusions children draw about themselves and others
in social contexts (e.g., about how lonely or dissatisfied they feel with
their peer relationships)? These questions are the focus of the present
chapter. Specifically, our goal is to generate a framework for understanding how children's actual peer experiences, and their interpretations of
those experiences, may affect their feelings of loneliness (see Figure 8.1).
This framework is based on a social-information-processing model of children's cognitive, emotional, and behavioral reactions to social contexts

---

[1] These responses are taken from 9- to 12-year-old participants in Crick, Bigbee, and
Howes, 1996, and Greener and Crick, in press.

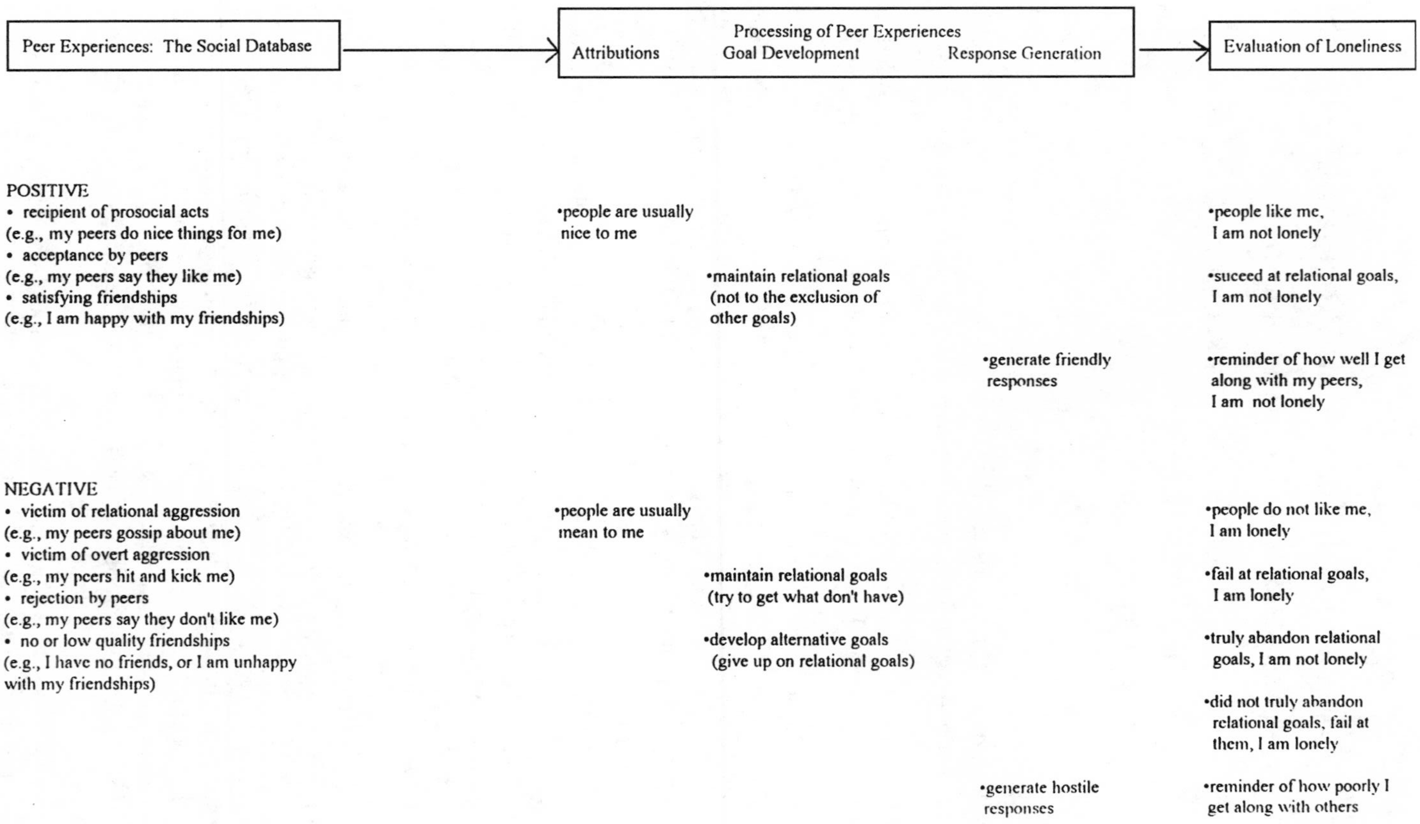

Peer Experiences: The Social Database

Processing of Peer Experiences

Attributions | Goal Development | Response Generation

Evaluation of Loneliness

POSITIVE:
- recipient of prosocial acts
(e.g., my peers do nice things for me)
- acceptance by peers
(e.g., my peers say they like me)
- satisfying friendships
(e.g., I am happy with my friendships)

- people are usually nice to me

- maintain relational goals (not to the exclusion of other goals)

- generate friendly responses

- people like me, I am not lonely
- suceed at relational goals, I am not lonely
- reminder of how well I get along with my peers, I am not lonely

NEGATIVE:
- victim of relational aggression
(e.g., my peers gossip about me)
- victim of overt aggression
(e.g., my peers hit and kick me)
- rejection by peers
(e.g., my peers say they don't like me)
- no or low quality friendships
(e.g., I have no friends, or I am unhappy with my friendships)

- people are usually mean to me

- maintain relational goals (try to get what don't have)
- develop alternative goals (give up on relational goals)

- generate hostile responses

- people do not like me, I am lonely
- fail at relational goals, I am lonely
- truly abandon relational goals, I am not lonely
- did not truly abandon relational goals, fail at them, I am lonely
- reminder of how poorly I get along with others

Figure 8.1. A social-information-processing approach to loneliness.

(Crick & Dodge, 1994). In this model, it is posited that children's social experiences serve as a "social database" that provides them with important feedback about their peers, about themselves, and about their peer relationships (e.g., "My classmates do things to be mean to me" and "My classmates don't like me"). Children then process this feedback, as social information, and during this processing they may draw inferences about their particular social situations (e.g., "People don't like me," "I don't have enough friends," and "I feel lonely"). In this way, it is hypothesized that children's feelings of loneliness may be influenced by their interactions with peers and by the ways they think about those interactions. In the sections that follow, we address each of these factors and discuss ways in which they may be linked to each other and to loneliness.

Peer Relationships: The Need to Belong

The importance of peer relationships to children's well-being has been demonstrated repeatedly in both the developmental and the clinical psychology literatures (e.g., see Asher & Coie, 1990, and Parker & Asher, 1987, for reviews). Successful peer relationships can enhance the quality of children's lives in many ways, but perhaps the most basic and significant function concerns their potential to satisfy children's needs for belongingness. Many theories of individual functioning have addressed the issue of belongingness needs in one form or another (e.g., Bowlby, 1973; S. Freud, 1930; Maslow, 1968; Rogers, 1961; Sullivan, 1953). Although the specifics of these theories differ vastly, they share the common thesis that humans are motivated, as least in part, by a desire to initiate and maintain relationships on both a group level (e.g., feeling accepted by peers) and a dyadic level (e.g., feeling valued by a friend or partner; Baumeister & Leary, 1995; Lyons-Ruth, 1995). One important implication of this hypothesis is that the inability to satisfy this need (whether because of personal or situational constraints) is likely to result in personal difficulties such as negative conclusions or feelings about the self, others, or both (e.g., feelings of exclusion by peers). Support for this hypothesis can be found in research on children, which has shown that difficulties in group and in dyadic peer relationships are significantly related to feelings of loneliness (e.g., Asher & Wheeler, 1985; Crick & Grotpeter, 1996; Crick & Ladd, 1993; Parker & Asher, 1993; Renshaw & Brown, 1993). Clearly, the evidence indicates that successful achievement of both types of relationships (i.e., peer-group acceptance and dyadic friendship) are important for the satisfaction of children's belongingness needs (Weiss, 1973).

In young children, belongingness needs are met primarily through family relationships with the parent–child relationship being particularly salient during these years. However, as children approach middle childhood and beyond, they increasingly rely on peers to satisfy their desires for meaningful connections with individuals and with communities or groups. Consequently, establishing mutually satisfying friendships and gaining at least a moderate level of acceptance by a relevant peer group become particularly important issues to children during this period (Bukowski & Hoza, 1989; Sullivan, 1953). Like any important developmental milestone, the emphasis on peer relationships results in a number of significant challenges and opportunities for children. The first challenge is to acquire the skills needed to establish and maintain the desired relationships with peers. However, because age mates are also engaged in this relationship acquisition process and are likely to highly value friendships and peer acceptance, some children may come to view relationships as a commodity to be sold, traded, or negotiated (e.g., "I'll be your friend if you do my homework for me"). In support of this hypothesis, recent evidence demonstrates that children sometimes use their ties with peers as vehicles for both harming and helping others (e.g., Cairns, Cairns, Neckerman, Ferguson, & Gariepy, 1989; Crick & Bigbee, 1998; Crick, Casas, & Ku, in press; Crick & Grotpeter, 1996; Greener & Crick, in press).

Using Relationships to Harm Others: Relational Aggression

In recent research, we have found that some children harm others through manipulation and damage to their peer relationships (e.g., Crick et al., 1996; Crick & Grotpeter, 1995). For example, these children may use social exclusion or rumor spreading as ways to punish or get even with another child (e.g., by not inviting her to an important party or by spreading lies that will make peers not like her), or they may threaten to withdraw acceptance or friendship to gain control over another child (e.g., "You can't be my friend unless you do what I tell you to do"). We have labeled these types of behaviors *relational aggression* to emphasize that it is relationships that are the instrument of harm. Evidence from three studies indicates that children view relationally aggressive behaviors as hostile, mean acts that are likely to produce feelings of distress in the targets (Crick, 1995; Crick et al., 1996, two studies). In one of these studies, we asked 9- to 12-year-old children to describe what most of their peers do when they want to "be mean" to another child. For contexts in which the actor was a girl, relationally aggressive behaviors were cited by boys and girls more often than any other type of response. These findings provide evidence that attempts to damage relationships (i.e., acts that are likely to get in the way of satisfying belongingness needs) are highly salient to children and are viewed in negative terms.

Using Relationships to Help Others: Relational Inclusivity

In most of the past research on children's prosocial behavior, acts such as sharing, caring, and comforting have been emphasized as exemplars of interpersonal strategies that are aimed at helping others (e.g., Burleson, 1982; Eisenberg & Mussen, 1989). Interestingly, however, we found in two recent studies that middle-childhood-age children were much more likely to cite providing relationship help as a way to assist others than they were to cite the more traditionally assessed prosocial behaviors (Greener & Crick, in press). Specifically, in two independent samples ($n = 468$ and $n = 393$), we asked 9- to 12-year-old children to open-endedly describe the kinds of things that most of their peers do when they want to "be nice" to other children (i.e., act prosocially). Content analyses of children's responses revealed that most of the responses (e.g., 63% in Study 2 for girl-to-girl interactions and 72% for boy-to-boy interactions; 56% in Study 1 for girls and 52% for boys, in which the sex of the target was not specified) were classified as relationally inclusive behaviors (i.e., behaviors that offer friendship or group inclusion to another child). These findings seem to support the hypothesis that behaviors that are likely to satisfy others' belongingness needs are highly salient to children of this age and are viewed as acts of kindness.

Belongingness Needs and Loneliness

The previously described research on relational aggression and relational inclusivity highlights the importance of peer relationships to children. Clearly, however, the importance that children place on their alliances with peers can be both a blessing and a curse. Their desires for intimate ties with others may motivate them to develop important social skills and social networks; however, they may also place children at risk for difficult feelings if their interpersonal goals are not achieved (e.g., feelings of loneliness). Working from a cognitive framework, Perlman and Peplau (1982) have defined loneliness as the state when one's actual social contacts and relationships fall short of one's desired interpersonal goals. If so, it seems likely that children's feelings of loneliness and social dissatisfaction in the peer group (or, conversely, feelings of social satisfaction) involve an assessment of one's interpersonal goals (i.e., the types and numbers of relationships one desires) versus one's actual interpersonal achievements (i.e., the actual types and numbers of relationships one has achieved). We propose here that this assessment begins during peer interaction, as children encounter a diverse population of peers – friends, enemies, classmates, and so forth – and, in the process, confront different types of peer experiences.

Children's Peer Experiences: The Social Database

What kinds of social encounters are likely to occur in children's peer groups on a daily basis? In particular, which of these social events is most likely to affect children's feelings of belongingness? Researchers who have addressed this question have frequently focused, not surprisingly, on negative social events that are likely to be problematic or troubling for children such as peer rejection or peer conflict (Dodge, McClaskey, & Feldman, 1985). There is diversity in terms of children's exposure to negative experiences with peers. That is, it is quite common for most children to be treated poorly by peers from time to time (e.g., being picked last for the kickball team or being excluded from a group activity); however, some children suffer from negative peer treatment on a more consistent basis (Olweus, 1993a).

A number of types of negative peer treatment have been assessed in past research, including peer rejection (i.e., being actively disliked by other children), physical victimization (i.e., being the consistent target of peers' physically aggressive acts), and relational victimization (i.e., being the frequent target of peers' relationally aggressive acts). The impact of negative peer treatment on children is supported by results from studies that demonstrate that it predicts a host of concurrent and future adjustment difficulties (Crick & Bigbee, 1998; Crick & Grotpeter, 1996; Boivin et al., 1995; Olweus, 1993a; Parker & Asher, 1987). Perhaps this is not surprising given that mistreatment by one's peers is relatively clear feedback that one does not fit into the peer group, a situation that is likely to hamper satisfaction of belongingness needs. Relative to the study of these negative peer experiences, less attention has been paid to children's positive peer experiences, such as peer acceptance (i.e., being highly liked by other children) and being the recipient of prosocial behavior (i.e., being the consistent target of peers' prosocial acts). Clearly, positive peer treatment provides feedback to children that they are important to peers and well liked, a situation that makes the satisfaction of belongingness needs more likely. Recent evidence suggests that the failure to receive positive treatment from peers may be viewed just as negatively by children as receiving negative treatment (e.g., not being the target of prosocial acts may be as unsettling for some children as being the target of hostile acts, Crick &

Grotpeter, 1996). Thus, it may be that exposure to positive treatment and lack of exposure to negative treatment are both necessary for children to develop a sense of belongingness in their peer groups.

The previously discussed peer experiences primarily reflect children's treatment by a group of children, and this is the focus of the present chapter. In contrast, recent investigators have begun to assess children's treatment within their dyadic peer relationships (Bukowski & Hoza, 1989). These dyadic relationships include mutual friendships, which are identified when two children nominate each other as best friends (e.g., Bukowski, Hoza, & Boivin, 1993; Parker & Asher, 1993a,b), and mutual antipathies, which are identified when two children mutually reject each other (Hembry, Vandell, & Levin, 1995). Similar to negative and positive treatment by groups of peers, treatment by friends and enemies is also likely to provide children with important information about their fit with others (see Parker et al., this volume). In fact, because of the emotional salience that is likely to be attached to such one-to-one relationships, it seems likely that friendships and mutual antipathies may provide more direct and frequent information about belongingness than about group relationships. Unfortunately, because of constraints in our data (see description later), we were not able to directly test these hypotheses. Future research is needed to address dyadic peer experiences (e.g., friendships and mutual antipathies) in relation to the proposed model.

The Role of Social Information Processing

The types of social experiences described previously provide children with feedback about themselves and about their competency in peer relationships. As such, these peer encounters serve as a kind of "social database" that provides children with important information about their social achievements. One way that children can use this information is to evaluate whether they feel lonely. That is, they can use this data as the basis for the comparison proposed by Perlman and Peplau (1982), which they hypothesize to be instrumental in determinations of loneliness – the comparison of children's interpersonal goals (e.g., the kinds of relationships that they desire) with the state of their current peer relationships (e.g., the kinds of relationships that they have actually obtained).

To understand better how children might make this important comparison, we propose a social information-processing approach to the study of children's loneliness. Cognitive approaches to loneliness have successfully been applied in past loneliness research (e.g., see Asher et al., 1990, and Perlman & Peplau, 1982, for reviews). Generally, investigators working from this perspective have assessed how individuals' (primarily adults have been studied) attributions about their social experiences are related to their behavior in social interaction. That is, social cognitions have been used as a tool for understanding why some lonely individuals engage in behavior that is likely to alleviate their loneliness, whereas other individuals do not. Although study of these social cognition–behavior links is very important, the focus of the present chapter lies in a different domain (i.e., how experiences in the peer group affect social cognitions rather than how social cognitions affect behavior in the peer group). Specifically, in the cognitive model of loneliness proposed here (see Figure 8.1), we are concerned with understanding the processes involved in children's determinations of loneliness. That is, we are interested in how children make the comparison proposed by Perlman and Peplau (1982), which forms the basis for their feelings of loneliness. We propose that to make sense of the information gained through peer contacts, children must first process and interpret the social cues that they encounter in these peer interactions (Crick & Dodge, 1994). These interpretations are hypothesized to influence the meaning that children ultimately assign to their peer experiences. Also, over time, the types of peer experiences that children tend to accrue may influence the nature of the interpretations they make (as illustrated in Figure 8.1).

Social-information-processing models have guided a great deal of research on children's peer relationships in recent years. This research has focused largely on the role that social cognitions play in the development or maintenance of social behavior patterns (e.g., aggressive behavior) and, subsequently, the types of peer encounters that children are likely to experience (e.g., rejection by peers; Dodge & Feldman, 1990). Little attention has been paid, however, to the role that children's peer experiences might play in the development of their social cognitions or to the role that social cognitions might play in mediating the relation between children's peer experiences and their feelings of loneliness (Crick & Dodge, 1994). However, the few studies that do exist provide evidence that such an approach is a useful one. Generally, these studies have shown that children's attributions about social events (i.e., their perceptions of the causes of their social failures and successes) are significantly related to their feelings of loneliness. Specifically, this research shows that children who attribute social failure to internal stable causes (e.g., they blame themselves for peer rejection) are more likely to feel lonely both concurrently and in the future (Bukowski & Ferber, 1987; Renshaw & Brown, 1993). Furthermore, the link between attributions and loneliness may vary as a function of the types of peer experiences children encounter (e.g., highly accepted and popular children feel more lonely when they fail to take credit for their social successes than when they do take credit for their social achievements; Crick & Ladd, 1993).

To expand on this past research and to explore further how this type of social cognitive approach might enhance the understanding of childhood loneliness, we apply a social-information-processing model developed by Crick and Dodge (1994). In this model, it is posited that children process social cues (e.g., those involved in an interaction with a peer) as a series of cognitive steps. Specifically, these steps involve encoding and interpreting social cues (e.g., generating attributions), formulating a social goal, accessing or generating ideas about how to respond to the situation, evaluating the generated responses, and selecting one for enactment (Crick & Dodge, 1994). Although this model has typically been used to focus on how social information processing affects behavior, it allows for the study of how experience affects social information processing (Crick & Dodge, 1994). One advantage of applying this type of processing model to the study of loneliness is that it allows for the evaluation of attributions (i.e., the focus of past research) plus additional social–cognitive processes (e.g., the construction of social goals). Thus, it may expand our knowledge of the role that cognition plays in children's determinations of loneliness.

A number of the social–cognitive processes described in the above-mentioned model might be affected by children's peer experiences in ways that have implications for their feelings of loneliness. For example, during the encoding and interpretation process, children who are consistently treated poorly by peers (e.g., peers are physically abusive to them or consistently exclude them from peer activities) may develop the tendency to interpret peers' behavior as hostile, even when hostility is not intended by other children (i.e., they may develop hostile attributional biases). In turn, viewing peers' intentions as hostile or mean may negatively affect children's perceptions of the quality of their peer relationships (e.g., "My classmates don't like me"), perceptions that are likely to result in loneliness.

At the goal development step of processing, several possibilities appear plausible. It seems likely that children who are generally treated well by their peers would maintain relational goals for their interactions with peers; that is, they may place maintaining relationships as high or higher than succeeding in achieving instrumental goals. Two alternative hypotheses seem logical to interpret the goals of children who are not treated well by their peers. First, being treated poorly by peers may result in the development of friendship or acceptance goals (i.e., children may strive to achieve what they have been missing). If so, the inability to satisfy these belongingness needs may result in feelings of loneliness. It is also possible that negative peer treatment may result in the development of goals that do not involve the satisfying of belongingness needs. That is, consistent rejection by peers may lead children to give up on relationship goals and point them toward the achievement of other goals (e.g., getting their own way in a conflict or winning at games). If children have truly abandoned relationship goals in a particular context (e.g., their classroom at school) and have taken on other goals as more important, they may not express feelings of loneliness in that context.

Finally, at the response generation step of processing (i.e., formulating ideas about how to react to the situation), it seems likely that the nature of children's peer experiences may influence the responses they access or generate. For example, children who are treated well by peers may develop the tendency to generate friendly prosocial responses to reciprocate their peers' positive behavior. Generation of friendly responses may enhance children's feelings of closeness or connectedness with peers that, in turn, may decrease or alleviate feelings of loneliness. In contrast, children who are treated poorly by peers may develop hostile or aggressive response generation patterns in reaction to angry feelings or the desire to retaliate. Generating hostile responses may enhance feelings of distress (e.g., it may point out how emotionally distant children feel from their peers) that may contribute to feelings of loneliness.

Application of the Model to an Actual Sample

To provide initial information regarding the hypotheses discussed previously (i.e., the relations among children's peer experiences, social information processing, and loneliness depicted in Figure 8.1), we drew on data collected on a sample of 919 third- through sixth-grade children (464 girls and 455 boys; 18% African American, 81% European American, and 0.8% other ethnicities). Children in this study were recruited through their elementary schools, and those with parental consent completed a battery of questionnaires during three, 1-hour group sessions administered in their classrooms (consent rate was 80%). During these group sessions, children completed a loneliness inventory, two social-information-processing instruments, two measures of children's peer experiences, and a number of additional instruments that were not a part of the present analyses (the sample described here represents a portion of a larger investigation of childhood aggression and victimization, The Peers and Pals Project, that we conducted in central Illinois; see Crick, 1997; Crick & Werner, 1998).

Assessment of Peer Experiences

Indices of children's peer experiences in this study included relational victimization, physical victimization, peer rejection, being the recipient of peers' prosocial acts, and peer acceptance. Specifically, to assess victimization and the receipt of prosocial acts, we used a peer nomination measure, the Social Experiences Questionnaire-Peer Report (SEQ-P), that we developed in a prior study (Crick & Bigbee, 1998). The measure consisted of 14 items, 4 of which assess physical victimization (e.g., kids who are hit by other kids a lot), 5 of which assess relational victimization (e.g., kids who other kids tell lies and mean rumors about), and 5 of which assess the receipt of prosocial behavior (e.g., kids who other kids do nice things for). Children's scores for each item of the SEQ-P were summed and then standardized within classroom; the standardized scores were summed to compute subscale scores. These scores have been shown to be reliable and valid in past research (Crick & Bigbee, 1998).

To assess peer acceptance and rejection status, children completed positive and negative sociometric nominations. Consistent with past research, the nominations that children received for each question were summed and standardized within classroom, resulting in a continuous variable for group acceptance and a continuous variable for rejection (Coie, Dodge, & Coppotelli, 1982).

Assessment of Social Information Processing

Indices of children's social cognitions in this study included intent attributions, social goals, and desires to enact relationally aggressive, physically aggressive, and friendly–assertive responses when confronted with peer conflict situations. Conflict contexts were chosen that described situations likely to be common in episodes of peer rejection, physical victimization, or relational victimization (i.e., so that episodes would reflect the types of negative treatment that are common in children's peer groups). Specifically, two conflict types were used: instrumental conflict (e.g., being pushed into a mud puddle by a peer) and relational conflict (e.g., discovering that you are the only child in your class not invited to a birthday party; Crick, 1995).

To assess children's intent attributions, children completed a hypothetical-situation instrument developed by Crick (1995; adapted from Fitzgerald & Asher, 1987). The measure consisted of 10 stories, each of which described a provocation in which the intent of the provocateur was ambiguous. Five of the stories depicted instrumental conflict (e.g., a peer has broken the participant's radio), and 5 of the stories depicted relational conflict (e.g., the participant overhears peers discussing a birthday party to which he or she has not been invited). Children's intent attribution scores for this measure have been shown to be reliable in past research (Crick, 1995; Crick, Grotpeter, & Bigbee, 1998). Children answered two questions for each story, each of which assessed their attributions of the provocateur's intent. The first question provided children with four possible reasons for the provocation: two of the reasons reflected hostile intent (e.g., "The child did not want me to come to the party"), and two of the reasons reflected benign intent (e.g., "The child hasn't had a chance to invite me yet"). For the second question, children were asked to tell whether the provocateur's behavior was intended to be mean to them or not to be mean to them. Although the attributions the child makes are about other children's reasons for acting, the attributions concern the provocateur's behavior toward the self (i.e., the responses were specific "The kid was being mean to me" and not general, such as "The kid is mean"). In this research, such attributions are considered to reflect children's self-view; that is, children who have a tendency to perceive others as mean toward them are considered to have a negative self-perception. This linkage is supported by Hymel, Woody, Ditner, and LeMare (1988), who provided evidence that children base their assessments of how well they are doing socially on inferences they make from how peers act toward them.

Children's social goals (i.e., instrumental goals vs. relational goals) were assessed with a measure developed in past research (Crick & Dodge, 1996). Participants were presented with six conflict events similar to the ones used in the intent attribution measure, except that in these vignettes, the hostile intent of the provocateur was clear. Three situations were of an instrumentally conflictual nature, and three stories were of a relationally conflictual nature. At the end of each story, children were asked to choose one of two presented goals: (a) an instrumental goal (e.g., "I would want my seat back") or (b) a relational goal (e.g., "I would want the kid to like me"). Children received two goal scores: one for instrumental versus relational goals in the instrumental stories and one for instrumental versus relational goals in the relational stories.

Finally, for each of the six stories presented previously, children were asked to rate how often they would like to use each of three strategies: (a) a physically aggressive strategy (e.g., "Push the kid out of the chair"), (b) a relationally aggressive strategy (e.g., "Tell the kid they can't come to your next party if they don't invite you to theirs"), and (c) a prosocial or assertive strategy (e.g., "Ask the kids a question to get into the conversation"). These questions were based on a measure adapted from past research (Crick & Dodge, 1996); the specific strategies included were based on children's open-ended responses obtained in pilot research.

Assessment of Loneliness

We used the Asher and Wheeler (1985) Loneliness and Social Dissatisfaction Scale to assess loneliness. This instrument consists of 16 items that tap loneliness at school (e.g., "I feel lonely at school") and 8 filler items. Children respond to the items by rating on 1 to 5 scales how true each descriptor is for them. Children's loneliness scores derived from this instrument have been shown to be reliable and valid in numerous prior studies (see Asher et al., 1990; Terrell-Deutsch, this volume).

Overview of Analyses

The theoretical model we have presented is directional in nature. Because our data are not longitudinal, as a first step toward empirically testing this model, we can only test relationships among the model's components. Thus, it is important to note that it is premature to draw causal inferences from the present data. Four sets of analyses were conducted to address the following goals: (a) evaluation of the relation between peer experiences and loneliness for the present sample, (b) assessment of the relation between children's peer experiences and their processing of social information, (c) evaluation of the relation between processing of social information and children's feelings of loneliness, and (d) assessment of the degree to which social-information-processing patterns account for unique variation in loneliness, beyond those accounted for by peer experiences.

Past research has demonstrated gender differences in the relations between many of the components of the model tested in the research reported in this chapter. In particular, gender differences have been demonstrated in the relations between (a) children's peer experiences (i.e., victimization) and loneliness (Boivin et al., 1995); (b) peer experiences (i.e., rejection) and processing of peer experiences (i.e., response generation; Feldman & Dodge, 1987); and, in adult samples, (c) processing of peer experiences (i.e., goal development) and loneliness (Schultz & Moore, 1986). Furthermore, significant gender differences have been obtained in past research for a number of the constructs under consideration in these analyses (e.g., physical aggression, relational aggression, and physical victimization). For these reasons, analyses were conducted separately for boys and girls.

Table 8.1. Correlations Between Children's Peer Experiences
and Loneliness

	Peer Experiences				
Loneliness	Peer Rejection	Peer Acceptance	Prosocial Treatment	Physical Victimization	Relational Victimization
Girls	***.35	***−.23	***−.28	***.32	***.30
Boys	***.34	***−.25	***−.25	***.29	***.33

*** $p < .001$.

Peer Experiences and Loneliness

In the first set of analyses, correlation coefficients were computed to evaluate the relation between children's peer experiences and their feelings of loneliness (refer to Table 8.1). These coefficients demonstrated that loneliness was significantly related to relatively high levels of negative peer treatment (i.e., peer rejection, physical victimization, and relational victimization) and relatively low levels of positive peer treatment (i.e., peer acceptance and being the recipient of peers' prosocial acts). These results confirm that the relation between loneliness and peer treatment was similar in the present sample to that obtained in past research (e.g., Asher & Wheeler, 1985; Crick & Grotpeter, 1996; Crick & Ladd, 1993).

Peer Experiences and Social Information Processing

In the second set of analyses, correlation coefficients were computed to assess the relation between children's peer experiences and their social-information-processing patterns (refer to Tables 8.2 and 8.3). Results showed that, for girls, negative peer experiences (i.e., peer rejection, physical victimization, and relational victimization) were positively associated with hostile attributional biases in instrumental conflict situations. Furthermore, positive peer treatment (i.e., being the recipient of peers' prosocial acts) was negatively associated with hostile attributional biases in instrumental conflict situations for girls. Additionally, physically aggressive response patterns in instrumental conflict situations were positively related to peer rejection and negatively related to prosocial treatment for girls. Analyses of processing in relational conflict situations revealed that being the recipient of peers' prosocial acts was related to relational, rather than instrumental, goal preferences for girls. Additionally, both physically aggressive and relationally aggressive response patterns were positively

Table 8.2. Study 1: Correlations Between Girls' Peer Experiences and Their Social-Information-Processing Patterns (SIP) in Instrumental and Relational Peer Conflicts

SIP	Peer Experiences				
	Peer Rejection	Peer Acceptance	Prosocial Treatment	Physical Victimization	Relational Victimization
	Instrumental conflict situations				
Hostile attributions	***.19	−.08	***−.17	**.14	**.13
Goals	.00	−.07	−.08	−.05	−.04
Physically aggressive strategies	***.18	−.07	***−.23	.05	.08
Relationally aggressive strategies	.09	−.01	−.09	.02	.07
Friendly assertive strategies	−.03	.02	.05	−.02	−.00
	Relational conflict situations				
Hostile attributions	.10	.05	−.03	.04	.08
Goals	.07	−.07	**−.13	−.00	−.02
Physically aggressive strategies	***.15	−.04	***−.18	.07	.08
Relationally aggressive strategies	***.15	−.02	**−.14	.02	.07
Friendly assertive strategies	−.02	.04	.05	.01	.01

* $p < .01$. *** $p < .001$.

associated with peer rejection and negatively associated with prosocial treatment for girls.

The obtained results for girls indicated that, in general, poor treatment from peers (peer rejection, physical victimization, and relational victimization) was associated with viewing peers as mean and with desires to

Table 8.3. Study 1: Correlations Between Boys' Peer Experiences and Their Social-Information-Processing Patterns (SIP) in Instrumental and Relational Peer Conflicts

SIP	Peer Experiences				
	Peer Rejection	Peer Acceptance	Prosocial Treatment	Physical Victimization	Relational Victimization
	Instrumental conflict situations				
Hostile attributions	.07	−.03	−.04	.07	−.01
Goals	.00	−.06	−.05	−.01	−.07
Physically aggressive strategies	.10	.06	−.04	.09	.06
Relationally aggressive strategies	**.13	−.07	−.08	.08	.10
Friendly assertive strategies	.07	−.08	.02	.02	.07
	Relational conflict situations				
Hostile attributions	.04	.01	.01	.05	.01
Goals	.06	−.08	−.09	.05	.01
Physically aggressive strategies	.06	.07	−.01	.07	.04
Relationally aggressive strategies	.06	.02	−.03	.04	.07
Friendly assertive strategies	.09	−.05	.03	.08	.11

** *p* < .01.

react in hostile, aggressive ways toward peers. In contrast, positive treatment from peers (peer acceptance and being the target of peers' prosocial acts) was associated with viewing peers in benign ways (i.e., as opposed to hostile), reporting relationship-oriented goals (i.e., wanting to be liked by peers), and tendencies not to respond in hostile, aggressive ways toward peers. Although cause cannot be determined from the present data, the results are consistent with the previously discussed hypothesis that hostile treatment from peers may result in the development of negative perceptions of peers and in desires for retaliation (e.g., "You got me and now I will get you"). For boys, results showed that peer experiences were largely unrelated to social information processing. Specifically, as can be seen in Table 8.3, the only significant association obtained was between peer rejection and endorsement of relationally aggressive responses to instrumental conflict situations.

Social Information Processing and Loneliness

Correlation coefficients were conducted to assess the relation between children's social-information-processing patterns and their feelings of (refer to Table 8.4). These analyses revealed that, for girls, loneliness was sig-

Table 8.4. Correlations Between Children's Social Information Processing and Loneliness

	Loneliness	
SIP	Girls	Boys
Instrumental conflict situations		
Hostile attributions	***.24	.05
Goals	.06	.02
Physically aggressive strategies	***.16	.02
Relationally aggressive strategies	***.14	.03
Friendly assertive strategies	−.02	−.09
Relational conflict situations		
Hostile attributions	***.23	.05
Goals	**.12	.04
Physically aggressive strategies	**.12	−.04
Relationally aggressive strategies	***.14	−.04
Friendly assertive strategies	−.02	−.08

** $p < .01$.   *** $p < .001$.

Table 8.5. Proportion of Variance in Loneliness Scores Accounted for by Peer Experiences and Social Information Processing (SIP)

Loneliness	R^2 for Peer Experiences Entered at Step 1	R^2 Δ for SIP Entered at Step 2
Girls	***.19	***.06
Boys	***.17	.02

*** $p < .001$.

nificantly related to hostile attributional biases (for both instrumental and relational conflict situations), instrumental goal preferences (for relational conflict situations), physically aggressive response patterns (for both instrumental and relational conflict situations), and relationally aggressive response patterns (for both instrumental and relational conflict situations). For boys, analyses revealed that loneliness was not significantly related to social information processing for either of the two conflict situations.

In summary, for girls, the obtained results indicated that viewing peers in negative ways, wanting to respond to peers in hostile ways, and not formulating peer acceptance goals were all associated with feeling more lonely. These associations are consistent with previously discussed hypotheses. That is, they suggest that girls who view their peers in negative ways may be keenly aware of the deficits apparent in their peer relationships, a view that would likely result in feelings of loneliness.

The Unique Contribution of Social Information Processing to the Prediction of Loneliness

To assess whether social information processing would account for unique variance in loneliness, beyond that accounted for by peer experiences, we computed hierarchical multiple regression equations in which loneliness served as the dependent variable. In these equations, children's positive and negative peer experience scores (i.e., peer acceptance, receipt of prosocial acts, peer rejection, physical victimization, and relational victimization) were entered at Step 1 and children's social-information-processing scores (i.e., hostile attributions, goals, physically aggressive responses, relationally aggressive responses, and friendly assertive responses for instrumental and relational conflict situations) were entered at Step 2 (refer to Table 8.5 for R^2 values). Results showed that social-information-processing patterns (i.e., children's interpretations of their peer experiences) added significantly to peer experiences in the prediction of loneliness for girls, $F(15, 446) = 3.6$, $p < .001$, but did not add significantly in the prediction of loneliness for boys, $F(15, 427) = 1.1$, *ns*.

Gender Differences in the Proposed Model

The obtained gender differences in the results described earlier were unexpected.[2] That is, we did not predict a priori that the findings would provide evidence (albeit descriptive) for the proposed loneliness model for girls, but not for boys. Before drawing inferences about why these gender differences might be operating, we decided to gather more information that might assist us in evaluating the validity of the current data set (i.e., to determine whether the obtained findings might be due to biases in this particular sample). Consequently, we drew on a second, independent sample of data in which we had assessed social information processing and indexes of children's peer experiences to see if relations similar to the first study would be obtained (we did not assess loneliness in the second study). The Study 2 sample included 341 third- through sixth-grade children (164 boys and 177 girls). Measures of social information processing and of children's peer experiences used in Study 2 were the same as those described previously for Study 1. Also similar to Study 1, correlation coefficients were computed to evaluate the social cognition–peer experience linkages (refer to Tables 8.6 and 8.7). Interestingly, the results of Study 2 confirmed the gender difference obtained in Study 1. That is, social information processing and peer experiences were significantly related for girls but were shown to be largely unrelated for boys. Although we were unable to evaluate the linkages that involve loneliness in the proposed model for Study 2, the obtained results offer some validity to support Study 1 findings.

The obtained results provide an interesting challenge for researchers interested in the role of gender in the study of loneliness, peer relations, and social information processing. Past research on social information processing in childhood has focused largely on the study of boys and on the links

---

[2] In a number of our analyses, correlations conducted on the girls' data were significant, whereas the correlations conducted on the boys' data were nonsignificant. To test whether the nonsignificant zero-order boys' correlations were significantly different from the low but significant zero-order girls' correlations we computed, z scores to test the differences between correlations. Results indicated that approximately half of these sets of zero-order correlations were significantly different from each other ($p < .05$).

Table 8.6. Study 2: Correlations Between Girls' Peer Experiences and Their Social Information-Processing Patterns (SIP) in Instrumental and Relational Peer Conflicts

	Peer Experiences				
SIP	**Peer Rejection**	**Peer Acceptance**	**Prosocial Treatment**	**Physical Victimization**	**Relational Victimization**
	Instrumental conflict situations				
Hostile attributions	*.15	−.09	*−.14	***.23	**.17
Goals	.03	.03	−.09	.04	.05
Physically aggressive strategies	.04	*−.13	***−.38	**.17	*.12
Relationally aggressive strategies	**.17	**−.17	***−.32	***.28	**.17
Friendly assertive strategies	.02	.10	.03	−.06	−.05
	Relational conflict situations				
Hostile attributions	.01	−.01	.06	.02	.03
Goals	.12	−.09	**−.17	.06	.11
Physically aggressive strategies	.09	−.10	***−.41	**.21	.11
Relationally aggressive strategies	.11	−.11	***−.35	*.16	.09
Friendly assertive strategies	.12	−.03	**.18	**.14	.12

* $p < .05$.   ** $p < .01$.   *** $p < .001$.

between processing and subsequent behavior (Dodge & Feldman, 1990). Results of this past research have consistently demonstrated the robustness of the cognition–behavior relation (primarily for boys because girls have often been excluded from these studies; Crick & Dodge, 1994). Thus, the gender difference obtained in the present research is in stark contrast

Table 8.7. Study 2: Correlations Between Boys' Peer Experiences and Their Social-Information-Processing Patterns (SIP) in Instrumental and Relational Peer Conflicts

	Peer Experiences				
SIP	Peer Rejection	Peer Acceptance	Prosocial Treatment	Physical Victimization	Relational Victimization
	Instrumental conflict situations				
Hostile attributions	.11	−.04	−.05	.10	.05
Goals	.02	.06	.00	−.03	.06
Physically aggressive strategies	.03	.01	*−.13	−.06	−.07
Relationally aggressive strategies	−.11	−.05	−.11	−.03	−.06
Friendly assertive strategies	*−.16	.05	.07	−.01	−.06
	Relational conflict situations				
Hostile attributions	.08	−.04	−.06	.00	.05
Goals	.06	−.05	**−.21	−.01	.04
Physically aggressive strategies	.01	.03	−.07	−.10	−.04
Relationally aggressive strategies	−.09	.07	−.07	−.12	−.07
Friendly assertive strategies	−.09	.02	−.01	.02	−.05

* $p < .05$.   ** $p < .01$.

to the patterns obtained in past studies. However, it is important to keep in mind that our focus was on a different pathway than that explored in past research. That is, we addressed the influence of peer experiences on social information processing (and subsequent loneliness), whereas past investigators have focused largely on the influence of social information processing on subsequent behavior and peer experiences (i.e., the two pathways are reciprocal). It seems likely that the pathway we assessed is more applicable for girls than for boys because of gender differences in internalizing and externalizing tendencies. That is, for peer experiences to influence social cognition, children must be reflective and introspective about those experiences. This process seems more internalizing than externalizing in nature, a characteristic that is more likely to be found in girls than in boys (Block, 1983). It also seems possible that because of the relative importance that girls place on establishing intimate connections with others (Block, 1983), events that threaten those connections (e.g., peer conflict situations like those assessed here) may be especially salient and likely to lead to more frequent introspection about those events for girls (e.g., to try to figure out what happened and why). Furthermore, Lyons-Ruth (1995) has proposed that girls' distress may be more influenced by life events than that of boys'. If so, girls may be more sensitive to social events (e.g., peer conflict) that are likely to induce distress (e.g., feelings of loneliness), and, thus, these events may be more likely to significantly affect girls' social–cognitive patterns and feelings of loneliness when confronted with those events. Perhaps this is why girls are (stereotypically) seen as more socially intuitive than are boys. Finally, because of the greater negative social consequences of being labeled as lonely for boys than for girls (Borys & Perlman, 1985), boys may be less willing to admit to their feelings of loneliness and may be more willing to replace relational goals with alternative goals. Or, boys' less willingness to admit to their loneliness would undermine the accuracy with which researchers can link male loneliness to a specific set of cognitive processes.

General Conclusion

Results of past research and of the new studies reported here provide initial evidence that a social-information-processing approach to the study of loneliness is a fruitful avenue for future research. However, longitudinal studies are needed before the model we proposed can be adequately tested. Additionally, studies are needed that assess children's experiences in dyadic peer relationships (e.g., friendships and mutual antipathies) in addition to the group indices (e.g., peer rejection and physical victimization) assessed in the research presented here. Further attention to the role of gender in the proposed model also seems warranted, given the results of the two studies reported here (see also Koenig & Abrams, this volume). It is our hope that the proposed model can serve as a basis for future research and conceptual creativity, as the study of loneliness is an important pathway for both understanding and helping children with social difficulties.

Acknowledgment

Preparation of this chapter was supported in part by grants from The Harry Frank Guggenheim Foundation, the National Institute of Mental Health No. MH53524, and the William T. Grant Foundation to Nicki R. Crick and by a Tilly Graduate Fellowship to Jennifer K. Grotpeter.

9 | Parental Antecedents of Children's Loneliness

KEN J. ROTENBERG

Interest in children's and adolescents' loneliness has increased dramatically over the past two decades (see the introductory chapter, this volume). One facet of loneliness that has received some attention is the parental antecedents of children's loneliness. This refers to parents' affective states and behavior that affect their children's loneliness; it is the topic covered by this chapter. I discuss how parents' loneliness, warmth, involvement, and promotion of peer relationships potentially affect their children's loneliness. Unless required, I use the term *children* to refer to both children and adolescents in this chapter.

Although the focus is on how parents affect their children's loneliness, this chapter is guided by the understanding that the relationship between parents and children is a reciprocal one (see Barnes & Olson, 1985; Bell, 1968; Belsky, 1981). Research indicates that infants' temperament affects how parents interact with their infants (i.e., Crockenberg, 1981; Thompson, Connell, & Bridges, 1988), and children's behavioral styles affect their parents' reactions to the children (Keller & Bell, 1977; Steinberg, 1987; Teyber, Messe, & Stollak, 1977). There is, of course, an extensive body of research that has documented the likely effects of parents' affect and behavior on their offspring (see Darling & Steinberg, 1993). Given that children's affective states and behavior affect, and are affected by, their parents' affective states and behavior, it seems reasonable to expect that children's loneliness is a product of complex reciprocal interactions between them and their parents.

There are various ways that loneliness has been defined and assessed, as indicated by Terrell-Deutsch's chapter in this volume. Research on loneliness in children has focused on loneliness as comprising (or arising) from their lack of satisfaction with their relationships with peers and the emotional experience of loneliness (see Asher et al., 1984; see also Parkhurst & Hopmeyer's chapter). It should be noted, though, that researchers such as Goossens and his colleagues (Marcoen et al., 1987; Goossens & Marcoen, this volume) have examined loneliness in children with respect to their relationships with their parents.

The present chapter is organized in the following fashion. First, I review each of the five major theories and hypotheses regarding the parental antecedents of children's loneliness and the research pertaining to each theory or hypothesis. After my review, I present a study that I have carried out to examine the implications of the theories or hypotheses. Finally, I discuss future directions for research.

Attachment Theory

Cassidy and Berlin (this volume) outline the application of attachment theory to children's loneliness. According to this theory, there are two distinct behavior systems: attachment to an adult caregiver and affiliation with peers. Each system is separate and serves different survival functions. The theory prescribes that differences in parental behavior (e.g., responsiveness to infants and affection) promote differences in the quality of children's attachment to their caregivers that, in turn, causes the children to form different internal working models, comprising representations of self and primary caregiver. This attachment to an adult system affects children's affiliation to peers because the children generalize the representational models (self and caregiver) to others, including peers.

With regard to loneliness, Cassidy and Berlin (this volume) drew on Weiss's (1973) hypothesis to propose that children primarily experience emotional loneliness within the context of their attachment to the caregiver, whereas they primarily experience social loneliness within the context of their peer social relationships. According to Cassidy and Berlin, because insecure attachment arises from the lack of acceptance and sensitivity on part of the caregiver, the insecurely attached child develops a working internal model in which the caregiver is represented as an unavailable source of comfort and affection. The child generalizes that mental representation to others, including peers. The authors describe various paths of modest strength that potentially connect the internal working model and loneliness. In one case, the child would experience an emotional void and a perpetual longing for something missing, an orientation that becomes manifested in their peer relationships and results in heightened loneliness with respect to those relationships. As alternatives, the child could experience loneliness in peer interactions because (a) he or she views him- or herself as unappealing or unworthy of care and therefore not likeable by peers or (b) has formed internal working models of others as generally hostile, rejecting, or unavailable and therefore believes that

Attachment Theory Paths and Correlations

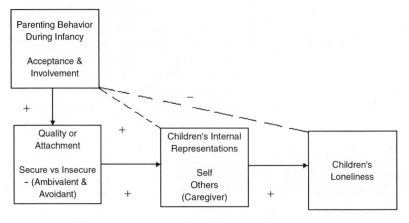

Parental Style Hypothesis Paths and Correlations

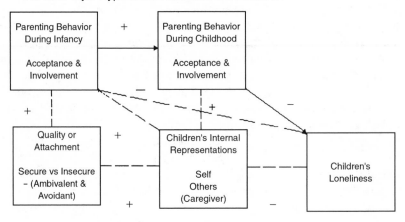

Note:
Solid lines = Paths
Dot lines = Correlations

Figure 9.1. Paths and correlations predicted by attachment theory and parenting style hypothesis.

he or she will not find companionship with others. It is interesting to note that a similar hypothesis about the origins of (chronic) loneliness was advanced by Hojat (1987) from a psychodynamic perspective. Nevertheless, attachment theory predicts that the development of insecure attachment in infancy contributes to loneliness during childhood and adolescence. The hypothesized paths are shown in Figure 9.1.

Berlin, Cassidy, and Belsky (1995) have examined the implications of attachment theory for loneliness in a longitudinal study. This study was designed to determine whether the quality of infants' (12-month-olds) attachment to their mothers predicted subsequent loneliness during childhood (5–7 years of age), as assessed by Cassidy and Asher's (1992) Loneliness and Social Dissatisfaction Questionnaire for Young Children. Cassidy and Belsky found that children who had formed insecure–ambivalent attachment to their mothers during infancy were more lonely than were children who had formed secure attachments during infancy. Additionally though, children who had formed insecure–avoidant attachment during infancy showed less loneliness than children who had formed secure attachments with their mothers. The findings provide support for attachment theory, in so far as insecure–ambivalent attachment during infancy was predictive of high loneliness during childhood. The pattern found for avoidant attachment, however, violated the expectations derived from the theory.

Berlin, Cassidy, and Belsky (1995) attempted to explain the unexpected finding by drawing on the principle that children who form an insecure–avoidant attachment during infancy experience high levels of rejection by their parents. The researchers suggested that the parental rejection caused the children to form a model of relationships in which they defensively excluded attachment-related information from attention and memory. As a result of this defensive cognitive style, it was proposed that the children habitually denied emotional vulnerability to themselves and others, including the experience of loneliness. These hypotheses about the defensive processes of children who formed insecure–avoidant attachments are interesting and warrant investigation. Nonetheless, the study confirmed only one of the expectations derived from attachment theory and yielded a pattern that was contrary to the theory.

Some researchers have examined the implications of attachment theory for loneliness during adulthood (see Shaver & Rubenstein, 1980). Hazan and Shaver (1987) examined the relation between adults' (college students') current state–trait loneliness and their reports of their relationships with their parents during childhood. The latter served as the measure of attachment history and included the college students' reports of the caring, warmth, and acceptance of mothers and fathers during their (the students') childhood. It was found that college students with an anxious/ambivalent attachment history reported higher current state and trait loneliness than did those with a secure attachment history; college students with an avoidant attachment history reported levels of state and trait loneliness that were of intermediate value. In a more detailed analysis, Hazan and Shaver found that college students with an anxious/

ambivalent attachment history reported greater loneliness on items assessing the self-ascription of loneliness traits (e.g., "I am a lonely person") than did individuals with the other two types of attachment histories. By contrast, it was found that college students with insecure attachment histories (both anxious/ambivalent and avoidant) reported more loneliness than those with a secure attachment history when the items pertained to more ambiguous aspects of loneliness (e.g., "During the past few years, no one has really known me well"). According to Hazan and Shaver (1987), individuals with avoidant attachment history admit to having considerable distance from others but may not be willing to admit being lonely people, potentially because of their defensive avoidance style.

Some additional support for the implications of attachment theory for loneliness was yielded by another study by Hazan and Shaver (1990). On the basis of responses to a questionnaire published in a local newspaper, the researchers found that adults with insecure attachment histories (both anxious/ambivalent and avoidant) reported more combined symptoms of loneliness and depression (e.g., cries easily and feeling hopeless) than did adults with a secure attachment history.

The adult research converges in some respects with the child research (Cassidy & Belsky, 1995) regarding the relation between attachment to parents and loneliness. Both lines of research indicate that anxious/avoidant attachment is associated with high loneliness, as expected on the basis of attachment theory. Both lines of research may be taken to suggest that insecure–avoidant attachment is less strongly associated with high loneliness than is insecure–ambivalent attachment. Nevertheless, the adult research yielded modest support for the notion that insecure–avoidant attachment is associated with high loneliness, as is expected on the basis of attachment theory. As noted earlier, the opposite pattern was found in the child research.

The Narcissistic Intrusion Hypothesis

Andersson and his colleagues (Andersson, 1990; Andersson, Mullins, & Johnson, 1987) have proposed that parental intrusion promotes narcissism in children that, in turn, contributes to the propensity to be lonely. Intrusive parenting is apparently a complex pattern. According to the formulations, the intrusive parent displays parenting strategies entailing (a) love withdrawal, (b) personality absorption, and (c) a "conflict between initial adjustment of submissive propitiation and the later assumption of goal achievement" (p. 84, Andersson, 1990). The proposed relations are as follows. The intrusive parent tends to use love withdrawal as a discipline technique that causes the child to manifest a host of difficulties: He or she conforms to expectations because of guilt, becomes unaware of his or her real needs, displays a lack self-consciousness, and suppresses the expression of anger in family interactions. Because the child is often regarded as an extension of the intrusive parent, the parent absorbs (in a sense) the child's personality. Overall, the family with intrusive parents is warm and secure, but only in appearance, because the family interactions are characterized by child conformity and imposed lack of parent–child conflict. Indeed, family members tend to withdraw from contact with others from outside the home because they could dispell the myth of the family as warm and secure. Actual seclusion complements that tendency and, thereby, enhances the effects of intrusive parenting.

Andersson and his colleagues (Andersson, 1990; Andersson, Mullins, & Johnson, 1987) have outlined the consequences of the intrusive parenting for the child, in some detail. Such a parenting style is presumed to predispose the child to (a) experience difficulty in differentiating from one or both parents, thereby inhibiting the development of him or her as an independent autonomous person; (b) develop an exaggerated sense of importance; and (c) (hence) acquire a narcissistic personality trait. These are believed to interfere with the individual's ability to form healthy bonds with others, thus resulting in loneliness. Also, Andersson (1990) describes a two-step model in which family withdrawal and parental intrusion contributed to narcissism in the offspring who, when becoming a parent, promotes the experience of anxiety in his or her offspring.

To investigate the narcissistic intrusion hypothesis, Andersson (1990; Andersson et al., 1987) required 207 older women to report the extent to which their parents displayed warmth and security, and their family was secluded, during childhood. Loneliness was assessed by a shortened and modified version of the UCLA Loneliness Scale (Russell et al., 1980). In support of the narcissistic intrusion hypothesis, Andersson found that individuals who reported having a warm and secure, but secluded, family life during childhood displayed greater loneliness than did individuals who reported having other types of family life during childhood collectively (i.e., the combinations of warm/secure and not secluded, not warm/secure but secluded, and not warm/secure and not secluded).

There are various limitations with Andersson's (1990) study. The researcher himself noted that the study was limited by the reliance on retrospective reports of childhood and the distinctiveness of the participant sample. Let me add that there was no evidence in the study for the reliability or validity of the measures of family warmth–security and seclusion. Also, Andersson did not examine the specific parenting style presumed to be responsible for intrusive parenting (e.g., love withdrawal discipline) nor for the narcissistic characteristics of the individual (the offspring) presumed to be responsible for loneliness. Finally, there is one notable problem with analysis of the loneliness data; because a single forced comparison was used (i.e., the targeted intrusive group vs. others), it is not clear whether there were main effects of warmth–security of family life, main effects of the seclusion of family life, and a significant interaction between two variables. Finding the two-way interaction would lend credibility to the conclusion that the combination of the effects of warmth–security and the effects of seclusion is linked to high loneliness.

Intergenerational Transmission of Loneliness Hypothesis

Various authors have speculated on the possibility that parents transmit their loneliness to their offspring, such that lonely parents tend to have children who are lonely as well. Most notably, Lobdell and Perlman (1986) examined the issue of whether parents "handed down" their loneliness to their offspring, or what was called the "intergenerational transmission" of loneliness (as a hypothesis). Lobdell and Perlman administered the revised UCLA Loneliness Scale to college-age daughters and their parents, both mothers and fathers. In support of the intergenerational transmission of loneliness hypothesis, Lobdell and Perlman found that loneliness in daughters was correlated with their mothers' loneliness, $r(128) = .26$, $p < .01$. They also found a modest correlation between the daughters' and their fathers' loneliness, $r(128) = .19$, $p < .05$. Some similar relations have been found in elementary school children; Henwood and Solano (1995) found that first-grade children's loneliness was significantly correlated with their mothers' loneliness ($r = .25$, $p < .05$). In this study, parents' loneliness was assessed by an abbreviated version of the UCLA Loneliness Scale, and children's loneliness was assessed by a modified version of Asher et al.'s (1984) Loneliness and Social Dissatisfaction Scale.

Drawing on attachment theory, Lobdell and Perlman (1986) speculated on the factors that potentially accounted for the intergenerational transmission of loneliness. The researchers proposed that children's failure to establish strong emotional bonds and secure attachment early in development resulted in their tendency to show various forms of distress across development, such as depression, emotional detachment, and loneliness. The relation between attachment and loneliness was attributed to the children's formation of an internal working model of self and other (caregiver). As support for these hypotheses, Lobdell and Perlman reported that the daughters' loneliness was correlated with (a) reports of their depression, (b) reports of the number of their friends, and (c) reports of their parents' closeness and positive involvement with them (the daughters). Also, parents' loneliness was correlated with their depression and reports of the number of their friends. On this basis, Lobdell and Perlman proposed that the parent–child relation emerged first, potentially establishing a proclivity to form a "depressive personality" (p. 595) and a high risk of loneliness. Later in development, loneliness became associated with the number of friends and that varied, in part, as a function of individuals' current social situation.

There are some limitations with Lobdell and Perlman's (1986) article that should be noted. For one, Lobdell and Perlman examined the relations between parents' and their offspring's loneliness when the latter were in college, as part of a cross-sectional design. More definitive evidence for the intergenerational transmission of loneliness would be provided if it was found that parents' loneliness is predictive of loneliness in their offspring across the course of development, beginning in childhood.

Furthermore, the intergenerational transmission of loneliness hypothesis pertains to the relation between parents' and their offspring's loneliness. To explicate the mechanisms responsible for the relation, Lobdell and Perlman (1986) primarily drew on the attachment theory because they found it particularly helpful. The researchers stated that it was possible that other theories (and hypothesized processes) could account for the relation between parents' and their offspring's loneliness. It is now time to turn to those theories and hypotheses and describe how they account for the parental antecedents of children's loneliness.

The Parenting Style Hypothesis

Parenting style has been defined by Darling and Steinberg (1993) as "a constellation of attitudes toward the child that are communicated to the child and, taken together, create an emotional climate in which the parents' behaviors are expressed" (p. 488). The early research by Schaefer and Bayley (1963) has contributed much to the knowledge of parenting style. They found that maternal behavior, specifically mothers' expression of love–hostility toward their children, affected their children's behavior concurrently and later in development (i.e., from infancy through adolescence). Furthermore, individual differences in mothers' love–hostility toward their children were moderately stable across childhood and adolescence and there was comparable stability in the children's behavior (e.g., friendliness) across that period. During later research (see Schaefer,

1965b), the love-hostility dimension of parental behavior was relabeled as *acceptance–rejection*.

Recent research has replicated a number of Schaefer and his colleagues' findings. Mothers' parenting styles, notably acceptance–rejection, have been found to be modestly consistent across childhood through adolescence, although there is some inconsistency in parenting styles across time (McNally, Eisenberg, & Harris, 1991; Roberts, Block, & Block, 1984). Also, various studies have shown that mothers' and fathers' parenting styles predict social functioning across childhood through adolescence. Baumrind (1979, 1991), for example, found that authoritative parents – those whose parenting styles include both warmth and control – have children and adolescents who are more socially competent than children whose parents adopt either authoritarian or permissive parenting styles.

According to the parenting style hypothesis, lonely parents are inclined to be more rejecting and less positively involved with their children than are nonlonely parents. It may be possible that these differences in parenting style arise from a broader negative interpersonal orientation in lonely adults, as indicated by their tendency to hold negative perceptions of others (Hanley-Dunn, Maxwell, & Santos, 1985; Henwood & Solano, 1995; Jones, Freemon, & Goswick, 1981; Rotenberg, 1994; Wittenberg & Reis, 1986). Nevertheless, the parenting hypothesis prescribes that the lonely parents' tendency to reject and not be positively involved with their children increases the likelihood with which the children experience loneliness. Regarding Lobdell and Perlman's (1986) findings, lonely parents' parenting style may have directly contributed, either from an earlier period (i.e., childhood) or concurrently (i.e., adolescence), to their college daughters' loneliness. A similar principle can account for Henwood and Solano's correlation between first-grade children's and their mothers' loneliness. In this case, lonely parents' parenting styles during their children's first grade or earlier may have contributed to loneliness in the children. The paths corresponding to the parenting style hypothesis are shown in Figure 9.1.

The parenting style hypothesis has been examined by M. H. Davis and Franzoi (1986) and Franzoi and M. H. Davis (1985). In two studies, 16-year-old high school students completed the short version of the UCLA Loneliness Scale and rated their current relationships with mothers and fathers regarding how much each parent was warm, loving, and rejecting. The adolescents were tested in 1 year, as part of the first study, and then again in the next year, as part of the second study. This procedure yielded cross-sectional analyses for each of the 2 years and a

1-year, longitudinal design. For the first year of the study (Franzoi & M. H. Davis, 1985), the cross-sectional path analyses indicated that mothers' warmth predicted loneliness in male but not in female adolescents. An even stronger set of relations was found in the second year of the study (M. H. Davis & Franzoi, 1986), the cross-sectional path analyses indicated that (a) fathers' warmth predicted loneliness in female and male adolescents, and (b) mothers' warmth predicted loneliness in male adolescents. When the path analyses were assessed longitudinally across the 1-year period, however, neither mothers' nor fathers' warmth was predictive of the adolescents' loneliness. In effect, the findings did not support the conclusion that parental warmth predicted, and presumably caused, loneliness in adolescence across a 1-year period. On the basis of M. H. Davis and Franzoi's discussion, it would appear that the *instantaneous causal lag* model provides the best account of the relation between parental warmth and loneliness in adolescents. According to that model, parental behavior affects loneliness over a short time span, such as days or weeks.

As an account for the pattern of findings, M. H. Davis and Franzoi (1986) proposed that "not surprisingly, warmer and more loving parents lead to reduced feelings of social isolation" (p. 608). Rather unfortunately, the researchers did not describe the mechanisms potentially underlying the observed relations in greater detail. Perhaps parental rejection (e.g., low warmth and low positive involvement) causes children to experience a dissatisfaction with those relationships that, through generalization, increases their experience of dissatisfaction with peer relationships and hence increases loneliness. Greater attention needs to be given to the precise mechanisms by which parenting style affects loneliness in children.

There is one particularly critical methodological problem with the research on the parenting style hypothesis. In all the studies to date, children reported their parents' behavior. This poses a problem because, as previously reported, lonely adults and children hold more negative perceptions of others (Hanley-Dunn et al., 1985; Henwood & Solano, 1995; Wittenberg & Reis, 1986) than do nonlonely individuals. Indeed, lonely adults believe that they are viewed negatively by others even though those perceptions are not accurate (see Rotenberg, 1994). As a result, lonely children may tend to negatively evaluate their parents' behaviors (i.e., low in warmth and positive involvement) and that could account for the correlations between parental behaviors and loneliness. This constitutes the *negative perception* hypothesis.

One solution to the preceding problem is to use multiple observers of parental behavior, including parents' reports of their own behavior. This resolution is complicated by research indicating that there is a very modest correspondence between parents' reports of parental behaviors and children's reports of those same behaviors (Barnes & Olson, 1985; Schwartz, Barton-Henry, & Pruzinsky, 1985). On the basis of such findings, some researchers have concluded that the parents' perspectives and children's perspectives are both important sources of information and that the perspectives may reflect different social "realities" (see Barnes & Olson, 1985). It should be pointed out that the negative perception hypothesis and the different social realities are by no means exclusive; lonely children's negative perceptions may contribute to the difference between their social reality and their parents' social reality (at least when parents are not lonely).

Given the aforementioned issues, it is certainly necessary to assess whether parents' reports of their warmth and involvement are associated with their children's loneliness. If the pattern of correlations is found when both parents and children report parental behavior, then the negative perception hypothesis would not be supported. If the pattern of correlations is found with children's report of parental behavior but is not found with parents' report of parental behavior, then the findings support (a) the negative perception hypothesis, (b) the hypothesis that parents' and their children's reports reflect different social realities, or (c) both hypotheses.

There are some important differences between attachment and parenting style theories and hypotheses that should be highlighted at this juncture. The thrust of the attachment theory is on the formation of the attachment bond during infancy and the resulting internal working model (internal representations) that predispose individuals to form given patterns of social relationships across the course of their development. It should be noted, here, that attachment theorists are divided on how individuals' internal working models affect their later occurring social relationships (see Bretherton & Waters, 1985; Waters, Vaughn, Posada, & Kondo-Ikemura, 1995). Nevertheless, on the basis of the attachment theory, parental loneliness should be correlated with their offspring's loneliness to the extent that lonely parents demonstrate a lack acceptance (including warmth) and involvement with their infants and thereby promote insecure attachment. As a result of insecure attachment, the children form working internal models that cause an intense longingness, the perception that they are not likeable, or the belief that they cannot find companionship. These are manifested in peer relationships and result in heightened loneliness. According to this theory, parental acceptance and involvement may be negatively correlated with children's loneliness at various ages but that would occur because of continuity in parenting style from infancy. (The corresponding paths and correlations are shown in Figure 9.1.) The attachment theory of loneliness cannot account for the instantaneous causal lag pattern of relations that M. H. Davis and Franzoi (1986) found between parental warmth and loneliness.

The parenting style hypothesis, in contrast, highlights the impact of parenting behaviors on children and adolescents at various periods in, as well as across, development. According to the parenting style hypothesis, parental behavior is associated with the formation of the attachment bond during infancy, but it is the parental behavior (i.e., the lack of acceptance and involvement) that causes loneliness in children – behavior that changes to some extent over the course of the parents' and the children's lives. Because of the links among parent acceptance–involvement during infancy, quality of attachment, and children's internal working models (representations), these may well be negatively correlated with children's loneliness. The parenting style hypothesis can account for the instantaneous causal lag pattern of relations found by Davis and Franzoi (1986). The paths and correlations for this hypothesis are shown in Figure 9.1 as well and can thus be readily contrasted with those for attachment theory.

There is a major limitation with both attachment and parenting style theories and hypotheses as accounts of loneliness in children. Both theories and hypotheses do not appear to recognize the possibility that parents' role of orchestrating and shaping the social interactions of their children likely affect the children's experience of loneliness. It should be mentioned that Cassidy and Berlin discuss that possibility in their chapter in this volume, but those speculations were derived from a transactional framework rather than from attachment theory. The following hypothesis is advanced to address that issue.

Parents' Promotion of Peer Relationships Hypothesis

The focus of this hypothesis is on the parenting practices that affect children's loneliness; *parenting practice* is used here to refer to parental behaviors that are designed to socialize children (see Darling & Steinberg, 1993). As reported earlier in this chapter, loneliness in children has been conventionally defined as the children's dissatisfaction with their relationships, primarily their peer relationships. Indeed when framed in that fashion, previous research may be taken to suggest that children's loneliness is anchored in actual peer relationships and is, to some extent, veridical (i.e., perception matches reality). Specifically, children's loneliness has been found to be linked to a low quality of peer relationships – both in terms of lack of friendships and peer rejection (Asher & Wheeler, 1985; Cassidy & Asher, 1992; Parkhurst & Asher, 1992; Renshaw & Brown, 1993).

The significance of parents' promoting peer relationships or children's loneliness becomes apparent in that context. Specifically, parents' tendency to promote positively the children's relationship with peers should decrease the likelihood with which the children experience loneliness. This may occur for two reasons. First, as research indicates, parents (notably mothers) can increase their children's success in peer relationships by arranging children's contacts with peers (Parke & Bhavnagri, 1989) and by facilitating children's cooperation and synchrony within peer-group activities (Parke et al., 1989; Russell & Finnie, 1990). Such parenting practices may increase the children's satisfaction with their peer relationships (even promote friendships) and consequently reduce loneliness. Second, as a result of parentally enhanced and appropriately guided peer interaction, children should increase their social skills (see Ladd & Golter, 1988), which would promote success in peer relationships and result in a sustained low level of loneliness.

The above-mentioned processes may account for the intergenerational transmission of loneliness. Research indicates that lonely adults tend to distrust others (Rotenberg, 1994), assume passive social roles in social interactions (Vitkus & Horowitz, 1987), display limited social skills (Jones, Hobbs, & Hockenbury, 1982; Wittenberg & Reis, 1986), and have limited social networks (Stokes, 1985). As parents, lonely adults likely display those orientations toward their children during peer interactions, thereby demonstrating a lack of positively promoting peer relationships with their children and increasing loneliness in them. For example, lonely parents would be inclined to distrust potential peer playmates for their children, not help children initiate social contacts with peers because of passivity, and not provide a network of peer playmates because of the lack of social networks (including other adults who would have children). As a result, children of lonely parents may have limited contacts with peers and be at risk, at least, for experiencing loneliness. Also, children may adopt their lonely parents' distrusting beliefs (Henwood & Solano, 1995; Rotenberg, 1995) and therefore not be inclined to develop intimate peer friendships and thus experience loneliness (see Rotenberg & Whitney, 1992). Finally, because of lonely parents' limited social skills, they would not be adept at facilitating children's cooperation and synchrony within peer-group activities, thus increasing the likelihood that children would acquire poor social skills and, as a consequence, sustained loneliness.

There is some limited support for the parents' promoting peer relationships hypothesis. Henwood and Solano (1995) examined the relations between first-grade children and their parents on loneliness and related measures of size of social network, mean closeness with individuals in the network, relationship enhancement strategies as a social skill, and attitudes toward others. As previously noted, the researchers found a significant correlation between mother's and their child's loneliness. Additionally, the researchers found that size of the children's social network was correlated with the size of their fathers' social networks. Also, for both children and mothers, loneliness was correlated with fewer relationship-enhancing strategies and negative attitudes toward others. Interestingly, parents' loneliness was not significantly correlated with their reports of how much time they spent outside of the home nor with the opportunity for social contact time outside of the home.

The findings yielded by Henwood and Solano's (1995) study are, in general, supportive of the parent promotion of peer relationships hypothesis. The findings are consistent with the hypothesized links between children's loneliness and both lonely parents' lack of social skills and limited social networks. Rather unfortunately, however, Henwood and Solano did not report the correlations between the children's loneliness and their parents' social networks, social facilitation (social skills), and attitudes. As a consequence, it is unclear whether these aspects of the parents potentially contributed to the children's loneliness.

The study that I have carried out was designed to test the adequacy of the five major theories and hypotheses as outlined (attachment, narcissistic intrusive, intergenerational transmission of loneliness, parenting style, and parental promotion of peer relationships) regarding the parental antecedents of loneliness in children. Because the various theories and hypotheses indicate that the parental antecedents of children's loneliness are constant across development, the study was designed to examine those processes for each of two age periods: middle childhood and adolescence.

The participants in the study were 97 children (54 boys and 43 girls) from second through eighth grade and their mothers ($n = 97$) and fathers ($n = 64$). The children and parents lived in predominantly low- and middle-class neighborhoods in Thunder Bay, Ontario, Canada. The children were divided into two groups on the basis of a median split (11 years, 5 months). This yielded a middle childhood sample that had a mean age of 9 years, 9 months (ranging from 7 years, 8 months to 11 years, 5 months) and an adolescent sample that had a mean age of 13 years (ranging from 11 years, 6 months to 15 years, 4 months).

Loneliness in both children–adolescents and their parents was assessed by self-report measures that have widely been used in the literature. The children–adolescents completed Asher et al.'s (1984) Loneliness and Social Dissatisfaction Scale (for the present sample, $\alpha = .81$), whereas the parents completed the revised UCLA Loneliness Scale – the short form (for the present sample, $\alpha = .84$). Parental behavior was assessed by a shortened form of Schaefer's (1965a) Children's Reports of Parental Behavior Inventory (CRPBI). Each child–adolescent completed the short form of the CRPBI twice: once to report the behavior of his or her mother and once to report the behavior of his or her father. Each parent, mother and father, completed the short form of the CRPBI to report his or her own behavior. The parents' and children's–adolescents' reports on the CRPBI yielded the following three scales: (a) Parental Warmth scale, assessing mothers' and fathers' display of warmth to their children–adolescents (e.g., "My mother–father smiles at me often" and "My mother–father almost always speaks to me in a warm and friendly voice"); (b) Parent Involvement scale, assessing the positive involvement of mothers and fathers in their children's activities (e.g., "My mother–father often speaks about the good things I do" and "My mother–father enjoys talking things over with me"); and (c) Parent's Promotion of Peer Relationships scale, assessing mothers' and fathers' tendency to positively promote their children's peer relationships (e.g., "My mother–father helps to give parties for me and my friends" and "My mother–father enjoys it when I bring my friends home"). Of course, the items in the scales were changed for parents so that they judged their own behavior toward their children–adolescents.

The parents' were sent the packet of questionnaires to their home accompanied by instructions for each parent to complete his or her questionnaire separately and individually. Parents returned the completed questionnaires by mail. The children completed the questionnaires at school. Although the children were tested in small groups, they completed the questionnaires individually.

Preliminary analyses did not yield gender differences in the correlations among the measures for both childhood and adolescence, and, therefore, the data were collapsed across gender for each age group. The correlations among the measures for adolescence are shown in Table 9.1 and those for middle childhood are shown in Table 9.2. Two-tailed tests of significance were used.

Table 9.1. Correlations Among the Measures for Adolescence

Measure/Parent	PL M	PL F	PPPR-CR M	PPPR-CR F	PI-CR M	PI-CR F	PW-CR M	PW-CR F	PPPR-PR M	PPPR-PR F	PI-PR M	PI-PR F	PW-PR M	PW-PR F
Children's Loneliness	.33*	.05	−.20	−.16	−.52**	−.65**	−.49**	−.51**	−.31*	.10	−.23	−.02	−.25	−.24
Parents' Loneliness (PL)														
M	.40*		−.01	−.05	−.20	−.20	−.20	−.19	−.30*	−.05	.20	−.15	−.26	−.00
F			−.01	−.05	−.15	.11	−.09	.02	.00	−.26	.12	−.33	−.14	−.20
Parents' Promotion of Peer Relationships – Child Rated (PPPR-CR)														
M				.75**	.63**	.54**	.62**	.44**	.13	.01	−.06	−.04	.06	−.08
F					.35*	.42**	.29	.43**	−.07	.13	.03	−.01	.02	−.05
Parental Involvement – Child Rated (PI-CR)														
M						.66**	.89**	.57**	.31*	−.06	.03	−.06	.18	.03
F							.62**	.74**	.44**	−.09	.30	−.14	.32*	−.15
Parental Warmth – Child Rated (PW-CR)														
M								.63**	.25	−.33	−.09	−.03	.18	.02
F									.10	−.34	.04	−.20	.04	−.14

(Continued)

Table 9.1. (*Continued*)

Measure/Parent	PL		PPPR-CR		PI-CR		PW-CR		PPPR-PR		PI-PR		PW-PR	
	M	F	M	F	M	F	M	F	M	F	M	F	M	F
Parents' Promotion of Peer Relationships – Parent Rated (PPPR–PR)														
M										.20	.55**	.36	.45**	.23
F											.27	.40*	.35	.27
Parental Involvement – Parent Rated (PI–PR)														
M												.32	.71*	.12
F													.33	.69*
Parental Warmth – Parent Rated (PW–PR)														
M														.12
F														

Note. M = mother (*n* = 47); F = father (*n* = 33).
* *p* < .05. ** *p* < .01.

Table 9.2. Correlations Among the Measures for Middle Childhood

Measure/Parent	PL		PPPR-CR		PI-CR		PW-CR		PPPR-PR		PI-PR		PW-PR	
	M	F	M	F	M	F	M	F	M	F	M	F	M	F
Children's Loneliness	-.18	-.26	-.10	-.02	-.17	-.03	-.21	-.11	-.15	.16	.30*	.11	.34*	.32
Parents' Loneliness (PL)														
M			.29	-.16	-.03	-.08	-.06	-.06	-.33*	-.70**	.28*	-.44*	-.35*	-.33
F			.17	-.28	-.14	-.33	-.06	-.09	.29	-.29	-.06	-.20	.28	-.20
Parents' Promotion of Peer Relationships – Child Rated (PPPR-CR)														
M				.51**	.53**	.27	.53**	.54**	.23	.03	-.10	-.04	.06	.01
F					.48**	.59**	.38*	.56**	.01	.32	.08	.22	.15	.29
Parental Involvement – Child Rated (PI-CR)														
M						.42**	.76**	.64**	-.03	-.13	.10	.01	.12	-.02
F							.47**	.82**	.00	.17	.25	.16	.21	.40*
Parental Warmth – Child Rated (PW-CR)														
M								.83**	.16	-.05	.01	-.05	.20	-.02
F									.21	.06	.20	.09	.27	.28

(Continued)

Table 9.2. (*Continued*)

Measure/Parent	PL M	PL F	PPPR-CR M	PPPR-CR F	PI-CR M	PI-CR F	PW-CR M	PW-CR F	PPPR-PR M	PPPR-PR F	PI-PR M	PI-PR F	PW-PR M	PW-PR F
Parents' Promotion of Peer Relationships – Parent Rated (PPPR-PR)														
M										.36	.03	−.11	.00	−.09
F											.11	.46**	.38*	.39*
Parental Involvement – Parent Rated (PI-PR)														
M												.38*	.66*	.56*
F													.58**	.69*
Parental Warmth – Parent Rated (PW – PR)														
M														.66*
F														

Note. M = mother (*n* = 47); F = father (*n* = 31).
* *p* < .05. ** *p* < .01.

The findings yielded by the study are consistent with the previously observed lack of correspondence between parents' reports and children's reports of parental behavior (i.e., Barnes & Olson, 1985). When considered for each of the age groups in the present study, there was a lack of a significant correlations between children's–adolescents' reports of parental behaviors and their parents' (mothers' or fathers') reports of parental behaviors; the correlations between different sets of reports ranged from $-.14$ to $.32$ ($M = .11$). The findings are consistent with the notion that the parents' perspectives and children's perspectives reflect different social realities (Barnes & Olson, 1985).

There were strong relations among the children's and adolescents' reports of the different parental behaviors (i.e., warmth, involvement, and promoting peer relationships); all of the correlations among the reports of the three behaviors for the two age groups were significant. There were similar correlations among the parents' reports of their parental behaviors, but the correlations were not as consistently strong. The correlations among the three behaviors may be taken to suggest they share some common factor, likely the acceptance versus rejection dimension of parental behavior (see Schaefer, 1965b).

The present study was designed to examine whether the parental antecedents of loneliness were the same for middle childhood and adolescence. The pattern of correlations is reported for adolescence first in this chapter. Next, the pattern of correlations for middle childhood is reported, accompanied by a comparison between the two age groups. The comparison of the correlations between the two age groups was limited to the correlations that had attained statistical significance for either group.

Adolescence

The correlations among the measures for adolescence were consistent with a number of the hypotheses. Consistent with the intergenerational transmission hypothesis, adolescents' loneliness was positively correlated with their mothers' loneliness. There was a lack of a correlation between adolescents' loneliness and their fathers' loneliness. These findings are consistent with previous observations that adolescents' loneliness is primarily related to mothers' rather than fathers' loneliness (Henwood & Solano, 1995; Lobdell & Perlman, 1986). Also, similar to Lobdell and Perlman's study, a positive correlation was found between the spouses' (mothers' and fathers') loneliness. This finding is consistent with the notion that loneliness may serve as a normative pattern among family members.

Consistent with the attachment and parenting style hypotheses, adolescents' loneliness was negatively correlated with their reports of their mothers' warmth, fathers' warmth, mothers' involvement, and fathers' involvement. Adolescents who reported that their parents were warm and involved in their lives were less likely to report being lonely. These findings replicate previous studies (M. H. Davis & Franzoi, 1986; Franzoi & M. H. Davis, 1985; Lobdell & Perlman, 1986) that have yielded correlations between adolescents' loneliness and their reports of their parents' warmth (the adolescents).

The findings yielded by this study are consistent, however, with the negative perspective hypothesis. Adolescents' loneliness was not significantly correlated with mothers' or fathers' reports of their warmth or involvement. It should be noted, though, that those correlations were in the expected direction and of a modest magnitude (most in the mid-.20s). Statistical significance could be attained with a reduction in error of the measures or even a modest increase in sample size. As a consequence, it is not reasonable to dismiss the parenting style hypothesis in favor of the negative perspective hypothesis at this stage of investigation.

Consistent with the parents promoting peer relationships hypothesis, mothers' loneliness was negatively correlated with their reports of positively promoting their adolescents' peer relationships and that was negatively correlated with their adolescents' loneliness. The statistical analyses recommended by Baron and Kenny (1986) were carried out to examine whether mothers' lack of promoting peer relationships mediated the relation between mothers' loneliness (the independent variable) and adolescents' loneliness (the dependent variable). The three recommended regression analyses yielded the following. Mothers' loneliness was negatively associated with promoting peer relationships ($\beta^* = -.30$, $p < .05$) and promoting peer relationships was negatively associated with adolescents' loneliness ($\beta^* = -.31$, $p < .05$). Mothers' loneliness was positively associated with their adolescents' loneliness ($\beta^* = .33$, $p < .05$), but that was no longer evident when promoting peer relationships was included in the regression analysis ($\beta^* = .11$). The findings are consistent with the hypothesis that mothers' hand down their loneliness to their adolescents by tending not to promote peer relationships positively.

Middle Childhood

The correlations among the measures for middle childhood were substantially different from those observed for adolescence. Most of the prevailing hypotheses were not supported by the pattern of correlations observed. Contrary to the intergenerational transmission hypothesis, neither mothers' nor fathers' loneliness was correlated with their children's loneliness. Indeed, the correlations were negative and of modest strength. The correlation between mothers' and their children's loneliness was significantly different from the correlation between mothers' loneliness and their adolescents' loneliness ($z = 2.47$, $p < .05$). Also, the findings did not support the parenting styles hypothesis; there were no appreciable correlations between children's loneliness and their reports of their mothers' or fathers' warmth and involvement. Again, these correlations were significantly different from the correlations between adolescents' loneliness and their reports of parental warmth and involvements ($z = 2.55$, $p < .01$ and $z = 2.64$, $p < .01$, respectively).

Consistent with the promoting the peer relationship hypothesis, however, mothers' loneliness was negatively correlated with the reports of their promotion of peer relationships. Nevertheless, this hypothesis was not supported because neither mothers' loneliness nor their promotion of peer relationships was appreciably correlated with their children's loneliness. Finally, a pattern of correlations emerged that was contrary to the parenting style hypothesis. Children's loneliness was positively correlated with their mothers' reports of their warmth and involvement. These correlations were significantly different from the corresponding correlations between adolescents' loneliness and mothers' reports of their warmth and involvement ($z = 2.55$, $p < .025$ and $z = 2.86$, $p < .01$, respectively).

The pattern of correlations may be considered as providing support for the narcissistic intrusion hypothesis advanced by Andersson and his colleagues (Andersson, 1990; Andersson et al., 1987). According to the hypothesis, parents' warmth and overinvolvement with their children results in their acquisition of a narcissistic personality that, in turn, predisposes the children to experience loneliness. In the current middle childhood sample, mothers' reports of their warmth and involvement with their children was positively correlated with the children's loneliness. Unlike the previous studies on this matter (Andersson, 1990; Andersson et al., 1987), these findings may be regarded as showing that that pattern is evident during childhood, as suggested by the hypothesis. One difficulty with this interpretation, however, is that the findings for adolescence are inconsistent with the narcissistic intrusion hypothesis. According to Andersson (Andersson, 1990; Andersson et al., 1987), the narcissistic intrusion hypothesis accounts for individuals' loneliness throughout the life span.

A more complete account of the observed pattern of correlations rests on the developmental changes in parenting roles, particularly the role adopted by mothers. It may be that during childhood, mothers assume some responsibility for their children's emotional state, including loneliness. In particular, lonely children likely display loneliness to their mothers at least, either verbally (e.g., saying they are lonely) or behaviorally (e.g., moping around). In response, mothers may increase their involvement and warmth with their children in an effort to decrease the apparent loneliness. In effect, mothers attempt to "compensate" for their children's loneliness during middle childhood (a *compensatory parental warmth–involvement* hypothesis). Such a strategy may relieve children's experience of loneliness but only temporarily, because it results, in large part, from the low quality of the children's peer relationships (as reflected in the measure of loneliness used in the current study). If this strategy was completely effective, for example, then there would be a lack of a correlation between parents' behavior and the children's loneliness. Furthermore, because children expect parents to be a source of comfort, the children may seek out their parents when lonely to relieve that loneliness. This pattern would complement parents' compensatory tendencies, resulting in a reciprocal interaction. Later in development, however, mothers assume less responsibility for providing compensatory contact for their children's – now adolescents' – loneliness. During that period, other factors may contribute to adolescents' loneliness, such as parents' (a) loneliness, (b) reported lack of warmth and involvement, and (c) failure to promote peer relationships.

The preceding account of the developmental changes in parenting roles is consistent with several lines of research. For example, there is some evidence to suggest that, from middle childhood through adolescence, parents' tend to exert less control over some aspects of their children's behavior (Roberts et al., 1984) and display less warmth toward their children (McNally et al., 1991). In effect, parents may be less inclined to assume responsibility for their adolescents' than children's affective state and less likely to demonstrate warmth as a compensatory strategy. Moreover, the proposed hypothesis is consistent with current notions that children affect their parents' behavior and that they engage in reciprocal patterns of interaction (see Belsky, 1981).

I would like to mention that the findings regarding middle childhood are not compatible with those obtained by Henwood and Solano (1995); they found that first-grade children's loneliness was positively correlated with their mothers' loneliness. The children in Henwood and Solano's study were, on average, younger than those in the middle-childhood sample in the current study, which may have contributed to the different findings. For example, it is possible that children may not be inclined to verbally express their loneliness at younger ages (first grade and even younger), and, hence, parents may not engage in compensatory strategies. Such divergent findings should prompt researchers to examine closely the types of interactions between parents and children that contribute to the children's loneliness.

There was one pattern that was evident across the two age periods: middle childhood and adolescence. The observed parent–child correlations were largely between mothers and their children rather than between fathers and their children. For example, mothers' parenting styles (warmth and involvement) and practices (promotion of peer relationships) were correlated with their children's or adolescents' loneliness. This was not found for fathers, with the notable exception that adolescents' loneliness was correlated with their reports of fathers' warmth. These findings are consistent with attachment theory and research, suggesting that mothers play a more dominant role than fathers as caregivers and, therefore, as attachment figures for children (see Bowlby, 1977; Cassidy & Berlin, this volume). These findings are also consistent, though, with the observations that mothers play a more dominant role than fathers in the socialization of children (see Putallaz, 1987).

Future Directions for Research

Researchers should undertake longitudinal research to investigate the causal paths predicted by the prevailing hypotheses about the parental antecedents of children's loneliness. Only with longitudinal designs, can researchers adequately test the expected paths. The research may be complicated, however, by the possibility of reciprocal causality, such as that between children's loneliness and their mothers' warmth and involvement. Also, researchers need to reexamine the negative perception interpretation of the correlations between adolescents' loneliness and their parents' warmth and involvement. For example, it may be worthwhile to use other observers of parent–child interactions to augment the data set.

Finally, the various hypotheses about the parental antecedents of children's loneliness were compared and contrasted in this chapter. Research may ultimately show, though, that children's loneliness is the result of multiple factors that are suggested by the different hypotheses. For example, quality of attachment, parenting styles of warmth and involvement, parents' promotion of peer relationships, and compensatory parental warmth–involvement may each independently contribute to children's loneliness. Moreover, the contribution of each factor may vary as a function of the children's age.

Acknowledgment

I thank Brenda Lucas for her help in the research. Thanks are also extended to the Lakehead Public School Board for its assistance.

10 Dimensions of Children's Friendship Adjustment: Implications for Understanding Loneliness

JEFFREY G. PARKER, JILL L. SAXON,
STEVEN R. ASHER, AND DONNA M. KOVACS

> Friends are hard to get for me
> If you were me, you would see
> But since you're not me, you can't see
> A friend is hard to get for me
>
> Friends are wise
> Friends are guys
> Friends are cool
> Friends are not cruel
>
> If I had a friend
> I would recommend
> friends for any other friend

Chad, the 10-year-old boy who wrote this opening verse in response to a routine class writing assignment, is lonely. Chad is not unpopular with his classmates. However, Chad's best friend moved away over the summer and, although it is December, Chad has not formed a comparable friendship with anyone else. According to his teacher, several of Chad's classmates are fond of him and have made social overtures, but thus far none of these potential relationships has taken root. As a consequence, far from the energetic and happy child of last year, this year Chad is frustrated or sad much of the day. Chad's teacher believes that Chad's loneliness has compromised his schoolwork, and she is worried enough to have recommended him to the school psychologist for counseling.

The fact that children experience loneliness when things are not going well in their friendships is evident to anyone who has ever attempted to console a child in Chad's circumstances. Yet, only recently have researchers directly addressed friendship as a factor in children's loneliness, or for that matter, children's friendships more generally (see Bigelow, Tesson, & Lewko, 1996; Bukowski et al., 1996; Gottman & Parker, 1986;

Laursen, 1993). Instead, most attention has been given to studying loneliness in relation to children's general acceptance versus rejection from
social groups. In general, loneliness has been shown to be a reliable
concomitant of low acceptance by peers. This is true whether accep-
tance is measured with a sociometric rating-scale measure (Asher,
Hopmeyer, & Gabriel, 1998; Asher et al., 1984; Asher & Wheeler, 1985;
Cassidy & Asher, 1992; Hymel et al., 1990; Parker & Asher, 1993b; Parker &
Seal, 1996; L. C. Quay, 1992; Renshaw & Brown, 1993) or with "like
most" and "like least" sociometric nominations (Asher & Wheeler, 1985;
Boivin & Hymel, 1997; Boivin et al., 1995; Boivin et al., 1994; Crick &
Ladd, 1993; Parkhurst & Asher, 1992; Sanderson & Siegal, 1995; Sletta,
Valas, Skaalvik, & Sobstad, 1996). Furthermore, this pattern has been
found not only in school contexts (the context that characterizes virtually all research conducted in this area) but in a summer camp context as
well (Parker & Seal, 1996). Also, although the majority of studies in this
area have been conducted with 8- to 11-year-old children, the relation between children's peer acceptance level and their feelings of loneliness has
been found to hold for children of ages ranging from 5 to 7 years of age
(Cassidy & Asher, 1992; L. C. Quay, 1992) to adolescence (Parkhurst &
Asher, 1992; Sanderson & Siegal, 1995; Sletta et al., 1996). In addition,
this relation has now been obtained in at least four different countries:
United States, Canada, Australia, and Norway. Finally, loneliness does
not appear to be an experience that unpopular children can easily shed
by changing their activities or social settings: Asher et al. (1998) queried
children about their loneliness in a variety of school contexts (i.e., classroom, physical education, lunchroom, and recess on the playground).
Regardless of the activity context they were asked to consider, rejected
children reported greater levels of loneliness than better accepted children. Put simply, wherever children are rejected, loneliness appears to
follow.

In short, there can be little argument that children who enjoy acceptance
among the members of a valued group experience an important sense of
belonging and enhanced social satisfaction. Yet, the associations in these
studies can be modest, leaving an intriguing level of heterogeneity in the
loneliness experience among children unexplained. We contend that in
neglecting friendship, loneliness researchers have overlooked much of
what is psychologically salient to children about their social lives with
peers and, consequently, are not addressing the particular explanation for
the distress experienced by children such as Chad.

Our purpose in writing this chapter is to examine the current state
of knowledge concerning the role of friendship in children's feelings of
loneliness and to highlight a number of key issues that must be addressed

if research on this issue is to significantly advance. As noted, our emphasis on children's friendships represents a departure from the emphasis on children's general acceptance versus rejection by peers that is so prevalent in past writing about this topic. Accordingly, before turning to our primary focus, we begin with a first section that briefly discusses the conceptual distinction between friendship and group acceptance. Space limitations prevent a comprehensive treatment of this topic, particularly its important methodological implications. Interested readers are invited to consider lengthier reviews by Bukowski and Hoza (1989); Parker and Asher (1993a); Parker, Rubin, Price, and DeRosier (1995); Asher, Parker, and Walker (1996); and K. H. Rubin, Bukowski, and Parker (1997) for further details, however.

Friendship experiences are astonishingly variable across children, even if one only considers children who are close in age. To meet the challenge of such diversity, researchers have generally taken one of two alternative approaches to the study of children's friendships. A first approach has been to focus on children's friendships in aggregate and to conceive of them as social networks. This network approach emphasizes the differences children typically display in how many friends they have and how interconnected and stable their friendship network is as a whole. The structure of an aggregate network does not reveal much about the characteristics of its component relationships, however. Consequently, an alternative but complementary approach to the study of friendship has been to study children's closest friendships one or a few at a time to uncover their salient properties as personal relationships. An overall sense of the extent of children's friendship involvement is lost through the personal relationships approach, but this approach is useful in highlighting how the interpersonal experience of close friendship varies across children, particularly with regard to the expression of intimacy, conflict, companionship, and other significant dyadic processes.

Both approaches provide insight into the relation between children's friendships and other important adjustment variables, including loneliness. Accordingly, in the second and third major sections of the chapter, we focus on individual differences at the network and personal relationship levels of analysis, respectively. Throughout, our intent is to summarize the work that has been done on loneliness to date and to suggest areas for future research.

Peer-Group Acceptance Versus Friendship

Friendship and group acceptance are closely related dimensions of children's experiences with peers, and perhaps for this reason researchers have sometimes been prone to treat them as nearly synonymous constructs. However, the two dimensions should not be confused with one another. Conceptually, they represent distinctly different levels of description of children's social circumstances and experiences (Asher & Hymel, 1981; Asher et al., 1996; Bukowski & Hoza, 1989; Furman & Robbins, 1985; Gottman, 1983; Hartup, 1996; Parker & Asher, 1993a, 1993b; Renshaw & Brown, 1993; Parker et al., 1995; K. H. Rubin et al., 1997; Vandell & Hembree, 1994).

Children who are liked by most members of a particular group of children enjoy acceptance in that group. That is, most children in the group have come to feel that there are many more things to like than dislike about these individuals, and this favorable perception is the prevalent attitude among the members of the group as a whole. It is important to note that although the members of the group may hold a very positive attitude toward a particular child, they all may not consider that child a friend. Children may enjoy each other's company in school but never spend time together outside of school or in other ways have experiences together that lead them to think of each other as friends. Indeed, sometimes children have only limited direct contact with other children they report liking. For example, children can admire another child from a distance, can be grateful to someone who is only an acquaintance, or may look up to someone for their leadership and facilitation of the group's functioning.

An important feature of group acceptance is that it describes the collective opinion of a group of children about a target child. In the assessment of group acceptance, each child's opinion of a particular target child is given equal weight, and the construct is a summary of the group opinion. Acceptance, then, should be considered a unilateral construct, because the feelings of the focal child about particular class members do not enter into the calculation of group acceptance (Asher et al., 1996; Bukowski & Hoza, 1989; Parker et al., 1995). The dimension of group liking–disliking, or group acceptance–rejection, therefore, specifies the relation of a child to a group of peers, but not the child's relationships with specific others.

Friendships, in contrast, are interpersonal relationships of a specific type between two particular peers. Friendship generally implies that the individuals involved in the relationship like one another and have some shared history together. Thus, unlike group acceptance, friendship is necessarily bilateral and particularized: The views of specific peers are not interchangeable, and one must assess or assume that both parties to the relationship feel similarly toward one another (Asher et al., 1996; Bukowski & Hoza, 1989; Parker et al., 1995).

The above-mentioned distinctions suggest the need for careful differentiation between these two constructs in the assessment of individual children's social adjustment. Indeed, recent research suggests that children's adjustment can be somewhat disparate across domains. Therefore, researchers who generalize too readily from one construct to the other can be led to erroneous conclusions about the adjustment of specific individuals. Consider, for example, the prevalence of friendship among groups of children with varying levels of overall group acceptance. Comparisons of the rates of friendship among well-accepted versus highly rejected children support commonsense perceptions that general acceptance within the peer group increases the likelihood of children's involvement in friendships as well (e.g., Asher & Parker, 1989; Parker & Asher, 1993b; Saxon, 1996). Yet, in these studies, the reported rates of involvement in mutual friendship among otherwise low-accepted children are consistently about 50%. Clearly, then, children who are poorly accepted by the majority of their peers do not necessarily lack friends. Indeed, these children have friends almost as often as they do not. Moreover, in these studies, a sizable minority of well-accepted children (6%–10%) are also found to have no mutual best friends. Thus, even being generally well liked by peers does not guarantee that children will have friends. In the next section, we take up the issue of how involvement in friendship relates to loneliness, including the specific issue of whether having friends affords rejected children any protection against the loneliness they might otherwise experience.

Friendship Experiences and Children's Feelings of Loneliness: The Friendship Network Approach

Although some children have no friends, other children may have three or four, or even a considerably larger number. Moreover, over time, some children's friendships can be seen to be highly enduring, whereas other children's friendship are more short-lived. Finally, children also differ in terms of the density of their friendship networks. That is, some children's friends are not friends with one another. However, within other children's friendship networks, nearly every member is also a friend of every other member.

Friendship Network Size and Children's Loneliness

Friendship network size differences are almost invariably present among the members of children's groups. These differences can be easily and reliably quantified by sociometric techniques (see Bukowski & Hoza,

1989; Hallinan, 1981; Parker et al., 1995). What is more, many personal and behavioral traits of children have been reported to be correlated with the size of children's friendship networks (see Parker et al., 1995). Thus, it would appear that the differences children show in the size of their social networks are not haphazard or accidental; instead, size differences would appear to reflect differences in individual children's social competence, or, in the very least, differences across children in their preferred manner of relating to others.

Are differences in the size of children's friendships network associated with differences in children's experience of loneliness? To address this issue properly, it is important to separate the distinction between having friends versus having no friends at all from the issue of whether small friendship networks consisting of only one or two friends are more likely to lead to loneliness than are larger networks of many friends.

Having Versus Not Having Friends. If friendships play any role at all in buffering children from loneliness, differences in the levels of loneliness expressed by friendless versus friended children are certainly to be expected. To date, this issue has received attention in at least five studies (Bukowski et al., 1993; Parker & Asher, 1993b; Parker & Seal, 1993; Renshaw & Brown, 1993; Saxon, 1996), with remarkably consistent results. Without exception, comparisons of children with and without close friendships indicate that friendless children report greater levels of loneliness than children who have at least one friend. The magnitude of the effects in these studies is often large, and, when the issue has been examined, a pattern of increased loneliness has been found for friendless children of both sexes. Moreover, from the age range studied thus far (roughly 8–15 years across all studies), it also does not appear that age is an important determinant of whether differences are present.

Finally, the issue of children's broader acceptance by the peer group has been given consideration in this area. As noted earlier, children with friends do tend to enjoy greater and broader acceptance in the peer group as well. Thus, loneliness differences between friended and friendless children might be dismissed as simply an outgrowth of the differences in general acceptance that also exist between these groups. This does not appear to be the case, however. Evidence on this point is clearest in studies in which, through either regression or covariance analyses, the distinct influence of group acceptance versus rejection on loneliness has been evaluated before the effects of friendlessness are considered (Parker & Asher, 1993b; Renshaw & Brown, 1993; Saxon, 1996). The results of these studies indicated that having a friend continues to decrease children's vulnerability to loneliness, even when group acceptance levels are controlled statistically. The results of the Renshaw and Brown study are particularly noteworthy in this respect, as this study included a longitudinal component. Concurrent assessments of loneliness and participation in friendship revealed that, even after controlling for group acceptance, children with friends were less lonely than were children without friends. What is more, longitudinal analyses showed that even short-term changes in participation in friendship were associated with changes in children's levels of loneliness. Specifically, comparisons conducted as short as 10 weeks apart showed that when friendless children subsequently made friends, their loneliness declined concomitantly. Conversely, children who went from being friended to friendless over this time showed concomitant increases in loneliness between these time points. Again, these changes were revealed despite the implementation of statistical controls for overall group acceptance.

A related issue concerns whether children at differing levels of overall group acceptance gain the same advantage from having a friend with respect to loneliness. At least one study has examined this issue to date. Among their large sample of third- through fifth-grade children, Parker and Asher (1993b) distinguished poorly accepted children from children of average group acceptance and from children of high group acceptance. Within each group, they then compared the levels of loneliness expressed by friendless children with those of children with friends. Results indicated that having a friend reduced children's loneliness at every level of overall acceptance and that the magnitude of the friendship effect was similar at each level of acceptance. Thus, having a friend appeared to buffer poorly accepted children from loneliness to the same degree as it did for better accepted children.

Large Versus Small Friendship Networks. Children with friends experience less loneliness than children without friends. However, is there any additional value to having many friends versus only one or two friends? The idea that children would accrue emotional benefits from participation in multiple friendships is intuitively attractive. It seems unlikely that having one friend would provide children with all of their relationship needs. For example, a child may derive companionship from one friendship and derive intimacy from another friendship. Thus, additional friends should help children meet their interpersonal needs more completely, thereby reducing their loneliness.

On the other hand, large friendship networks increase not only the opportunities for social support but also the responsibilities and work necessary to maintain one's relationships (Rook, 1988). Furthermore, large friendship networks may increase opportunities for conflict, jealousy, and rivalry among members of the network. Perhaps, then, for each individual, there is an optimal size to the friendship network, beyond which costs increase disproportionately and benefits diminish in terms of loneliness.

Almost no research exists on the role of large versus small friendship networks in children's loneliness. Thus, researchers' understanding of the significance of network size for children's loneliness is seriously limited. It is important to keep in mind that to evaluate this variable correctly, it is necessary to exclude from analyses children who lack friends completely. Unless children without friends are excluded from comparisons, the well-established link between friendlessness and loneliness may give an inappropriate impression of a strong positive relation between number of friends and loneliness.

A recent study by Parker and Seal (1996) appears to represent the sole exception to the neglect of this issue in the literature. In a study of the evolution of children's social relationships over the course of a month-long summer camp, Parker and Seal assessed the reciprocal friendships of 215 8- to 10-year-old children at several time points. At every point of assessment in the study, children with more friends were less lonely than children with fewer friends. However, when children who were chronically friendless were removed from these analyses, number of friends was not significantly related to children's feelings of loneliness. These results suggest that the ability to predict loneliness from number of friends is largely a function of the distinction between children without friends and children with one or more friends.

Parker and Seal's (1996) results, then, suggest that having a friend helps children to avoid feeling lonely, but there do not appear to be particular benefits of having a greater number of friends. As we have noted, there are reasons to assume that children would accrue emotional benefits from participation in multiple friendships. Thus, in some ways, this is a surprising finding. Perhaps there is a developmental aspect to this issue that needs attention. Although the research on the development of friendship expectations and needs (e.g., Bigelow & LaGaipa, 1980; Buhrmester, 1996; Furman & Bierman, 1983) is somewhat sparse and sometimes difficult to interpret because of methodological problems, it is likely that children's friendship expectations and needs become more complex as children develop (see Parkhurst & Hopmeyer, this volume). In particular, although all children expect companionship from their friends, older children begin to expect intimacy, loyalty, and emotional support as well. If younger children require principally companionship from their friends, a single friend may be sufficient for this purpose. As children get older and friendships are required to fulfill new and more complex needs in their lives, the likelihood that any single friendship could meet all needs is reduced. The correlation between friendship network size and loneliness may thus increase with age. Research is needed, therefore, on the possible effects of multiple-friendship participation among older individuals such as adolescents.

Friendship Stability and Children's Loneliness

Along with differences in friendship network size, children also differ in the stability of their friendships. Some children's friendships tend to be short-lived, whereas other children are clearly capable of sustaining friendships over even very long periods of time. The stability of children's friendship networks has received comparatively less empirical attention than have differences in network size. Instability in a network may be reflected in its size, at least when viewed over time. Children's network size can grow over time as new friends are added. On the other hand, children who have made many friends may find themselves friendless at some future point if they have difficulty keeping these relationships and difficulty forming new friendships. Accordingly, the trajectory of children's network size over time can augment information that is available through a one-time measurement of size alone (Parker & Seal, 1996).

Few studies to date have examined the issue of whether loneliness is associated with individual differences in the durability of children's friendships or in the rates or ease with which children form new friendships. The research reviewed previously suggests that initially friendless children who subsequently make a friend show improvements in their loneliness over time (Renshaw & Brown, 1993). Conversely, when children with friends become friendless, their loneliness appears to increase over time (Renshaw & Brown, 1993). These findings are suggestive, but they do not separate the effects of change within the network per se from the disruptive effects of friendlessness itself. When children have several friends, they may be less affected by friendships that do not last. Moreover, although probably very few children are likely to enjoy seeing a friendship end, this circumstance may be less upsetting to children who find it easy to make new friends or who have a habit of changing friends frequently.

Parker and Seal's (1996) recent summer camp study provides data on this point by tracking preadolescents' friendships on multiple occasions over a 4-week period. With this design, it was possible to observe whether children's existing friendships were likely to last and whether children were likely to make new friends as opportunities arose. Two composite variables were formed: one to characterize children's likelihood of forming friendships and the other to index the stability of their friendships. In addition, the overall size of children's friendship networks was averaged over time.

Results indicated that, after controlling for loneliness at the start of camp, age, and children's friendship network size, the two temporal variables of durability and formation helped improve the prediction of loneliness at the end of camp. The friendship formation variable, in particular, was related to changes in loneliness. Specifically, children who developed more new friendships or who renewed more old friendships reported less loneliness over time than children with low friendship formation. Parker and Seal (1996) emphasized that, because the size of children's friendship networks was controlled, it was the formation of new friendships, and not the existence of many friendships per se, that reduced children's loneliness over time.

However, the trend for friendship formation to predict changes in loneliness was qualified by a significant interaction between friendship formation and duration. The inverse relation between friendship formation and loneliness held true only for children whose friendships tended to be more durable. That is, forming new friendships at camp only reduced loneliness for children who maintained those friendships. Thus, when friendships did not typically last, new friendships did not give children an advantage when it came to loneliness.

In summary, it appears that there are important individual differences in the temporal characteristics of children's friendship networks; that is, how stable children's friendships are and how many new friendships children form in a given time period. Moreover, these individual differences have implications for children's feelings of loneliness in school and in nonschool contexts. Children who tend to have longer-term friendships and who are able to form new friendships that endure over time tend to report lower levels of loneliness than children with other friendship network characteristics. Significantly, these effects hold true regardless of children's overall network size.

Network Density and Children's Loneliness

Dense friendship networks consist of networks in which most individuals are friends with each other. In less dense networks, particular friendships tend to be isolated from other friendship pairs. To date, research in this area (e.g., Karweit & Hansell, 1982) has rarely used network density as an individual-difference variable. Nonetheless, some existing research (e.g., Benenson, 1994; Parker & Seal, 1996) demonstrates that individual children do tend to show reliable differences in the density of their friendship networks, and it is possible that this structural variable has important implications for children's feelings of loneliness. A relatively connected, or dense, social network may reduce children's loneliness by fostering a greater sense of community, a greater sense of belonging, and a stronger feeling of security than a less dense one that pulls children in different, and perhaps competing, directions. Of course, just the opposite may also be the case. It is possible that density contributes to loneliness by heightening the tensions, rivalries, and jealousy of network members.

Despite such intriguing hypotheses, network density has almost been completely ignored in the study of children's loneliness. Thus far, only Parker and Seal (1996) appear to have addressed this issue. They reported few significant correlations between friendship network density and children's loneliness. As noted, these investigators examined children's friendships in a summer camp setting. Future research should examine these hypotheses in other settings, such as classrooms, where friendship networks have a longer time period in which to develop and may be somewhat more entrenched.

In this section, we have discussed approaches that differentiate among children on the basis of the extent of their friendship participation. As we have seen, children who completely lack friends or cannot keep friends are understandably more lonely than children with stable friendships. However, among children with friends, it appears that children with fewer friendship ties are not necessarily more lonely than children with many friends. In the next section, we address the question of whether even among children with many stable friends, some may still experience loneliness. Specifically, we turn to the issue of the possible role that deficiencies in existing friendships play in the origins of loneliness.

Friendship Experiences and Children's Feelings of Loneliness: The Friendship Features Approach

Almost nonexistent a decade ago, research on the salient properties of children's best friendships has grown rapidly recently. Methodologically, studies in this area have used self-report questionnaires and, to a lesser extent, observations of friends together (see Furman, 1996, for a recent review). The developmental significance of various specific interpersonal processes has been demonstrated through correlations between these processes and important outcomes and characteristics of children (see Berndt, 1996; Parker et al., 1995). In particular, children with more supportive friendships have been found to be better accepted in the peer group, more socially competent, and more motivated and involved in school, as well as to exhibit fewer behavioral problems. Conversely, less friendship support or more unresolved conflict is associated with lower self-esteem, more negative self-perceptions, and greater school difficulties.

The relevance of friendship features to children's loneliness is suggested by research on the close relationships of lonely adults (see reviews by Rook, 1988, and Shaver & Hazen, 1985, for example). This work indicates that lonely adults' social relationships tend to be characterized by lower levels of intimacy and social support than those of nonlonely individuals. In addition, lonely adults report greater conflict and disagreement in their close relationships than do nonlonely adults.

Are there links between the particular features of children's friendships and the degree to which children experience loneliness? Several studies have assessed potential connections. The strategy most often used in these studies is to identify a child's best friend and then to give the child a questionnaire in which he or she describes their friendship on various dimensions. Parker and Asher (1993b) gathered data on the friendships and loneliness of more than 800 third- through fifth-grade children. The supportive features these investigators studied included the children's perceptions of the extent to which their closest friendship was characterized by validation and caring, help and guidance, intimate self-disclosure, and companionship and recreation. In addition, relationship difficulties, as manifest by high interpersonal conflict and betrayal or poor resolution of disagreements, were also investigated. Children with more supportive and less conflicted friendships were found to report less loneliness than children with less supportive or more conflicted relationships. This was equally true of boys and girls. What is more, regression analyses indicated that each friendship feature was predictive of loneliness, even after controlling for children's level of overall acceptance by the peer group. Thus, positive friendship experiences appeared to play a unique role in buffering children from loneliness.

In another investigation, Bukowski et al. (1993) evaluated several alternative models of the links among group acceptance, friendship quality, and children's loneliness by using a sample of 169 fifth- and sixth-grade children. In contrast to Parker and Asher's (1993b) focus on several specific relationship features, Bukowski et al. used a single global index of friendship quality, primarily reflecting children's expressed security in the relationship and their sense of closeness. Consistent with the findings of Parker and Asher, higher friendship quality was significantly negatively associated with children's loneliness among both sexes. Moreover, this association was clearly independent of children's overall acceptance in the peer group. However, in contrast to Parker and Asher, who reported that friendship quality and general acceptance in the peer group made separate and roughly equal contributions to lowering children's loneliness, Bukowski et al. found a more complex, mediated relationship. Specifically, path analyses indicated that children's general acceptance by the peer group influenced loneliness only indirectly, through at least two distinct pathways. First, greater group acceptance increased children's likelihood of having a friend at all and was also associated with higher quality friendships. Both having a friend and having higher quality friendships, in turn, directly decreased children's loneliness. Second, Bukowski et al. distinguished the emotional experience of loneliness from children's broader perceptions of "fitting in" with their peer group. Not surprisingly, group acceptance was a strong direct correlate of children's sense of belonging and feeling part of a larger group. This sense of belonging, in turn, was directly associated with lower loneliness.

A third study to address this issue was conducted by Parker, Saxon, Houlihan, and Casas (1997) with 168 fourth- through eighth-grade children. In this study, to assess the features of children's friendships, the authors used a Q-sort technique in which children sorted 67 features of friendship into seven piles according to how extremely characteristic or uncharacteristic each is of their friendship. From the resulting distribution of items, Parker et al. derived summary variables tapping eight facets of the quality of the friendships of the participating children: affirmation and personal support, reciprocal candor, loyalty and commitment, compatibility of attitudes and behavior, interdependence, exclusivity, rivalry and competition, and asymmetrical influence and status. Loneliness was unrelated to the level of exclusivity of either boys' or girls' best friendships. However, each of the remaining friendship features was linked to children's loneliness, although results depended somewhat on the sex of the children. Among both boys and girls, children with less interdependence and less loyalty and commitment in their friendships were more lonely than were children with friendships higher in these qualities. In addition, several other features were related to loneliness for girls: Girls whose friendships were higher in affirmation and support, reciprocal candor, and compatibility of attitudes and behaviors were less lonely than girls whose friendships were lower on these dimensions. Furthermore, girls who reported greater rivalry and competition between their best friends and themselves, and greater disparities between their best friends and themselves in influence and status, were also more lonely than were girls with lower levels of these features.

In a recent study, Saxon and Asher (1998) extended work in this area by broadening the range of friendship features considered. Moreover, Saxon and Asher introduced a further distinction that may be of great importance for the prediction of loneliness, namely, the distinction between the manifest behavioral features of children's friendships and children's affectively laden cognitions about these same relationships (see also Furman, 1996). As Saxon and Asher noted, what children do with their friends is important because children inevitably attach deeper meaning to specific behavioral events and are inclined to draw from them broader affectively laden cognitions about the relationship and its importance in their lives (e.g., "I feel close to this person" or "I can trust this person"). What is more, these two distinct ways of understanding children's experiences in their relationships need not coincide. For example, although children who share secrets and disclose private thoughts and opinions may come to feel close to one another, there are avenues to closeness besides intimate disclosure. Presumably, children can feel close to one another without frequently revealing their private thoughts or most personal perspectives to their partners. Yet, research on the features of children's friendships has rarely examined children's broader evaluations of their relationship separately from how children report or are observed to behave together.

To address these issues, Saxon and Asher (1998) modified the Parker et al. (1997) Q-sort and asked 256 fourth- and fifth-grade children to report on 10 behavioral features of their best friendships: affirmation and personal support, amusement, asymmetrical influence and status, betrayal, conflict resolution, exclusivity, general conflict, interdependence, reciprocal candor, and rivalry and competition. These features were intended to capture various important dimensions of the children's manifest experiences together. In addition to these 10 behavioral features, Saxon and Asher obtained children's self-reports of 9 broader, affective–evaluative dimensions of these relationships: closeness or attachment, comfort, security, trust or reliance, enjoyment, satisfaction, validation, commitment, and investment.

Regression analyses were conducted on the connections between behavioral features and loneliness. These analyses were performed while statistically controlling for children's level of acceptance. Findings indicated that children whose best friendships were characterized by greater amounts of general conflict, betrayal, and rivalry and competition were lonelier than children with lower levels of these negative behavioral features. In addition, children who characterized their best friendships as more asymmetrical in influence between partners also experienced greater loneliness than children who reported more of a symmetrical relationship.

Finally, children whose friendships were characterized by less interdependence were more lonely than children whose friendships were higher on this behavioral feature. None of the five remaining behavioral features were found to be significantly associated with loneliness. Most notably, the positive features of reciprocal candor and affirmation and personal support were not significantly related to lower loneliness.

Children's affectively laden cognitions about their friendships had a more consistent association with loneliness: Seven of the nine dimensions of children's broader evaluations of their friendships predicted children's loneliness. Specifically, children who felt closer, more satisfied, more comfortable, more secure, more trusting, more validated, and who experienced more enjoyment in their very best friendships reported less loneliness than other children. Significantly, in all seven instances, these relations between children's feelings about their friendships and their loneliness obtained, despite controlling for the manifest behavioral properties of the relationship. As Saxon and Asher (1998) noted, these results support the interpretation that, at least as far as loneliness is concerned, what appears to matter in children's relationships is how they come to feel about the relationship rather than the frequency or pervasiveness of specific interpersonal processes per se. That is, it may not be the frequency of betrayal per se that contributes to children's vulnerability to loneliness but the lack of closeness and trust that children come to feel as a result of betrayal. Indeed, Saxon and Asher reported that further path analyses of the data indicated that the behavioral features of friendships contribute little, if any, direct variance to children's loneliness. Rather, the role of these features is largely indirect, through their influence on children's underlying broader evaluations and feelings.

The results of these investigations underscore a link between loneliness and the behavioral and affective features of children's friendships. However, because these data are essentially correlational, it is difficult to make strong statements about causal direction. It is not difficult to imagine children's loneliness as an outgrowth of their difficulties in adjustment with peers, including deficits in the features of their close friendships. Indeed, this particular interpretation of the direction of effects is the one most consistent with theoretical models of the loneliness experience (Rook, 1988). Nonetheless, the literature on loneliness also includes the interpretation that lonely individuals sometimes contribute to their loneliness by undermining the smooth functioning of their relationships or by engaging in inappropriate self-disclosure (see Rotenberg & Holowatuik, 1995). Clearly, prospective studies that are capable of testing competing causal models of loneliness and friendship features would be valuable.

To date, the literature in this area has rarely used prospective designs. A recent study by Ladd et al. (1996) represents an exception. As part of a broader longitudinal study of kindergarten children's school adjustment, Ladd et al. examined how the features of children's best friendships were related to changes in loneliness over a 5-month period. Children reported on five features of their reciprocal best friendship (validation, aid, conflict, exclusivity, and disclosure of negative affect). A series of regressions was conducted predicting loneliness in the spring from each of the five friendship features, controlling for initial levels of loneliness. Thus, by controlling for children's initial loneliness, Ladd et al. were better able than past researchers to examine directly whether difficulties in friendships escalate the levels of loneliness children experience.

Ladd et al. (1996) reported results consistent with the interpretation that friendship difficulties may exacerbate children's loneliness while hinting at the complexity of disentangling these issues, at least at such young ages. Validation, aid, and exclusivity were unrelated to changes in children's loneliness over time. However, boys (but not girls) who reported greater conflict in their best friendship in the fall showed increases in loneliness over the school year. In addition, higher levels of disclosure of negative affect in the fall were associated with increases over time in the level of children's loneliness.

Because self-disclosure to friends is so often assumed to represent a positive aspect of relationship adjustment, the finding in this study that children who frequently discussed upsetting things with their friends increased their loneliness over time may seem surprising. However, the young age of the children involved in this study must be kept in mind. As Ladd et al. (1996) noted, the children in these relationships appeared to be experiencing early-school adjustment difficulties and already were displaying loneliness. These children's self-disclosure may well have represented an attempt to cope with their interpersonal and academic difficulties by discussing them with a close friend. Because of their young age, however, the friends of these children may have been ill prepared to receive these negative disclosures or to support their friend's efforts to resolve their difficulties successfully. Under the circumstances, these disclosing children may have been even more likely than other children to become discouraged by their friendships. As a consequence, their loneliness may have increased over time rather than decreased as it might have with older children. Regardless of the accuracy of this interpretation, however, an important implication of this finding is that attempts to characterize the direction of effects in this area in simple terms are likely to run into difficulty. Researchers in the future would be well advised to allow for the possibility of reciprocal influences among loneliness and the features of children's friendships.

In summary, several studies now support the interpretation that loneliness can be an outgrowth of problems within specific close friendships, as much as from a lack of close relationships per se. When children's close friendships lack supportive features or are characterized by higher levels of conflict, children feel lonely. A link between the features of friendships and loneliness certainly cannot be explained by other findings indicating that better acceptance within the larger peer group is associated with higher quality friendships as well as less loneliness. On the contrary, although acceptance may afford opportunities for more successful friendships, it is these friendship experiences themselves – or perhaps the conclusions that children draw from them about themselves and the relationship – that seem to matter. Clearly, however, researchers have much yet to discover about this relation.

In particular, there is a strong need to examine developmentally the linkages between friendship features and loneliness. Thus far, studies in this area have primarily involved children of late elementary school age. The research by Ladd et al. (1996) represents an exception, and, as has been shown, immediately raises developmental issues. The broader point, however, is that children's friendships undergo tremendous change with development. Development permits children to bring new skills to these relationships but also demands that these relationships change to accommodate new interpersonal needs and niches (Parker & Gottman, 1989). Thus, it is likely that the links between specific features of children's friendships and loneliness will differ depending on the age of the children considered. Properties of friendships that become more salient as children grow older, such as intimate exchange, may not become predictive of loneliness until children reach older ages, especially adolescence. Perhaps this is why in the studies we reviewed, intimacy features were not as strongly predictive of loneliness as were the companionship aspects of the relationship. For elementary-school-age children, companionship and fun may be more essential to satisfaction with friendships than intimacy.

A second point that might be raised is that studies in this area so far have invariably focused only on the quality of one relationship; namely, that of the child's best friendship. As Furman (1996) has recently noted, it is common practice throughout the study of children's friendships for researchers to study one friendship at a time rather than to summarize specific friendship features across a child's entire network. However, the one-friend-at-a-time approach can be limiting. Indeed, research on children's self-esteem suggests that stronger effects are found when a composite of friendships is examined than when just best friendships are (Berndt & Miller, 1992). In the future, work on single friendships should be complemented by research designed to examine children's loneliness in relation to the friendship features of several of their friends to gain a more comprehensive picture of their friendship experience.

Additional Suggestions for Future Research

In this chapter, we have reviewed research indicating that various aspects of children's involvement and experiences in friendships have implications for loneliness. Children who have at least one friend, who are able to form and maintain friendships, who have friendships high on positive features and low on negative features, and who derive positive feelings from their friendships tend to be relatively protected from loneliness as compared with other children.

A consistent aspect of research to date, however, is that all of the acceptance and friendship variables studied make significant but still modest contributions to the prediction of children's feelings of loneliness. This occurs because some children who are doing well on objective measures of peer adjustment nonetheless report elevated levels of loneliness, and other children who are not doing well on the basis of objective peer adjustment measures fail to report high levels of loneliness. Little is known about why some children who are accepted by their peers and have stable high-quality friendships nonetheless report some degree of loneliness. One possibility is that children's expectations for their relationships may not intersect well with the social context in which these relationships inevitably must be managed. For instance, children who stress exclusivity in their friendships are likely to be disappointed and jealous when, inevitably, their friends make other friends, even casual ones. In this instance, it may be difficult to point to specific properties of the relationship as a culprit in the disappointment and loneliness these children may feel. Rather, their loneliness stems from the circumstances in which they find themselves with their friend – specifically, that they cannot effectively prevent their much-valued partner from being influenced by and spending at least some time with others. Thus far, models of the social factors that contribute to loneliness include very little recognition of the fact that children's expectations for their friendships can be unrealistic for the social context in which they live. These unrealistic expectations can leave them vulnerable to loneliness.

Another potential explanation for why children who are doing well on measures of friendship adjustment still experience loneliness is that participating in friendships involves vulnerability (Rawlins, 1992). Even well-intentioned friends can sometimes disappoint – earlier commitments subsequently may need to be broken as circumstances change, promises may be forgotten, secrets can slip out, and some favors cannot be reciprocated. Such events mean more between individuals who regard one another as friends. Furthermore, circumstances sometimes conspire to keep children apart – illnesses happen, teachers rearrange classroom seating, and, sometimes, families relocate. Sadly, sometimes friends even die. In short, even competent children with healthy relationships cannot completely be protected from feelings of loneliness (see Hymel et al., this volume). Indeed, it is because children care about these relationships that they are vulnerable to feelings of loneliness. In fact, it could be argued that a child's indifference in the context of separation or loss should give greater cause for concern than loneliness under these circumstances.

Furthermore, it is likely that loneliness ebbs and flows, like other better understood mood states (see Larson, this volume). Although theoretical treatments of loneliness have recognized that loneliness can be situationally specific (Rook, 1988), researchers have been slow to consider the implications of short-term fluctuations in loneliness for assessments of individuals. There may be many days in which a child does not feel the need for a confidant. On these days, the relation between the intimate features of the child's best friendship may be poorly related to the child's loneliness. On the days in which the child does feel the need for a confidant, friendship intimacy may have a stronger effect on loneliness. Similar hypotheses could be made for other friendship features, such as instrumental help. When a child has no need for a friend's help, the amount of help and guidance in the relationship may be irrelevant to the child's loneliness. When help is needed, however, loneliness may be related to whether such assistance is forthcoming.

At the other end of the social adjustment spectrum, researchers also need to better understand why certain children who are doing poorly on objective measures of peer adjustment nonetheless report extremely low levels of loneliness. With respect to group acceptance, although studies consistently show that poorly accepted children are more lonely than other children, authors have sometimes noted considerable variability among rejected children in their expressed loneliness (see Asher et al., 1990). In particular, when rejected children who are behaviorally aggressive have been distinguished from rejected children who are timid, submissive, or withdrawn, the former have been found to report less extreme feelings of loneliness (Asher et al., 1998; Boivin et al., 1989; Parkhurst & Asher, 1992; Williams & Asher, 1987). Less attention has been paid to the possibility of variability in loneliness among children with problematic friendship adjustment (as opposed to variability among poorly accepted children). However, it is likely that such variability exists. That is, we suspect that, were researchers to address this issue with their data, they would surely discover, for example, that even among children who completely lack friends there are stable individual differences in loneliness, including some individuals who do not report loneliness at all. How should researchers interpret such seeming "resilience"?

One possibility worth exploring in the future is that children who do not feel lonely despite objective justification may be children who are dismissive of the importance of relationships or highly defensive about their difficulties and therefore unwilling to report sadness. Perhaps such children are more likely to report anger than sadness. This hypothesis could be tested by examining children's reactions to social disappointments. Children who are poorly adjusted on peer measures but do not report loneliness may respond to disappointment more with anger and blaming of the environment rather than with a sense of sadness or loneliness (see Asher et al., 1990; Weiner, 1985).

Another area that needs research attention concerns how the identity or characteristics of one's friends influence feelings of loneliness. Recently, Hartup (1996) proposed that in conceptualizing the nature of children's friendships, attention should be given not just to network characteristics or friendship features but to the identity or characteristics of children's friends. Children's friends vary on a variety of characteristics, such as sex, race, peer status, behavioral style, and social competence. The identity of children's friends is an important aspect of the friendship experience and may have an impact on the benefits of the friendships for the children involved. It may be that children who are doing well on the typical measures of friendship adjustment (the extent and stability of their network and the features of their friendships) are nonetheless vulnerable to loneliness because of some aspect of the identity of their friends.

There is no known research on the relationship between the identity or characteristics of a child's friends and a child's feelings of loneliness. We can speculate, however, about the ways in which the identity of a child's friends could affect loneliness. One possibility is that the peer acceptance level of a child's friends and the extent of a friend's network affects a child's loneliness. Having a popular friend might increase positive attention from the peer group, thus providing further protection from loneliness. Similarly, a friend's friendship network could be a source of additional friends, thus potentially decreasing feelings of loneliness. By contrast, having a friend who is disliked by the peer group may cause lower levels of peer interaction for the child, thus increasing a child's loneliness. Interestingly, having a popular friend could also have opposite effects on loneliness. Having a friend who is very popular or who has many other friends may create jealousy in the friendship, as this friend may be more likely to spend time with other children.

Another characteristic of children's friends that may affect their loneliness is the level of loneliness their friends are experiencing. A friend's loneliness may create a negative emotional tone to the children's interaction, thus inducing loneliness in the target child. Similarly, a friend's overall happiness may help to create a positive emotional tone to the interaction, thus buffering the child from loneliness. Indeed, a secondary analysis of Saxon and Asher's (1998) data revealed that the levels of loneliness that two very best friends report are significantly correlated ($r = .22$). These preliminary data suggest that further investigations into the effects of a friend's mood could be productive.

Conclusion

Over the past two decades, peer relationship researchers have come to appreciate that an important distinction exists between a child's level peer acceptance and a child's friendship relations. Indeed, the study of children's friendships has established itself as distinct from the study of children's acceptance by peers more generally, and behavioral scientists have begun to accumulate a research base from which they can glean insights into how friendships function, how they meet children's emotional needs, and how they contribute to children's feelings of social satisfaction and reduce their loneliness. Throughout this chapter, we have discussed the links between children's involvement and experiences in friendship and their feelings of loneliness. Although promising research has been done, many questions remain unanswered. We hope that the hypotheses offered in this chapter will stimulate others to join in the search for a more complete understanding of the relation among children's friendship involvement, friendship experiences, and their emotional lives.

IV | LONELINESS IN ADOLESCENCE

11 | Adolescent Loneliness, Self-Reflection, and Identity: From Individual Differences to Developmental Processes

LUC GOOSSENS AND ALFONS MARCOEN

The present chapter focuses on adolescence and illustrates some of the developments that have taken place in research on loneliness during the past few years. Historically, much of the previous research in this area takes the view that loneliness is a sad predicament that is primarily experienced by selected groups of children, such as rejected children (see Asher et al., 1990, for a review) or the learning disabled (Margalit, 1994). Poor relationships with peers are thought to be at the heart of the problem in both cases. The present chapter joins with other chapters in this volume and reflects a growing awareness that loneliness is experienced to a certain degree by everyone (e.g., Hymel, Tarulli, Hayden Thomson, & Terrell-Deutsch, this volume) and that these feelings of relational dissatisfaction are intimately related to various positive developmental changes that take place during adolescence in particular (Larson, this volume).

In line with recent developments in the domain, the present chapter also makes a sharp distinction between *loneliness* on the one hand and *aloneness* or *solitude* (i.e., the state of being alone) on the other. Several authors (Cassidy & Asher, 1992; Hymel et al., this volume; Youngblade, Berlin, & Belsky, this volume) have demonstrated that children and adolescents can and do distinguish between these two constructs. On the basis of these findings, an awareness that being alone does not necessarily imply loneliness is currently viewed as a necessary component of a true understanding of what loneliness is. In the present chapter, however, we take this line of reasoning one step further and suggest that individuals' attitude toward being alone be measured in addition to their feelings of loneliness. We further assume that some people at least adopt a positive attitude toward being on their own. More specifically, we claim that some adolescents, while initially feeling lonely when alone, come to appreciate the time they spend on their own for its own sake and begin to use solitude in purposeful and adaptive ways. This particular view does of course imply a multidimensional approach to the measurement of loneliness and attitude toward aloneness.

In this chapter, (a) our conceptualization of adolescent loneliness and adolescents' attitude toward being on their own is briefly described, and (b) two aspects of our ongoing research program on individual differences in adolescent loneliness are introduced. The contribution as a whole falls into five different parts. First, we introduce our multidimensional view on measuring adolescent loneliness and we describe the various age trends revealed for each of the different aspects of loneliness. We then go on to suggest that these trends may be accounted for by two developmental processes that characterize the second decade of life: the emerging sense of identity and the growing need for self-reflection. In the second part, therefore, we critically examine the associations between identity and feelings of loneliness in adolescence. A third part is devoted to the role of individual differences in adolescent self-consciousness as a concomitant of loneliness and solitude. In a fourth part, then, we explore whether these two lines of inquiry within our research program may converge in significant ways or whether they lend themselves to some sort of integration at a higher level. The overall picture on adolescent solitude being a positive one throughout this entire chapter, we expand in a fifth and final part of this chapter on additional findings regarding associations between loneliness and solitude on the one hand and other forms of negative emotionality (e.g., depression) on the other hand. The net result is a more balanced view on the complicated and essentially double-sided phenomenon of time spent alone in adolescence.

A Multidimensional Approach to Measuring Loneliness

In this first part we present the main features of our multidimensional measure of loneliness, followed by a brief description of the age trends observed when using the measure with adolescents.

A Multidimensional Loneliness Measure

In developing a loneliness scale, we decided to design a measure of both loneliness and a person's attitude toward being alone. With regard to loneliness, we hypothesized that the negative feelings that result from relational dissatisfaction may be relation specific. This is to say that some adolescents may be very satisfied with their relationships with their parents, but at the same time they may feel very lonely in their contacts with their friends. The converse may hold for other adolescents who feel satisfied with their friends, but who feel extremely lonely in their contacts with their parents. As a result of this consideration, we decided to distinguish between two types of loneliness as they are experienced in relationships with parents and peers, respectively. In regard to adolescents' attitude toward being alone, we basically distinguished between a positive attitude and a negative attitude.

Loneliness in adolescence, then, was seen as a multidimensional phenomenon, which comprises four different aspects, each of which was measured by means of a 12-item scale. These aspects (with sample items in parentheses) are (a) *parent-related loneliness* (L-PART; e.g., "I feel left out by my parents"), (b) *peer-related loneliness* (L-PEER; e.g., "I think I have fewer friends than others"), (c) *aversion to aloneness* (or negative attitude toward being alone; A-NEG; e.g., "When I am alone, I feel bad"), and (d) *affinity for aloneness* (or positive attitude toward being on one's own; A-POS; e.g., "I want to be alone"). An English translation of the entire scale, known as the Louvain Loneliness Scale for Children and Adolescents (LLCA; Marcoen et al., 1987; as used by Terrell-Deutsch, 1993, with Canadian preadolescents) is provided in the Appendix to Terrell-Deutsch's (this volume) chapter.

Research on both European (i.e., Belgian) adolescents (Marcoen & Goossens, 1993) and English-speaking Canadian children (Terrell-Deutsch, 1993, this volume) has revealed that the measure exhibits excellent psychometric properties (e.g., subscale alpha reliabilities of .80 and above). Most important, rather low subscale intercorrelations were observed, and the distinction between the four different aspects of loneliness and being alone was upheld in confirmatory factor analyses. In addition, rather different age trends were observed for each of the four aspects of loneliness and solitude.

Age Trends in Adolescent Loneliness

Most of our research on normative developmental trends in adolescent loneliness and aloneness has concentrated on the age range 10–17 years or Grades 5–12. Within this particular range, an increasing trend was found for loneliness as experienced in the relationships with parents (L-PART), accompanied by a clear decline in peer-related loneliness (L-PEER) from early adolescence onward. A decreasing trend was further found for adolescents' negative attitude toward being alone (A-NEG), whereas a clear increase was observed regarding their positive attitudes toward aloneness (A-POS; see Marcoen & Goossens, 1993, for additional information).

The trend toward greater affinity for aloneness among older adolescents was corroborated in research using alternative attitudinal measures, such as sentence completion tasks (J. C. Coleman, 1974; Kroger, 1985). An additional research technique, the experience sampling method (ESM; Csikszentmihalyi & Larson, 1987), which allows for the time sampling of adolescents' actual experiences of solitude (Larson, this volume), has yielded important data on the time that adolescents spend on their own and how they feel during those moments when there is no one else around.

This type of research has revealed that a rather dramatic shift occurs in early adolescence with respect to the incidence and the experience of solitude. Compared with fifth and sixth graders, seventh, eighth, and ninth graders spend more time on their own (Larson & Richards, 1991), they see solitude more as a voluntary state, and they evidence a positive aftereffect of being alone on subsequent emotional states, which is basically absent in the fifth and sixth graders (Larson, 1997). This positive aftereffect of being alone implies that older adolescents feel more happy and more cheerful when with others if they have been alone in the prior 2-hour period (Larson & Csikszentmihalyi, 1978).

In short, these findings on attitudes toward being alone (e.g., the A-POS subscale) and on adolescents' subjective reports on moments when they were actually on their own (ESM data) converge into a single conclusion. Throughout the second decade of life, adolescents actually spend more time on their own, they exhibit a more positive attitude toward being alone, and they begin to use the time they spend separated from others in a deliberate and purposeful way (Larson, 1990, 1997). At least two different functions may be attributed to adolescents' solitude. First, solitary moments may provide ample opportunities for self-reflection and for emotional self-renewal, as evidenced by the positive aftereffect on subsequent emotional states. A second possibility, not entirely different from the first one, is that adolescents use time on their own for identity work. That is, they tend to explore and experiment with alternative options regarding their future identity and reflect a lot about who they really are when they are alone, typically while listening to their favorite music (Larson, 1995).

The latter explanation in terms of identity exploration, which seems to account for the observed increase in affinity for aloneness, has also been advanced with regard to the developmental trend observed for peer-related loneliness. Several authors (Brennan, 1982; Perlman, 1988) have claimed that an important restructuring of the social world takes place during adolescence. In the course of this process, parents become less important and peers become more important. As a result of all these changes, the adolescent sense of personal identity is typically disrupted and this perturbation in turn calls for a complete reworking of one's identity, particularly in regard to the interpersonal self. As long as the adolescent has not arrived at a new equilibrium in his or her relational network and a new interpersonal self-concept, feelings of loneliness in one's relationships with both one's peers and one's parents are likely to emerge.

Following these leads from the literature, we decided to conduct two different sets of studies which concentrated on the role of identity and self-reflection, or, to be more precise, self-consciousness in the emergence of adolescent loneliness and attitude toward aloneness. Each of these different sets of studies is discussed in some detail.

Adolescent Loneliness and Identity

In this second part of this chapter, we present a first part of our research program, which comprises three studies. We first describe the theoretical framework for our study of adolescent loneliness and identity. The structural approach used in our research program assigns a central role to the basic dimensions of exploration and commitment in the process of identity formation and distinguishes between four different types of identity or identity statuses, which are actually combinations of particular levels of the two basic dimensions. After this brief theoretical introduction, our main findings regarding identity statuses (Samples 1 and 2) and the basic dimensions (exploration and commitment; Sample 3) are discussed, in that order (Goossens, 1995b, 1996b).

Before we embark on a description of our main findings, however, a preliminary remark seems to be in order. All of the studies reported in this chapter approach the issue of adolescent loneliness from a personality framework as opposed to a developmental framework. This means that the methods used allowed us to determine whether two variables, say loneliness and identity, are meaningfully related during adolescence. Researchers who are working within a developmental framework, by contrast, try to determine how adolescent loneliness develops or changes over time and how these age trends can be accounted for in terms of underlying developmental processes. (See Shaffer, 1994, for a similar personality vs. developmental framework distinction in the general domain of developmental psychology.) In practice, both frameworks or approaches may be viable and account to some extent (and perhaps jointly) for the loneliness experienced by adolescents. However, as we see in the closing paragraphs of this chapter, the methods used in our current work have to be complemented with "truly" developmental designs if we ever hope to explain why say peer-related loneliness and adolescents' affinity for aloneness develop in the way they do.

Identity: The Structural Approach

Borrowing heavily from Erikson's (1950, 1968) writings, Marcia (1966, 1980) has developed a theory about the underlying personality structures of different forms of identity in adolescence. As a first approximation of these underlying structures, Marcia has introduced two basic dimensions of the process of identity formation, and he has claimed that each and every adolescent who is dealing with the developmental task of identity formation may be situated on these two dimensions. The first of these refers to the amount of exploration of alternative identity options that the person engages in, and the second one deals with the strength of the convictions and personal viewpoints that the individual has arrived at. The latter dimensions are referred to as *commitments*. Marcia further argued that each of these aspects, exploration and commitment, can be either present or absent in any given adolescent. As a result, four types of identity may be distinguished that represent particular combinations of commitment and exploration of identity alternatives. These four identity types, which Marcia (1966) refers to as identity *statuses* or particular solutions to the developmental task of identity formation in late adolescence, are represented in Table 11.1.

Adolescents in the *identity achievement* status have developed strong commitments after a period of active exploration of alternative identity options. Individuals in the *foreclosure* status have equally strong commitments, but they have never gone through a period of active exploration of their emerging identity. In most cases, they have simply adopted their commitments from their parents or other significant adults. Adolescents in the *moratorium* status, by contrast, have not yet arrived at strong commitments, but they are going through a period in which they actively explore different identity options. Finally, individuals in the *diffusion* status have never gone through such a period of active exploration and have never come up with strong commitments. Although the actual ordering of the four statuses along a developmental line is still an issue of hot debate

Table 11.1. Four Identity Statuses as Defined by Marcia (1966)

Commitment	Exploration	
	Present	Absent
Present	Identity Achievement	Foreclosure
Absent	Moratorium	Diffusion

(Goossens, 1995a), it is generally assumed that diffusion and foreclosure are the least developmentally advanced statuses and that achievement and moratorium are the most developmentally advanced ones.

Identity statuses as described by Marcia (1966) may be determined by means of individual interviews or questionnaires, and adolescents may be assigned a global identity status (when information regarding different domains of identity formation is simply collapsed) or different identity statuses may be assigned to the same individual, one for each domain of identity formation under consideration.

The structural approach, as outlined in the previous paragraphs, allows researchers to formulate clear, testable hypotheses about the associations between identity formation on the one hand and adolescent loneliness and attitude toward aloneness on the other hand. One may expect, for example, if loneliness is associated with a weak sense of self, then individuals in the diffusion status (low commitment and low exploration) will score higher on peer-related loneliness than individuals in the two more advanced statuses: achievement (high commitment and high exploration) and moratorium (low commitment and high exploration). This association will be particularly evident in interpersonal domains of identity development (e.g., relationships with friends). Conversely, with regard to adolescents' attitude toward aloneness, one could expect that affinity for aloneness will be strongest in the moratorium and possibly the achievement status or that this particular attitude toward time spent in solitude will be associated with the underlying dimension of exploration.

Identity Statuses and Loneliness

Adolescents' identity status was determined by using a paper-and-pencil measure – the Extended Objective Measure of Ego-Identity Status (EOM-EIS; Adams, Bennion, & Hu, 1989). This instrument yields continuous scores for each of the four identity statuses (achievement, moratorium, foreclosure, and diffusion) for two broad domains of identity: ideological identity (which comprises issues of occupation, religion, politics, and general philosophy of life) and interpersonal identity (which combines information on the subdomains of friendship, dating, recreation, and gender roles). Sample items for each of the four statuses in the interpersonal domain (with each of these items referring to a different subdomain) may be found in Table 11.2. The four identity scales have been found to be internally consistent (Cronbach's alpha ranging between .60 and .80), and concurrent validity has been established through significant correlations with alternative questionnaire measures of adolescent identity (Adams et al., 1989). A whole set of objective rules allows one to classify a given

Table 11.2. Typical Items for Each of Four Identity Statuses

Status	Domain	Item
Achievement	Friendship	There are many reasons for friendship, but I choose my close friends on the basis of certain values and similarities that I've personally decided on.
Foreclosure	Gender roles	My ideas about men's and women's roles are identical to my parents'. What has worked for them will obviously work for me.
Moratorium	Dating	I'm trying out different types of dating relationships. I just haven't decided what is best for me.
Diffusion	Recreation	I sometimes join in recreational activities when asked, but I rarely try anything on my own.

group of adolescents into the four identity statuses. Comparisons of the EOM-EIS categorizations and interview ratings have yielded moderate-to-high agreement between the two instruments (Craig-Bray & Adams, 1986).

The association between adolescent loneliness and identity statuses was explored in two studies. A group of 10th and 12th graders ($N = 169$; Sample 1) and a group of first-year university students ($N = 350$; Sample 2) completed both the EOM-EIS and the LLCA. The participants were assigned to one of the four identity statuses for ideological and interpersonal identity separately, and in both cases the average scores of these four groups on the four loneliness subscales were compared by means of a set of one-way analyses of variance (ANOVAs). As expected, there were no significant between-group differences for ideological identity. However, significant associations were found for interpersonal identity. Adolescents in the foreclosure status had the lowest score on parent-related loneliness of all of the four groups, and individuals in the diffusion status scored significantly higher than did foreclosures on this particular scale. Adolescents in the diffusion status also obtained higher scores than both achievers and moratoriums on peer-related loneliness. No associations were found for attitudes toward aloneness.

These differences between the statuses, however, may be somewhat misleading. Because the four identity statuses represent specific combinations of low versus high scores on the basic dimensions of commitment and exploration, one can never arrive at a "true" estimate of the associations between these dimensions and the various aspects of adolescent loneliness. Several authors (Bosma, 1992; Matteson, 1977) have therefore suggested to use "pure" estimates of commitment and exploration, and they have cautioned that correlational results obtained with these continuous measures may well be different from the findings obtained with identity status classifications.

Exploration, Commitment, and Loneliness

As a complement to the first two studies, an attempt was made to measure the basic dimensions of exploration and commitment, which underly the four identity statuses, in continuous fashion. To this end, we decided to use an interview-based measure of adolescent identity – the Groningen Identity Development Scale (GIDS; Bosma, 1992). This measure yields information on three variables, which are referred to as (a) the content of the commitment, (b) the strength of commitment, and (c) the amount of exploration. In an individual interview on different identity domains that may last up to $2\frac{1}{2}$ hours, an adolescent is interviewed by an advanced psychology student about each of these domains in succession.

Once the participant has reached some sort of a conclusion regarding a given domain, the interviewer invites him or her to write down this commitment. (a) This written statement, which provides an expression of the adolescent's personal conviction on the issue at hand (e.g., "I just hate my parents" for the domain of parents), is referred to as the *content* of his or her commitment. The participant then completes a 32-item scale regarding this commitment, which comprises two subscales. (b) The Strength of Commitment Scale contains 18 items (e.g., "Could you change your mind regarding your view on your parents?" (reverse scored) or "Does this particular view of your parents influence your daily life?" (c) Finally, the Amount of Exploration subscale comprises 14 items (e.g., "Do you think about your parents?" or "Do you try to find out what others think about their parents?"). Participants choose from a number of alternatives (e.g., *yes, sometimes,* and *no* or *a lot, sometimes,* and *never*), and their scores are summed across the different items to yield highly reliable estimates for the strength of commitments and the amount of exploration in each of the six domains ($\alpha = .80$ or above in most cases).

A sample of high school students (Grade 12) and second-year university students (Sample 3; $N = 56$) completed both the LLCA and the GIDS. The latter measure comprises six identity domains, but the results for only three of these domains (friends, parents, and ideology) are what we chose to concentrate on. In line with earlier findings using identity status classifications, peer-related loneliness was significantly and negatively correlated with commitment regarding friendships (23% of shared common variance). Likewise, a highly significant negative correlation was found between parent-related loneliness and the commitment score in the domain of parents (56% of shared common variance). In other words, individuals who reported greater peer-related loneliness were less likely to have committed themselves within the friendship domain. Adolescents who were uncommitted in their relationships with their parents reported higher levels of parent-related loneliness.

The results further expanded on previous studies in that a significant positive association emerged between parent-related loneliness and exploration regarding parents (10% of shared common variance) and between peer-related loneliness and exploration regarding friendship (14% of shared common variance). Individuals who reported greater peer- and parent-related loneliness, respectively, were more likely to be engaged in extensive exploration of alternative identity options within these respective domains. The latter associations could be construed as evidence for a positive or healthy role for loneliness. In all probability, these associations reflect adolescents' natural tendency to think about their current relationships and to discuss their relational concerns with their age mates when they feel dissatisfied with their relationships with parents and peers. These positive associations between loneliness and identity exploration should certainly be examined in greater detail in future research.

Finally, a significant positive correlation was observed between the participants' positive attitude toward aloneness and the exploration scores for the domains of philosophy of life (or ideology; i.e., politics and religion combined) and friendship.

A clear picture then, emerges from these three studies that have used identity status assignments or continuous measures of the basic dimensions of commitment and exploration. Strong feelings of loneliness in relationships with peers are typically found among adolescents who exhibit the diffusion status (weak commitment and low levels of exploration) in the interpersonal domain and among those young people who exhibit an absence of commitments in their relationships with their friends. Low levels of loneliness in relationships with parents are encountered in those adolescents who are assigned to the foreclosure status (strong commitments but low levels of exploration) and who show strong commitments to their parents. Finally, affinity for aloneness fails to demonstrate significant associations with the identity statuses but proves to be associated with intensive exploration of identity alternatives, particularly in important domains such as ideology (i.e., politics and religion) and friendship.

In all, then, our series of three studies on identity has yielded considerable support for the idea, advanced earlier on in this chapter, that loneliness in adolescents' relationships with peers is typically found among those who have not yet found their interpersonal identity (in structural terms, those who are in the diffusion status). Also, adolescents may come to think of solitude in more positive terms, because time spent in separation from others allows for active exploration of alternative options regarding one's identity.

It may be added here that the associations between loneliness and identity are not easily explained in terms of content overlap between the various measures used. Diffuse individuals are undecided or uncertain about relational matters and are not necessarily the least satisfied with their relations with others. (Moratoriums, who score significantly lower on peer-related loneliness, may be equally dissatisfied with their relationships.) Likewise, the Strength of Commitment Scale does not measure relational satisfaction per se, but adolescents' sense that their personal convictions about their relationships (whatever their actual content may be) give meaning and direction to their lives.

Let us now turn to the next part of this chapter, which deals with the role of individual differences in self-reflection or self-consciousness in the emergence of adolescent loneliness.

Adolescent Loneliness and Self-Consciousness

This third part of the chapter presents the results of a second set of studies (Goossens, 1994) within our ongoing research program on adolescent loneliness. The basic hypothesis in this set of two studies (Samples 4 and 5) was that adolescents come to value time spent on their own because they can engage in extensive self-reflection when there is no one else around. This, however, was not the only hypothesis of interest in the research program.

Self-consciousness as a personality trait (as opposed to self-awareness, which has statelike characteristics) is generally defined as "the consistent tendency to direct attention inward or outward" (Fenigstein, Scheier, & Buss, 1975, p. 522). In psychology, a distinction is frequently made between reflection about the private self and attention directed toward the public self, that is, the way in which people appear in the eyes of other people. This distinction seemed a meaningful one for our present purposes, because private self-consciousness may be related to affinity for aloneness, whereas public self-consciousness may be associated with peer-related loneliness. Excessive concern over the way in which one is perceived by significant others is a characteristic that is frequently attributed to lonely people. Therefore, we set out to test, as a second hypothesis, whether public self-consciousness would exhibit a significant positive correlation with peer-related loneliness.

Two different steps may be distinguished in our approach in this third part of this chapter. First of all, we look for common dimensions that underly a variety of self-consciousness measures commonly used with adolescents. These dimensions or factors are assumed to reflect the distinction between private and public self-consciousness and possibly additional factors. In a second part, then, we analyze the associations between these empirically derived factors, on the one hand, and loneliness and solitude, on the other hand.

A Three-Dimensional Model of Adolescent Self-Consciousness

A group of 440 Belgian adolescents from Grades 7 to 11 (Sample 4) filled out Dutch versions of a whole set of self-consciousness scales. These instruments comprised the Self-Consciousness Scale (SCS; Fenigstein et al., 1975), the Body Consciousness Scale (BCS; Miller, Murphy, & Buss, 1981), the Introspectiveness Scale (IS; Hansell, Mechanic, & Brondolo, 1986), and the Imaginary Audience Scale (IAS; Elkind & Bowen, 1979; Goossens, 1984; Goossens, Seiffge-Krenke, & Marcoen, 1992).

The SCS (Fenigstein et al., 1975) is a widely used measure that comprises three different subscales, each of which focuses on a different aspect of self-consciousness. (a) *Private Self-Consciousness* is concerned with attending to one's inner thoughts and feelings (e.g., "I reflect about myself a lot"). (b) *Public Self-Consciousness* refers to a general awareness of the self that has an effect on others (e.g., "I'm concerned about the way I present myself"). Finally, (c) *Social Anxiety* is defined as discomfort in the presence of others (e.g., "I feel anxious when I speak in front of a group"). The latter scale does not represent an aspect of self-consciousness per se but is a reaction to the process of self-consciousness (particularly, public self-consciousness).

A personality trait closely related to self-consciousness is body consciousness. The BCS (Miller et al., 1981) addresses both the tendency to direct attention to the private and public aspects of the body. The two subscales, Private Body Consciousness (e.g., "I am sensitive to internal bodily tensions") and Public Body Consciousness (e.g., "I like to make sure that my hair looks right"), have been shown to be strongly related to the Private and Public Self-Consciousness subscales of the SCS, respectively (Miller et al., 1981).

Introspectiveness, or the tendency to devote diffuse attention to thoughts and feelings about the self, is thought to develop during adolescence. This tendency is measured by means of the Introspectiveness Scale (Hansell et al., 1986), which includes questions such as "How much do you pay attention to your own thoughts?"

The IAS, finally, measures self-consciousness, defined as "a reluctance to reveal oneself to an audience" (Elkind & Bowen, 1979, p. 38). This measure comprises two subscales, which probe adolescents' concern over the fact that transient aspects of the self (e.g., accidentally soiled clothing or a bad haircut) or abiding aspects of the self (e.g., low mental ability or undesirable personality traits), respectively, will become known to others.

A principal-component analysis with varimax rotation revealed a three-factor structure of adolescent self-consciousness. This structure has been represented in Table 11.3. One of these factors was clearly identifiable as the *Introspectiveness* factor (with substantial loadings for the Private Self-Consciousness and the Introspectiveness subscales, but not for the Private Body Consciousness subscale). The second factor was labeled *Public Self-Consciousness*. This factor is defined by high loadings for the Public Self-Consciousness, Public Body Consciousness, and Transient Self subscales. The Private Body Consciousness subscale (which had failed to load onto the Introspectiveness factor) also got a high loading on this factor. Finally,

Table 11.3. Three-Component Structure of Adolescent Self-Consciousness

Component	Scales
Introspectiveness	Private Self-Consciousness (SCS)
	Introspectiveness (IS)
Public self-consciousness	Public Self-Consciousness (SCS)
	Public Body Consciousness (BCS)
	Transient Self (IAS)
	Private Body Consciousness (BCS)
Social anxiety	Social Anxiety (SCS)
	Abiding Self (IAS)

Note. SCS = Self-Consciousness Scale; BCS = Body Consciousness Scale; IS = Introspectiveness Scale; IAS = Imaginary Audience Scale.

the third factor could easily be interpreted as a *Social Anxiety* factor (with high loadings for the Social Anxiety and Abiding Self subscales).

Why the Private Body Consciousness scale loaded onto the Public Self-Consciousness (and not on the Private Self-Consciousness) factor remains an open question. This finding may simply be a reflection of the fact that body consciousness is inherently a public issue in adolescence. An alternative explanation may be found in the actual content of some of the items in the Private Body Consciousness subscale. Adolescents may be more inclined to pay attention to the fact that their mouth is getting dry or to the beating of their heart when they are in the company of others. The important point for our present purposes is of course that a clear factor structure has been identified, which can be used when examining the associations between self-consciousness and adolescent loneliness.

Loneliness, Aloneness, and Self-Consciousness

The final set of analyses, which allows us to test our main hypotheses, was conducted on Sample 5. This sample was composed of 274 Belgian students from Grades 10–12. All of the participants in this sample completed the multidimensional loneliness measure used with Samples 1–3 (LLCA) in addition to the personality measures used with Sample 4 (SCS, BCS, IS, and IAS).

Earlier research on university students (Jones et al., 1981) and high school students (Moore & Schultz, 1983), in which the SCS (Fenigstein et al., 1975) and the UCLA Loneliness Scale (Russell et al., 1980) were used, revealed that loneliness demonstrated significant positive associations with social anxiety and public self-consciousness but was unrelated to private self-consciousness. Additional research on university students (Bruch, Kaflowitz, & Pearl, 1988; Segrin, 1993) and high school students (Inderbitzen-Pisaruk, Clark, & Solano, 1992), in which instruments such as the Interaction Anxiousness Scale (Leary, 1983) were used, has further corroborated the link between loneliness and social anxiety. These findings led us to expect that both the social anxiety and public self-consciousness components (but not introspectiveness) would exhibit significant positive associations with peer-related loneliness. With regard to affinity for aloneness, we expected to find the opposite pattern of associations: a significant correlation with introspectiveness and nonsignificant associations with both public self-consciousness and social anxiety.

Adolescents' score on the four subscales of the loneliness measure were correlated with their component scores for the three principal components. (These orthogonal component scores, which are by definition unrelated to one another, are comparable to factor scores.) Both the L-PART

Table 11.4. Summary of Significant Associations Between Loneliness
Scales and Self-Consciousness Components

Component	Shared Common Variance	Loneliness Subscale
Introspectiveness	.01	Peer-related loneliness
Public self-consciousness	.02*	
Social anxiety	.18***	
Introspectiveness	.12***	Affinity for aloneness
Public self-consciousness	.03**	
Social anxiety	.05***	

Note. Associations are in r^2s.
* $p < .05$. ** $p < .01$. *** $p < .001$.

and the A-NEG subscales generally proved unrelated to the personality components. A summary of the correlational results (r^2s) for the two other subscales, which basically confirm our initial expectations, has been provided in Table 11.4. The Social Anxiety component proved to be a significant and in fact the most important correlate of peer-related loneliness (L-PEER), followed by the Public Self-Consciousness component. The Introspectiveness component failed to emerge as a significant correlate of peer-related loneliness. This same component (Introspectiveness), however, was a significant and by far the most important correlate of affinity for aloneness (A-POS). Both the Social Anxiety and the Self-Consciousness components proved significant, yet somewhat less important correlates of adolescents' score on this particular subscale.

Combining these findings with earlier results on identity, we arrived at two important conclusions with regard to loneliness and solitude, respectively. First, loneliness in the relationships with both parents and peers is related to the restructuring of the social world in adolescence and to the ongoing search for a new interpersonal identity in particular. Social anxiety and, to a lesser extent, public self-consciousness contribute to the emergence, maintenance, and consolidation of peer-related loneliness (but not parent-related loneliness) in adolescence. Second, adolescents' positive attitude toward aloneness is related, in part, to their exploration of alternative identities. This affinity for aloneness is further associated with a stronger tendency to direct one's attention toward one's inner thoughts and feelings (i.e., greater introspectiveness). These conclusions naturally raise the question whether the findings on identity development and self-reflection can be integrated in one way or another.

Identity and Self-Consciousness: Toward an Integration?

The two different sets of findings reported in this chapter could be accommodated by a single theoretical framework if one were to show that (a) adolescents with weak forms of identity such as diffusion have high scores on public self-consciousness and social anxiety and that (b) identity exploration is correlated with private self-consciousness (or introspectiveness). Several studies, which have all used the EOM-EIS and various self-consciousness measures, have in fact provided support for these hypothesized relations.

In one of these studies, it was shown that identity-achieved individuals scored significantly lower on the Transient and Abiding Self scales of the IAS than the three other types of adolescents (Adams, Abraham, & Markstrom, 1987). Less developed forms of identity, then, are indeed characterized by higher levels of public self-consciousness and social anxiety. In addition, female university students in the developmentally more advanced statuses (i.e., achievement and moratorium) scored significantly higher on private self-consciousness than did students in the developmentally less advanced statuses (i.e., foreclosure and diffusion; Shain & Farber, 1989). Private self-consciousness was significantly related to the moratorium status in another group of university students (Hamer & Bruch, 1994) in which the continuous scores of the EOM-EIS were used (but see Piliavin & Charng, 1988). Pending further research, then, identity exploration and adolescent introspectiveness seem to be intertwined processes. A word of caution, however, is in order regarding the Affinity for Aloneness scale.

Loneliness, Affinity for Aloneness, and Negative Emotionality

The results described in this chapter paint a most positive picture of adolescents' affinity toward aloneness as an adaptive attitude in adolescents. However, one should never loose sight of the "dark side" of adolescents' affinity for aloneness, which, as one will recall, also proved associated in significant ways with higher degrees of social anxiety (5% of shared common variance, see Table 11.4).

Recent research on both early (Goossens, 1996a) and midadolescents (Marcoen & Goossens, 1995), in which instruments such as the Children's Depression Inventory (Kovacs, 1985), the Children's Depression Scale (Tischer, Lang-Takac, & Lang, 1992), the Beck Depression Inventory (Beck, Steer, & Garbin, 1988), and the Center for Epidemiological

Studies – Depression Scale (Radloff, 1977) were used, has expanded on the latter findings in significant ways. In line with earlier research (Koenig & Abrams, this volume), rather strong associations were found between peer-related loneliness and the various measures of depression. Affinity for aloneness exhibited somewhat lower, yet significant positive correlations (typical *r*s around .30) with the depression scales.

These results are strikingly similar to the results reported by Larson (this volume), who used self-reports of affective states when adolescents are actually alone. One potential way to explain this apparent contradiction between the positive functions of adolescent solitude and its association with negative emotional states is to refer to the positive aftereffects on emotional state of time spent alone in what has been labeled the *paradox of solitude* (Larson, 1997). This means that the temporary loneliness of solitude leads to better subsequent moods. An alternative explanation is of course that some adolescents only manage to use solitude for constructive purposes, whereas others fail to do so, or that the same adolescents will on some occasions put time spent alone to good use while completely failing to do so on other occasions. A final explanation is that an adolescent's score on affinity for aloneness as such is rather uninformative if one does not have concurrent information on sociability or affiliative tendencies of the adolescent. Solitude can only have a constructive role in adolescents' lives as a temporary or strategic retreat from an active social life, for purposes of self-reflection, identity exploration, or both. Extremely and exclusively negative effects are expected to arise when time spent alone is consistently preferred over time spent in the company of others. One way or the other, affinity for aloneness will remain a double-sided phenomenon as long as psychologists fail to discover the exact reasons why adolescents want to spend time on their own and, in so doing, fail to make the distinction between *healthy solitude* and *unhealthy solitude* (Larson, 1997).

Discussion: From Individual Differences to Developmental Processes?

By adopting a personality framework, the present chapter has clearly illustrated how peer- and parent-related loneliness and positive attitudes toward aloneness are significantly associated with adolescents' sense of identity and with their habitual levels of self-directed attention. A fourth aspect of loneliness and solitude in our multidimensional conceptualization of these phenomena, adolescents' aversion to being alone, proved largely unrelated to these same individual-difference variables.

Although our ongoing research program seems pivotal in current efforts to understand adolescent loneliness, because of its claim that loneliness and affinity for aloneness are part and parcel of normal development in this stage of life, it has at least three important drawbacks.

First, through our emphasis on concurrent associations between loneliness and developmental phenomena, important information gets lost on causal links between the variables under study. One should always keep in mind that our studies have only yielded correlations between loneliness and identity or between affinity for aloneness and introspectiveness. As a result, one should never infer causality from these correlations, but bear in mind that three different explanations may be advanced for these associations. Increases in adolescent introspectiveness could lead to greater affinity for aloneness, or greater affinity for being alone could lead to higher levels of introspectiveness, or both phenomena could be accounted for in terms of their associations with a third (as yet unknown) variable.

Second, stronger evidence for a developmental contribution to adolescent loneliness could be provided, for example, by showing that the associations between loneliness and the various measures used in this chapter are mediated by age. (The fact that the association between introspectiveness and affinity for aloneness is stronger among older adolescents as compared with younger adolescents [e.g., if corroborated by future research] could be construed as such a form of "stronger" developmental evidence.) Generally speaking, longitudinal efforts are needed to uncover cause–effect chains. The most convincing type of developmental findings could be obtained in longitudinal research, if one were to show, for example, that increases in the individual-difference measures (e.g., the sense of identity or introspectiveness) are tied to increases in loneliness and affinity for aloneness across the adolescent period. In effect, longitudinal studies are necessary to identify the developmental contributions, as distinct from personality contributions, to loneliness and affinity for aloneness during adolescence.

Third and finally, mild and transient forms of both loneliness and the desire to be alone are central to our concerns, but the measure used seems to pick up some of the more negative aspects of both loneliness and solitude, which border on depressive states and acute social withdrawal, respectively. The latter aspects are not easily accommodated by our current conceptual framework. In short, future research should distinguish temporary and stage-specific forms of loneliness from long-term, strongly debilitating forms of loneliness (such as the development of a lonely or solitary "life style").

Acknowledgments

The authors are greatly indebted to Ann Brits, Hans Grietens, Lieve Janssen, Helen Ducheyne, and Katrien Van Baelen for their assistance in data collection and data entry. Special thanks are due to Rob Stroobants, who conducted all of the statistical analyses.

12 The Uses of Loneliness in Adolescence

REED W. LARSON

Scholars from the Renaissance to the current era have pictured the individual in Western culture as torn between imperatives to participate in the collective and go it alone as an individual. On the one hand, the culture values membership in the group and the community; separation from the collective is understood to create the painful experience of loneliness, among other ills. On the other hand, there is an expectation in Western culture that impels each person to differentiate him- or herself; at the same time that people are given messages that they should be connected to others, they are also given messages that they should "break away from the pack" and become their own person.

At no point in the life span may the tension between these competing imperatives – to social connection and individuation – be greater than in adolescence. Expectations that a person conform to the peer group, have close and intimate friends, and become romantically involved reach a peak at this age period. Yet, independence is identified as a central developmental task: Becoming an individual is almost synonymous with coming of age. These disparate tasks would appear to pull adolescents in conflicting directions and set them up for the experience of social isolation. In this chapter, I investigate whether these seemingly opposing expectations create loneliness that puts adolescents' well-being at risk.

The orientation of my research is toward reconfiguring questions such as these in terms of the hour-to-hour "experiential ecology" of people's lives. This orientation focuses on the immediate subjective encounters that make up daily reality – what do children and adolescents experience as they get up in the morning, go to school, and come home to their families? In examining adolescent loneliness, then, I am interested in localizing where during daily life loneliness is felt: Is it most frequent in the school and peer contexts, where it is most often studied, or might it be more prevalent in other domains of their lives, such as with family members or when teens are alone in their bedrooms? In contrast to researchers who examine loneliness as a global condition or trait (e.g., as measured by the UCLA Loneliness Scale; Russell et al., 1978), the focus of my research is on loneliness as an emotion occurring at discrete moments in time.

In this chapter, I ask whether and how the cultural tension between social connection and individualism leads Western adolescents into daily experiences with loneliness. My theoretical position is that development is constituted in children's daily interactions with differing "experiential systems," or what Super and Harkness (1986) called "developmental niches." The various contexts of children's lives – family, peers, and school – are each associated with a distinct frame of cultural norms and expectations that lead to a distinct set of opportunities for interaction and probable experiences. My objective is to understand how teens' daily participation in these different niches shapes their experience. For this chapter the questions are as follows: (a) What contexts in adolescents' daily lives breed loneliness? (b) Are encounters with loneliness in these contexts associated with decrements in adolescents' well-being?

It will be shown that loneliness does not occur equally across all parts of adolescents' lives, and, interestingly, as Western children enter adolescence, they actively choose contexts of greater loneliness. This suggests that adolescents are indeed set up for loneliness. A key finding, however, is that loneliness has different significance when experienced in the contexts of peers, family, and alone. In certain settings, it appears to be less of a risk factor and may even be useful. However, before discussing these findings, the underlying expectations that generate adolescent loneliness need to be more fully considered.

The Imperative to Social Connection

Cultures often specify whom people affiliate with, how often, and what forms this affiliation takes; however, there may well be a universal underlying imperative for interpersonal connection. Early psychologists such as Murray (1938) and Sullivan (1953) theorized that humans have a fundamental need for social interaction. More recent evidence indicates that the human species, as well as most other mammalian species, have evolved a motivation system that promotes social attachment for reasons of safety and other benefits of social connection (Wentworth & Yardley, 1994). Indeed, the feeling of loneliness, created when needs for social attachment are not fulfilled, may be a manifestation of this motivational system (Schultz & Moore, 1989; Weiss, 1973).

As Western children move into adolescence, this social imperative becomes directed toward the world of peers. This is a time when relationships with friends become extremely important (Blos, 1962; Sullivan, 1953), when conformity to peers reaches a peak (Costanzo, 1970), and when youth begin to experience a strong interest and drive to be involved with romantic relationships. The high frequency of loneliness among Western adolescents (Brennan, 1982; Cutrona, 1982) suggests that the expectation for social connection is high and often unfulfilled.

The question is whether adolescents' need for affiliation is undercut by an expectation that they separate from others and become their own persons.

The Imperative to Individualism

Western individualism is characterized by its emphasis on the single person as the central unit of analysis (whether one's analysis is moral, social, economic, or psychological) and by a view of the self as, what Giddens (1991) termed, "a reflexive project." The centrality given to the individual project in Western society traces its historical roots to the independent merchants, explorers, and artisans of the Renaissance and to the strong emphasis given to individual achievement by the Protestant Revolution (Burckhardt, 1960; Shanahan, 1992; Weintraub, 1978). Early American "rugged individualism" was built around the economic self-sufficiency of the pioneer and the republican autonomy of the Jeffersonian land owner and small businessman (de Tocqueville, 1969). In contemporary Western mass society of large bureaucracies and interdependent systems, the material self-sufficiency of the frontier is no longer called for; however, commentators have recognized a new *psychological individualism* rooted in an ethos of emotional self-sufficiency and self-fulfillment (Bellah, Madsen, Sullivan, Swidler, & Tipton, 1985). In this new ethos, articulated by psychologists such as Maslow, Rogers, Erikson, Kohlberg, Loevinger, and numerous others, a psychologically healthy adult needs to achieve an internal sense of control over his or her life and to establish clear emotional boundaries between self and others (Sampson, 1988).

Socialization for psychological individualism begins at an early age in Western child-rearing practices. Western societies are unique throughout the world in requiring infants to sleep in separate beds – often separate rooms – from other family members (Morelli, Rogoff, Oppenheim, & Goldsmith, 1992). LeVine (1990) argued that frequent face-to-face interaction between American infants and their mothers (as opposed to skin-to-skin) promotes early internalization and autonomy. As Western children get older, they are exposed to children's books that focus on individuals as the unit of experience (Shannon, 1986, cited by Triandis, 1990) and they are taught a set of rights and responsibilities, such as those around material possessions, that stress individual values (Greenfield, 1994; Trueba & Delgado-Gitan, 1985). The individualism promoted in Western child training, however, is limited by children's lack of cognitive skills and by their continued dependence on parents for fundamental emotional needs. The psychoanalyst Winnicott (1958), for example, recognizes a "capacity to be alone" that begins in infancy, but in the early years this capacity takes the form of being "onto oneself" in the presence of others.

It is in adolescence that the Western expectation for individualism hits with full force. Psychoanalysts have recognized adolescence to be a time of "second individuation" (Blos, 1962) when the tasks of establishing emotional boundaries between self and parents and the task of forging an individual identity must be taken on (Erikson, 1968). Steinberg (1989) argued that this distancing from parents at puberty is partly a pan-human and pan-primate phenomenon that may have evolved as a mechanism to promote exogenous mating. Nonetheless, this emphasis on independence, emotional separation from parents, and becoming one's own person is greater among European and European American adolescents than among adolescents in cultural groups with more collective values (Cooper, Baker, Polichar, & Welsh, 1993; Erikson, 1968; Feldman & Quatman, 1988). The value placed on personal autonomy is graphically evident in the rebellious rock music, as well as rap music at present, that has been popular among Western teenagers for decades (Hebdige, 1979; Rose, 1994).

The development of analytic reasoning skills is undoubtedly a key factor that makes possible the emergence of individualism in adolescence. These cognitive skills allow teenagers to be critical of attachments they previously accepted without question and to construct psychological abstractions, such as self and psyche. These skills give adolescents the potential for awareness of the radical subjectivity (a la Descartes and Hume) that is at the intellectual core of Western individualism (Shanahan, 1992). Furthermore, these skills allow adolescents to begin to conceive of the reflexive project of constructing the images and trajectory of their own separate development. Yet, these very same skills may also make adolescents aware of their epistomological isolation, leading to increased loneliness (Chandler, 1975; Ostrov & Offer, 1980). This raises the question of whether this individualistic project might have an emotional price.

Reconciling Connection and Individualism

Individualism is credited with making possible the enormous technologi-
cal and cultural advances of Western society over the past 750 years. Like
the "splitting of the atom," individualism has been recognized to have
liberated tremendous creative energy that has been stymied by demands
of conformity and obligation in other societies (Maybury-Lewis, 1992).
At the same time, however, recent critics have argued that individualism
generates enormous costs, including alienation, social isolation, and loneliness. Bellah et al. (1985) argued that it leaves the individual "suspended
in glorious, but terrifying isolation" (p. 6). Sampson (1977) asserted that
"excessive individualism leads to alienation and estrangement; it isolates
person from person; it separates us from the very nutrient soil out of
which we were cast" (p. 780).

Empirical data appear to verify the link between individualism and
loneliness. Triandis (1990) finds that loneliness is more frequent in individualistic than collectivist cultures. Several studies suggest that, even
within a given culture, people with more individualistic tendencies experience greater loneliness (Jones, 1982; Wilson, Sibanda, Sibanda, & Wilson,
1989). These findings suggest that Western individualism promotes loneliness. The imperative to individualism would appear to be in conflict
with the need for social connection. Also, this tension might be expected
to be greatest in adolescence.

If adolescents lives are looked at closely, however, there is reason to suspect that these two imperatives are acted on in separate spheres of daily
experience. The imperative to social connection in Western adolescence
is largely oriented to the domain of peers. Adolescents do not evidence an
increased desire to be more closely connected to their families; if anything,
the reverse is the case (Steinberg & Silverberg, 1986). Also, this imperative
to be attached with peers is not undercut by individuation: Differentiating oneself from one's friends does not appear to be a major project, at
least of early and midadolescence (Steinberg & Silverberg, 1986). Adolescents often show limited concern with defining psychological boundaries
between themselves and their friends and often throw themselves into
relationships of wholesale merger (Douvan & Adelson, 1966; A. Freud,
1946). Peers, then, are a domain in which adolescents pursue the imperative of social connection.

The imperative to psychological individuation is largely oriented, not
to relationships with friends, but to home life and relationships with family. Triandis (1990) found that the key element differentiating individualistic cultures (especially the United States) from collective cultures is the

greater independence from family that comes with adulthood. In fact, he found evidence that people in individualistic cultures may be more involved with friends than are people in collective cultures. The process of individuation from family is evident in studies of American adolescents. Steinberg and Silverberg (1986) showed major declines between fifth and ninth grades in the degree of emotional dependency that youth report toward their parents. Smetana (1988) demonstrated that with age adolescents increasingly invoke rights to personal jurisdiction over matters at home – they assert, for example, that what goes on in their own room is their own business and is outside their parents' purview. Home is the domain where the agenda of individuation is pursued.

Thus, the imperatives to social connection and individualism may not be as directly at loggerheads as they originally seemed. In fact, if researchers look at the how youths allocate their time as they enter adolescence, it can be seen that they appear to be putting a priority on both agendas.

Social Connection and Individualism Within Daily Life

If you will recall, my orientation is to examine development in terms of children's and adolescents' daily participation in different contexts or experiential niches. If the age trends in how youth devote their time is looked at, it can be seen that, with entry into adolescence, the amount of time spent in contexts related to social connection and individualism both increase.

The findings I discuss come from time sampling studies in which people report on their immediate experiences. In this research, American youths of differing ages provided reports on their hour-to-hour activities and emotions when signaled by pagers at random times, following the procedures of the experience sampling method (ESM). I draw primarily on a study in which a random cross-sectional sample of 483 youths between 10- and 15-years-old provided over 18,000 such reports (Larson & Richards, 1989). This young adolescent sample included equal numbers of boys and girls across the 5th–9th grades. I also report on longitudinal data for a subset of 220 of these youths who provided ESM data at a second period in time, 4 years after the original study (Larson et al., 1996). For this longitudinal sample, there is ESM data for each individual at two periods in time spanning the 5th–12th grades (ages 10–19), with a total of over 16,000 self-reports. It should be cautioned that these samples were White, middle- and working-class youths in the United States, thus generalizations need to be limited to this population.

These data indicate that, far from separating themselves from peers, adolescents spend more of their waking hours with friends than do preadolescents. Because the ESM signals occur at random, they provide estimates of how participants spend their time. For the longitudinal sample, we (Richards, Crowe, Larson, & Swarr, 1998) found that amount of time with friends (excluding class time) rose from 18% of waking hours in 5th–6th grades to 25% in 11th–12th grades. This rise, which is most evident in the high school years, is related to more time spent away from home and to increased time with mixed-sex groups of friends.

This increased time with friends indicates that American adolescents are pursuing an agenda of social connection: They are responding to cultural expectations that they be deeply engaged with their peers. The students' reports of positive motivation during this peer time leave little doubt that this is a use of time that they have chosen (Larson, 1983; Larson & Richards, 1991). The priority given to the social agenda for American adolescents is indicated by the fact that they spend much more time with friends than do adolescents in collectivist cultures, such as Korea, Taiwan, and Japan (Fuligni & Stevenson, 1995; M. Lee, 1994).

Along with this increase in peer time, we found that adolescents spend increasing amounts of time physically alone, which appears to be a context of individuation. For the young adolescent sample, the amount of time both boys and girls reported being alone rose dramatically – by 50% – between the fifth and seventh grades. This rise is attributable to expanded solitary time at home and comes at the expense of time spent with family, which falls substantially across this age span (Larson & Richards, 1991). Parke and Sawin (1979) observed substantial changes at this age period in the emphasis given to privacy: Teens begin closing the bedroom and bathroom doors and become sensitive about others respecting their privacy. M. Wolfe (1978) also found that teens, more than children, begin to value being alone to have greater autonomy and to limit the information others have about them. This time alone at home, then, may serve partly to sharpen the emotional boundaries between adolescents and their parents.

Adolescents appear to also value this time alone for its own sake. Across this age period, youths reported increased desire to be alone and gave more intrinsic reasons for being alone – they wanted to be alone to concentrate on an activity, to think, or to pull themselves together (Larson, in press). Other researchers have also found that adolescents describe aloneness as less aversive and more desirable than do preadolescents (C. C. Coleman, 1974; Kroger, 1985; Marcoen & Goossens, 1993; M. Wolfe & Laufer, 1974). This rise in time alone, of course, may be unique to working- and middle-class adolescents in Western culture. Teens in less affluent families, in the United States and elsewhere, are likely to have more crowded households and are less likely to have private bedrooms (e.g., S. S. Davis & Davis, 1989; M. Wolfe, 1978). Evidence shows that the amount of time teens spend alone is less in non-Western, more collectively oriented societies (Malik, 1981; Saraswathi & Dutta, 1988), with the exception of economically developed Asian societies where solitary studying fills a large segment of discretionary time (Fuligni & Stevenson, 1995; M. Lee, 1994).

As a whole, these findings suggest that American adolescents can "have their cake and eat it too": They devote more time to peers – a context of social connection – and to solitude – a context of individuation. However, what happens in these contexts and what teenagers feel should be examined. Research suggests that American teenagers are more lonely than teens in other cultures (Ostrov & Offer, 1980; Medora, Woodward, & Larson, 1987). Might the cultural expectations that promote peer interaction and send teens into their room increase their loneliness? To answer this question, researchers need to ask where loneliness is experienced and whether this changes with age.

Daily Patterns of Loneliness

From reading the literature on childhood loneliness, one might think school and peer interactions are the setting of highest risk for experiencing loneliness. Most research on childhood loneliness focuses on the school context and asks youths to report on feelings of social isolation from their peers. Yet this increased time that adolescents spend alone – often alone in their bedrooms – might also be a major context where social isolation is frequently felt. When during daily life do teens experience loneliness?

Our time sampling research allows us to answer this question for the young adolescent sample. On every other ESM self-report form, participants were asked whether they felt lonely on a 4-point scale, with responses ranging from *not at all* to *a little bit* to *kind of* to *very much*. These responses provide in situ data on an adolescent's immediate experiences of loneliness at multiple points in time during daily life. It should be noted that this approach differs from the more global assessments of loneliness obtained by most researchers, which are typically obtained at only one point in time and depend on children's ability to remember and reconstruct accurately what they typically feel.

I was interested, first, in whether these young teens felt more lonely when alone or with people, and, second, whether loneliness differed

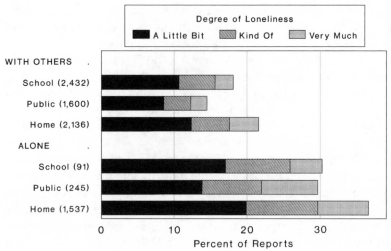

Figure 12.1. Rates of loneliness by context. In this figure, the number of self-reports for each context is indicated in parentheses.

across the locations of school, other public locations (friends' houses, parks, stores), or home. Together these two dimensions, companionship and location, define six cells for a 2 × 3 analysis of variance (ANOVA). It should be noted that the people adolescents were with in the three locations differed. At school and in other public locations, they reported primarily being with peers. At home, the people they were with were nearly always family members. In a two-way ANOVA, I evaluated whether loneliness differed across these contexts. For this ANOVA, I standardized the loneliness responses, z scoring them within person, so that values represented an adolescent's loneliness at a given moment relative to his or her overall mean and standard deviation for this item.

The results showed that feelings of loneliness did indeed differ across contexts and that they were more frequent when adolescents were alone and at home. In the ANOVA, loneliness differed significantly by social companionship, $F(1, 8169) = 128.44$, $p < .001$, and location, $F(2, 8169) = 8.77$, $p < .001$, with no significant interaction. To examine the differences between contexts, I present in Figure 12.1 the rates at which teens reported each level of loneliness on the raw item (before z scoring). One can see, first, that the adolescents reported much greater loneliness when alone than with others, irrespective of location. Second, they reported somewhat greater loneliness at home and less loneliness at school and in public locations. Combining these two trends, it can be seen that being with others – typically peers – at school or other public locations is the least lonely part of these youth's lives. If the frequency of feeling lonely very much is considered, the rates are almost three times lower when they are with others at school and in public, 3%, as compared with when they are alone at home, 7%.

In summary, being alone, especially being alone at home, is the loneliest part of young adolescents' lives. This has also been found to be true in ESM studies of older adolescents and adults (Larson, Csikszentmihalyi, & Graef, 1982).

This finding suggests that the increased time that Western adolescents spend alone should increase their overall loneliness. One would think that spending more time in a lonely context would boost teenagers' feelings of loneliness. Remarkably, however, this is not the case. The data show no change in overall rates of reported loneliness across the entry into adolescence. To determine this, I calculated the percentage of time that each of the 483 students reported feeling loneliness (of any degree), then I transformed these percentages with a square root function to achieve a normal distribution for these scores. Finally, I evaluated whether these transformed percentages were related to grade. They were not, $r(477) = .05$, *ns*. Despite spending much more time alone, eighth and ninth graders reported no greater frequency of loneliness than fifth and sixth graders. Overall rates of loneliness remained stable at 23% of the ESM reports across the fifth to ninth grades. Rates of feeling lonely *very much* also were not related to grade, $r(479) = -.01$, *ns*, and were stable at about 4% of all reports across grades. This stability in overall rates of loneliness, despite more time alone, is explained by nonsignificant trends for all contexts to be less lonely with age. This lack of an age trend in loneliness is particularly striking given that rates of reporting other negative emotions, such as unhappiness, anger, and boredom, increased across this age period (Greene & Larson, 1991; Larson & Lampman-Petraitis, 1989).

Adding to the surprise, the data show that individual teens who spent more of their time alone did not experience more frequent loneliness. Among the preadolescents – the fifth and sixth graders – spending more time alone was correlated with more frequent loneliness, $r(207) = .14$, $p = .04$. However, among the seventh to ninth graders, this correlation was not significant, $r(270) = .01$, *ns*. Adolescents who spent more time in this lonely context were not more lonely.

The quantum of adolescents' loneliness, then, seems to be unrelated to their time in this more lonely context. It appears to be constant across variations in amount of time spent alone. This unanticipated finding suggests that the cultural expectations that encourage teens to withdraw into their bedrooms do not put teens at risk for greater loneliness – at least as a "feeling state" in the way that we measured it in this research.

There is one exception to this pattern, however, that is worthy of note: Friday and Saturday nights. In a prior ESM study with 75 high school students, Larson et al. (1982) found that when adolescents were alone on Friday or Saturday night they reported extremely high rates of loneliness. Likewise, for our longitudinal sample, I found this accentuated loneliness on weekend evenings, but only for youth in eighth grade and above. When alone after 6:00 PM on Friday and Saturday night, the 5th–8th graders reported a mean loneliness score of $z = -.06$, whereas the 9th–12th graders reported a score of $z = .40$, $t(237) = 2.70$, $p = .007$. Signaled on one of these occasions an older girl wrote, "I feel lonely because I used to go out every weekend until my best friend moved to Georgia. I want to go out, I don't want to stay home." The intense loneliness that older adolescents report when alone on weekend evenings reflects the expectations in teenage subculture that Friday and Saturday nights are the social and emotional climax of the week (Larson & Richards, 1996). Youths who are alone during this time period feel the pain of not meeting a strong cultural expectation that they be with their peers at this segment of the week.

Aside from weekend evenings, however, solitude does not appear to increase directly adolescents' risk of loneliness. Perhaps because of the support for individuation present in Western culture, being alone is tolerated and may even provide benefits for adolescents. Suedfeld (1989) argued that being alone produces a different, less innocuous kind of loneliness, which in some cases may be constructive. Indeed, my research has suggested that this is the case for American adolescents.

The Benefits of Aloneness

The constructive side of adolescent solitude can be seen both in the subjective states that surround being alone and in individual differences between teens who spend varying amounts of time alone. I have just shown that the subjective experience of solitude includes a high probability of feeling lonely; it also includes lower rates of happiness and a more passive, drowsy, and vegetative mood. Yet, although the emotional states of being alone are typically less positive, the cognitive states that teens report are more favorable. In two earlier ESM studies, Larson and Csikszentmihalyi (1978, 1980) found that when alone, adolescents rate themselves as much less "self-conscious" – a significant benefit during an age period when self-consciousness is quite high. Teens also indicate higher levels of concentration when alone than at other times (Larson & Csikszentmihalyi,

1978, 1980). In fact, in interviews, the adolescents in those studies reported that being able to concentrate – to work on a project or just to think – is one of the reasons why they like to be by themselves (Freeman, Csikszentmihalyi, & Larson, 1986; Tenbrink, 1990).

The immediate benefits of this reduced self-conscious and more attentive state are suggested by findings on what teenagers feel after a period of being alone. In two separate studies (Larson & Csikszentmihalyi, 1980; Larson, in press), I have found that the emotional states that teens report after solitude are more positive than at other comparable times. To conduct these analyses, I evaluated the emotional states reported for the first ESM self-report after a report when they had been alone. Their emotional state for these reports were compared with occasions when they had not just been alone. The finding in both studies was that it was significantly more positive than during the other occasions. This suggests that they obtain a positive emotional bounce from an interval of solitude.

My recent analysis of data from our young adolescent study indicates that this positive aftereffect is not present prior to the seventh grade. It is only in adolescence that this benefit appears (Larson, in press). In interviews with a subsample of youth in the young adolescent study, we also found a significant grade trend, with seventh–ninth graders more likely to report a positive aftereffect from being alone than fifth–sixth graders. In response to the question "Do you feel any different after you have been alone for a long period of time?" only 5% of the fifth–sixth graders reported a positive aftereffect, whereas 22% of the seventh–ninth graders did, $\chi^2(1, N = 119) = 5.60$, $p = .018$. One student mentioned that he felt calm; another said, "I feel older. I feel like I'm on my own." These findings suggests a developmental change: That adolescents learn to use time alone to restore their mood, that they are beginning to use solitude for emotional self-sufficiency, which is an important trait in an individualistic society.

The long-term, cumulative benefits of using solitude are suggested by my repeated finding that American teenagers who spend some amount of time alone are better adjusted than those who are never or rarely alone. This is a finding that I have verified in three studies (Larson & Csikszentmihalyi, 1978, 1980; Larson, in press): Adolescents who spend an intermediate amount of time alone – 20%–35% of waking hours – show more favorable adjustment than those who are rarely alone or are alone more often. These youths reported more positive average emotional states on the ESM and lower alienation and depression on a questionnaire measure. They were also rated as having fewer problem behaviors by their parents and had higher grade point averages (GPAs) in school (Larson & Csikszentmihalyi, 1978, 1980; Larson, in press). Perhaps because of the restorative effect on mood, among other things, being alone is associated with improved adjustment.

I argue elsewhere that this solitary time provides the context for adolescents' reflexive project of developing a personal identity (Larson, 1990, 1995). A voluntary retreat into solitude, sometimes accompanied by music, provides the opportunity for exploring the new and tentative private selves that are discovered in adolescence. It provides the chance for exploring multiple identities, including those desired and feared, and for cultivating skills of emotional regulation, which contemporary psychoanalysts see as central to the self (Larson, 1990, 1995). Steele and Brown (1995) showed how this identity work is often represented in "bedroom culture," in the posters and other items that adolescents put up on their walls.

Support for the idea that Western adolescents use solitude for psychological individuation is provided by two studies. Marcoen and Goossens (1993) found that a positive disposition toward aloneness to be related to Belgian adolescents' identity achievement (also see Goossens & Marcoen, this volume). McCormack (1984) found that spending time alone was correlated with adolescents having life goals justified by intrinsic as opposed to extrinsic rationales.

Surviving the Loneliness of Being Alone

Yet, while showing signs of positive benefits, the fact remains that solitude is frequently lonely. Is this solitary loneliness innocuous? Might it be less correlated with adjustment than loneliness in other contexts? Or is it still a risk factor? This can be investigated by looking at differences between adolescents who experience more versus less loneliness in solitude, and in other contexts.

My analyses asked whether the extent of a person's loneliness in each context was correlated with measures of psychological adjustment. The adjustment measures included internalizing variables, such as depression and self-esteem, and externalizing variables, such as school GPA and teacher and parent ratings of behavioral adjustment. Because the benefits of aloneness appear to be manifest only among youth in seventh grade and above, these analyses were focused on the 270 seventh–ninth graders from the young adolescent study.

The independent variables for these analyses were loneliness in four contexts, corresponding to four of the six cells in the previous figure: being with others at school, being with others in public, being with others at home, and being alone at home. Unfortunately, the number of ESM reports in the other two cells – alone at school and alone in public – was insufficient to allow for meaningful estimates for each individual. The actual variables for these analyses were the mean levels of loneliness (for the raw 4-point item) for all of an adolescents' self-reports in each of the four contexts. Correlations among these four loneliness means ranged from .41 to .51, indicating that there is substantial overlap between the adolescents who report loneliness in one context and loneliness in another. Given this overlap, the results of the subsequent analysis were particularly interesting.

Feeling lonely in the peer context was clearly correlated with poorer adjustment (Table 12.1). Adolescents who reported feeling more lonely with others in school and in public settings were more depressed, reported lower self-esteem, were rated as less adjusted by parents and teachers, and had lower GPAs. So even though base-rate loneliness is comparatively rarer in these peer contexts (as was seen in Figure 12.1), when loneliness occurs, it is associated with maladjustment.

It should be pointed out that these finding are consistent with research using global measures of loneliness (see Asher et al., 1990; Crick et al., this

Table 12.1. Correlates of Feeling Lonely in Different Contexts for Seventh to Ninth Graders

| Mean Loneliness in This Context | Measures of Adjustment | | | | |
	Depression	Self-Esteem	Parent Rating of Problem Behavior	Teacher Rating of Adjustment	School GPA
With others					
School	.37***	−.23***	.14*	−.20**	−.14*
Public	.31***	−.15*	.29*	−.13	−.12*
Home	.31***	−.26***	.11	−.16*	−.12
Alone					
Home	.13	−.10	.10	−.14*	−.09

Note. Table displays correlation coefficients. The sample for these analyses is 270 youths, though sample size is smaller for some analyses because of incomplete data. These measures were the Child Depression Inventory (Kovacs, 1986); the Rosenberg (1965) index of self-esteem; the Child Behavior Checklists (Achenbach & Edelbrock, 1986); an adaption of Stevenson, Parker, Wilkinson, Hegion, and Fish's (1976) measure of school adjustment; and GPA for academic classes for the four quarters leading up to the present one. GPA = grade point average.

* $p < .05$. ** $p < .01$. *** $p < .001$.

volume; Parker et al., this volume; Koenig & Abrams, this volume). They show that peer-related loneliness is associated with adjustment. This is important because it suggests convergence between loneliness as measured by one-time global assessment and by the ESM. The findings are also important in reaffirming that past research has been correct in focusing on loneliness in relationships with peers – because it is associated with psychological risk.

The analyses indicate that loneliness with others at home (i.e., with family members) is also associated with risk, and this risk is somewhat separate from the risk of peer-related loneliness. Rates of feeling lonely with others at home were found to be significantly correlated with depression, lower self-esteem, and teacher ratings of poorer adjustment (Table 12.1). In additional analyses, I evaluated these correlations, partialling out the rate of loneliness that each adolescent felt in the school and public contexts. With these values for peer-loneliness controlled, there remained a significant correlation between loneliness with others at home and depression, $r(203) = .21$, $p = .01$, and self-esteem, $r(225) = -.19$, $p = .02$. In other words, the effects of feeling lonely with family members appeared to be separate from the effects of loneliness in the two other contexts. These findings suggest that family-related loneliness may be as worthy of investigation as peer-related loneliness, a point Marcoen and Goossens (1993) have argued (also see Goossens and Marcoen, this volume).

These correlations, of course, do not prove causality. They do not establish that loneliness in these peer or family contexts cause maladjustment – certainly maladjustment may generate loneliness. Nonetheless, the findings indicate that feelings of loneliness in these peer and family contexts are clear and strong markers of risk for maladjustment.

What is striking, then, is that the correlations for feeling lonely when alone at home were much less strong. In fact, they were significant for only one measure (Table 12.1). Although loneliness in the school setting strongly predicts depression ($r = .37$), loneliness when alone at home is a weak and nonsignificant predictor of depression ($r = .13$). Similar differences are suggested for prediction of self-esteem.[1] The only criterion of adjustment correlated with solitary loneliness was teachers' rating of adjustment, and this correlation was weak. In summary, although loneliness

---

[1] R to z tests were computed to compare the correlations for time alone at home with those for time with others in the three different locations. For depression, the comparisons to being with others in all three locations were significant at the .05 level. The correlations for parent ratings of problem behavior were also significantly different between alone at home and with others in public. All other comparisons were not significant.

with others is clearly a predictor of adolescent adjustment, loneliness when alone at home is not a substantial indicator of risk.

I would not go so far as to conclude that loneliness when alone at home is innocuous. As I mentioned previously, I have repeatedly found that adolescents who spend large amounts of time alone are generally less well adjusted, and perhaps loneliness contributes to their maladjustment. Nolen-Hoeksema and Girgus (1994) showed that among adolescents, especially adolescent girls, a ruminative coping style is associated with greater depression. It is possible that some solitary teens dwell in a maladaptive lonely passive state that is self-perpetuating (van Buskirk & Duke, 1991). This pattern, however, does not leap out of these data.

Our findings indicate that, when alone at home, degree of loneliness per se is not a strong predictor of adjustment. These findings also suggest that the benefits associated with spending an intermediate amount of time alone occur independently of how lonely an adolescent typically feels when alone. I computed partial correlations between a term for intermediate amount of time spent alone and the adjustment variables, controlling for the mean loneliness a teen experienced when alone. These analyses showed that, irrespective of loneliness, spending an intermediate amount of time in solitude was correlated with lower ratings of problem behavior by parents, $r(227) = .21$, $p = .001$, more favorable teachers ratings of adjustment, $r(205) = .17$, $p = .01$, and higher GPA, $r(235) = .13$, $p = .04$. Although it may be painful, feeling loneliness when alone does not appear to be at odds with an adolescent experiencing the benefits of solitude.

Conclusion

This chapter began with the question of how the imperatives in Western society to social connection and individualism might create loneliness within the daily contexts of adolescents' lives. Because I have not directly compared cultures, of course, it cannot conclusively be said how patterns of loneliness for these U.S. adolescents might differ from those for teens in other cultural settings. Also, because I have not measured these imperatives, it should be recognized that they are, at this point, theoretical variables. Within these limitations, however, the findings provide useful information about the daily ecology of adolescent loneliness.

What the findings suggest is that the classic tension between social connection and individual autonomy may not be as great as has often been portrayed, at least for adolescents, because these two imperatives are addressed in different contexts of their daily lives. The Western imperative to individualism may generate more frequent feelings of loneliness, but all loneliness is not created equal.

The peer and school setting, I argue, is the context in which the agenda of social connection is addressed. As youths move through adolescence, they spend more time in this context, particularly with mixed-sex peers. In these peer settings, feelings of loneliness are comparatively rare; however, the implications of this loneliness are great. The teens who feels more lonely during this time is more likely to show depression, lower self-esteem, lower GPA, and have more problem behaviors as rated by parents and teachers. The reason loneliness in these contexts is more salient may be because the underlying stakes are high. Parkhurst and Hopmeyer, this volume, suggested that these strong correlations for peer contexts may be attributable to a mixture of shame and humiliation with the loneliness. Teens do not just feel alienated from peers; they feel like they have failed a critical task of being socially connected. Loneliness in this context, then, is a significant risk factor for Western adolescents, possibly because it is an indicator that the cultural imperative to social attachment has not been fulfilled.

The loneliness experienced with family members at home is largely a separate issue. The family is a context in which the adolescent task of individuation is addressed. The findings show, first, that loneliness occurs at a higher rate in this family context than in peer contexts. Second, individual differences in this context loneliness are a comparable risk factor to loneliness in peer settings: Individuals who report high rates of loneliness in this context are also more likely to be depressed, have lower self-esteem, and be rated by teachers as being less well adjusted. A possible explanation for these findings lies in current thought that adolescents' relationships with family change with age. There is a consensus among adolescents scholars that the optimal path in family relationships involves, not a radical break of family connectedness, but rather a gradual renegotiation of separation within a continued relationship of connectedness (e.g., Grotevant & Cooper, 1986; Youniss & Smollar, 1985). Yet, this balancing of connection and individuation may be difficult to achieve, especially in early adolescence, and it seems likely that feelings of alienation – and loneliness – would be common and that teens who cannot maintain this balance act would be at greater risk.

The loneliness that adolescents report when they are alone – mostly at home – is clearly yet a different category of loneliness – one that has not often been studied. This is a context in which, I believe, adolescents are most directly addressing the issue of becoming an individual. Our data suggests that this time alone can play a positive function in development, when it comes in limited quantities. It is used for personal emotional regulation – adolescents describe seeking solitude for restorative purposes and regularly show moods after being alone that are improved. It also appears to be a context for the reflexive project of identity exploration and development – they may put on their headphones and transport themselves to a private world of reflection and self-analysis (see Goossens & Marcoen, this volume). Perhaps because of these positive functions, the loneliness experienced when alone at home is less innocuous: It is less strongly associated with psychological problems.

Do these findings redeem Western individualism? Do they refute the arguments of Sampson (1977, 1988), Bellah et al. (1985), and others that individualism does not have costs? No. The teens here reported feeling lonely for a large amount of time – close to one quarter (23%) of their waking hours. Other studies suggest that Western adolescents experience higher net levels of loneliness than youths in other cultures (Medora et al., 1987; Ostrov & Offer, 1980). Even though these data indicate that the loneliness of solitude is pretty innocuous, the loneliness of peer and family time are not, and loneliness in these contexts may be partly attributable to individualism. Compared with collective cultures, Western adolescents are under more pressure to distance themselves from emotional ties to their families and seek acceptance from peers (Triandis, 1990). This situation may set them up for more frequent and more consequential loneliness in family and peer contexts. During interactions with family and friends, the awareness of separation as a possibility might increase Western adolescents' likelihood of feeling lonely.

All the same, the findings provide a clearer picture of how individualism is enacted within adolescents' lives and suggest benefits that derive from it. Evidence suggests that adults who attain the individualistic traits that are valued in Western society are psychologically healthier, irrespective of the loneliness they may have endured. Waterman (1984) reviewed a large volume of research indicating that, within Western culture, those adults with individualistic traits, such as an internal locus of control and a secure personal identity, show lower rates of psychopathology, are more effective in their lives, and, curiously, are also more accepting of others and more altruistic. In this chapter, I have proposed that adolescent solitude, despite its loneliness, is a context in which adolescents cultivate these healthier individualistic traits; and that the benefits associated with spending an intermediate amount of time alone appear to outweigh the costs.

Curiously, beyond adolescence, I have found little evidence that solitude continues to have this constructive function. In several studies I have found that spending time alone or feeling comfortable alone is correlated with worse, rather than better, adjustment in adulthood (Larson, 1990; Larson & Lee, 1996). In adulthood, as in childhood, aloneness appears to be more like a deficit state. Of course, these findings may be due to many other factors in adults lives – being unmarried, job factors, and misanthropy – that are confounded with aloneness and obscure underlying relationships. However, I believe that aloneness becomes less significant in adulthood because healthy adults achieve a synthesis of their private and public selves and thus have less need for a private sanctuary to sort out new and untried thoughts and feelings (Larson, 1990).

Time alone may also be less functional for adolescents outside the European American samples I have studied thus far. The opportunity to withdraw into solitude is a luxury not available to most adolescents in the world, whose homes are often smaller and families larger. Among adolescents living in inner cities, feelings of danger when alone (Bhana, 1995) may also prevent solitude from being used constructively. Also, irrespective of whether the opportunity to be alone is present or not, aloneness may have little value apart from the cultural tradition of individualism – it may be just lonely. My argument, then, is that it might only be within the Western individualistic tradition that the loneliness of being alone is tolerable, in limited doses, and can provide a context for adolescents' reflexive project of constructing the much-valued personal self. Under these conditions loneliness may be useful.

Acknowledgment

This research was partially supported by National Institute of Mental Health (NIMH) Grant 1R01MH38324 awarded to Reed W. Larson and NIMH Grant 5R01MH53846 awarded to Maryse H. Richards.

13 | Social Self-Discrepancy Theory and Loneliness During Childhood and Adolescence

JANIS B. KUPERSMIDT, KATHY B. SIGDA,
CONSTANTINE SEDIKIDES, AND
MARY ELLEN VOEGLER

In this chapter, we are interested in loneliness in children and adolescents and its relevance to their adjustment. The subjective experience of loneliness as a negative affective state associated with deficits in the formation of social relationships has long been recognized as an important area of study in adults (see Marangoni & Ickes, 1989, for a review). However, until the past decade, loneliness was relatively neglected in the child and adolescent literature. In recent years, a growing body of literature has emerged to suggest that children and adolescents experience feelings of loneliness related to problems in social relationships. Indeed, approximately 10% of children between kindergarten through eighth grade report feeling very lonely (Asher et al., 1984; Asher & Wheeler, 1985; Cassidy & Asher, 1992; Parkhurst & Asher, 1992). These and other studies highlight the fact that loneliness can occur with alarming frequency across child and adolescent development.

Loneliness is related to a range of emotional, social, and behavioral problems for children, adolescents, and adults. Emotional problems include low self-esteem (Hymel et al., 1990), depression (Goswick & Jones, 1981), and social anxiety (Moore & Schultz, 1983). Social problems include peer rejection and victimization, lack of friendships, and lack of high-quality friendships (Asher et al., 1990; Asher & Wheeler, 1985; Boivin & Hymel, 1996; Crick & Ladd, 1993; Kochenderfer & Ladd, 1996; Parker & Asher, 1993b). Behavioral problems include shyness, social withdrawal, spending more time alone (Horowitz, French, & Anderson, 1982; Jones et al., 1981; Russell et al., 1980), dating frequency (Brennan, 1982), and decreased participation in religious and extracurricular school activities (Brennan, 1982). Thus, feeling lonely, in and of itself, is a negative outcome for children and adolescents, but it is also associated with other adjustment problems. Taken together, these findings underscore the importance of understanding the factors associated with loneliness.

Despite the fact that research on the implications of loneliness for the adjustment of youth has been an area of growing interest, theories about the etiology of loneliness in children and adolescents and about developmental differences in the factors related to the onset of loneliness are only recently being developed. Thus, the goal of the present chapter was to develop a theoretical model relating social cognitions about the self to loneliness in children and adolescents. The chapter is organized into four sections. In the next section, we discuss previous efforts to explain the phenomenon of loneliness in children and adolescents within theoretical and empirical contexts. In the second section, we examine the association between peer relationship problems and loneliness in the context of self-discrepancy theory and propose the relevance of examining self-discrepancies in the social domain. We provide a review of the peer relations literature and its relation to loneliness that provides initial support for this theory. In the third section, we describe a study we conducted to test the applicability of social self-discrepancy theory to the understanding of self-reports of loneliness in adolescents. Finally, we discuss the implications of social self-discrepancy theory and our study for future research efforts that attempt to understand the etiology of feelings of loneliness.

Theoretical and Empirical Explanations of Loneliness

Two theoretical models have emerged regarding the etiology and implications of loneliness for the adjustment of youth: the social needs model and the cognitive discrepancy model. According to the social needs model (Bowlby, 1973; Fromm-Reichman, 1959; Sullivan, 1953; Weiss, 1973), human individuals have a universal, basic need for social contact (e.g., affiliation, companionship, intimacy, and attachment). When this need is not met, individuals experience loneliness. Thus, loneliness is the result of an actual deficit in the extent or closeness of social contact.

In contrast, the cognitive discrepancy model (Paloutzian & Janigan, 1987; Peplau & Perlman, 1979; Peplau et al., 1982) distinguishes between actual and desired level of social contact. Individuals will experience loneliness only to the extent to which their actual degree of interpersonal contact falls short of their desired degree of contact. The larger this discrepancy, the stronger the feelings of loneliness will be.

In addition to these two theoretical perspectives, a host of other approaches have attempted to identify predictors of loneliness. One approach has distinguished between different aspects of loneliness. Marcoen and Goossens (1993) pointed out the importance of distinguishing between parent-related and peer-related loneliness when studying children and adolescents. In addition, Weiss (1973) distinguished between emotional and social loneliness. Weiss defined emotional loneliness in terms of the feelings that emanate from the lack of a close, intimate attachment dyadic relationship; he defined social loneliness in terms of the feelings that emanate from the lack of strong association with a meaningful group. This approach views negative social experiences as critical antecedent conditions for loneliness. The assumption underlying this approach is that certain aspects of peer relationships are normative, and that any deviation from these norms is associated with loneliness. In support of this approach, aspects of peer relationships have been shown to be associated with loneliness. Specifically, absence of positive relationships (i.e., lack of friendship and lack of high-quality friendship) and presence of negative relationships (i.e., peer rejection and peer victimization) predict loneliness (Asher et al., 1990; Asher & Wheeler, 1985; Crick & Ladd, 1993; G. A. Williams, Ladd, & Asher, 1996). Four peer contexts were examined simultaneously in structural equation models in relation to self-reports of loneliness (G. A. Williams et al., 1996). Feelings of loneliness were predicted by both the absence of positive relationship qualities with peers and the presence of peer victimization. Thus, both the way a child was treated by his or her peers and the quality of his or her relationships were associated with loneliness. Although unexamined in the loneliness literature, other aspects of peer relationships have been shown to increase in importance in adolescence, such as romantic relationships (Furman & Buhrmester, 1992) and social networks (Cairns, Leung, & Cairns, 1995). As such, these relationships may have important implications for the study of loneliness.

A second approach points to personality characteristics such as shyness, anxiety, social withdrawal, and submissiveness (Hymel et al., 1993; Boivin et al., 1989; Parker & Asher, 1993b) as predictors of loneliness. Passive socially withdrawn children report feeling lonelier than more sociable children (Hymel, Woody, & Bowker, 1993; K. H. Rubin et al., 1993; K. H. Rubin & Mills, 1988). In addition, social withdrawal in early childhood is predictive of loneliness in middle childhood (Hymel et al., 1990). Rejected children who are submissive in their behavior have also been found in several studies to report more loneliness and social dissatisfaction than average-status children (Boivin et al., 1989; Boivin et al., 1994; Parker & Asher, 1993b; Williams & Asher, 1987).

A third approach is concerned with attributions for success and failure. The tendency to attribute success to external and unstable factors and to attribute failure to internal and stable factors is associated with loneliness across age groups (Anderson, Horowitz, & French, 1983; Bukowski & Ferber, 1987; Renshaw & Brown, 1993). Consistent with this perspective, Bukowski and Ferber found that children who attribute peer relationship problems to internal and stable causes are more lonely. Likewise, Crick, Grotpeter, and Rockhill (1996) have adopted the social-information-processing model to explain self-reports of loneliness (also Crick et al., this volume). According to this model, children incorporate feedback gained through their social experiences into their "social database." This database stores information about individuals, their peers, and their peer relationships, and it influences their processing of information in specific situations. In a study of elementary-school-age children, Crick et al. (1996) reported a relation between social information processing and peer experiences, supporting the notion that peer experiences affect social information processing. With regard to loneliness, they found that, for girls, social information processing predicted loneliness and added to the prediction obtained by peer experiences. For boys, however, social information processing was unrelated to loneliness. Thus, awareness of one's peer status, expectations for social interactions with peers, and attributions for social successes and failures may interact with social experiences to produce loneliness.

Finally, another line of research has pursued a cumulative approach to the identification of predictors of loneliness. This research has examined the relative influence of the above-mentioned predictors simultaneously and within a single sample. For example, personality characteristics (e.g., social withdrawal), problematic peer relationships (e.g., peer rejection), and self-deprecatory attributional patterns (e.g., attributing personal failure to internal and stable factors) each predict the presence of loneliness. Empirical support has begun to emerge to support this more complex model. For example, Bukowski and Ferber (1987) reported that unpopular children who attributed peer rejection experiences to internal and stable causes were the loneliest. Also, Renshaw and Brown (1993) combined the factors listed earlier in a single study, and they reported that withdrawn behavior, low peer acceptance, lack of friendships, and internal and stable attributions were related to later loneliness. Thus, these different factors uniquely contributed to the prediction of loneliness within a single sample. Finally, Boivin and Hymel (1997) considered the personality characteristics of aggression and withdrawal as well as the peer group factors of victimization and affiliation in a single sample. They reported that the impact of social withdrawal on loneliness was mediated in part, by peer rejection and by peer behaviors directed toward the target child (victimization).

Although these more complex approaches have recently received empirical support, the theoretical basis underlying the social–cognitive component of these models has been less well developed (Renshaw & Brown, 1993). This focus, then, formed the primary goal of the present chapter, namely, to develop a theoretical model relating social cognitions about the self to loneliness in children and adolescents.

We have noted in the past that although problematic peer relations can have negative consequences for concurrent and subsequent adjustment such as feelings of loneliness, negative outcomes do not necessarily generalize to all children with peer problems (Kupersmidt, Buchele, Voegler, & Sedikides, 1996). For example, as Renshaw and Brown (1993) pointed out, studies assessing peer factors account for a low-to-moderate amount of variance in loneliness scores. Several explanations for these observed individual differences have been proposed, such as the attributional bias approach, whereby some children may blame themselves for their social failures. Asher et al. (1990) provided several additional possible explanations for the relation between peer factors and loneliness, including the ideas that some children may receive social support from individuals other than their peers, some children may have experienced social problems for relatively short periods of time and therefore may not experience associated loneliness, and some children classified as having peer problems may in fact have one high-quality friendship. In addition, children may place differing levels of importance on aspects of social relationships. For example, some children may have a relatively low level of interest in affiliation with peers or high peer status. Such children may describe themselves as not caring what others think about them or not wanting or needing friends. Also, these children may have other means of satisfying their social needs, such as through a positive affiliation with a pet, parent, or sibling. For these children, peer problems may be unrelated to their emotional adjustment. Thus, knowledge of normative cognitions about desirable or ideal social conditions, experiences, and resources would provide researchers with a benchmark for evaluating social functioning and may improve researchers' ability to predict children's reactions to different kinds of interpersonal successes and failures with peers.

The aim of this chapter is to propose and develop a theoretical model relating children's and adolescents social self-cognitions to feelings of loneliness. Social–cognitive factors represent individual-difference variables that may help to account for the differential impact of peer relations problems on loneliness. In this chapter, we develop a framework that explains individual differences in the impact of the type, quality, and quantity of children's peer relations problems on loneliness. The theoretical model that we describe in this chapter conceptualizes social cognitions about the self as a moderator of the associations between peer relationship problems and loneliness. We also present the results of an empirical study that we conducted with children and adolescents to begin to examine this theory.

Self-Discrepancy Theory Applied to Social Relationships and Feelings of Loneliness

Description of the Theory

Social cognitions about the self have been examined extensively in the social psychological literature. In particular, Higgins and his colleagues have developed a framework for understanding different cognitions about the self, known as *self-discrepancy theory* (Higgins, 1987; Higgins, Bond, Klein, & Strauman, 1986; Strauman & Higgins, 1987). This model evolved separately from the cognitive discrepancy model of loneliness described previously. Nonetheless, the two models are similar to one another in that they both consider cognitive discrepancies as predictors of emotional states. This self-discrepancy model adds to the literature on loneliness in that it provides a context within models of the self by which the social–cognitive underpinnings of loneliness can be better understood. Self-discrepancy theory distinguishes among several domains of the self. For the purposes of understanding loneliness, two of these domains are relevant, namely, the *actual self* (representations of attributes actually possessed) and the *ideal self* (representations of attributes that might ideally be possessed).

We have described an important difference between Higgins's (1987) theory and our adaptation of the theory to understanding individual differences in peer relations problems on children and adolescents (Kupersmidt et al., 1996). Briefly, in Higgins's conceptualization, all aspects of the self are examined, whereas we have focused our interests on examining only the social realm of the self. Thus, we have termed our adaptation of this theory, *social self-discrepancy theory*. We define the *actual social self* as children's perceptions of their actual social resources (e.g., the actual type, quality, and quantity of peer relations), and we define the *ideal social self* as children's reported desired social resources, or social needs (e.g., the desired type, quality, and quantity of peer relations).

In our model, an ideal social self cognition is a broad conceptualization of the desire for and importance of social relationships. For example, a child who reports that being popular is very important would be said to have a high ideal for popularity. Ideal social self-cognitions are distinguished from the construct of social goals by their relatively broad nature.

We conceptualize a *social goal* in the context of the social-information-processing model as a type of social cognition that may determine the choice of strategies used to solve a specific social problem. Social goals have been operationalized in terms of the proximal and immediate goals for specific social situations (e.g., Renshaw & Asher, 1983). Ideal peer relationships reflect cognitive structures representative of the social self. These cognitive structures are thought to be accessible in memory and can influence social goals and behavior in specific situations (Sedikides & Skowronski, 1990, 1991; see also Higgins, 1990).

We have organized our understanding of the actual and ideal social selves into three broad peer contexts of the type, quality, and quantity of peer relationships. First, social self-cognitions may vary with regard to the type of relationship, such as dyadic same-sex or dyadic opposite-sex friendships. For example, a child may have a high level of desire for a best friend, but may have a low level of desire for a romantic partner. Second, social self-cognitions may vary with regard to the qualities or provisions of the relationship. For example, a child may want to have a best friend for companionship but may place less importance on sharing secrets or intimacy. Another example is that a child or adolescent may really want a low-conflict best friendship and may not care about having high levels of support. Third, social self-cognitions may vary with regard to the perceived quantity of relationships. For example, a person may want many close friends but may believe that he or she has only one close friend.

Researchers examining similar constructs in adults have conceptualized the desire for social relationships or the ideal social self as global personality variables such as sociotropy or need for relatedness (Baumeister & Leary, 1995; Beck, 1983). Thus, the ideal social self of adults is viewed as a stable personality trait that, in the extreme, may be representative of psychopathology. In contrast, we propose that in children and adolescents, social self-cognitions are context specific and vary both within and across individuals. We expect that social self-cognitions in one context are relatively independent of social self-cognitions in other contexts. High levels of importance in one social domain may be unrelated to high levels of importance in another social domain. In addition, adult models are typically presented as relatively static models, whereas we conceptualize social self-cognitions in children and adolescents as operating within a dynamic developmental framework. Thus, we would expect to find individual differences as well as developmental differences in social cognitions about features of children's peer relationships. For example, the ideal social cognition of wanting a best friend (as opposed to playmates) may increase across elementary school and may stabilize throughout adolescence. Likewise, wanting a boyfriend or girlfriend may be relatively less common in childhood and may become increasingly more important across adolescence as well.

As the name suggests, self-discrepancy theory is primarily concerned with differences or discrepancies among the different domains of the self. The theory suggests that discrepancies between different domains of the self will be related to adjustment. For example, if an individual's actual self does not match his or her ideal self (he or she does not have what he or she would like), the individual should experience some adjustment-related outcome as a result of this discrepancy. Specifically, self-discrepancy theory proposes that discrepancies between actual and ideal selves result in dejection-related affect. This affective reaction to an ideal–actual discrepancy signifies the absence of positive outcomes, or the nonattainment of goals, desires, and hopes. In support of this idea, research with adults has found that ideal–actual self-discrepancies are associated with sadness, disappointment, and discouragement (Higgins et al., 1986; Higgins, Klein, & Strauman, 1985; Strauman & Higgins, 1987). In addition, discrepancies between actual and desired relationships in adults have been suggested as predictors of loneliness in adults (Peplau & Perlman, 1982; Rook, 1988). Although this model has been less well examined with children and adolescents, we would expect to find a similar pattern of findings to those reported with adults. In the case of the present chapter, the dejection-related affect examined with children and adolescents was loneliness.

Empirical Findings Relating Social Self-Discrepancy Theory to Loneliness

The relation between social self-discrepancy theory and loneliness has received some prior theoretical attention in the adult literature. Loneliness has been thought to be dependent on the degree of discrepancy between individuals' desired and actual social relationships (Peplau & Perlman, 1982; Rook, 1988). The discrepancy between perceptions of ideal and actual social relationships is thought to be a cognitive mediator between social relationships and psychological adjustment. Self-discrepancy theory has empirically been examined in children and adolescents in only a few studies and has rarely been examined with respect to loneliness. Nevertheless, these studies provide some support for the notion that ideal–actual discrepancies in children may be related to their experiences in social relationships (Archibald, Bartholomew, & Marx, 1995; Higgins, Loeb, & Moretti, 1995; E. C. Rubin, Cohen, Houston, & Cockrel, 1996). The ideal social self has been examined, to some extent, in studies of children's subjective experiences with peers or in their reports of different types of desirable or ideal peer relations.

The importance of distinguishing between those children who are alone by choice and those who prefer to be with others and are alone because of peer rejection has previously been discussed (K. H. Rubin & Asendorpf, 1993; Rubin et al., 1990). For example, K. H. Rubin (1993) reported that 5-year-olds who exhibited socially withdrawn behavior tended to report that interactions and relationships with others were not important to them. One might interpret these findings as suggesting that for these socially withdrawn children, their ideal social self would include cognitions that being alone was important and that affiliating with peers is less important or not important to them.

In a recent study, adolescents rated a variety of social goals that factor analyzed into six scales, including dominance, intimacy, nurturance, leadership, popularity, and peer victimization (Jarvinen & Nicholls, 1996). An examination of this new measure indicated that, in fact, the items could also be described as assessing aspects of the ideal social self. For example, items were constructed with the root phrase "When I am with people my own age, I like it when" or "I don't like it when." An example stem for the popularity scale is "I'm the most popular" and for the avoidance scale is "they pick on me." These six social goals or aspects of the ideal social self were examined in relation to self-reports of loneliness and social dissatisfaction on Asher et al.'s (1984) scale. Loneliness items were reverse scored so that high scores indicated less loneliness and greater social satisfaction. Jarvinen and Nicholls reported that the goals or ideals of popularity and intimacy and nurturance from friends were positively correlated and that dominance was negatively correlated with social satisfaction. Hence, the more adolescents endorsed dyadic quality and group acceptance ideal self-cognitions or goals, the less lonely they reported that they were. Also, the more they desired to be dominant with peers, the more lonely they were.

The cognitive discrepancy model was compared with the social needs model in a study of loneliness in 10th-grade students (Archibald et al., 1995). Students' reports of loneliness were predicted by actual levels of social contact and by discrepancies from a personally defined ideal standard and a socially defined normative standard of social activity. The domains of social activity that were examined included social friends, close friends, and special activities such as attending parties or going to movies. This measure focused on levels of social contact or activities with peers but did not examine other features of peer relations such as size of social network, quality of peer relations, status in peer group, or social experiences such as peer victimization. Actual social activity was determined on the basis of summed scores across the three domains. Likewise, ideal social relations were examined through a composite measure of social satisfaction summed across the domains. The relation between the actual levels of social activity and loneliness were hypothesized to reflect the social needs model and hence, this was controlled for in each model. Although actual–ideal and actual–normative discrepancies were associated with loneliness, they only added minimally to the prediction of loneliness after controlling for level of social activity. Archibald et al. concluded that their findings provided more support for the social needs rather than for the cognitive discrepancy model, but they cautioned about limitations in the study because of the restricted range of social relations that were examined. Taken together, these studies provided initial evidence of the importance of examining broader social goals or ideal social self-cognitions in terms of their measurability and their relation to loneliness.

Examination of the Self-Discrepancy Model for Loneliness

Goals of the Study

We conducted a study to examine Higgins's (1987) self-discrepancy model as a means of explaining loneliness in adolescents. The existing literature on the relationship between problematic peer relations and loneliness led us to focus on the social domain in the present study. Given that problems in friendship have already been found to be associated with loneliness in children (see Parker et al., this volume), we expected to replicate and extend these findings in the context of the self-discrepancy model for adolescents. In addition, other types of peer relationship problems may be associated with negative outcomes in adolescents and constitute additional domains of inquiry within the rubric of social functioning. For example, considering the normative nature of social network involvement across childhood and adolescence, one hypothesis is that lack of involvement in a desired social network might additionally be associated with loneliness in children. Similarly, romantic relationships become increasingly more common across adolescence so that lack of desired involvement in a romantic relationship might also be associated with adolescent loneliness. By using a recently developed measure of the social self, we were able to examine the relative strengths of association between each discrepancy and loneliness. On the basis of the prior findings of the additive relationship between different types of peer problems and loneliness, we also hypothesized that social self-discrepancies were additively associated with loneliness in a cumulative risk model.

Description of Study Methods and Results

A study was conducted with 212 African American and Caucasian 7th- and 11th-grade students enrolled in a rural southern public high school. Participating students completed several paper-and-pencil questionnaires during the regular school day including the Social Selves Questionnaire (SSQ; Kupersmidt et al., 1996), the Loneliness and Social Dissatisfaction Questionnaire (LSDQ; Asher & Wheeler, 1985), and other measures not relevant to the current study.

The LSDQ is a 16-item measure that assesses children's self-reports of loneliness and social dissatisfaction on a 5-point rating scale, with higher summed scores indicating greater feelings of loneliness. Scores for this sample ranged from a low of 16 to a high of 59. Previous studies have demonstrated adequate internal reliability and validity of this questionnaire (Asher & Wheeler, 1985; Asher et al., 1990; Parkhurst & Asher, 1992; Terrell-Deutsch, this volume). Because this measure has been used more often with children, we examined its psychometric properties with the current sample of adolescents. Internal consistencies of the LSDQ for 7th graders was .90 and for 11th graders was .87, findings that are consistent with prior research. The LSDQ had convergent validity with the Mood and Feelings Questionnaire (Angold et al., 1987) designed to measure depression in children and adolescents (.53, $p < .0001$, for 7th graders and .42, $p < .0001$, for 11th graders) and the Revised Children's Manifest Anxiety Scale (Reynolds & Richmond, 1978; .52, $p < .0001$, for 7th graders and .57, $p < .0001$, for 11th graders). Because of the significant positive correlations found across studies between depression and anxiety, we expected loneliness to be correlated with both types of negative affect (V. V. Wolfe et al., 1987). Discriminant validity was also examined by using the Trait Scale of the State–Trait Anger Scale (Spielberger, Jacobs, Russell, & Crane, 1983). Loneliness was not correlated with trait anger (.05 for 7th graders and .10 for 11th graders). Although some researchers suggest that adolescents, on average, report higher levels of loneliness than children (Parkhurst & Asher, 1992; Peplau & Perlman, 1982), mean levels of loneliness in this sample did not appear to be unusually high (7th grade: $M = 26.59$, $SD = 9.90$; 11th grade: $M = 27.75$, $SD = 8.69$).

The SSQ is a new self-report measure designed to assess the type, quality, and quantity of ideal, actual, and ought social self-cognitions in children and adolescents. For the purpose of the present study, six subscales on the actual and ideal sections were utilized and are described later. Each actual social self item began with the stem "I have." A parallel form of the actual section was developed to assess the ideal social self. Each ideal social self item was identical to each of the actual social self items, except that each began with the stem "It is important to me or I want." Each item was rated on a 5-point rating scale ranging from 1 (*not true for me*) to 5 (*the most true for me*).

Six subscale scores were created for the following social contexts including having a best friend, having a good quality best friendship, having a romantic relationship, experiencing peer acceptance, being in a social network, and not being victimized by peers. Except as noted later, each scale item was presented with both the actual stem and the ideal stem described previously. All scale items are described later, using the actual stems as examples. Three scales contain one item per scale because they indicate solely the presence or absence of a particular type of peer relationship. The Presence of a Best Friend Scale included one item, "I have a best friend." Similarly, the Romantic Relationship Scale included one item, "I have a boy/girlfriend." The Social Network Membership Scale included one item, "I have a group of friends." The Best Friendship Quality Scale consisted of seven items, "I have a best friend who will be my friend for a long time," "I have a best friend who I can trust," "I have a best friend who I can talk to about my problems," "I have a best friend who I can share my thoughts and feelings with," "I have a best friend who keeps my secrets," "I have a best friend who sticks up for me," and "My best friend and I do not have arguments with each other." The Peer-Group Acceptance Scale consisted of five items, "I am popular," "I am liked by a lot of kids," "I hang out with more than one group of kids," "I spend a lot of time around other kids," and "I am the kind of person other kids want as their leader." Finally, the Not Being Victimized by Peers Scale consisted of four items, "I am not picked on or bullied by other kids," "I am not talked about behind my back by other kids," "I am not rejected or disliked by other kids," and "I am not left out by other kids."

Internal consistencies of scales were acceptable and ranged from a low of .67 to a high of .94. The seventh-grade sample was retested 2 weeks after the original testing. Test–retest correlations were low to moderate, ranging from .34 to .77 for actual self and from .45 to .78 for ideal self, suggesting that children's conceptualizations of their actual and ideal social selves are moderately stable across time. These findings are consistent with arguments that self-perceptions are reflective of children's social experiences that vary over time (Crick & Ladd, 1993) and with reports on the stability of self-concepts across childhood and adolescence (Damon & Hart, 1986).

Correlations among the scales described previously were examined separately for 7th and 11th graders. In general, students distinguished among the peer context scales within a domain of the self and among the domains of the self within a peer context. Within the Actual domain, correlations among the different peer contexts ranged from .03 to .27. Within the Ideal domain, correlations ranged from .14 to .67. The correlations for each peer context scale between Actual and Ideal Social Selves scales were .43 for Presence of Best Friend, .25 for Romantic Relationship, .31 for Social Network Membership, .64 for Best Friendship Quality, .47 for Peer-Group Acceptance, and .15 for Not Being Victimized by Peers. Taken together, these mild-to-moderate interscale correlations suggest that adolescents could distinguish among the different domains of the self and the six peer contexts.

To test the discrepancy hypothesis, we first examined ideal scores. Because these scores were not normally distributed, we were unable to analyze the data using continuous raw scores. Instead, we chose to classify ideal scores for each of the six social domains into one of two groups, namely, being a domain of high importance or being a domain of low importance to each individual. We decided that a median split on the six scale scores might underestimate the level of importance of the domain. Thus, we adopted an absolute cutoff point reflecting the descriptive anchors on the rating scales. High importance was indicated by a scale score of greater than or equal to three, which represented ratings of moderate importance or better. Low importance was classified by a mean scale score of less than three, which represented that the social context was not at all important or a little important to the student. The majority of students reported that the six social domains were important to them when using this definition, as can be seen in Table 13.1. In fact, low importance was endorsed by 20 or more students for only three of the peer context scales including the Peer Group Acceptance, Romantic Relationship, and Not Being Victimized by Peers. High importance was found to be normative in this adolescent sample for the scales of Having a Best Friend, Best Friendship Quality, and Social Network Membership.

In the cases in which all students classified a domain as being of high importance, the discrepancy hypotheses is implied by a significant negative correlation between scores in the actual social subscale and loneliness. Hence, low actual scores implicitly suggest a discrepancy with the normatively high ideal for that peer context. Because of a small number of students in the low-importance group for three of the domains, only correlations are reported for the high-importance group between the actual social self and loneliness (see Table 13.1). Consistent with self-discrepancy

Table 13.1. Correlations of Mean Actual Social Self and
Loneliness Scores as a Function of Ideal Social Self Level for
Each Social Domain

| | Level of Ideal Social Self | | | |
| | Low | | High | |
Social Domain	r	n	r	n
Have a best friend		11	−.38***	201
Quality of best friendship		10	−.48**	202
Have a romantic relationship	−.05	44	−.16*	162
Peer acceptance	−.40**	54	−.63***	158
Not victimized by peers	−.26	32	−.36***	180
Have a social network		14	−.46***	198

*$p < .05$.   **$p < .001$.   ***$p < .0001$.

theory, the less a student has a best friend, a high-quality best friendship,
or a social network, the more lonely the student reports that he or she is.

The correlation between actual social self and loneliness for each domain for students who rated the domain as low versus high in importance
can also be seen in Table 13.1. The difference in the magnitude of correlations for the two ideal groups (low vs. high) is readily obvious. For
example, the actual social self is more strongly correlated with loneliness
for the Peer Group Acceptance and Not Being a Victim Scales. Thus, for
adolescents who report that peer group acceptance is important, the less
well liked they are by the peers, the lonelier they say that they are. For
students who report that peer-group acceptance is relatively less important to them, the correlation between the actual Peer Group Acceptance
and Loneliness Scales is less strong. Likewise, for students who report
that peer victimization is very undesirable, being a victim is associated
with loneliness. This association was not found for students who reported
that being a victim of peer aggression is not that important to them. The
magnitudes of the correlations for the low-versus-high groups for having
a romantic relationship did not differ. The results of these correlations
provide support for the discrepancy hypothesis in the social domain for
adolescents.

Given recent interest in the cumulative risk model and the findings
reported by Renshaw and Brown (1993), we also tested the hypothesis that the number of social domains with an ideal–actual discrepancy
would be significantly and positively related to loneliness. Children were

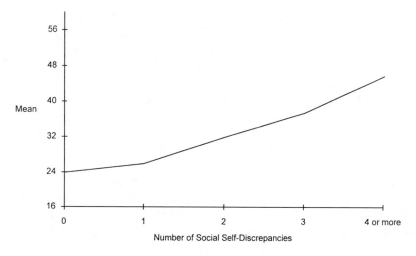

Figure 13.1. Mean loneliness scores as a functions of number of social self-discrepancies.

classified on each scale as being discrepant for that scale if they had a high ideal mean score greater than or equal to three and an actual mean score less than three. For the purpose of this analysis, all other students were classified on each scale as nondiscrepant if they did not meet this criteria. The number of ideal–actual discrepancies was summed for each study participant and ranged from 0 to 6. Only six students had four or more discrepancies so that the range of scores was changed to range from 0 to 4. The sum ideal–actual discrepancy score was significantly correlated with the sum loneliness score ($r = .50$, $p < .0001$). As the number of social self-discrepancies increased, the mean level of loneliness also increased. These findings are graphically represented in Figure 13.1, which suggests that discrepancies are additively related to one another in the prediction of loneliness. In addition, the mean scores for the students who reported three or more discrepancies were among the highest sum scores reported in the literature and exceed the mean scores reported for children who were rejected by their peers using peer report measures (Asher & Wheeler, 1985; Cassidy & Asher, 1992; Crick & Ladd, 1993; Parkhurst & Asher, 1992; Parker & Asher, 1993b).

Conclusions

The self-discrepancy model that we have adopted in this chapter to explain loneliness in children and adolescents represents an attempt to integrate previous research on self-cognitions with the peer relationships literature. We summarized different theoretical approaches to understanding the conditions under which loneliness has been reported in youth and focused on a possible mechanism that may underlie the observed relation between social problems and loneliness. We have proposed one broad framework within which these mechanisms may be understood and tested. We applied the self-discrepancy framework to examining cognitions about the social self and have argued that discrepancies between various aspects of the social self can be powerful elicitors of negative affect such as loneliness.

In the present framework, our goal has been to focus on peer problems and their relation to loneliness; however, self-discrepancy theory may also be applicable to explaining the relation between social experiences and other negative emotions such as depression, anxiety, and anger. In addition, the theory may be applied to examining the relation between social successes and emotional well-being and life satisfaction. This approach is not incompatible with other research on the self, social behavior, social experiences, and emotional adjustment and may be one of several mechanisms that may operate to produce negative affect in the developing child or adolescent. The social self-discrepancy model undoubtedly operates within a network of other social and self-cognitions to produce an affective outcome. In addition, these processes may vary as a function of competing needs and resources, as well as developmental, ethnic, and gender differences.

In one sense, social self-discrepancy theory may be conceptualized as an example of a cognitive discrepancy theory with particular relevance for negative affect such as loneliness regarding social relations. In addition, the discrepancy approach may provide an explanatory framework for explaining prior support for the social needs theory. Consistent with the social needs theory, certain types of peer relationships were nearly universally desired by adolescents. Hence, the correlation of any measure of actual social contact in those specific, universal domains with loneliness would be hypothesized to be significant. The discrepancy score would not be needed in the sense that the actual would be subtracted from a "universal constant." On the surface, this type of analysis would appear to provide support for the social needs theory; however, at its root, a discrepancy with the universal ideal is implied. In the present study, for example, for each of the universal social needs or ideals, there were significant correlations between the actual social self and loneliness. In addition, we did find several domains of peer relationships that demonstrated variability in responding. This variability in the ideal social self allowed for the direct examination of the discrepancy model that resulted in empirical support for that theory.

In conclusion, the ideas contained in this chapter suggest new directions for research on loneliness that more carefully examine the self as part of the prediction model. Relations between social behavior and social experiences have provided important advances in understanding loneliness in youth. However, cognitions about the self in social relationships across different developmental levels and their relationship to loneliness are less well-known. We have proposed that discrepancies between the ideal and actual social self for various types, qualities, and quantities of peer relations may play an important role in predicting loneliness and warrants additional investigation. The use of a theoretical framework such as social self-discrepancy theory will provide one avenue for moving beyond the description of social behavior and social relationships and their effect on youth to the development of explanatory models of the cognitive processes involved.

Acknowledgment

This research was supported in part by a William T. Grant Faculty Scholars Award and a University of North Carolina at Chapel Hill University Research Council Grant to Janis B. Kupersmidt. We would like to thank the students and staff of the Chatham Public School Systems for their help in conducting the study reported in this chapter.

14 | Self, Other, and Loneliness From A Developmental Perspective

LORRIE K. SIPPOLA AND WILLIAM
M. BUKOWSKI

In this chapter, we explore the construct of loneliness from a developmental perspective. Our goal is to show how feelings of loneliness during adolescence derive from developmental processes regarding the resolution of the self–other dialectic. The basic point of this chapter is that loneliness in adolescence results from struggles with both interpersonal and intrapersonal issues and with the tension between them (i.e., the dialectic of self and other). There are two important features to this point. First, we argue that loneliness results from normal developmental processes of adolescence, and therefore some degree of loneliness is to be expected in adolescents. A corollary to this view is that variations in how well particular adolescents resolve these developmental challenges will account for individual differences in feelings of loneliness. Second, we propose that much of the association between loneliness and *inter*personal processes (e.g., the association between some aspects of friendship experiences and loneliness) can be attributed to the mediating effects of *intra*personal processes such as adolescents' feelings about the self.

We have chosen to focus on the adolescent period for two main reasons. The first reason is that adolescence still appears to be an understudied part of the life span. With some notable exceptions (M. H. Davis & Franzoi, 1986; Goossens & Marcoen, this volume; Koenig & Abrams, this volume; Koenig, Isaacs, & Schwartz, 1994; Larson, this volume; Marcoen et al., 1987; Ostrov & Offer, 1978), researchers interested in loneliness have largely overlooked the adolescent years, preferring to focus instead on school-age children or adults. Second, we propose that particular processes related to development during adolescence may predispose the individual to feelings of loneliness that are particular to this age. Loneliness may be a more frequent or a more intense experience during adolescence than during either childhood or adulthood. This is seen in both research and theory on adolescence (see Brennan, 1982; Sullivan, 1953) and in fictional accounts of the adolescent story. Indeed, Joyce's Stephen

Dedalus (*Portrait of the Artist as a Young Man*), Salinger's Holden Caulfield (*Catcher in the Rye*), and Richler's Duddy Kravitz (*The Apprenticeship of Duddy Kravitz*) are all alone and lonely, split off from their worlds and from themselves. Autobiographical accounts, such as those written by John Cheever, Virginia Woolf, Irving Howe, and Gertrude Stein, also often portray adolescence as a time of loneliness and alienation.

We begin our chapter with a discussion of the concept of loneliness. Next, we adopt a developmental perspective to explore the phenomenon of loneliness in early and mid-adolescence. Our view is that particular developmental transformations regarding the concepts of self and other create a vulnerability for feelings of loneliness in adolescence. For adolescents, resolving the dialectic between self and other is a particularly challenging task. In this regard, although the self and other are distinct, they are very much interrelated. Adolescents strive to understand how the self fits into the broader social context. However, much of this understanding comes from the experiences of the self embedded within an interpersonal context that inform the adolescent how the self is viewed by others.

Following our discussion of self/other, we discuss developmental changes in cognitive abilities that have direct repercussions for adolescents' understanding of the self and describe how these changes may lead to feelings of loneliness. After this, we discuss how interpersonal events are linked to the intrapersonal. That is, we discuss how feelings of loneliness are linked to changes in adolescents' concepts of self. In the final section of this chapter, we report initial findings from our research program that help to elucidate some of the processes described in this chapter.

What is Loneliness?

Loneliness refers to feelings that derive from a sense of isolation. Ultimately, the concept of loneliness is linked to the concept of self in that it refers to a sense of separateness or isolation of the self. In so far as the concept of the self is tied to the concept of the other (Mahler, Pine, & Bergman, 1975; Zukier, 1994), loneliness has been studied from the perspective of self vis-à-vis from interpersonal experiences. From this perspective, the self can be separated from others in a *physical* sense, such as when one is not in the same place or location as one's friends or peers (Archibald et al., 1995). Or, the self can be separated from others in a *psychological* sense, such as when one is out of touch with or distant from someone in an emotional sense (Bukowski et al., 1993). Embedded within this interpersonal perspective is the argument that loneliness results from experiences at either the group or the dyadic level. That is, one can be alienated from one's social group (Asher et al., 1990; Parkhurst & Asher, 1992) or from particular others (Bukowski, Hoza, & Boivin, 1994; Weiss, 1973). Regardless of the level of analysis, however, the main theme of most research on loneliness is that loneliness occurs when the self becomes isolated from the other.

In this chapter, we wish to add to this perspective by presenting the argument that loneliness during adolescence may also result from intrapersonal processes. The basic premise of our perspective is that just as the self can be isolated from the other as a result of interpersonal experiences, one can also feel alone in reference to one's self per se. That is, feelings of loneliness can result from "separations" that occur within the self. These separations may be experienced when one feels that the various components that make up the self are out of touch with each other or when one sees the separateness between the features of the self or even experiences an alienation from these features. This sense of separateness is more likely during adolescence than at other times of life because it is during this developmental period that the self becomes a more complex and differentiated structure. As a consequence, adolescents face several poignant developmental challenges that may contribute to increased feelings of loneliness. These challenges include (a) the development of a sense of coherence between the various components of the self and (b) the reconciliation of the "true" inner self and the self presented to others. These challenges, and the interplay between them, constitute important developmental events. However, they also provide and perhaps even require opportunities that are likely to lead to feelings of alienation and separateness.

Loneliness From a Developmental Perspective

Much of the research on loneliness in childhood and adolescence has been based on concepts and studies from the literature on adult social psychology, most notably the ideas of Weiss (1973). There is no doubt that the social psychological literature has had a positive and stimulating effect on the study of loneliness during childhood and adolescence. Nevertheless, the use of a model developed to explain a phenomenon observed during adulthood to explain the same construct during childhood or adolescence presumes that the structures and processes from adulthood are equivalent to those of these earlier developmental periods. We argue that this presumption is not true. Even between childhood and adolescence, there are differences in social and personal needs, skills, orientations, and supporting structures (Grotevant, 1998). Consequently, a developmental perspective is essential for a complete understanding of the phenomenon of loneliness within a particular age group.

One important aspect of the developmental perspective we adopt concerns the interdependency between systems. Cognition, social needs, personal experiences, and the self are neither conceptually nor experientially independent of each other. Accordingly, the goal of a developmental model should be to account for the interactions between these phenomena. As Hinde (1979, 1987) has shown, a person's experience of relationships derives not only from one's interactions within the relationship but also from one's interpretation or understanding of these interactions. A corollary of such a position is that as a person's cognitive abilities change so will a person's experience within interpersonal relationships. This interactionist or systems orientation is central to the arguments we present in this chapter. Indeed, we propose that loneliness occurring in adolescence is due to the adolescent's struggle with the self–other dialectic and that this struggle reflects an interaction between the self-system and the social domain. With these views in mind, the following sections explore the particular developmental challenges of early and mid-adolescence and develop a model for understanding feelings of loneliness during this age period.

Cognitive Development During Adolescence: *A Précis*

The cognitive skills that emerge in adolescence are a powerful force – they free the adolescent from a concrete, quotidian existence and launch them into new realms of existence. In children, concepts of events, people, and objects are largely based on concrete, readily observable characteristics (Keating, 1990). However, in early adolescence, concrete representations no longer dominate cognitive activities. Instead, adolescents become capable of abstract representations, and they can engage in processes constructed entirely on abstract properties.

Part of the movement away from an emphasis on the here and now is due to the increasing ability to think in terms of hypotheses or possibilities (Flavell, 1963). In adolescence, the cognitive system becomes multidimensional and relativistic rather than narrow and absolute. As a result of this multidimensionality, adolescents become aware of the complexity in simple things. They see that even simple ideas or objects can have a nearly endless range of possibilities or features, albeit that these phenomena are situated in time and space. That is, adolescents see that phenomena are in part defined by where and when they exist or occur. This attention to time and context increases adolescents' concerns with the stability of phenomena across time and to how a particular phenomenon might vary across situations.

Changes in the Understanding of Self

The changes in cognitive functioning that are observed to occur during adolescence have direct implications for adolescents' sense of self. The sense of self can be thought of as a theory about the self that individuals maintain on the basis of their experiences and past histories. These theories include a description of the particular features that make up the concept (i.e., the content or the features of the self), as well as an account of the structure or organization among these features.

Developmental changes have been observed in both content and structure of self theories (Harter, 1983). Children tend to define the content of self according to concrete phenomenon such as hair color, gender, and abilities or skills (Harter, 1983). Thus, children's sense of themselves are generally defined according to outwardly observable characteristics. In contrast, on entering formal operations, adolescents acquire a powerful tool that allows them to think about the self in more complex and differentiated ways. That is, they can now think about and reflect on their own thoughts, desires, and motives. As they turn increasingly inward for self-definition, adolescents begin to structure their definition of the self according to beliefs, values, and psychological traits and characteristics. This reorganization of adolescents' self-descriptions reflects their ability to categorize specific patterns of beliefs or behaviors according to higher order abstract structures (Harter, 1983). Thus, in adolescence, the self becomes a richer and more pluralistic concept.

The structural changes occurring in adolescents' understanding of self reflect development in the adolescents' understanding of self as unique from others and the integration of different features into a coherent theory of self. The self is experienced as unique when adolescents see that features of the self distinguish themselves from others (Chandler, 1975). The self is experienced as integrated when adolescents see a unity and coherence among the different, and sometimes conflicting, aspects of the self (Broughton, 1981). In the following sections, we describe the changes that occur in these two structural dimensions of the self and examine the implications of these changes for feelings of loneliness during adolescence.

The Unique Self and Loneliness

The notion that separation or individuation of the self from others is an important developmental task of adolescence is ubiquitous in the developmental literature. According to several authors (Blos, 1967; Cooper &

Grotevant, 1987), successful resolution of this particular developmental task requires balancing identification of the self as separate or unique from other selves with a sense of closeness or connection to important others, such as parents or friends (see Larson, this volume).

In parallel to an increased awareness of their own inner world of thoughts and feelings, adolescents become more acutely aware that others also possess such an inner world. A consequence of this heightened inner awareness is a sense of the ultimate isolation of one's inner world from the inner worlds of others. Elkind's (1967) notion of the "personal fable" suggests that adolescents become increasingly focused on the uniqueness of the self from other selves. Indeed, Blos (1967) has argued that in contrast to the stereotypical view of teenage rebellion, much of the struggle to individuate occurs on a cognitive rather than a behavioral level. For this reason, adolescents may initially view separation from others as a fundamental condition of human experience. Consequently, the adolescent may feel alone in the struggle to achieve the particular developmental task of individuation.

The ability to engage in complex abstract reasoning helps adolescents' resolve the developmental challenge of separation–individuation by redirecting their focus for justifications of self as unique and distinct. In childhood, observable physical features (e.g., "Nobody else has a nose that is shaped like mine") form the basis for justifications of a unique self. In contrast, adolescents focus on the unique combination of psychological and physical qualities to justify the self as unique and distinct from others (D. Hart, Maloney, & Damon, 1987). At the highest level of development, the self is differentiated from others on the basis of the inner experiences of thoughts and emotions. That is, the self is differentiated from others by one's own unique, subjective experiences and interpretations of the world (e.g., "Nobody else sees things or feels the same way about things as I do"; D. Hart et al., 1987, p. 128). To some extent, the emphasis on internal features that form the basis for adolescents' unique-self justifications enables them to conform to others' expectations without losing their sense of uniqueness. For example, an adolescent who differentiates the self from others on the basis of internal psychological experiences may, at the same time, present an outward appearance of conformity to the peer-group's or parents' standards for behavior. However, this ability presents its own challenge to the adolescent. Specifically, the challenge is to maintain a precarious balance between an outward appearance of conformity and an inner sense of a unique and distinct self.

Broughton (1981) took this perspective when he proposed that adolescents may become "philosophically invested in loneliness" to maintain the balance between conformity and distinct self. He suggested that, for an adolescent, revealing inner self to others threatens the very existence of a self because once the self is known to others, it is no longer unique or distinct. Thus, as the adolescent begins to perceive that one's own inner worlds of thoughts and emotions are ultimately separate from the inner worlds of others, she or he may acquire the belief that the self can never be known or understood by others (Harter, 1990). Feelings of isolation and alienation may result, then, from the sense that these inner worlds of self and other constitute a "plurality of solitudes" (Sartre, in Chandler, 1975).

Divided Self and Loneliness

One of the struggles confronting adolescents that was identified in the previous section concerns the balance between a unique sense of self with the demands for conformity to others' perceptions of self. As adolescents struggle to separate the values and beliefs of others from their own values and beliefs, they may not only feel isolated from others but may also begin to feel separated from various core dimensions of the self. That is, as adolescents become aware of the complexity of the self and of the many "possible selves" that one could present, there is an increased recognition of the separation between the inner self and the self that is presented to others. Thus, adolescents are confronted with the task of integrating and coordinating these various dimensions of the self.

The sense that the self lacks integration can be exacerbated by the many new domains in which adolescents spend their time. Indeed, adolescents often make a school transition moving from a smaller elementary school to a larger high school. This transition leads to an abrupt change in the structure and organization of the peer group. New friends are added to the group and, occasionally, supplant the role of old friends from childhood. Importantly, the peer group begins to include members of the other-sex as adolescents face increasing pressure to participate in heterosocial situations (Dunphy, 1963). These friends may have different expectations of the adolescent and, consequently, treat the adolescent as she or he has never been treated before (e.g., as a "boyfriend" or as a "girlfriend"). In contrast, parents have a continuous history with the adolescent and may continue to have similar expectations of the adolescent as they had of the child (see, for example, Smetana, 1988a). As a result, adolescents often feel as if the self were split (i.e., divided) across different domains (Broughton, 1981).

As part of this sense of divided self, adolescents can experience a separation between true and false selves (see Broughton, 1981). This sense of having a divided self may be manifested by expressing things that one does not really believe or feel or by changing oneself to conform to others' expectations. This sense of divided self may be a normal developmental process that helps adolescents learn to integrate the multiple roles that they must adopt in response to changing societal expectations and roles (Harter et al., 1993). Nevertheless, the experience of a divided self may have consequences for feelings of loneliness in so far as it implies that the true self can never really be known by others. That is, because of the structural changes occurring in adolescents' conceptualization of the self, adolescents may perceive the self as "doomed to eternal isolation within the cell of the body" (Broughton, 1981, p. 22). Thus, the divided self makes adolescents vulnerable for feelings of loneliness as it reinforces the view that one's true inner self is alienated or split off from experience with the outer world.

It is conceivable that opportunities for forging a coherent sense of self are available in interactions with friends. Sullivan (1953) argued that one of the specific ways that friendship contributes to development is by giving an adolescent the chance "to see oneself through the other's eyes" (p. 248). This experience is useful not only because it helps adolescents clarify their sense of self but also because it would provide a powerful validation of the self as they come to recognize the positive regard that the friend holds for them. Talking to a friend about issues that really matter to oneself, thereby exposing one's innermost thoughts and feelings to another, provides adolescents with the opportunity to clarify exactly how they are similar and different from others. In this respect, the impact of friendship on self-clarity functions as a counterweight to the processes that challenge adolescents' sense of coherence of the self.

One must, however, examine the potentially negative effects of the peer network on adolescents' self-development. Although friendship may have a positive impact on adolescents who are striving to form an integrated self, other aspects of the peer system may have the opposite effect. During early adolescence, peer expectations can have a nearly tyrannical or coercive impact on youngsters' behaviors and attitudes (Berndt, 1982). The norms of the peer group can be a constant reminder to an early adolescent of how others expect him or her to be. This may force an adolescent to experience a deep gulf between how he or she sees him- or herself and how others want him or her to be. This task of comparing one's self to external expectations makes the process of seeing a coherence in the self more difficult, and makes it harder to arrive at a clear sense of what is part of the self and what is not.

Summary

In the previous sections, we have suggested that changes in the structural organization of the self-concept may have important implications for feelings of loneliness in adolescence. From a theoretical perspective, integrating the concurrent changes in the physical, social, and cognitive domains during adolescence may temporarily create a sense of uncertainty concerning the integration of various dimensions of the self-concept. That is, until these changes have been integrated into the adolescent's sense of self, the question "Who am I?" becomes problematic. We have also suggested that this problem has specific consequences for feelings of loneliness during adolescence. This is in part due to the increased feelings of isolation and alienation of the self from other selves and in part is also due to feelings of alienation of the different dimensions of the self from each other (i.e., inner feelings and outer appearance).

Currently, the ideas we have presented earlier have generally not been subjected to empirical investigation. Thus, we have embarked on a program of research designed to assess some of the theoretical links between the self and feelings of loneliness in early and mid-adolescence that we have outlined. In the following section, we report the results of two studies conducted to examine a specific component of the self-concept (i.e., the divided self) and loneliness in adolescent girls and boys.

Research on Self-Concept and Loneliness in Early Adolescence

In the following studies, we were interested in clarifying the processes through which certain relational experiences influence feelings of loneliness in adolescence. Previously, researchers have observed that greater intimacy in self-disclosure to peers is associated with lower feelings of loneliness in adults (Berg & Peplau, 1982; Chelune, Sultan, & Williams, 1980; Solano, Batten, & Parish, 1982). We suggest that this association occurs as a result of helping adolescents integrate the divided self. That is, adolescents who are able to reveal their innermost thoughts and needs to their peers are more likely to experience an integration between their inner and outer selves and, consequently, feel less lonely. In the first study, we examined self-disclosure and feelings of divided-self in early adolescents' same-sex friendships. In the second study, we examined both same- and other-sex friendships in early adolescence.

Both studies were conducted with students attending one of two high schools located in middle-class suburbs of Montreal, Canada. These high schools contained a large, multiethnic, and multi-socioeconomic status population. In each study, students completed a version of the Measure of Relational Authenticity (MRA). On the basis of a measure previously designed to assess women's experiences in romantic relationships (Jack & Dill, 1992), we developed the MRA to assess adolescents' experiences in their friendship relations. The measure used in this study consists of two subscales: (a) Divided-Self scale (DS) and (b) Authentic Self-Disclosure scale (ASD). Two versions of the measure were used.

In the first version of the measure (used in the first study), the DS scale consists of seven items designed to assess the degree to which adolescents feel they can reveal the true self to their friends (e.g., "In order for my friend to like me, I cannot reveal certain things about myself to them" and "I feel that my friends do not really know who I am"). The second scale, ASD, consists of nine items designed to assess the degree to which adolescents feel they can express their inner feelings and opinions to their friends (e.g., "I think it is better to keep my feelings to myself when they conflict with my friend's" and "I try to bury my feelings when I think they will cause trouble with friends"). The ASD subscale was used as an indicator of self-disclosure in that it assesses adolescents' willingness to reveal highly intimate events (i.e., "feelings") to others.

On each of the scales students indicated how true each item was for them on a Likert-type rating scale. Higher scores on the DS subscale indicate a greater split between the inner-self and the self presented outwardly to friends. Higher scores on the ASD subscale indicate greater willingness to disclose one's feelings in the friendship.

The second version of the MRA was very similar to the first, except that it contained fewer items per scale and students were asked to complete one measure for their same-sex friendships and another measure for their other-sex relationships. In the second version of the MRA, therefore, the DS subscale consisted of four of the original items, and the Authentic Self-Disclosure subscale consisted of three of the original items.

In both studies, loneliness was assessed using a 23-item measure developed by Asher et al. (1984). For the purpose of the current study, average ratings on three items that focus on distinct feelings of loneliness were used as the dependent measure. Table 14.1 presents a summary of the means, standard deviations, and reliability coefficients for the measures used in both studies.

Study 1: Divided Self and Loneliness

In the first study, 93 students from Grade 7 participated (boys, $n = 46$ and girls, $n = 47$). Nine boys and 3 girls did not complete the MRA, therefore, the final sample was reduced to 81. The MRA and loneliness questionnaires were completed as part of a larger longitudinal study examining adolescents' expectations about the transition to middle school. All questionnaires were completed in groups during a regularly scheduled class period. Analyses focused on (a) gender differences in feelings of

Table 14.1. Means (Standard Deviations) and Correlations between Loneliness, Emotional Self-Disclosure (ESD), and Divided-Self (DS)

Boys

| | Study One | | | Study Two | |
	M (SD)	Reliability Coefficient		M (SD)	Reliability Coefficient
Loneliness	1.48 (.78)	0.90	Loneliness	1.51 (.76)	0.85
Emotional Self Disclosure (ESD)	3.27 (.67)	0.74	ESD Same-sex	2.76 (.85)	0.47
			ESD Other-sex	2.67 (.96)	0.44
Divided-Self (DS)	2.41(.84)	0.87	DS Same-sex	2.27 (.91)	0.68
			DS Other-sex	2.26 (.84)	0.68

Girls

| | Study One | | | Study Two | |
	M (SD)	Reliability Coefficient		M (SD)	Reliability Coefficient
Loneliness	1.54 (.74)	0.87	Loneliness	1.79 (.86)	0.85
Emotional Self Disclosure	3.44 (.68)	0.63	ESD Same-sex	2.62 (.95)	0.56
			ESD Other-sex	2.64 (.91)	0.63
Divided-Self	2.00 (.78)	0.87	DS Same-sex	2.29 (.91)	0.7
			DS Other-sex	2.53 (.87)	0.72

loneliness and in self-concept in early adolescence and (b) the mediating effects of divided self on the association between emotional self-disclosure and feelings of loneliness.

First, gender differences were examined for each of the measures used in the study. As indicated in Table 14.1, no gender differences in mean ratings of loneliness were observed, $F(1, 85) = 0.14$, $p > .05$. In general, these ratings were fairly low ($M = 1.51$, $SD = .76$). Similarly, no gender differences were observed on the ESD subscale, $F(1, 80) = 1.26$, $p > .05$.

Both boys and girls felt capable of revealing their feelings and opinions to their friends. Gender differences were observed, however, on the DS subscale. In this study, boys felt less able to reveal the true self to their friends when compared with girls, $F(1, 79) = 5.13$, $p < .05$.

In our next analyses, we examined the mediating effects of feelings of divided self on the association between emotional self-disclosure and loneliness using the method described by Baron and Kenny (1986). In this approach, hierarchical multiple regression is used to assess the association between a predictor variable (i.e., self-disclosure) and a criterion variable (i.e., loneliness) after the effects of a mediating variable (i.e., divided self) have been accounted for. Consistent with previous research (e.g., Davis & Franzoi, 1986), self-disclosure was negatively related to reported loneliness (boys, $r = -.34$ and girls, $r = -.32$; $p < .05$). Also, feelings of divided self were significantly related to feelings of loneliness (boys, $r = .49$ and girls, $r = .58$) and to emotional self-disclosure (boys, $r = -.69$ and girls, $r = -.70$; all $ps < .05$). However, as shown in Figure 14.1, the association between self-disclosure and loneliness was almost entirely explained by feelings of divided self for both boys and girls.

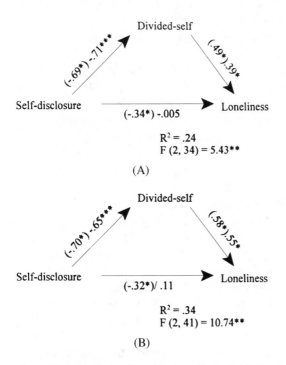

Figure 14.1. Mediational models from Study 1. (A) Boys' mediational model. (B) Girls' mediational model.

Study 2: Loneliness and Divided Self in Same- and
Other-Sex Relationships

Early adolescence is characterized by important changes in the structure of the peer group. One of these changes involves the inclusion of
members of the other sex in adolescents' friendship networks (Feiring &
Lewis, 1991). This transition may be a difficult task for some adolescents,
with specific consequences for their self-concept and, subsequently, for
feelings of loneliness. For a variety of underlying reasons (see Maccoby,
1988), adolescents may feel a greater split between the true inner self
and the false outer self that is presented to other-sex peers. Moreover,
considering observed gender differences in relational and conversational
styles (Tannen, 1990), self-disclosure to other-sex peers may be difficult to
achieve and contribute to heightened feelings of loneliness.

As part of a larger study examining the interpersonal factors underlying the onset of gender differences in affective well-being, 239 students
from Grades 7 and 9 (boys, $n = 100$ and girls, $n = 139$) participated in
Study 2. Students completed a number of questionnaires that included
the revised version of the ASD and DS subscales in addition to the loneliness measure. In this study, we asked boys and girls to complete the ASD
and DS subscales, thinking first of their relationships with same-sex peers
and then with other-sex peers. Means, standard deviations, and internal
consistency of the measures used in Study 2 are presented in Table 14.1.

As in Study 1, no gender differences were observed in feelings of loneliness, $F(1, 263) = 3.06$, $p > .05$. Similarly, no gender differences were
observed on the ASD subscales for the other-sex form, $F(1, 199) = 0.04$
or for the same-sex form, $F(1, 234) = 1.39$ ($ps > .05$). However, gender
differences in feelings of divided-self with other-sex peers were observed,
$F(1, 202) = 4.77$, $p < .03$. In this study, boys reported feeling a greater
sense of divided self with girls than girls reported feeling with boys (see
Table 14.1 for means). No gender differences were observed in feelings of
divided self with same-sex peers, $F(1, 234) = 0.04$, $p > .05$.

The next set of analyses for Study 2 examined the mediational models
for boys and girls separately. We also examined the models separately
for same-sex and other-sex peers. It should be noted that the strength
of the associations between the variables in Study 2 is attenuated because of low internal consistency of the ASD and subscales. However, in
spite of this attenuation, the results of Study 2 provide additional support for the mediational effects of divided self on the association between self-disclosure and loneliness. Figure 14.2 illustrates the mediational models for boys and girls with same- and other-sex friends. In

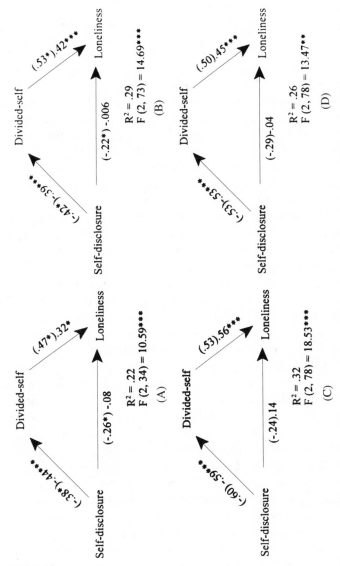

Figure 14.2. Mediational models from Study 2. (A) Boys' mediational model: Same-sex friends. (B) Boys' mediational model: Other-sex friends. (C) Girls' mediational model: Same-sex friends. (D) Girls' mediational model: Other-sex friends.

all of these models, the association between emotional self-disclosure and loneliness was almost entirely accounted for by feelings of divided self.

Conclusion

G. S. Hall (1904) compared adolescence with the historical period of revolutions (i.e., the political and economic revolutions of the eighteenth and nineteenth centuries). In this chapter, we have likened adolescence to a more recent epoch, namely, the twentieth-century period known as *modernism* (Howe, 1967a, 1967b). The essential feature of modernism was a search for meaning and identity in an ambiguous world lacking the certainties and shared convictions of previous times. One of the compelling experiences of modernists is the recognition that people are split off from each other, each is engaged in his or her own struggle to make sense of his or her own experience. This modernist perspective can be seen in many expressions. John Berger (1973), the art critic, showed how the modernist perspective was manifested in the sticklike, highly textured iron statues of isolated human beings created by the sculptor Alberto Giacommetti. For Giacommetti, the loneliness of these figures reflects a basic condition of human existence, specifically that people are ultimately unknowable to each other and that the inner reality that they experience as individuals cannot be shared. In this chapter, we have made the same claim about adolescence. We propose that processes of development, especially those regarding conceptions of self and other, lead adolescents to the same worldview of the modernist age.

The essential point of our proposal is that feelings of isolation and alienation during adolescence may derive from two interrelated sources, namely (a) a sense of being separated from others (e.g., one's parents or one's peers) or (b) a sense of being alienated from the different dimensions of the self (e.g., feelings of divided self). Although each of these perceptions may make a unique contribution to the experience of loneliness, it is possible that the *intra*personal factors are influenced by *inter*personal experiences. In this regard, the intrapersonal processes may be the pathway by which interpersonal experiences have their effect on loneliness. Together, these intrapersonal and interpersonal factors may cause a crisis of loneliness that certainly challenges the adolescent's internal resources.

Although loneliness is generally viewed as a negative experience by developmental psychologists, it is important to consider the positive effects of these feelings for adolescent development. The internal crisis and the potential external conflict that these feelings create for adolescents may provide them with the opportunity to develop mature and constructive coping strategies for future experiences of solitude. Moreover, feelings of loneliness may open a path for adolescents to gain greater self-insight and to become more thoughtful and reflective adults (see Larsons, this volume; Goossens & Marcoen, this volume). Clearly, however, one cannot overlook the difficulty that these experiences cause for adolescents nor the potential for long-term maladaption if the experience is extremely adverse. Consequently, it is important to illuminate the normative processes of development that may influence this experience to better understand when the experience warrants intervention. In our research, we have begun to focus on links between the various structural features of the adolescent's self-concept and feelings of loneliness. Although at this time, we have focused primarily on the links between the self-concept and the peer group, it will be important to understand the association between changes in the parent–child relationship, the self-concept, and feelings of loneliness in adolescence.

We have shown that loneliness is linked to a set of complex human processes, linking the interpersonal with the intrapersonal and embedding them within the developmental processes of adolescence. For adolescence, resolving this tension between internal and external forces and processes is a major developmental challenge. In the short term, this aspect of development may have negative affective consequences. In the long run, it creates engaged modernists – individuals who are secure with themselves and with others.

Acknowledgment

Work on this chapter was supported by grants to Lorrie K. Sippola and William M. Bukowski from the Social Sciences and Humanities and Research Council of Canada and by an award from the Seagram's Fund for Innovative Teaching and Research. William M. Bukowski was also supported by the William T. Grant Foundation, and the Fonds Pour la Formation des Chercheurs et Pour l'aide à la Recherche. Each author contributed equally to this project.

15 Adolescent Loneliness and Adjustment: A Focus on Gender Differences

LINDA J. KOENIG AND ROBIN F. ABRAMS

Historically, adolescence was thought of as a period of upheaval, emotional turmoil, and "storm and stress" (A. Freud, 1958; Hall, 1904). According to Anna Freud, it was the teenager who did not experience this turmoil who was abnormal. Contemporary research supports a balanced view of the psychological problems occurring during adolescence. On the one hand, epidemiological studies confirm that the majority of individuals pass through adolescence without marked disorder, and only about 20% experience some form of diagnosable disturbance (e.g., Kashani et al., 1987; McGee et al., 1990; Offord et al., 1987; Whitaker et al., 1990). At the same time, studies examining the developmental patterns of certain syndromes (e.g., depression and dysthymia, drug and alcohol abuse, and anorexia and bulimia nervosa) and symptoms (e.g., dysphoria, anxiety, self-deprecation, suicidal ideation, and negative body image) confirm their increased prevalence during the adolescent years, indicating that adolescence is indeed a time of heightened emotional discomfort and negative affectivity.

Perhaps more striking than the increased prevalence of certain specific psychopathologies and emotional distress symptoms is the shift in gender distribution that occurs with adolescence. Before adolescence, it is boys who experience more psychopathology. During adolescence, this gender distribution reverses, with girls showing higher rates of disorder. This reversal can be accounted for by girls' increased risk for a number of specific disorders, including unipolar depression and dysthymia, anxiety disorders, and anorexia nervosa and bulimia nervosa (see, for example, Kashani et al., 1987; Kashani & Orvashel, 1988; Lewinsohn, Hops, Roberts, Seeley, & Andrews, 1993; McGee et al., 1990; Nolen-Hoeksema, 1987; Whitaker et al., 1990). Studies of self-reported problems and symptoms show a similar pattern of gender distribution. Adolescent girls report higher levels of dysphoria, self-consciousness, negative self- evaluations, negative body image, and somatization – symptoms that are related to the mood and eating disorders – than do adolescent boys (see Schonert-Reichl & Offer, 1992, for a review).

Like these other unpleasant experiences, loneliness also seems to increase during adolescence when, in fact, it may be most widespread (Brennan, 1982; Rubinstein & Shaver, 1980). Several factors may account for this. First, this may be in part a function of the increased amount of time adolescents spend by themselves. Time usage studies indicate a sharp increase in the time adolescents spend alone (26% of the time) compared with time spent alone during late childhood (17% of the time; Larson & Csikszentmihalyi, 1980; Larson & Richards, 1991). This would not provide a complete explanation however, as loneliness is more than just spending time alone; people can be alone without feeling lonely. Adults, in fact, spend more time alone than adolescents, even though it is adolescents who are more likely to experience this time as unpleasant (Larson, 1990).

Thus, researchers also need to know what happens when adolescents spend time alone that does not happen for adults. According to Larson (1990; this volume), adolescents (at least those in Western cultures) use time alone to pursue the important developmental tasks of individuation and identity formation; that is, separating one's identity from that of one's parents and consolidating the many different aspects of one's private and public personna into a cohesive, integrative-self system. During the adolescent years, before the self is fully autonomous, time alone is often experienced as painful and lonely, rather than as the peaceful solitude often experienced by adults. Poet Mary Sarton may have aptly captured this distinction when she stated that "solitude is the richness of self, and loneliness is the poverty of self." Together with the time usage studies, this suggests that the phenomenon of increased adolescent loneliness results from the increasing amounts of time adolescents spend alone, focusing inward and working to resolve the essential developmental tasks of self-exploration and identity integration.

Loneliness and Psychological Adjustment

The previous discussion suggests the importance of distinguishing between objective and subjective experiences (i.e., time alone vs. the pleasantness of that time) when trying to identify the aspects of loneliness that may or may not be related to psychological adjustment. Another important consideration should be the chronicity of that experience. That is, how long has this unpleasant state of loneliness been occurring? Most individuals experience loneliness from time to time, for example, when

starting at a new school, moving to a new town, or losing an important relationship (see Hymel et al., this volume). In these situations, loneliness is
a transitory and probably normative experience. Loneliness can serve as a
challenge to people – to extend the ability to tolerate temporary isolation,
to soothe and console themselves in the face of loss, and to develop new
social networks actively. Individuals who cannot grow with these challenges are likely to experience continued loneliness, and possibly more
severe emotional problems. Although experienced as distressful, temporary loneliness, or even developmentally appropriate loneliness, may not
be associated with any significant maladjustment.

Several authors have attempted to operationalize or define chronic
loneliness and examine whether its underlying causes and correlates are
distinct from those of temporary or situational loneliness. Young (1982)
suggested that chronic loneliness, characterized as a lack of satisfaction
with social relationships for 2 or more consecutive years, probably involves more cognitive and behavioral deficits related to social skills and
interpersonal relations than temporary loneliness. Hanley-Dunn et al.
(1985) attempted to examine this interpersonal hypothesis by determin-
ing whether the chronically lonely were more likely than the temporarily
lonely to attribute hostile or negative intentions to others. To define chronic
loneliness, Hanley-Dunn et al. asked participants to identify whether they
experienced four loneliness symptoms at any point during their life and
to identify how long these symptoms persisted. They also measured how
much time had passed since participants experienced the chronic loneliness. Although the authors found that loneliness was correlated with
greater negative inferences, chronicity of loneliness was no better predictor than general loneliness scores (the revised UCLA Loneliness Scale
[R-UCLA]; Russell et al., 1980). Moreover, if chronic loneliness had not
been recent (defined as less than 5 years in the past), it was not as good
a predictor as was general loneliness. Gerson and Perlman (1979) also
distinguished between chronic and situational loneliness by asking participants to complete two forms of the UCLA Scale, with one indicating
how they had felt in the past 2 weeks, and one indicating how they felt
"in their life." Participants scoring in the upper third for recent loneliness
but the lower third for general loneliness were designated *situationally
lonely*, those scoring in the upper third of both were labeled *chronically lonely*, and those scoring in the bottom third of both were labeled *nonlonely*.
Gerson and Perlman found that the situationally lonely were better communication senders than the chronically or nonlonely participants and
suggested that this was due to increased motivation arousal on their
part that was created by attributing their loneliness to unstable causes.

However, the chronically lonely and the situationally lonely were equally depressed, with levels of dysphoria in the moderate-to-severe range. In summary, although the distinction between situational–temporary loneliness and chronic–persistent loneliness appears a reasonable one, there is little empirical evidence to date to support the notion that they are differentially related to adjustment.

To best understand the relation between adolescent loneliness and psychological adjustment, we believe it is important to consider the larger clinical picture in which loneliness may be a part. One reason is that the emergence of gender differences in distress symptoms during adolescence might shed light on researchers' understanding of crucial aspects of loneliness during this period. A second reason is that loneliness shares a number of features with depression and dysthymia, common adolescent disorders. According to Peplau and Perlman (1982b), there are three essential characteristics of loneliness. First, it results from deficiencies in social relationships. Although deficits in social relationships are not a defining feature of depression, current conceptualizations of the etiology and maintenance of depression have placed a strong emphasis on the role of social skills deficits and dysfunctional interpersonal behaviors (e.g., Coyne, 1976; Youngren & Lewinsohn, 1980), as well as the protective features of social support (Cohen & Wills, 1985). Second, as previously noted, loneliness represents a subjective experience. Although experts consider clinical depression to be more than a subjective state (with observable somatic, motivational, cognitive, and affective symptoms), cognitive models of depression etiology (e.g., Abramson, Metalsky, & Alloy, 1989; Beck, 1967) place a strong emphasis on the role of interpretive processes and the subjective, rather than the objective, evaluation of one's circumstances. Third, loneliness is by definition unpleasant and emotionally distressing, and this is clearly similar to the negative affectivity that characterizes depression, dysthymia, and anxiety.

Despite these similarities, depression and loneliness are not the same construct. Correlations between the two are moderately high (rs ranging from the .40s to .60s in high school students; Koenig et al., 1994; Moore & Schultz, 1983) but certainly less than perfect. They do share a common emotional distress component, but Jackson and Cochran (1991) found that the relationship between the two remained strong, even when the effect of emotional distress was statistically controlled. Using structural equation modeling and a short-term longitudinal design to explore the causal links between loneliness and depression, Weeks, Michela, Peplau, and Bragg (1980) found that the two were distinct constructs and that neither one caused the other. More likely, their findings suggested that the two shared a common cause. Poor social skills are often suggested as a candidate for this common component, leading first to loneliness and then to depression. Another candidate might be explanatory style, or the way people understand and interpret personal failures (Young, 1982). Anderson et al. (1983) and Anderson and Riger (1991) found that both lonely people and depressed people attributed interpersonal failures to internal causes (traits or abilities) that they believed to be uncontrollable and stable over time, though this association was stronger for loneliness. Clearly, loneliness is a more circumscribed phenomenon than clinical depression, a disorder in which heterogeneity and multiple causal pathways are often noted (Abramson et al., 1989).

Plan for the Chapter: Gender and Adolescent Loneliness

The purpose of this chapter is to consider the relation between adolescent loneliness and psychological adjustment, with a particular focus on the role of gender. Having already briefly touched on the literature examining gender differences in psychological symptoms and disorders during adolescence, we begin this section by reviewing the literature on gender differences in severity of self-reported loneliness. Do such differences exist and are they similar to those found for other emotional distress symptoms? Child, adolescent, and to some extent college populations are considered to evaluate whether these relationships are unique to adolescence. Second, we review the literature on gender and the correlates of adolescent loneliness, considering the possibility that loneliness may be associated with different psychosocial variables for male and female adolescents. After identifying several important issues that have not yet been considered, we present new data from our own research to examine some of these emerging issues and questions.

Gender Differences in Loneliness Severity

At first glance, the research on gender differences in severity of loneliness appears inconsistent and equivocal. However, when studies are divided on the basis of participant age, a pattern emerges (see Table 15.1). Studies of children consistently report an absence of gender differences in loneliness. Reports by Asher et al. (1984), Parkhurst and Asher (1992), Renshaw and Brown (1993), Rotenberg and Whitney (1992), and K. H. Rubin et al. (1993) all examined self-reported loneliness as a function of gender in children ranging in grade from three to eight. In all of these studies, some version of the Asher et al. loneliness and dissatisfaction scale was used.

Table 15.1. Results of Studies Examining Gender Differences in Self-Reported Loneliness

Study	Ages (in Years)	Grades	Sample Size M	Sample Size F	Measure of Loneliness	Outcome	Comments
Children							
Asher et al. (1984)	—	3rd–6th	261	242	Asher-O	ns	
Parkhurst & Asher (1992)	—	7th–8th	231	219	Asher-R	ns	
Renshaw & Brown (1993)	7–12	3rd–6th	66	62	Asher-R	ns	
Rotenberg & Whitney (1992)	11–13	6th–7th	37	47	Asher-O	ns	
K. H. Rubin et al. (1993)	10.6 (mean age)	5th	75	71	Asher-O	ns	
Adolescents							
Allen et al. (1994)	—	9th–12th	935	980	UCLA-R	M > F	
Archibald et al. (1995)	14–17	10th	116	101	UCLA-R	F > M	
Avery (1982)	12–18	7th–12th	137	88	UCLA-O	M > F	
Brage et al. (1993)	11–18	7th–12th	62	94	Woodward	ns	
M. H. Davis & Franzoi (1986)	—	9th–12th	171	161	UCLA-Short	M > F	
Franzoi & M. H. Davis (1985)	16 (mean age)	9th–12th	177	173	UCLA-Short	ns	Trend ($p < .10$) for M > F

(Continued)

Table 15.1. (*Continued*)

Study	Ages (in Years)	Grades	Sample Size M	Sample Size F	Measure of Loneliness	Outcome	Comments
Interbitzen-Pisaruk et al. (1992)	13–16	9th	107	79	UCLA-R	ns	Trend for M > F
Koenig et al. (1994)	14–18	9th–12th	152	245	UCLA-R	ns	Controlling for denial of distress, trend for M > F
Lonigan et al. (1994)	—	9th–12th	185	185	UCLA-R	M > F	
Marcoen et al. (1987)	—	5th–11th	222	222	LLCA	ns	
Moore & Schultz (1983)	14–19	9th–12th	45	54	UCLA-R	ns	
Page (1990)	15.3 (mean age)	9th–12th	654	630	UCLA-R	M > F	
van Buskirk & Duke (1991)	14–17	—	16	17	UCLA-R	ns	
Young adults							
Berg & Peplau (1982)	—	College	89	129	UCLA-R	ns	Introductory psychology
Booth (1983)	18–43	—	—	—	UCLA-R	M > F	N = 57
Green & Wildermuth (1993)	17–29	College (years 1–4)	44	51	UCLA-R	ns	
Jackson & Cochran (1991)	17–26	College (years 1–2)	146	147	UCLA-R	ns	
Maroldo (1981)	18–40	—	157	155	UCLA-O	ns	
Newcomb & Bentler (1986)	19–24	—	221	518	UCLA-R, DLS	ns	Trend F > M in family and romantic relationships

Pierce et al. (1991)	—	College	94	116	UCLA-R	ns	Introductory psychology
Rotenberg & Morrison (1993)	—	College	229	314	UCLA-R	M > F	Introductory psychology
Russell et al. (1978)	—	College	76	151	UCLA-O	ns	Introductory psychology
Russell et al. (1980, Study 1)	—	College (year 1)	64	98	UCLA-R	M > F	Introductory psychology
Russell et al. (1980, Study 2)	—	College	107	130	UCLA-R	ns	Psychology courses
Schultz & Moore (1986)	—	College	59	53	UCLA-R	M > F	Introductory psychology
Solano (1980)	18–22	—	151	107	UCLA-O	ns	
Solano et al. (1982, Study 1)	—	College (years 1–4)	37	38	UCLA-O	ns	Trend ($p < .10$) for M > F
Solano et al. (1982, Study 2)	—	College	—	—	UCLA-O	ns	Introductory psychology, $N = 246$
Adolescents and adults							
Schultz & Moore (1988)	—	—	127	137	UCLA-R	M > F	High school, college, retirees

Note. Dashes indicate data not available. Asher-O (Original Asher Scale); Asher-R (Revised Asher Scale for middle-school students); DLS (Differential Loneliness Scale); LLCA (Louvain Loneliness Scale for Children and Adolescents); UCLA-O (Original UCLA Loneliness Scale); UCLA-R (Revised UCLA Loneliness Scale); UCLA-Short (Revised UCLA Loneliness Scale-Short form); Woodward (Woodward Loneliness Inventory); M = male; F = female; *ns* = not significant.

Three studies used the original 1984 version (Asher et al., 1984; Rotenberg & Whitney, 1992; K. H. Rubin et al., 1993), one study used Asher and Wheeler's (1985) adaptation (Renshaw & Brown, 1993), and one study used the 1985 adaptation with modifications (Parkhurst & Asher, 1992). Although none of these studies reported mean scores for boys and girls separately (and thus there is no way to determine whether there is a pattern to the direction of the means), all reports indicated the absence of statistically significant differences. In one case (Rubin et al., 1993), a significant Gender × Peer Rating effect emerged. The authors reported that boys rated as withdrawn were lonelier than boys rated as aggressive or average, whereas no differences were found between the three groups of girls. Although it is not clear whether post hoc tests directly comparing boys and girls were conducted, the pattern of means is of interest. Girls rated as aggressive reported higher loneliness scores than boys rated as aggressive ($Ms = 33.2$ vs. 26.25), whereas boys rated as withdrawn reported higher loneliness scores than girls rated as withdrawn ($Ms = 37.33$ vs. 29.56). However, consistent with other studies, boys and girls rated as average reported virtually identical loneliness scores ($Ms = 30.77$ vs. 29.12, for boys and girls, respectively).

If there is a gender difference in loneliness, it emerges during the period of adolescence. Of the thirteen studies we identified that reported loneliness scores for male and female adolescents on the basis of self-report questionnaires, five studies (Allen, Page, Moore, & Hewitt, 1994; Avery, 1982; M. H. Davis & Franzoi, 1986; Lonigan, Kistner, Risi, & Balthazor, 1994; Page, 1990) clearly found boys to be significantly lonelier than girls. All utilized some version of the UCLA Loneliness Scale. (Avery [1982] used the original form [Russell, Peplau, & Ferguson, 1978], M. H. Davis & Franzoi [1986] used the short form of the R-UCLA [Russell et al., 1978], and the four remaining studies used the R-UCLA [Russell et al., 1980].) Moreover, of the eight remaining studies, a marginally significant tendency for male adolescents to score higher than female adolescents occurred in two studies (Franzoi & M. H. Davis, 1985; Inderbitzen-Pisaruk et al., 1992), and a third study (Koenig et al., 1994) also reported this trend once the tendency to deny emotional distress was statistically controlled. Each of these studies also used a version of the UCLA (the revised version in Inderbitzen-Pisaruk et al., 1992, and Koenig et al., 1994, and the short form in Franzoi & Davis, 1985).

Of the thirteen previously identified studies, only four studies (Brage, Meredith, & Woodward, 1993; Marcoen et al., 1987; Moore & Schultz, 1983; van Buskirk & Duke, 1991) found a complete absence of gender differences. Two of these studies (Moore & Schultz, 1983; van Buskirk &

Duke, 1991) used the R-UCLA Scale. However, small sample sizes ($n = 33$ for van Buskirk & Duke, 1991, and $n = 100$ for Moore & Schultz, 1983) may have limited the ability to detect differences. (Means are not reported in either study, so it is not possible to determine whether they fall in the predicted direction.) Also, no gender differences were found in the two studies using alternate questionnaires (Brage et al. [1993] using the Woodward Loneliness Scale [Woodward, 1988], and Marcoen et al. [1987] using their Louvain Loneliness Scale). However, Marcoen et al. (1987) did report a significant Gender × Age interaction for the Peer subscale. The authors did not examine the main effects of gender at each grade (Grades 5, 7, 9, and 11), but they did indicate that a developmental trend toward decreased peer-related loneliness occurred at an earlier age for girls than it did for boys. This suggests less peer-related loneliness for girls as they age and progress from elementary to high school.

Finally, in only one of the 13 studies of adolescents (Archibald et al., 1995) were girls found to be lonelier than boys (using the R-UCLA Scale). Thus, although the findings are not completely consistent, the overall pattern suggests a difference between the childhood and adolescent studies, with the emergence of a gender difference in loneliness during adolescence. Although the effect may be small, adolescent boys appear to be lonelier than adolescent girls.

It is not clear whether these differences persist into late adolescence/ young adulthood. Again, several studies of college students have found college men to score higher (e.g., Booth, 1983; Borys & Perlman, 1985; Rotenberg & Morrison, 1993; Russell et al., 1980, Study 1; Schultz & Moore, 1986), or tend to score higher (Solano, Batten, & Parish, 1982, Study 1, $p < .07$), on the R-UCLA than college women. Schultz and Moore also found male participants to be lonelier than female participants in a sample that combined adolescents with college and older adults. However, other studies have failed to find gender differences by using this scale (Berg & Peplau, 1982; Green & Wildermuth, 1993; Jackson & Cochran, 1991; Newcomb & Bentler, 1986; Pierce, Sarason, & Sarason, 1991; Russell et al., 1980, Study 2; Solano et al., 1982, Study 2). Using an alternate scale, Solano (1980) also found men to be lonelier than women on the total score and several subscale scores of the Belcher Extended Loneliness Scale (Belcher, 1973). In one of only two studies to find women scoring higher than men, Newcomb and Bentler (1986) reported a tendency ($p < .10$) for women to score higher on two subscales (Familial and Romantic Relationships) of the Differential Loneliness Scale (Schmidt & Sermat, 1983). However, this study had a large number of participants ($N = 739$), and a close examination of the correlations indicates that the relation between gender and loneliness was extremely weak (both point-biserial $rs = .07$).

Overall, gender differences appear in about 50% of the studies, but they are always in the same direction. That is, with only one true exception (Archibald et al., 1985), it is always male participants who report higher levels of loneliness.

The change from equal levels of loneliness among girls and boys in childhood to increased relative loneliness on the part of boys during adolescence suggests the presence of a developmental shift. It is important to note, however, that this does not necessarily indicate that boys are experiencing increased loneliness as they make the transition into adolescence. In the first place, if there is a change, it could also be due to decreased loneliness on the part of girls as they make this transition. Marcoen et al's. (1987) findings that girls experience decreased peer-related loneliness at an earlier age than do boys would support such an hypothesis. Second, statements about shifts and changes will require longitudinal studies that follow children across this developmental period, and such studies have not yet been reported.

In addition, the apparent shift in gender ratios could actually be a methodological artifact attributable to the use of different scales with children versus adolescents. All of the research on children's loneliness used the Asher Loneliness and Dissatisfaction scale, whereas the majority of studies in adolescent and young adult populations utilized the UCLA Scale. On the one hand, a cursory examination of the items in the Asher Scale compared with those in the R-UCLA suggests that there is considerable construct overlap. For example, both have items tapping self-labeled loneliness (e.g., "I'm lonely" or "I do not feel alone"), friendships (e.g., "I have lots of friends" or "I lack companionship"), social support (e.g., "There's nobody I can go to when I need help" or "There is no one I can turn to"), and social inadequacy (e.g., "I'm good at working with other children" or "I can find companionship when I want it"). On the other hand, there are also notable differences. Although the Asher scale focuses predominantely on the presence of friends (and the 1985 revision asks only about friendships at school, thus avoiding loneliness that may stem from family relationships), the R-UCLA also taps feelings of alienation (e.g., "I feel in tune with the people around me") and dissatisfaction with the intimacy of one's social relationships (e.g., "My social relationships are superficial"). Clearly, the phenomenological experience of loneliness is likely to change with maturity and the development of social agendas and cognitive abilities. Failure to assess these more cognitively sophisticated aspects of loneliness may indicate a failure to understand the experience in older participants. The use of the same or a similar scale for all participants would address this methodological continuity problem but might fail to capture these qualitative differences. Unfortunately, until the literature in this area can report consistent findings for children and adolescents across a variety of loneliness measures, it may not be possible to determine conclusively whether there is a real shift in gender ratios for loneliness at the transition to adolescence.

Explanations for Findings

In considering the findings just reviewed, two important questions arise. First, what might account for teenage girls' lower likelihood of being lonely relative to that of boys? Second, why does this change occur at the transition from childhood to adolescence? As previously mentioned, changes in amount of time spent alone may play a role in adolescents' increased loneliness. Research on older children and adolescents indicates that with age, there is not only an increased amount of time spent alone but also a decreased amount of time spent with families. For example, in a study of children aged 9 to 15, Larson and Richards (1991) found that older students spent about half as much time with their families as did the younger students. However, the nature of this change was different for boys versus girls. Although all adolescents spent more time alone and less time with family than did children, this pattern was stronger for boys than it was for girls (Richards & Larson, 1989). Moreover, male adolescents replaced family time with time spent alone, whereas female adolescents replaced it with time spent with peers (Larson & Richards, 1991). These findings correspond to those of Montemayor (1982), who found that among 10th-grade students, time spent with parents was negatively correlated with time spent alone for male teens, and time spent with peers for female teens. In addition, girls are more social than boys, and this gap widens with adolescence. Rafaelli and Duckett (1989) found that the increased social time of girls relative to boys could be explained by the increased amount of time girls spend talking with friends. Not only do girls spend more time talking to their friends, but compared with boys' peer conversations, girls were more likely to be discussing people or personal concerns. In other words, even girls' conversations were more interpersonally focused.

Taken together, these data suggest that the emergence of gender differences in severity of adolescent loneliness may be a function of both increased loneliness on the part of boys and decreased loneliness or minimized increases on the part of girls. That is, at the same time as teenage boys begin to spend less time with their families (who are likely to have provided some refuge from loneliness), they are also spending an increased amount of time pursuing solitary activities – time that is typically experienced as lonely (see Larson, this volume, for an alternative interpretation). Girls, on the other hand, replace their family support with peer support and in fact, spend increased amounts of time talking to peers and engaging in interpersonally focused activities. Although it is not clear whether this could actually decrease girls' loneliness, it is likely to at least attenuate potential increases.

Gender and the Correlates of Adolescent Loneliness

Teenage boys experience more loneliness than teenage girls. Nevertheless, many teenage girls are lonely, and the role of gender in the experience of adolescent loneliness remains an important but relatively unexplored question. More specifically, it might be asked whether the experience of loneliness is qualitatively different for boys than it is for girls. For example, is being lonely more distressful or more personally meaningful to one gender than the other? One way to explore this is to examine the pattern of correlations between loneliness and experiential variables. Several studies have reported gender differences in the correlates of adolescent loneliness. Some suggest that there might be a greater association between loneliness and distress among male adolescents. For example, in a study of college students, Schultz and Moore (1986) reported a greater association between the severity and frequency of loneliness and anxiety, happiness, life satisfaction, and negative self-evaluation among male than female students. Rauste-Von Wright and Von Wright (1992) reported that in their sample of Finnish adolescents, lonely boys had higher levels of psychosomatic complaints than nonlonely boys, a relationship that was not present for girls. Similarly, studies of depressed adolescents indicate that mild depression is associated with more loneliness (Koenig et al., 1994) and more social isolation (Larson, Raffaelli, Richards, Ham, & Jewell, 1990) for boys than it is for girls. In contrast though, Lonigan, Kistner, Risi, and Balthazor (1994) reported that hopelessness was associated with loneliness more for girls than for boys.

In addition, there may also be gender differences in the behaviors associated with adolescent loneliness. Some studies do suggest that girls' loneliness has a stronger link to interpersonal functioning. Although Inderbitzen-Pisaruk et al. (1992) found that both boys' and girls' loneliness was associated with poor social skills, girls' loneliness was best predicted by a combination of variables that included social anxiety and attributions for interpersonal situations, whereas boys' loneliness was best predicted by a combination of variables that included low self-esteem and attributions for noninterpersonal situations. Research by Koenig et al. (1994) supports the notion that teenage girls' use of interpersonally based coping may serve as a buffer against loneliness. The authors used a five-item scale to assess the extent to which teenagers utilized social support to cope with feelings of sadness. Use of this strategy, which was more likely to be endorsed by girls than by boys, was not correlated with current depressive symptoms; however, it was negatively correlated with loneliness.

Similarly, several studies point more directly to gender differences in the role of disclosure processes in loneliness. Two studies have found adolescent loneliness to be associated with self-disclosure to peers for girls but not for boys (Franzoi & M. H. Davis, 1985; M. H. Davis & Franzoi, 1986). More specifically, Rotenberg and Whitney (1992) found that variations in the intimacy of disclosures were associated with preadolescents' reports of loneliness but that the nature of these norm violations regarding self-disclosure differed by gender. That is, relative to their nonlonely peers, lonely boys were more likely to be less intimate in their disclosures to opposite sex partners, whereas lonely girls were more likely to be overly intimate in their disclosures to same-sex partners.

Overall, there is not yet enough evidence at this point to suggest a greater association between adolescent loneliness and emotional distress for one gender versus the other. However, these studies do suggest that adolescent loneliness in girls may have a stronger link to problems with peer relationships than loneliness in boys. However, this conclusion should be treated with caution, as some evidence for inappropriate interpersonal behavior among lonely boys has also been reported. Of course, correlational studies suggest variables that might be differentially related to the onset or maintenance of loneliness. However, these must remain suggestions; in the absence of prospective longitudinal studies, it is not determine whether loneliness is a cause or consequence of distress, poor interpersonal skill, or both. Indeed, one longitudinal study (M. H. Davis & Franzoi, 1986) suggests that the relationship is likely reciprocal, with loneliness leading to poor relationships and poor relationships leading to loneliness.

Remaining Questions and Empirical Study

One problem with the current research on loneliness and adjustment is that it fails to consider more serious forms of maladjustment. Typically, researchers have asked adolescents to complete a loneliness inventory concurrently with one or more symptom inventories. Consequently, little is known about the relation between loneliness and more serious forms of psychopathology or other aspects of adjustment. A second limitation of the current body of research is that it fails to consider whether the loneliness that is being assessed is a temporary phenomenon or part of a more stable condition.

In the following section, we present data from a longitudinal study of adolescent mental health that addresses some of these questions. One purpose of the current study was to consider the relation between adolescent loneliness and other aspects of psychological adjustment. In addition to measures of depression and anxiety symptoms, we also assessed clinical psychiatric syndromes and academic functioning. In addition, loneliness was assessed at two points in time, initially during high school and then 2 1/2 years later. In this way, we were able to consider two important questions. First, does adolescent loneliness predict emotional distress at a later point in time? Second, what kind of adjustment is associated with chronic, rather than temporary loneliness? Of course, gender differences in the patterns of these relationships remained a central focus.

During the spring semester of 1991, 397 public high school students completed a series of self-report questionnaires as part of a larger study on adolescent adjustment. The sample was from a mixed suburban–rural district outside a major metropolitan area in the southeast. Individuals who participated ranged in age from 14 to 18, with grade distribution as follows: 27% in Grade 9, 26% in Grade 10, 29% in Grade 11, and 18% in Grade 12. Participants were predominantly White (91%), Protestant (84%), and from middle- to lower-middle socioeconomic groups (Hollingshead & Redlich, 1958). Approximately two thirds were female adolescents. (For a more detailed description of the sample, see Koenig et al., 1994, or Schwartz & Koenig, 1996.)

Questionnaire data were collected in three sessions across a 6-week period, and grade point averages (GPAs) were obtained through school records. Because of absences and missing data, 367 participants remained at the end of this first assessment period. All but 30 individuals gave permission to contact them at a future time.

Two and a half years later, in the summer and fall of 1993, we contacted approximately half of the original group of students ($n = 164$) who agreed to participate in a followup study. Virtually all participants who could be located agreed to take part. (This assessment period will be referred to as Time 2.) Statistical tests indicated that there were no differences between those participants who were included in the Time 2 study and those who were not, on initial measures of loneliness, emotional distress (our measures of depression and anxiety symptoms), or socioeconomic status.

At Time 2, participants were mailed a packet that contained self-report questionnaires and other survey materials. These were completed at home and returned to the examiner at the time of the interview. Participants were then individually interviewed using a structured clinical interview for current and past psychopathology.

The following questionnaires were completed at Time 1, Time 2, or both assessment periods. Loneliness was measured at both Time 1 and Time 2 using the R-UCLA (Russell et al., 1980).

Three self-report scales and a clinical interview were used to measure emotional distress. The Beck Depression Inventory (BDI; Beck, Ward, Mendelson, Mock, & Erbaugh, 1961), given at Time 1 and Time 2, is a 21-item self-report questionnaire that assesses the presence and severity of cognitive, affective, motivational, and physical symptoms of depression. Higher scores indicate greater symptom severity but do not necessarily indicate the presence of depressive disorder. It has been found to have adequate reliability and validity in repeated assessments across a wide variety of populations (Beck et al., 1988). The Beck Anxiety Inventory (BAI; Beck, Epstein, Brown, & Steer, 1988), also given at Time 1 and Time 2, contains 21 items that assess cognitive, behavioral, and physiological symptoms of anxiety. The measure has been shown to have high internal consistency and test–retest reliability over a period of 1 week (Beck et al., 1988). Finally, Time 1 participants also completed the Depression scale from the General Behavior Inventory (GBI-D; Depue, Krauss, Spoont, & Arbisi, 1989), a 45-item scale designed to assess frequent or chronic–intermittent unipolar (dysphoric) conditions. Thus, although the BDI assesses severity of current depressive symptoms, the GBI-D can capture low level but chronic depressive experiences. Respondents rate the frequency, duration, and changeability of each item over the course of their life. The GBI has been shown to have high internal consistancy among adolescents (Schwartz & Koenig, 1996), adequate test–retest reliability over a 12- to 16-week period, and high predictive power and specificity for diagnostic groups (according to interview diagnosis) in several university populations (Depue et al., 1989).

Several other important psychosocial variables associated with depression were also assessed. One of these was perceived social support, measured at Time 1 by the Perceived Emotional/Personal Support Scale (PEPSS; Slavin, 1991), a 36-item adolescent self-report measure. Individuals are asked to list three important relationships in each of three categories: family members, nonfamily adults, and friends. For this study, we used only the family (PEP-Fam) and friends (PEP-Friend) subscales. Participants then describe the emotional support provided by each relationship by answering four questions on a 4-point Likert-type scale. A subscale score is formed by averaging the ratings within each category, with higher scores indicating greater perceived support. PEPSS scores have been found to have adequate internal consistency (alphas rang- ing from .83–.91) and predictive validity (e.g., PEPSS scores are associ- ated with BDI and Children's Depression Inventory scores; Gladstone & Koenig, 1994; Slavin, 1991; Slavin & Rainer, 1990).

In addition, we also included several measures of depressive cognition. Explanatory style, the characteristic way individuals interpret positive and negative life events, was assessed at Time 1 by the Attributional Style Questionnaire (ASQ; Peterson et al., 1982). For each hypothetical situation, participants identify what they believe would be the main cause of the event if it happened to them, and then rate that cause with respect to its internality, globality, and stability. (Slight changes in wording were made so that the items would be understandable and meaningful to our adolescent population; see Schwartz and Koenig, 1996, for a description.) Two composite scores, ASQ-Neg and ASQ-Pos, were created, with higher scores indicating greater interpretive pessimism for ASQ-Neg and greater interpretive optimism for ASQ-Pos.

At Time 1, we also asssessed hopefulness about the future using the Hope Scale, an eight-item measure designed to assess two aspects of opti- mism – agency, the "sense of successful determination in meeting goals," and pathways, the "sense of being able to generate successful plans to meet one's goals" (Snyder et al., 1991). Adequate internal consistency has been reported for both subscales, with alphas of .71–.76 for agency and .63–.80 for pathways in college students (Snyder et al., 1991) and .75 and .73 for agency and pathways, respectively, in adolescents (Koenig & Embry, 1993). The Hope Scale has been found to be moderately correlated with other measures of general optimism and pessimism, such as the Life Orientation Test and the Hopelessness Scale, in high school and college student samples (Koenig & Embry, 1993; Snyder et al., 1991).

At Time 2, participants were interviewed by trained research assistants using the Structured Clinical Interview for the *Diagnostic and Statistical Manual of Mental Disorders* (3rd ed., revised), nonpatient edition (SCID; Sptizer, Williams, Gibbon, & First, 1990). This identified individuals who met criteria for clinical disorders either currently or in the past. All mod- ules, with the exception of somatoform disorders, were included. Thus, participants were screened for psychosis and assessed for mood disorders, anxiety disorders, substance use disorders, and eating disorders. An addi- tional module assessing conduct disorder, patterned after the Diagnostic Interview for Children, was also administered.

Finally, academic achievement was measured in two ways. At Time 1, GPA was obtained through school records. At Time 2, participants were asked to provide information on their current school status. Specifically, at the Time 2 assessment, all but the original first-year students had graduated from high school. These individuals were asked if they were now attending college or were matriculating in the fall. For the purposes of this study, all forms of postsecondary education (i.e., including vocational and technical school, full or at least half time) were considered to be participation in postsecondary education.

Correlates of Loneliness in Adolescent Boys and Girls

Following Inderbitzen-Pisaruk et al. (1992), we examined whether there were cross-gender similarities in the relation between loneliness and depressive symptoms, anxiety symptoms, grades, and other relevant psychosocial variables. Two stepwise regression analyses – one for boys and one for girls – were performed by using Time 1 R-UCLA scores as the dependent variable and the Time 1 variables as the predictors (see Table 15.2). Our results indicated that for both boys and girls, determination regarding one's future goals (hope–agency), depressive symptoms (BDI for boys and GBI-D for girls), and social support from friends (PEP-Friend) were selected as significant predictors. Although there were some differences in the order of selection and the strength of association, each of these variables made a unique contribution to the prediction of loneliness for both boys and girls. Thus, greater loneliness was associated with less optimistic determination, more dysphoria, and poorer perceived peer social support for both boys and girls. Moreover, for both genders, these variables predicted about 42% of the variability in loneliness scores. There were, however, some differences. Problem-solving optimism (hope–goal) and explanatory style (ASQ-Pos) were also significant predictors for girls, allowing us to account for an additional 5% of the variability in girls' loneliness scores.

In summary, these data provide only limited support for the notion that there are different correlates of loneliness for boys and girls. However, for girls, there were additional significant predictors, suggesting that a depressive cognitive style may be an important part of girls' loneliness.

Gender Differences in Loneliness Severity

Gender differences in loneliness for this sample were previously examined and reported in Koenig et al. (1994). Although boys scored higher than girls (*Ms* = 37.74 and 36.82 for boys and girls, respectively), the difference was not statistically significant.

Table 15.2. Standardized Regression Coefficients (betas), Partial Correlations (*prs*), and Increments in R^2 From Stepwise Regression Analyses Predicting Concurrent R-UCLA Scores for Girls and Boys

	Girls			Boys		
Step	**Predictors**	β	*pr*	**Predictors**	β	*pr*
Step 1	Agency	−.19	−.18*	Agency	−.37	−.39**
	$R^2 = .29$			$R^2 = .31$		
Step 2	PEP-Friend	−.28	−.35**	BDI	.32	.34**
	R^2 increment = .07			R^2 increment = .08		
Step 3	GBI-D	.25	.31**	PEP-Friend	−.19	−.24*
	R^2 increment = .07			R^2 increment = .03		
Step 4	Goal	−.24	−.24**			
	R^2 increment = .03					
Step 5	ASQ-POS	−.15	−.19*			
	R^2 increment = .02					
	Summary $R^2 = .48$			Summary $R^2 = .42$		

Note. Betas and *prs* are based on final equation. Agency = Hope Scale – Agency subscale; Goal = Hope Scale – Goal subscale; PEP-Friend = Perceived Emotional/Personal Suport Scale – friend subscale; ASQ-POS = Attributional Style Questionnaire – Positive events composite; BDI = Beck Depression Inventory; GBI-D = General Behavior Inventory – Depression subscale; R-UCLA = revised UCLA Loneliness Scale.
* $p < .01$.   ** $p < .001$.

Gender Differences Among the Severely Lonely

Although there were no gender differences in loneliness severity, we wondered whether there might be gender differences among the severely lonely. That is, we considered the possibility that mild or moderate levels of loneliness might represent more normative or transient loneliness experiences and that those individuals who were extremely lonely might be a qualitatively distinct group. If this were the case, might gender differences exist among these severely lonely individuals? To address this question, we first identified the extremes of our loneliness distribution by selecting those participants who fell into the upper or lower quartiles on the R-UCLA. (Recall that significant gender differences in severity did not emerge, and a chi-square analysis indicated no significant differences in the gender makeup of our lonely vs. nonlonely group.) Each predictor was then examined in a series of 2 × 2 analyses of variance (ANOVAs), comparing these severely lonely and nonlonely participants as a function of Gender. Statistically significant Gender × Loneliness interactions

Table 15.3. Means for Time 1 Major Dependent
Variables With Significant Gender × Loneliness
Interactions

	ASQ-NEG		Hope–Goal		GPA	
Participant	Boys	Girls	Boys	Girls	Boys	Girls
Nonlonely	4.15	3.97	13.54	13.34	2.76	2.91
Lonely	4.12	4.33	12.20	10.65	2.24	2.78

Note. ASQ-NEG = Attributional Style Questionnaire – Negative events composite (higher scores = greater attributional pessimism); Hope–Goal = Hope Scale – Goal subscale (higher scores = greater problem solving optimism); GPA = high school grade point average at Time 1.

($p < .05$) emerged only for the cognitive variables of hope–goal and ASQ-Neg (see Table 15.3). Simple effects tests indicated that lonely girls were the most attributionally pessimistic (i.e., the most likely to attribute negative outcomes to internal, stable, and global causes) and the least optimistic about finding ways to meet their goals. These results indicated that a depressive cognitive style characterized by attributional pessimism and the lack of problem-solving optimism are specific to extreme loneliness among girls.

Although none of the symptom or psychosocial variables were uniquely associated with loneliness for boys, we did find a tendency for extremely lonely boys to have poorer academic performance than their peers. That is, when we subjected the GPA scores to the same 2 × 2 ANOVA as indicated previously, a marginally significant ($p = .069$) Gender × Loneliness interaction emerged. Simple effects tests indicated that lonely boys tended to have poorer grades than girls, or nonlonely boys (see Table 15.3). In summary, although lonely girls are more likely to suffer from self-defeating and depressogenic cognitions, lonely boys tend to have more problems with their school functioning.

Loneliness and Outcomes at 2-Year Follow-Up

Loneliness and Achievement. Perhaps the most important question we can ask is whether adolescent loneliness is associated with serious negative consequences. Given the tendency for lonely boys to do poorly in school, we first began by examining the potential consequences to academic achievement. During the follow-up evaluation, participants who had completed 12th grade at the time of the Time 2 assessment (i.e.,

Table 15.4. Number of Time 2 College and Noncollege Attenders Who Were Lonely or Nonlonely During High School

	Women		Men	
Participant	College	Noncollege	College	Noncollege
Lonely	22	13	10	10
Nonlonely	20	19	21	6

10th, 11th, and 12th grade students at Time 1) were asked whether they were attending college. We performed two chi-square analyses for proportions – one for female participants and one for male participants – comparing lonely and nonlonely college attenders or nonattenders. No significant effects emerged for the female participants (see Table 15.4). That is, for girls, there was no relationship between high school loneliness and college attendance. Approximately 50% of college attenders had been lonely in high school, and about 50% of those not attending college had been lonely in high school. For the male participants, however, there was a statistically significant relationship ($p < .05$) between these two variables. Among the college attenders, only about one third had been lonely compared with two thirds who were nonlonely. Among those not attending college, the pattern was reversed (one thirds nonlonely compared with two thirds lonely). Thus, there were disproportionately more lonely high school boys among the group that was not attending college. (A simple correlation indicated that for boys, high school loneliness accounted for about 10% of the variability in college attendance [$r = -.31$, $p = .011$] whereas it accounted for virtually no variability for girls [$r = .06$, $p = .57$].) Of course, the nature of our design prevents us from drawing conclusions about causation. Nevertheless, these data do suggest that relative to nonlonely boys, extremely lonely boys tend to do poorly academically, and not surprisingly, they are at risk for not pursuing postsecondary education.

Loneliness and Mental Health. The experience of loneliness is obviously not a pleasant one. As the previous analyses suggest, it is associated with depressive symptoms and other negative experiences. Nevertheless, it might be transitory with no implications for future mental health. To examine this question, we conducted a series of analyses using the Time 2 data as outcome measures. First, we examined whether lonely teens would be more depressed or anxious than nonlonely teens at Time 2 follow-up if we controlled for their initial levels of depression or anxiety symptoms. We performed two similar 2 (lonely vs. nonlonely) × 2 (male vs. female) analyses of covariance using the Time 2 depression (BDI) and anxiety (BAI) scores as dependent variables. In each analysis, Time 1 depression or anxiety scores, respectively, were entered as the covariate to control for initial levels of distress.

As expected, initial distress (i.e., Time 1 depression when predicting Time 2 depression and Time 1 anxiety when predicting Time 2 anxiety) accounted for significant variability in Time 2 distress scores. This is to be expected, as initial levels of symptoms are typically the best predictors of these same symptoms at follow-up. However, for depression, but not anxiety, a significant main effect of loneliness remained, even after initial Time 1 symptoms were controlled. This suggested two things. First, there was a relation between initial loneliness and follow-up depressive symptoms that could not be accounted for by a common distress factor. That is, despite the generally strong correlation between measures of anxiety and depression that are due to general distress, loneliness only predicted depressive symptoms. Second, because initial symptom levels were controlled, extreme loneliness was related to an increase in the level of depressive symptoms over time. Thus, for those teens who experienced extreme loneliness, this loneliness (or factors that were associated with it) served as a vulnerability for future depressive symptoms. Finally, there were no main effects or interactions involving gender. The relationship between extreme adolescent loneliness and future depressive symptoms was similar for both male and female adolescents.

Perhaps most important, we wanted to consider the question of whether loneliness was associated with more serious mental health problems. In other words, was there an association between loneliness and psychopathology that extended beyond symptom levels? To address this question, we first began by examining the psychiatric diagnoses of those participants who fell into the upper or lower quartiles on the R-UCLA at either Time 1 or Time 2. This produced no observable pattern, suggesting that loneliness assessed at any given point in time is not related to diagnosable psychopathology. Moreover, when we examined the test–retest reliability of the R-UCLA from Time 1 to Time 2, we noted that the scores were only mildly stable, with a test–retest correlation of .38 (.33 for girls and .46 for boys). Many participants, particularly girls, experienced transient loneliness. Consequently, we performed a second analysis in which we compared those participants who scored in the upper or lower quartiles on the R-UCLA at both Time 1 and Time 2. We labeled these

Table 15.5. Psychiatric Diagnoses for Participants Scoring in Upper (Lonely) or Lower (Nonlonely) Quartiles on R-UCLA at Both Time 1 and Time 2

	Consistently Nonlonely			Chronically Lonely	
Participant	Gender	Diagnosis	Participant	Gender	Diagnosis
1	F	No diagnosis	1	M	No diagnosis
2	F	No diagnosis	2	F	Major depression, conduct disorder, alcohol dependence, polysubstance dependence (all past)
3	M	Conduct disorder (past)	3	M	No diagnosis
4	F	Generalized anxiety disorder	4	F	Major depression (past)
5	F	No diagnosis	5	F	Major depression (past)
6	M	No diagnosis	6	M	Agoraphobia simple phobia
7	F	No diagnosis	7	M	Dysthymia (past) conduct disorder (past)
8	F	No diagnosis	8	F	Major depression (past)
9	M	Alcohol abuse	9	M	No diagnosis
10	M	No diagnosis	10	F	Major depression (past)
11	F	No diagnosis	11	F	No diagnosis
12	F	No diagnosis	12	F	Agoraphobia
13	F	No diagnosis	13	F	Major depression (past)
14	F	No diagnosis	14	F	Major depression (past)
15	M	Social phobia (past), simple phobia	15	F	No diagnosis
			16	M	No diagnosis

Note. Diagnoses based on Structured Clinical Interview for *DSM–III–R* Axis 1, excluding somatoform and including conduct disorders. Disorders are current unless otherwise noted. M = male; F = female; R-UCLA = raised UCLA Loneliness Scale.

participants the *chronically lonely* or the *consistently nonlonely*, respectively. The female : male proportion was equivalent for both groups. In this case, a striking pattern emerged (see Table 15.5).

Chronically lonely adolescents had a greater overall history of psychiatric disorder than those who were consistently nonlonely. Almost two thirds of the chronically lonely adolescents (63%), versus approximately one fourth (27%) of the consistently nonlonely adolescents, had a history of a psychiatric disorder. That is, the chronically lonely adolescents were more likely than the consistently nonlonely adolescents to have met clinical criteria for a psychiatric disorder at some time during their lives. In addition, the type of disorder they experienced was not random. Specifically, a larger percentage of the chronically lonely disturbed participants had a history of major affective disorder (i.e., the unipolar depressive conditions of major depression or dysthymia) compared with the consistently nonlonely disturbed participants. Among the lonely participants, 80% of those with a psychiatric disorder, or 50% of the total group, had a history of major affective disorder. Not one of the nonlonely adolescents had experienced an affective disorder. Finally, the pattern of diagnoses did not appear to be random with respect to gender. All but one of the participants with affective disorder (or 88% of the sample) were female, with a previous history of major depression. That is, of the 10 female participants with chronic loneliness, 7 (or 70%) had experienced a major affective disorder. Of the 6 male participants with chronic loneliness, only 1 (or 17%) did so.

Thus, these data suggest two things about the predictive utility of loneliness scores for emotional adjustment. First, loneliness does confer some vulnerability for both boys and girls to experience future depression, but not anxiety, symptoms. Second, loneliness is not highly stable across this period of time, and one-time assessments do not allow for the prediction of more severe psychopathology. Chronic loneliness, however, is related to clinical disorder, but given the nature of our data, it is not possible to determine whether loneliness preceded or followed the onset of psychopathology. Nevertheless, chronic loneliness appears to be a signal of more serious emotional problems, particularly for adolescent girls. Those who experience persistent loneliness are also likely to have experienced depression in its most severe form.

Conclusion

We began this chapter briefly reviewing the adolescent psychopathology literature, noting that disorders and symptoms characterized by emotional distress and discomfort rise markedly during this time. Not surprisingly, so too does the painful experience of loneliness. Are these two phenomena related, or is loneliness a developmentally normative experience with little connection to psychological adjustment? Our first approach to answering this question was to consider whether loneliness displayed patterns and shifts in gender ratios similar to those evidenced in surveys of psychopathology. Our review indicated that although no evidence of a gender difference in loneliness exists during childhood, a shift occurs with the transition to adolescence. The direction of the shift, however, is in the opposite direction to that which occurs for psychopathology. Although adolescent girls are more dysphoric and exhibit higher rates of psychopathologies characterized by depression, emotional distress and self-deprecation than do adolescent boys, adolescent boys appear to be lonelier than adolescent girls. In this way, loneliness is quite different from distress symptoms and internalizing emotional disorders.

Despite this gender difference in loneliness, we did not find such a difference in our own sample. However, also consistent with the larger body of literature for studies not finding boys to be significantly lonelier than girls, mean loneliness scores were in the predicted direction. In fact, previous analyses conducted on this sample (Koenig et al., 1994) indicated a marginally significant difference once the tendency to deny emotional distress was controlled.

A second way in which gender might play a role in adolescent loneliness is by moderating the association between loneliness and its experience. Some studies suggest that lonely adolescent girls may have more difficulty with interpersonal skills than nonlonely girls. Again, findings from our study did not support such a distinction, nor did it support a differential relationship between loneliness and emotional distress (at least as it was measured cross-sectionally). Although cognitive style variables added to the predictive power of the model for girls but not boys, distress and peer social support were related to loneliness for both genders. To some extent, differences between study findings often reflect the different variables included in the models being tested. For example, Inderbitzen-Pisaruk et al. (1992) found distress (i.e., anxiety) to be a predictor of loneliness for girls but not for boys, yet their measure tapped social anxiety, whereas ours tapped general anxiety. Moreover, the same variable may or may not emerge as a significant predictor in one versus another multiple regression model, depending on the other variables that are included in the equation. For example, anxiety may have emerged in the Inderbitzen-Pisaruk et al. model but not in ours because we included measures of depression, which entered the equation first and accounted for their shared variance with loneliness. Replication of findings across samples by using similar variables will be necessary before conclusions about differential predictors can be drawn. Finally, it is important to note that few studies of adolescent loneliness provide strict tests in which the predictive power of a variable is compared for boys versus girls. Some, like our study here, present common factors that predict for both genders; others report differential predictors for boys and girls. Still, indicating that a variable is a significant predictor for one gender but not for the other is different than indicating a significant difference in the predictive power of a variable for one gender versus the other. These strict tests are not typically provided and limit our ability to determine whether such differences exist.

Our second approach to considering the loneliness – adjustment relationship was to focus on extreme groups, reasoning that maladjustment would probably have its greatest relationship to either severe loneliness or chronic loneliness. With respect to the severely lonely teens, we identified certain gender differences that, in fact, appeared to relate somewhat to the nature of the difficulties they experienced at follow-up. Severely lonely boys tended to have poor grades. They were probably disenfranchised from the school environment, and thus it was not surprising that they were at risk for not pursuing postsecondary education. To our knowledge, this is the first study to relate loneliness to high school academic performance (but see Rotenberg & Morrison, 1993, and Olmstead, Guy, O'Malley, & Bentler, 1991, for a discussion of loneliness and college attendance). Severely lonely girls had more depressogenic cognitive styles; they were more likely to attribute failure to stable internal factors and to be more pessimistic about their ability to accomplish goals. Although severe loneliness was related to future depression symptoms for both boys and girls, depression was the most common psychological disorder among the chronically lonely girls.

Chronicity of loneliness is not a variable that has received much study in the adolescent literature, despite the fact that the issue was raised at least 15 years ago. However, chronicity is a dimension that probably distinguishes normative from abnormal loneliness and forms the link between loneliness and psychopathology. Our own data provided the opportunity to examine the stability of loneliness over a long period of time and an important developmental transition (i.e., the transition out of high school). Loneliness was not highly stable during this time, and associations with diagnosable psychopathology were only possible when we identified individuals who were severely lonely at both time points. This suggests that one-shot loneliness assessments may correlate with adolescents' other negative feelings, beliefs, and behaviors at the time but are not likely to provide much information about significant maladaptation. Though we were not able to measure loneliness continu-ally over the $2^1/_2$-year span (as suggested by Young's, 1982, definition), we suspect that by identifying those adolescents in the upper quartile at both time points, we captured those most likely to have experienced long loneliness durations. Unlike Moore and Schultz (1983), who found ado-lescent females to experience longer periods of loneliness than adolescent males (but who did not describe the way in which duration was defined or measured), the proportion of girls in the chronically lonely group was equivalent to that of the nonlonely group, and similar to the proportion of girls in the sample as a whole. What we did observe, however, was a link not only between loneliness and maladjustment but with gender as well. The psychopathology most highly associated with chronic loneliness was unipolar depression, and this was particularly true for women.

In summary, it appears that although the pattern of gender differences in adolescent loneliness severity distinguishs loneliness from other dis-tress symptoms, longitudinal assessments (i.e., chronicity assessments or predictions from initial assessment to follow-up) link loneliness to dys-phoria and depression. One likely explanation for this connection is that both loneliness and depression result from poor social skills. Although this explanation is certainly reasonable, a variety of other complex processes and interactions between loneliness and depression could also exist. For example, early manifestations of a genetically inherited vulnerability for depression could interfere with the learning of social skills or could lead to other behavioral deficits that then inhibit friendships and encourage loneliness but that are not related to the onset of the depression itself. Alternatively, episodes of clinical depression early in life may interfere with the developmental course of social skill aquisition, which may lead to feelings of isolation and loneliness. More elaborate research designs will be necessarily to tease apart such complex interactions. Furthermore, methodologies and designs that allow researchers to link the childhood and adolescent research areas will help to provide a clearer picture of the developmental course of loneliness and its associations.

Acknowledgment

This research was supported in part by a grant to Linda J. Koenig from the University Research Committee of Emory University. We would like to thank the Cobb County School District and the students, teachers, and administrators of South Cobb High School for their help and participation. We would also like to thank Leanne Embry, Tracy Gladstone, Bonnie Moscovich, and Jennifer Schwartz for their assistance with the clinical interviews.

V | PROSPECTIVE

16 | Examination of Loneliness in Children–Adolescents and in Adults: Two Solitudes or Unified Enterprise?

DANIEL PERLMAN AND
MONICA A. LANDOLT

Loneliness cuts across the life cycle, affecting children, adolescents, midlife adults, and senior citizens. While loneliness is experienced by people of various ages, one can legitimately ask to what extent conceptual analyses and empirical studies of loneliness span different age periods of life or are limited to specific age ranges. Recently, Goossens and Hymel tried to assemble a symposium for the 1996 International Society for the Study of Behavioural Development meeting in Quebec, Canada to bring together child and adult loneliness researchers. Unfortunately, those individuals invited to speak on adult loneliness were not able to attend for various reasons, so only the researchers on loneliness in childhood and adolescence presented at the symposium. Goossens and Hymel's initial aim for the symposium and the difficulties they encountered in reaching it underscore that there are two camps of loneliness researchers – those concerned with loneliness in childhood and those concerned with loneliness in adulthood.

Stated broadly, our goal for this chapter is to examine points of continuity and discontinuity between childhood and adult loneliness literatures. In doing so, we hope to highlight and reflect on some of the themes we see in the childhood literature as represented in the current volume and to further illuminate the phenomenon of loneliness at all points in the life cycle. Consistent with our goal, we consider the following: (a) the evolution of work on loneliness since the 1930s to see historically how the study of loneliness in childhood and in adulthood has been intertwined, (b) several of the core loneliness topics to identify how they have been treated similarly or differently in the childhood and the adult literatures, (c) the uniquely developmental aspects of loneliness, and (d) the conclusions that can be drawn from our observations and comparisons.

Developmental Versus Adult Concerns in the Early Study of Loneliness

Sippola and Bukowski (this volume, p. 282) contend that "much of the research on loneliness in childhood and adolescence has been based on concepts and studies from the literature on adult social psychology, most notably the ideas proposed by Weiss (1973)." Hymel, Tarulli, Hayden Thomson, and Terrell-Deutsch (this volume) echo this view, seeing the increasing concern for children's loneliness as "inspired by efforts in the area of adult loneliness" (p. 80).

In line with these remarks, our sense is that the adult loneliness literature became prominent in the 1970s and 1980s and has been one important influence shaping current research on children's loneliness. Yet, we believe that throughout most of the twentieth century, there has been at least some concern with childhood and developmental aspects of loneliness.

Social science examination of loneliness dates back at least as far as Stoddard's 1932 volume *Lonely America*. Available bibliographies (see Peplau & Perlman, 1982a) list only a dozen or so psychologically oriented, English-language publications on loneliness prior to 1960. Another 64 identifiable articles and books appeared in the 1960s. Approximately 170 known items on loneliness were published in the 1970s, and over 750 more were published between 1980 and the summer of 1997. Thus, there has been a noticeable increase in the rate of publication on loneliness. The early 1970s mark what might be called the beginning of the contemporary era for loneliness research, the era that serves as the primary point of comparison in this chapter.

Rotenberg (this volume) provides data on the number of publications on childhood and adolescent loneliness in each biennial period since 1950. Rotenberg's Figure 1.1 shows that this number was quite low prior to the early 1980s and then rose noticeably. We believe the increase in publications on children's loneliness trailed slightly behind a detectable increase in the number of publications on loneliness in general. One might argue that Rotenberg's data show very little concern about childhood and adolescent loneliness prior to the early 1980s, but given the low rate of publication on loneliness in the mid-twentieth century, we contend that even before the 1980s, childhood loneliness was one ongoing strand of interest.

In examining the substantive interrelationships between the study of loneliness in childhood and adulthood, Zilboorg (1938) published an article on the personality attributes associated with loneliness in adulthood. He identified these as narcissism, megalomania, and hostility. However, in common with many of his early psychodynamically oriented colleagues, he saw loneliness as stemming from early childhood experiences. Foreshadowing the parental intrusion model discussed by Rotenberg (this volume), Zilboorg felt that overindulgence (coupled with frustration) in early childhood leads to later loneliness. In the late 1970s, Ellison (1978) returned to the question of the developmental factors leading to loneliness. He identified insecure attachment, interpersonal rejection, and poor social skills as the key variables.

Two very prominent contributors to the literature, Sullivan (1953), an early analyst, and Weiss, whose 1973 book had a seminal influence, addressed the developmental question of when loneliness can first be experienced. As others in this volume have noted, neither Sullivan nor Weiss believed that children could experience loneliness. Although not all early writers shared their view (see Bakwin, 1942; cf. Illingsworth, 1955), their position appears to have become dominant among adult loneliness researchers by the late 1970s.

Peplau and Perlman's (1982b) edited volume, which reflected the state of the field in the early 1980s, is often classified as a contribution to the adult loneliness literature. Review of the book's contents indicates, however, that it included a section on developmental aspects of loneliness, with chapters on loneliness in childhood and in adolescence by Z. Rubin (1982) and Brennan (1982), respectively. On the basis of his observations at his son's preschool, Rubin argued for a much earlier age of the onset of loneliness than was then thought to be the case. Brennan examined how the unique aspects of adolescence contribute to loneliness being acute at that period of the life cycle.

From these early writings, we conclude that concern with developmental issues extends throughout the history of the modern loneliness literature. Three focal questions for early analysts of loneliness were as follows: (a) What are the childhood antecedents of adult loneliness? (b) At what age can loneliness first be experienced? (c) Are there unique, age-related aspects of loneliness? Nonetheless, the late 1970s and the early 1980s were a period in which loneliness research, primarily focused on adults, gained a new legitimacy. That literature helped set the stage for the burgeoning of research on children's loneliness that Rotenberg's Figure 1.1 (this volume) shows as having begun in the early to mid-1980s.

The Treatment of Several Core Topics in the Childhood and Adult Loneliness Literatures

To illuminate some of the context from which the recent work on childhood loneliness emerged, and to have one framework for comparing the adult and childhood literatures, it is helpful to introduce briefly the foci of adult loneliness work in the 1970s and 1980s. Undoubtedly, some topics are omitted, but it is fair to say (see Perlman & Peplau, 1984; McWhirter, 1990b) that during the period from the mid-1970s until the late 1980s, authors dealt with the following matters:

- Definitions: At a conceptual level, what is loneliness?
- Measurement: How can loneliness be reliably and validly measured?
- Types: What are the different varieties or kinds of loneliness that exist? Is there a generic loneliness experience common in most cases of loneliness?
- Social problems: What social and personal problems accompany loneliness?
- Prevalence: How widespread is loneliness? In what demographic groups is it most common?
- Correlates: What correlates or antecedents (e.g., personality, social, or contextual) are associated with loneliness?
- Theoretical explanations and processes: What models or theoretical frameworks are available to help researchers best understand loneliness? What processes are involved with loneliness?
- Reactions, coping, and overcoming loneliness: How do people respond to and cope with loneliness? Do they naturally recover from being lonely? What are the interventions available to help people overcome loneliness? Do they work effectively?

Definition

Perlman and Peplau (1981) defined loneliness as "the unpleasant experience that occurs when a person's network of social relations is deficient in some important way, either quantitatively or qualitatively" (p. 31). In the current volume, some contributors allude to extant definitions of loneliness such as Perlman and Peplau's (see Crick, Grotpeter, & Rockhill, this volume); others offer their own definitions of loneliness (see Table 16.1). Consistent with definitions found in the adult literature, the definitions formulated with reference to childhood loneliness emphasize that loneliness results from being alone or isolated and feeling sad.

We believe that definitions of loneliness are seminal for at least two reasons. First, as Parkhurst and Hopmeyer note, theoretical explanations of loneliness are often based on how one understands to what loneliness refers. Second, to the extent that various definitions of loneliness refer to different underlying phenomena, the variables useful in empirically predicting loneliness undoubtedly partially depend on what definition is used. Along these lines, Burgess, Ladd, Kochenderfer, Lambert, and

Table 16.1. Definitions of Loneliness

Definition	Authors	Chapter/Page Number
Consistent with young children's own conception of loneliness, we similarly define this construct as being alone and feeling sad.	Burgess, Ladd, Kochenderfer, Lambert, and Birch	Chapter 6, p. 109
Loneliness is a negative feeling, resulting from a belief that others are unavailable when desired.	Cassidy and Berlin	Chapter 3, p. 34
Loneliness is a sad or aching sense of isolation; that is, of being alone, cutoff, or distanced from others. This is associated with a felt deprivation of, or longing for, association, contact, or closeness.	Parkhurst and Hopmeyer	Chapter 4, p. 56
Loneliness refers to feelings of sadness from being alone.	Sippola and Bukowski	Chapter 14, p. 280
[Loneliness is] a sad subjective state resulting from dissatisfaction with one's social experiences.	Youngblade, Berlin, and Belsky	Chapter 7, p. 135

Birch (this volume) raise the possibility that "a phenomenon such as loneliness can change as children grow older, and ... the factors underlying its expression can also change with age" (p. 133). Aspects of loneliness may truly be age-related, but one cannot expect the childhood and adult correlates of "loneliness" to be the same if the underlying phenomena at different ages are not the same. Although there are undoubtedly nuances in the different ways loneliness is conceptualized, we are heartened that there is considerable similarity in how child and adult researchers define the phenomenon of interest.

Measurement

In as much as measures are designed to operationalize constructs as they have been conceptually defined, definitions and measurement are interrelated. The development of the UCLA Loneliness Scale (Russell et al., 1978) in the late 1970s has often been credited as one force that lead to the flourishing of adult loneliness research at that time. The development of the Asher et al. (1984) Illinois Loneliness Scale (ILQ) undoubtedly played a similar role in the childhood loneliness literature.

The construction of the UCLA Scale began with an initial pool of 75 items written by psychologists to describe the experience of loneliness. These items were refined by item analysis and other techniques. Various forms of reliability and validity were determined. One particularly useful step taken by Russell et al. (1980) in developing the revised UCLA Scale was the innovative use of factor analysis to demonstrate that loneliness has discriminant validity vis-à-vis depression (Russell et al., 1980). Russell (1996) has continued to refine and develop the UCLA Scale. One controversy in the literature on the UCLA Scale has been its factor structure (Austin, 1983; Hartshorne, 1993; Knight & Chisholm, 1998; McWhirter, 1990a). Some studies have found more than one factor, but Russell (1996) contended that the best solution involves two method factors (corresponding to positively and negatively worded items) that combine into a bipolar global loneliness factor.

According to Terrell-Deutsch (this volume) "Much of the work in the development of the ILQ was inspired by the work of the team who developed the adult UCLA (University of California, Los Angeles) Loneliness Scale" (p. 14–15). Like the UCLA Scale, the ILQ has a high Cronbach alpha, which signifies its high internal consistency and is consistent with the Illinois group's (Asher et al., 1984) presentation of loneliness as a unidimensional concept. The Illinois group also marshaled considerable reliability and validity evidence, although perhaps less (especially in the discriminant validity area) than the UCLA group (Russell et al., 1978; 1980). Koenig and Abrams (this volume) note some differences in the content of the items on the UCLA and Illinois Scales, with the UCLA Scale doing more to tap feelings of alienation and dissatisfaction with the intimacy of relationships, and the Illinois scale dealing more with the presence of friends. These authors, however, perceive "considerable construct overlap" between the two scales.

Overall, we see substantial similarity in the leading techniques for measuring children's and adults' loneliness. As one would hope, these techniques are consistent with the conceptual definitions depicting loneliness as a sense of discomfort associated with social deficiencies. That childhood and adult researchers have come to define and operationalize loneliness in quite similar ways points to the possibility that the core aspects of loneliness are constant across the life cycle.

Types

Although the UCLA and Illinois loneliness measures are predicated on the assumption of a unidimensional construct (cf. Parkhurst &

Hopmeyer's conceptual views, this volume), other scholars have advanced multidimensional scales, and theorists have postulated different types of loneliness. Three important distinctions in the adult loneliness literature have been between state versus trait (or temporary vs. enduring) loneliness (Gerson & Perlman, 1979; Hojat, 1983; Shaver et al., 1985; Young, 1982); between loneliness in different interpersonal domains such as friendships, romantic relations, and family (Schmidt & Sermat, 1983); and between social and emotional loneliness. According to Weiss (1973), emotional loneliness stems from the absence of emotional attachments provided by intimate relationships. Social loneliness stems from the absence of an adequate social network.

Terrell-Deutsch (this volume) laments that "in the childhood loneliness literature, there has been a failure to differentiate between the emotional 'state' of loneliness and the 'trait' of loneliness" (p. 25). We would, however, contend that the childhood loneliness literature has investigated both trait and state loneliness. The response format of the Illinois Scale asks children how true various descriptive statements are of them, ranging from *always true* to *not at all true*. Presumably *always true* responses reflect a persisting, traitlike quality. Larson's (this volume) pager studies, which tap how participants are feeling at the time they are beeped, assess state loneliness.

Indicative of the temporal persistence of loneliness in adolescence, Koenig and Abrams (this volume) report a moderate correlation ($r = .38$) between teenagers' loneliness levels measured $2^{1}/_{2}$ years apart. Burgess et al. (this volume) cite a correlation of .41 between children's loneliness scores in the fall and spring of their year in kindergarten. Among college students tested over time periods ranging from 6 to 11 weeks, correlations have been considerably higher (range = .71 to .85; Jones & Moore, 1987; Shaver et al., 1985; Spitzberg & Hurt, 1987). Over longer periods, Sarason, Sarason, and Shearin (1986) reported 1 and 3 years test–retest correlations among a university sample of .68 and .64, respectively. De Jong Gierveld and Dykstra (1994) administered the De Jong Gierveld Loneliness Scale to 3,107 Dutch senior citizens at an interval of approximately 11 months. In that study, the test–retest correlation was .72. The differences in the magnitude of the correlations might be due to methodological factors such as the time interval between administrations or the loneliness measure used. More germane for a developmental analysis is the equally plausible possibility that loneliness is more stable for older adults than for young children and teenagers. Whichever interpretation one selects, moderately high temporal stability of loneliness is consistent with conceptual models that claim loneliness is due to a combination of stable individual difference and changing situational factors.

As for the other two dimensions of the adult literature, Goossens and Marcoen (this volume) have examined children's loneliness in different interpersonal contexts, and Hayden (1989) developed the Relational Provision Loneliness Scale to be consistent with Weiss's (1973) distinction (see Terrell-Deutsch, this volume) between emotional and social loneliness. Thus, it is evident that contributors to the childhood loneliness literature have been thinking about some of the same distinctions among varieties of loneliness as have been made in the adult literature. In the adult literature, these distinctions have stimulated modest lines of research (e.g., DiTommaso, & Spinner, 1997; Russell et al., 1984); in the childhood literature, they do not seem to be directing major streams of research.

Goossens and Marcoen (this volume) offer a multidimensional view of loneliness that appears to be unique in its inclusion of the dimensions of aversion and affinity for aloneness. We share Goossens and Marcoen's view that one should distinguish " 'loneliness' from 'aloneness.' " (p. 225). Having asserted the distinction of these phenomena, it is not altogether clear to us why Goossens and Marcoen then proceed to include affinity for aloneness as a dimension in their multidimensional loneliness model. We are not surprised that the aversion and affinity scales generally have low correlations with other measures of loneliness (see Terrell-Deutsch, this volume, Table 2.1). We would prefer to treat affinity for aloneness as a separate variable that moderates the relationship between the condition of solitude and the experience of loneliness.

Personal and Social Problems Associated With Loneliness

In the adult literature, loneliness has been associated with a variety of problems including physical illnesses and overuse of the health-care system (Lynch, 1977), nursing home admissions (Cutrona, Russell, & Wallace, 1997), age-adjusted morality rates (Niemi, 1979; Russell & Cutrona, 1985), suicide (Diamant & Windholz, 1981; Wenz, 1977), alcohol use (Akerlind & Hornquist, 1992; Sadava & Thompson, 1986), poor psychological adjustment (Jones & Carver, 1991), aggression (Check, Perlman, & Malamuth, 1985; Diamant & Windholz, 1981), and low grades in university (Booth, 1983; cf. Brennan & Auslander, 1979). A similar pattern is evident among children and adolescents. For instance, a study done in the 1970s reported a link between loneliness and both stealing and vandalism (Brennan & Auslander, 1979). In the present volume, Youngblade, Berlin, and Belsky report associations between loneliness and aggressive behavior; Koenig and Abrams (this volume) found that lonely students do less well academically (see also Larson, this volume) and are more prone toward psychiatric disturbances. Complementing Koenig and Abrams's mental health findings, Cassidy and Berlin conclude that "independent observers are strikingly consistent in portraying lonely children as less well adjusted" (p. 36), and Larson found that "feeling lonely in the peer context was clearly correlated with poorer adjustment" (p. 257).

So, again in this domain, a basic similarity between the childhood and the adult literatures is seen. We do, however, believe that the prevalence of the links between loneliness and specific problems may be age linked. For instance, the tendency of lonely individuals to "run away from home" is probably a phenomena most common in adolescence (Brennan & Auslander, 1979). The health correlates of loneliness are most likely more pronounced in the later phases of the life cycle (Schmitt & Kurdek, 1985). Childhood, adolescence, and young adulthood are the periods when people are most likely to be involved in educational pursuits. So it is at those times that poor academic performance is apt to be associated with loneliness.

Prevalence of Loneliness

In a representative sampling of U.S. citizens, 26% said they had felt "very lonely or remote from other people" in the past few weeks (Weiss, 1973, p. 23). Naturally, survey results vary as a function of the exact wording of the question posed to respondents. Asked if they have ever been lonely in their lives, more people answer affirmatively. Asked if they see themselves as a "lonely person," fewer people respond affirmatively.

Adult loneliness researchers have demonstrated that loneliness varies as a function of several demographic variables and life experiences (see Perlman & Peplau, 1984, and McWhirter, 1990b, for further references and more detailed evidence). For instance, married individuals are less likely to report loneliness than single or divorced individuals. Several studies have found that loneliness is more prevalent among lower income groups. A large scale National Institute of Mental Health survey found that Blacks were more apt to report loneliness than Whites (L. Radloff, personal communication, 1982). European studies have found nationality differences, with, for example, southern Europeans being more prone to loneliness than northern Europeans (Jylha & Jokela, 1990). Childhood and adolescent researchers appear to have generally been less interested than adult researchers in demographic predictors of loneliness. They have, however, examined at least two factors.

Age. For the purposes of this chapter, age is an especially important correlate of loneliness. The media often portray old age as a time of loneliness. Contrary to this stereotype, young adulthood is actual a peak

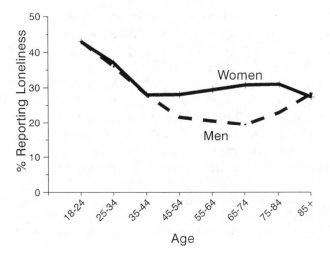

Figure 16.1. Age trends in loneliness.

period for loneliness. This can be seen in Figure 16.1, which is based on an unweighted aggregation of male and female respondents ($N = 18,682$) from six surveys containing similar self-labeling questions about loneliness (Perlman, 1991). In each of these surveys, there were both younger and older adult respondents. As seen in the figure, loneliness appears to have a "backward" check-shaped curve, dropping from young adulthood through middle age and then seeming to increase again slightly. The shape of the curve is influenced by gender, and there is some controversy over exactly what happens in later life. In other studies restricted to just older adults (aged 55+), findings on the association between age and loneliness vary, some studies showing marked increases, others showing none at all. Examination of these findings suggests that the magnitude of any possible increase in loneliness among older adults may depend on the proportions of widowed and incapacitated people in older subgroups (Townsend, 1968).

Contributors to this volume address the questions of when does loneliness first appear in childhood and how does it change over time. We believe that one of the main advances underscored by this volume and related work is that the age of onset of loneliness is much earlier than writers in the 1950s, 1960s, and 1970s presumed. Parkhurst and Hopmeyer (this volume) speculate that loneliness may actually be experienced during infancy, although infants clearly would not have the necessary cognitive and verbal abilities to label the emotion. Parkhurst and Hopmeyer assert that the strange situation paradigm, commonly used by researchers to assess attachment in children as young as 9 months of age (e.g., Ainsworth & Bell, 1970), could conceivably be eliciting loneliness responses in children, as well as anxiety and fear.

Regardless of exactly how early loneliness is experienced, we are convinced that it is well before the age Sullivan (1953), Weiss (1973), and others have claimed. Our conclusion is based on at least three points. First, a number of authors in this collection (e.g., Parkhurst & Hopmeyer) have referred to the Cassidy and Asher (1992) finding that the majority of children at a very early age (as young as age 5) seem to understand the nature of loneliness; in some cases, this may stem from their personal experience with the emotion. Along these same lines, Hymel et al. (this volume) were able to get 8-year-olds to define and describe loneliness. Second, the internal consistency of answers to the ILQ has been established in studies involving children as young as those in kindergarten. This testifies that something, presumably loneliness, is being reliably assessed. Finally, even at that age, scores on the ILQ are relating to other factors as one might expect. This provides a form of construct validity to the measure and gives encouragement that it is measuring what it was designed to assess.

After children begin experiencing loneliness, Larson (this volume) found that the aggregated frequency of feeling lonely is relatively constant between Grades 5 and 9. At both Grades 5 and 9, respondents indicated they were lonely in 23% of their daily reports. From Grade 5 until the end of high school, Goossens and Marcoen (this volume) conclude "an increasing trend was found for loneliness as experienced in the relationships with parents (L-PART); accompanied by a clear decline in peer-related loneliness (L-PEER) from early adolescence onwards" (p. 227). Schultz and Moore (1988) found that high school students ($n = 96$) reported higher loneliness than college students ($n = 110$).

Gender. The other demographic correlate of loneliness that contributors to this volume consider is gender. As part of the adult literature, Borys and Perlman (1985) did a meta-analysis of gender differences in loneliness. They found that the outcome depended on which measure was used to assess loneliness. The UCLA Scale, the most widely used multiitem measure, assesses loneliness indirectly without explicitly asking respondents if they are lonely. Many surveys, however, use a single item to ask respondents to acknowledge their "lonely" feelings or label themselves as a lonely person. The meta-analysis showed that women were more likely to label themselves as lonely. Very few studies involving the UCLA Scale obtained gender differences in loneliness, but those few that did generally showed men to be more lonely than women. With supportive findings from a person perception type experiment, Borys and Perlman argued that it is more stigmatizing for men to admit loneliness than it is for women.

In the current volume, Koenig and Abrams include a meta-analysis of studies reporting children's and adolescents' loneliness as a function of gender. The studies they analyzed used multiple-item loneliness scales, usually the Illinois index for younger children and the UCLA measure for adolescents. They conclude that, despite some inconsistent findings, the overall pattern suggests that a gender difference in loneliness emerges during adolescence, with boys reporting more loneliness than girls. Thus, the UCLA measure gender difference that they report is similar to what Borys and Perlman obtained. Another team of contributors to this volume, Hymel et al. report finding significant mean differences in their data on expected loneliness ratings for boys and girls. Interestingly, these latter findings are consistent with those reported in the adult literature by Borys and Perlman (1985) that it is usually men (boys) who are more reticent in admitting their loneliness.

Besides examining mean differences in loneliness between boys and girls, several contributors to this volume also report on the gender-dependent correlates of loneliness. This is manifest in at least four chapters including those by Burgess et al.; Crick et al.; Sippola and Bukowski; and Koenig and Abrams. For instance, each of the following findings held for only one gender:

- at higher levels of friendship, conflict was associated with increased loneliness in boys (Burgess et al.);
- boys who had experienced high levels of parental warmth and responsiveness reported lower levels of loneliness (Burgess et al.);
- for girls, poor treatment from peers (low peer acceptance) was associated with the development of negative peer perceptions, and this was linked to loneliness (Crick et al.);
- for girls, having a sense of a divided self in their same-sex relations was a useful predictor of their loneliness (Sippola & Bukowski); and
- adolescent women with chronic loneliness were likely to experience major affective disorders (Koenig & Abrams).

The gender-specific correlates of loneliness may partially be explained by the variability in predictor variables. When the range of scores on a predictor variable is restricted for one gender, the association may not be found in that group. Beyond this, researchers have not identified any single substantive principle that would help understand and predict when gender differences are likely. Most of the authors who report gender differences in correlations provide only post hoc explanations of these findings. We believe continued attention to gender specific correlates of loneliness, especially at the stage of hypotheses formulation, is warranted in the future. Through such an approach, researchers can hope to develop a more comprehensive understanding of such effects.

Correlates of Loneliness

A large number of correlates of loneliness have been identified in the adult literature. Although the list is too long to cover each one adequately, these include such classes of factors as

- personality attributes (see Jones & Carver, 1991);
- the nature of people's social skills and their social relationships (see Jones, 1982);
- interpersonal judgments (see Jones, 1982); and
- childhood familial relations, life transitions (e.g., going to college and death of a spouse), and the like (see Perlman, 1988).

Several findings in the adult literature have been replicated or approximated in the childhood literature. For example, in this volume, authors report on the associations between loneliness and: shyness (Youngblade et al.), depression (Goossens & Marcoen; Koenig & Abrams), insecure attachment (Cassidy & Berlin), and social anxiety and public self-consciousness (Goossens & Marcoen). Similar findings have been reported in the adult literature (shyness, Maroldo, 1981; depression, Weeks et al., 1980; social anxiety, Anderson & Harvey, 1988; self-consciousness, Schmitt & Kurdek, 1985; and insecure attachment, Hazan & Shaver, 1987). In his chapter on parental antecedents of loneliness, Rotenberg re-examined the ideas from the adult literature (Lobdell & Perlman, 1986) that there is an association between the loneliness reported by mothers and their offspring and that parental warmth is associated with children being less lonely (cf. Burgess et al. this volume). He found both these notions supported among adolescents, but not among his midchildhood sample.

As with social problems, some correlates of loneliness may be age specific. For example, Burgess et al. (this volume) also reported a study by Ladd and Burgess (in press) that indicates that negative personality traits do not seem to be associated with an increase in loneliness until middle childhood. Similarly, Youngblade et al. (this volume) argue that the commonly found social withdrawal of early childhood is normative and therefore not associated with loneliness until middle childhood. Looking at the correlational patterns across adulthood, Schmitt and Kurdek (1985) speculated that loneliness of older women "apparently results from more permanent losses," whereas that of college women may "be related to transient changes in identity and relationship status" (p. 494). Complementing this conclusion, Schultz and Moore (1988) found that personality and adjustment factors were less predictive of loneliness among retirees than among younger adults.

We see at least one central area of concern in the childhood literature that has been largely, if not totally, ignored in the adult literature. That is the area of peer status. The childhood literature is replete with various studies of peer acceptance, friendship, and rejection among school children. In the adult literature, there have rarely been opportunities to collect data from closed social groups in which every member could rate all others, although in one study, personal network information was collected from both college students and their friends (Williams & Solano, 1983). In that study, lonely college students listed as many friends as did nonlonely students, but lonely students felt less intimate with their friends. Turning to how the "friends" of the college students felt toward them, the friends of lonely students were less likely than the friends of nonlonely students to return the friendship choices.

In this volume, sociometric data are reported, discussed, or referred to by several authors. Burgess and her associates, for example, report a number of studies which show a modest correlation between loneliness and sociometric status ($-.23$ and $-.29$). Parker, Saxon, Asher, and Kovacs (this volume) review evidence showing the generality of the association between various aspects of friendship and loneliness across different cultures, settings and contexts (e.g., camps as well as schools), age groups, and measurement methodologies.

Although it is not their primary focus, Hymel et al. (this volume) shed light on the dynamics that might be involved in the relationship between sociometric status and loneliness. In their study of popular, average, and unpopular children, they found that neither the expectation of being lonely in potentially loneliness producing situations nor the percent of children reporting ever having been in such situations varied as a function of sociometric status. Their null findings, however, lead these authors to speculate that peer-rejected children may report more loneliness in their actual daily lives because they experience loneliness-producing situations "more frequently and with greater intensity." In part, less-accepted children may find themselves in loneliness-producing situations because their peers exclude them from social activities. Another possibility for why unpopular children are lonely is that they are treated less well (e.g., less positively or more punitively) when they do participate in peer activities (see Burgess et al.).

Cassidy and Berlin (this volume) offer possible insight into why the correlation between sociometric status and loneliness is modest rather than strong. They hypothesize that variability in loneliness and relationship status might readily be explained by attachment theory. They postulate that some unpopular children who are rejected by their peers have an avoidant–attachment style (associated with ego-defensiveness) and, therefore, deny or rationalize their experiences of loneliness. Conversely, popular children who have anxious–ambivalent attachment styles (associated with feelings of unworthiness) may experience elevated levels of loneliness because they fail to recognize that they are accepted by their peers. Thus, even though there is a general tendency for peer rejection to be associated with loneliness, this association may not hold equally strongly for all subsets of children.

Regardless of the magnitude of the correlation, an important feature of childhood sociometric studies of particular interest is that they use measures of interpersonal ties based on outsiders' reports, not on the participants' own reports. This circumvents the question that must be considered in many adult studies of whether reported differences in sociability reflect the participants' perceptual biases, actual differences, or both. The childhood studies join with that of Williams and Solano (1983) in suggesting that actual differences in relationships are probably part of the equation-producing loneliness.

Theoretical Views of Loneliness

In synthesizing theoretical views of loneliness in the adult literature, Perlman and Peplau (1982) summarized eight perspectives (i.e., cognitive discrepancy, existential, interactionist, phenomenological, privacy, psychodynamic, sociological, and systems). Marangoni and Ickes (1989) organized their review of theoretical approaches around three perspectives: the social needs (or psychodynamic) approach, the behavioral (social skills)/personality approach, and the cognitive processes (discrepancy) approach. As suggested by Parkhurst and Hopmeyer (this volume), arguably the two most influential frameworks in the adult loneliness literature in the late 1970s and the 1980s were the social needs and the cognitive approaches, associated, respectively, with such scholars as Weiss (1973) and Peplau et al. (1982). Weiss's analysis of loneliness was rooted in the Bowlby (1982) attachment tradition. For Weiss, loneliness stems from failure to fulfill specific interpersonal needs. He underscored that sometimes people's failure to satisfy their needs may be related to life circumstances such as moving or becoming widowed. Depending on which relational needs are unfilled, individuals experience either social or emotional relationships. Weiss argued that the emotions associated with loneliness and the ways people might cope with it are a function of which type of loneliness they encounter.

For Peplau et al. (1982), loneliness is "a response to the perception that one's social relations fail to measure up to some internal yardstick" (p. 137). This perspective focuses attention not only on the provisions of relationships but also on how these provisions do or do not match needs and desires. Peplau et al. contended that cognitive processes including attributions and perceived control moderate between the desired versus achieved discrepancies in social relations and the experience of loneliness, making it more or less intensive and aversive.

The influence of social needs and cognitive discrepancy perspectives can be seen in the work being done on loneliness among youths. These perspectives are offered as a starting or interpretative framework at specific points in several chapters in the present volume (e.g., Cassidy & Berlin; Crick et al.; Hymel et al.; Kupersmidt, Sigda, Sedikides, & Voegler; Parkhurst & Hopmeyer). Orientation toward solitude, implicitly a key factor in discrepancy models but not extensively investigated in the adult literature, is central to some of the work being done on childhood loneliness (Goossens & Marcoen; Youngblade et al., this volume). The role of attributions, a facet of discrepancy analyses, continues to be investigated in the childhood and adolescent literatures (e.g., Crick et al.; Koenig & Abrams, this volume). In both the adult and the adolescent literatures, there is some evidence that internal and stable attributions for failures are associated with greater loneliness (see Anderson, Miller, Riger, Dill, & Sedikides, 1994; Koenig & Abrams, this volume; Bukowski & Ferber cited in Kupersmidt et al., this volume).

Although central theoretical aspects of the adult literature continue to emerge in the childhood literature, we also perceive new emphases in the childhood work. First, with regard to the attachment tradition, Weiss (1973) drew primarily on Bowlby's (1982) normative notions of attachment. Since the 1970s, the individual-difference aspects of attachment processes (i.e., secure vs. insecure attachment styles) have become considerably more prominent. This interest is manifest in the present volume (see Cassidy & Berlin) as well as in the more recent adult literature (see Hazan & Shaver, 1987). In particular, Cassidy and Berlin report their findings that 5- to 7-year-olds who had been insecure–ambivalent in infancy reported more loneliness when compared with secure and insecure–avoidant children (who reported the least loneliness). This makes sense, given that insecure–ambivalent children typically have experienced inconsistent parental support. As with any intermittent reinforcement, such inconsistencies in the availability of support results in chronically activated attachment needs, which most probably makes the ability to be alone more difficult and loneliness more prevalent. Similarly, in the adult literature, Hazan and Shaver (1987) found that insecure (anxious–avoidant and avoidant) attachment was also associated with higher levels of both state–trait loneliness.

Second, the contributions that cognitive processes and the self make to loneliness have been further articulated and taken in new directions. For instance, Crick et al. (this volume) analyze loneliness in terms of an information-processing model. They make notions such as encoding, formulating social goals, and generating ideas about how to respond to situations more prominent than they were in earlier cognitive discrepancy models. Similarly, Sippola and Bukowski (this volume) discuss cognitive development during adolescence and how this influences teenagers' understanding of self and other, which in turn is linked to loneliness.

Sippola and Bukowski (this volume) chide past researchers for not trying to understand loneliness from a developmental perspective. We agree with this point. Contributors to the adult literature addressed childhood antecedents of loneliness, speculated on reasons why loneliness might be high in specific periods (Brennan, 1982), discussed loneliness and life transitions (Perlman, 1988), and checked for age-related correlates of loneliness (Schmitt & Kurdek, 1985; Schultz & Moore, 1988). They did not, however, to our knowledge, articulate truly developmental theories of loneliness. They were not especially sensitive to the ways adults change and develop. Thus, a final and noteworthy advance in this volume is that Parkhurst and Hopmeyer offer a developmental theory of loneliness. We discuss aspects of that model in the next section.

Coping, Treatment, and Overcoming Loneliness

In the adult literature, there have been various analyses of how people react to and cope with loneliness (see Jones & Carver, 1991). For instance, Rubenstein and Shaver (1982) reported four reactions to being lonely: sad passivity, active solitude, spending money, and social contact. In what we believe is a study representative of findings in this area, Cutrona (1982) reported that first-year university students become less lonely between their initial arrival on campus and the end of the academic year (see also

Shaver et al., 1985). Unfortunately, however, she did not find definitive patterns between how students tried to overcome loneliness and their success in doing so.

Jones and Craver (1991; see also McWhirter, 1990b) have reviewed studies of the efficacy of therapy for treating people with loneliness. They note that a variety of therapeutic interventions have been used. Jones and Carver concluded that "these studies suggest . . . that various approaches result in significant reductions in loneliness both simultaneously and at follow-up" (p. 409). Most of these studies have used designs that demonstrated greater improvement than occurred because of spontaneous recovery (or regression artifacts).

Save for one or two passing references (see Terrell-Deutsch), interventions for alleviating loneliness have been largely ignored in the present volume. Given the effectiveness of psychotherapeutic treatment for lonely adults and the benefits of social skill training for low-accepted children (Coie & Koeppl, 1990), there is reason to be optimistic that interventions will help alleviate loneliness among children. At least one study done by child researchers not involved in this volume has shown promising preliminary results (King et al., 1997). We believe more work in this area is warranted. The priority to give to interventions in helping children overcome loneliness may be informed by additional evidence on the extent to which childhood loneliness leads to adult loneliness and other detrimental outcomes such as those found for low peer acceptance (Parker & Asher, 1987).

The Uniquely Developmental Focus of the Childhood and Adolescent Literature

Having discussed several topics considered in both of the adult and childhood loneliness literatures, we believe there are uniquely developmental aspects of loneliness identified in the childhood and adolescent literature. Specifically the contributors to this literature identify four domains that are worthy of being examined developmentally: cognition, social skills, emotion, and self-identity. Covering both childhood and adolescence, we summarize each domain in turn.

Cognitive

Parkhurst and Hopmeyer (this volume) explain that children's very understanding of loneliness develops in accordance with their changing cognitive abilities. Drawing on Fischer's (1980) work, they identify five steps in children's and adolescents' cognitions about what they want in relationships and what makes them lonely. Specifically, as children move from the stage of concrete thinking to the stage of more abstract representations typical in adolescence, so too do their cognitions related to loneliness. In childhood, temporary physical separation is a sufficient antecedent of loneliness, whereas in adolescence the causes of loneliness may be more complex and reflexive in nature. For example, Parkhurst and Hopmeyer (this volume) indicate that in adolescence, sources of loneliness may be associated with the more abstruse issue of failing to know one's own identity (see also Goossens & Marcoen; Sippola & Bukowski, this volume).

Social Skills

Maturation of social skills, associated with evolving cognitive development, is a second correlate of loneliness offered by Parkhurst and Hopmeyer (this volume). They propose that, for a given age, specific social skills are required to foster successful relationships. The necessary skills change with development (e.g., abilities to engage in group activities during middle childhood and intimacy in adolescence). Furthermore, Parkhurst and Hopmeyer believe that children who were previously successful at one stage, but who failed to meet the skill requirements at the next, are likely to experience increased loneliness. Consistent with this view, a number of authors in this collection have reported that peer-group acceptance, evidence of acquired stage-specific social skills, was negatively associated with loneliness, whereas peer victimization was positively associated with loneliness (e.g., Burgess et al.; Youngblade et al.).

Emotion

A further developmental correlate of loneliness proposed by Parkhurst and Hopmeyer (this volume) is emotion. More specifically, these authors comment on the fact that as emotional development advances, there may be a corresponding change in felt loneliness. Parkhurst and Hopmeyer go on to assert that a relationship between other emotions and loneliness can occur because new negative emotions may change an individual's criteria for closeness or produce cognitions that make closeness more difficult. As well, evolving emotions can produce new behaviors that may damage social relationships.

Self-Identity

Unlike the other three domains that occur during the childhood period, achievement of autonomy and attainment of identity assume greater prominence as developmental tasks in adolescence. A number of authors in this collection have focused on the evolution of loneliness during adolescence. Larson (this volume) claims that in the period of adolescence, loneliness may actually serve as a restorative function; that is, it facilitates the developmental demands of individuation and identity formation. In fact, he found that adolescents who spent an intermediate amount of time alone showed better adjustment than those adolescents who were rarely alone or were alone quite often.

Larson's (this volume) claims have an even greater implication, given Sippola and Bukowski's (this volume) assertion that the identity development process itself may lead to an increase in loneliness. More specifically, Sippola and Bukowski contend that adolescents have a particularly onerous task of assimilating their multiple conceptions of self into one coherent identity. Loneliness is apt to persist in those individuals who feel that their new identity is too precarious to share with others or that others can never fully come to know the nascent self. Indeed, Sippola and Bukowski's research bears out these hypotheses; they found that having a divided self was strongly associated with loneliness, and a concomitant decrease in loneliness was observed for those adolescents who did engage in self-disclosure.

Interesting work by Goossens and Marcoen (this volume) pulls together research on adolescent identity formation and the increased need in adolescence for time spent among peers. Recall that they assessed identity formation (based on Marcia's, 1966, identity types), along with peer-related and family-related loneliness. Results of their research indicated that adolescents who achieved identity status or were at moratorium (high-level identity status) had higher scores on parent-related loneliness (as would be expected following from Larson's work). Conversely, diffused adolescents, who had a less-advanced identity status, experienced the highest levels of peer-related loneliness. This last finding indicates that adolescents who fail to proceed according to the developmental script of separating from parents and developing their own identity are most vulnerable to feelings of loneliness in the relationship domain, which is of increasing importance to this age group.

Summary and Conclusion

Two Solitudes or Unified Enterprise?

At the beginning of this chapter, we stated that our goal was to examine points of continuity and discontinuity between the childhood and adult loneliness literatures. We noted anecdotal evidence that childhood and adult loneliness researchers formed separate circles, even though contributors to this volume view the current research on childhood and adolescent loneliness as being based on concepts and studies from the adult literature. As we look at the chapters in this volume, we see both points of continuity and points of difference.

For example, in terms of continuity, in the two literatures, there are comparable definitions of loneliness, highly related measures of the phenomenon, use of similar typologies of loneliness, common personal and social problems that have been linked to loneliness, similar sets of correlates, and reference to common theoretical perspectives. We consider these substantial threads of continuity.

Nonetheless, we also see several important points of difference. For instance, the childhood literature is based on the assumption that loneliness occurs earlier in life than was commonly believed by influential earlier scholars concerned with adult loneliness. We believe the work represented in this volume supports the view that loneliness can be experienced considerably before puberty. Second, some of the problems associated with, and predictors of, loneliness are age-related. Third, loneliness may be less stable and persisting in childhood than it is in adulthood. Fourth, investigators of childhood loneliness seem less concerned with some topics than do adult researchers (e.g., life transitions such as loss of a loved one, demographic variables, and the efficacy of therapeutic interventions). On the other hand, childhood researchers have extensively developed a sociometric approach to loneliness that has been virtually nonexistent in the adult literature. Finally, adult researchers have largely ignored stages of adult development and how they might be intertwined with loneliness. Especially in Parkhurst and Hopmeyer's chapter (this volume), childhood loneliness researchers are offering a theoretical analysis of how developmental changes in cognitions, emotions, social skills, and identity can influence loneliness.

As we look at these differences, some seem to occur because of the childhood literature incorporating intellectual traditions (e.g., sociometry) that are not present in the adult literature. Along with this, childhood researchers have collected much of their data in school settings, which has probably shaped aspects of their work (e.g., an interest in or particular concern with children who are disruptive in classrooms). Other differences between childhood and adult literatures (e.g., the attention to attachment styles and new emphases on information processing) probably reflect larger changes within the field. Still others appear to be refinements of notions (or work) advanced earlier in the loneliness literature. Crutchfield and Krech (1962) once characterized the history of psychology by saying, "We seem to detect a tendency for thinking on a problem to go full cycle . . . there is a kind of spiral, a recurrence of older conceptions but a more advanced level of complexity and sophistication" (p. 10). We think such spirals can be found in the loneliness literature. For instance, 20 years ago Ellison (1978) briefly described the role of attachment, interpersonal rejection, and social skills in the development of loneliness. His key factors are still discussed in the literature but in new ways with greater refinement of concepts and with more evidence to assess the validity of various claims.

Perhaps to some extent childhood and adult loneliness researchers attend different conferences, work in different departments, and publish in different journals. Yet, in terms of the life of ideas, they tie into a common pool of knowledge and share a common vocabulary.

Comparison With Attachment: Another Area Involving Childhood and Adult Literatures

Both the loneliness and the attachment literatures can be divided into their childhood and adult facets. In the attachment domain, work on childhood attachment generally preceded interest in adult attachment. Although the underlying dynamics of attachment are presumed to operate across the life cycle, attachment changes in significant ways as people get older. For one thing, the manifestations of separation distress change. Furthermore, the structure of attachment changes in at least three ways (Weiss, 1982a): (a) In infancy, but not in adulthood, attachment involves an intransitive provision of security (from caregiver to child, but not vice versa), (b) a person's most common attachment partner shifts over the life cycle (from parents to romantic partners), and (c) sex is typically a component of adult (but not childhood) attachment relationships. Mental models offer a mechanism by which childhood attachment styles persist into adulthood.

Akin to the changing nature of attachment partners, perhaps the types of relationships most likely to be associated with loneliness change over the life course. However, as far as we are aware, the loneliness literature does not have either comparable discussions of the differences between childhood and adult loneliness or articulation of the mechanism akin to mental models by which loneliness persists over time. The absence of prominent distinctions between childhood and adult loneliness is another factor influencing us to see the important continuities between the ways childhood and adult researchers approach loneliness.

Cross-Fertilization of Ideas

By looking at both childhood and adult loneliness, one hopes to get a broader and better understanding of the phenomenon. It is not only the similarities that are reassuring but also the gaps and points of difference in the two literatures that can prompt creative reconciliation and suggest further avenues for research. As we look at the childhood and adult literatures, we see major areas in each in which we would like to encourage further integration. In the childhood literature, we would like to see more work done on interventions to help lonely children overcome their feelings of being lonely. Related to this, we would like to see long-term longitudinal studies of the persistence of, and later problems associated with, childhood loneliness. In the adult literature, we would like to see more emphasis on how adult development influences loneliness.

In the early to mid-1980s, many of those engaged in the study of adult loneliness felt it had moved from being an avoided or perhaps devalued topic to one in good standing. The contributions in this volume testify to the vitality of research on children's loneliness over the past 10–15 years. We take pride in these advances yet appreciate that science constantly strives to move forward. For scholars participating in the next generation of loneliness research, a key question is what routes will lead to the most important future advances. In the spirit of Crutchfield and Krech's (1962) aforementioned observations, we look ahead to work on loneliness spiraling forward to more complex, sophisticated, valid, and useful formulations. Certainly, a developmental approach, blending together insights and information from both the childhood and the adult loneliness literatures, is one promising pathway for getting there.

References

Abramson, L. Y., Metalsky, G. I., & Alloy, L. B. (1989). Hopelessness depression: A theory-based subtype of depression. *Psychological Review, 96,* 358–372.

Achenbach, T. M., & Edelbrock, C. (1986). *Manual for the teacher's report form and teacher version of the child behavior profile.* Burlington: University of Vermont, Department of Psychiatry.

Adams, G. R., Abraham, K. G., & Markstrom, C. A. (1987). The relations among identity development, self-consciousness, and self-focusing during middle and late adolescence. *Developmental Psychology, 23,* 292–297.

Adams, G. R., Bennion, L., & Hu, K. (1989). *Objective measure of ego-identity status: A reference manual* (2nd ed.). Unpublished manuscript, Utah State University.

Ainsworth, M. D. (1989). Attachments beyond infancy. *American Psychologist, 44,* 709–716.

Ainsworth, M. D. (1990). Some considerations regarding theory and assessment relevant to attachments beyond infancy. In M. T. Greenberg, D. Cicchetti, & E. M. Cummings (Eds.), *Attachment in the preschool years: Theory, research and intervention* (pp. 463–488). Chicago: University of Chicago Press.

Ainsworth, M. D., & Bell, S. M. (1970). Attachment, exploration, and separation: Illustrated by the behavior of one-year-olds in a strange situation. *Child Development, 41,* 49–67.

Ainsworth, M. D., Blehar, M., Waters, E., & Wall, S. (1978). *Patterns of attachment.* Hillsdale, NJ: Erlbaum.

Ainsworth, M. D., & Eichberg, C. G. (1991). Effects on infant–mother attachment of mother's unresolved loss of an attachment figure or other traumatic experience. In P. Marris, J. Stevenson-Hinde, & C. Parkes (Eds.), *Attachment across the life cycle* (pp. 160–183). New York: Routledge.

Akerlind, I., & Hornquist, J. O. (1992). Loneliness and alcohol abuse: A review of evidences of an interplay. *Social Science and Medicine, 34,* 405–414.

Allen, O., Page, R. M., Moore, L., & Hewitt, C. (1994). Gender differences in selected psychosocial characteristics of adolescent smokers and nonsmokers. *Health Values, 18,* 34–39.

Alsaker, F. D. (1993, March). *Bully/victim problems in day-care centers: Measurement issues and associations with children's psychosocial health.* Paper presented at the biennial meeting of the Society for Research in Child Development, New Orleans, LA.

Alsaker, F. D. (1989). Perceived social competence, global self-esteem, social interactions, and peer dependence in early adolescence. In B. H. Schneider,

G. Attili, J. Nadel, & R. P. Weissberg (Eds.), *Social competence in developmental perspective* (pp. 390–392). Boston: Kluwer Academic.

Anderson, C. A., & Arnoult, L. H. (1985). Attributional style and everyday problems in living: Depression, loneliness, and shyness. *Social Cognition, 1,* 16–35.

Anderson, C. A., & Harvey, R. J. (1988). Discriminating between problems in living: An examination of measures of depression, loneliness, shyness, and social anxiety. *Journal of Social and Clinical Psychology, 6,* 482–491.

Anderson, C. A., & Riger, A. L. (1991). A controllability attributional model of problems in living: Dimensional and situational interactions in the prediction of depression and loneliness. *Social Cognition, 9,* 149–181.

Anderson, C. A., Horowitz, L. M., & French, R. D. (1983). Attributional style of lonely and depressed people. *Journal of Personality and Social Psychology, 45,* 127–136.

Anderson, C. A., Miller, R. S., Riger, A. L., Dill, J. C., & Sedikides, C. (1994). Behavioral and characterological attributional styles as predictors of depression and loneliness: Review, refinement, and test. *Journal of Personality and Social Psychology, 66,* 549–558.

Andersson, L. (1990). Narcissism and loneliness. *International Journal of Aging and Human Development, 30,* 81–94.

Andersson, L., Mullins, L. C., & Johnson, D. P. (1987). Parental intrusion versus social isolation: A dichotomous view of the sources of loneliness. In M. Hojat & R. Crandall (Eds.), Loneliness: Theory, research and applications [Special issue]. *Journal of Social Behavior and Personality, 2,* 125–134.

Angold, A., Costello, E. J., Pickles, A., et al. (1987). *The development of a questionnaire for use in epidemiological studies of depression in children and adolescents.* Unpublished manuscript, London University.

Archibald, F., Bartholomew, K., & Marx, R. (1995). Loneliness in early adolescence: A test of the cognitive discrepancy model of loneliness. *Personality and Social Psychology Bulletin, 21,* 296–301.

Arend, R. A., Gove, F. L., & Sroufe, L. A. (1979). Continuity of individual adaptation from infancy to kindergarten: A predictive study of ego-resiliency and curiosity in preschoolers. *Child Development, 50,* 950–959.

Asher, S. R., & Coie, J. D. (Eds.) (1990). *Peer rejection in childhood.* New York: Cambridge University Press.

Asher, S. R., & Dodge, K. A. (1986). Identifying children who are rejected by their peers. *Developmental Psychology, 22,* 444–449.

Asher, S. R., Hopmeyer, A., & Gabriel, S. W. (1998). *Children's loneliness in different school contexts.* Manuscript submitted for publication.

Asher, S. R., & Hymel, S. (1981). Children's social competence in peer relations: Sociometric and behavioral assessment. In J. D. Wine & M. D. Smye (Eds.), *Social competence* (pp. 125–157). New York: Guilford Press.

Asher, S. R., Hymel, S., & Renshaw, P. (1984). Loneliness in children. *Child Development, 55,* 1456–1464.

Asher, S. R., & Parker, J. G. (1989). Significance of peer relationship problems in childhood. In B. H. Schneider, G. Attili, J. Nadel, & R. P. Weissberg (Eds.),

Social competence in developmental perspective (pp. 5–23). Amsterdam: Kluwer Academic Publishing.

Asher, S. R., Parker, J. G., & Walker, D. L. (1996). Distinguishing friendship from acceptance: Implications for intervention and assessment. In W. M. Bukowski, A. F. Newcomb, & W. W. Hartup (Eds.), *The company they keep: Friendship during childhood and adolescence* (pp. 366–406). New York: Cambridge University Press.

Asher, S. R., Parkhurst, J. T., Hymel, S., & Williams, G. A. (1990). Peer rejection and loneliness in childhood. In S. R. Asher & J. D. Coie (Eds.), *Peer rejection in childhood* (pp. 253–273). New York: Cambridge University Press.

Asher, S. R., & Wheeler, V. (1985). Children's loneliness: A comparison of rejected and neglected peer status. *Journal of Consulting and Clinical Psychology, 53,* 500–505.

Asher, S. R., & Williams, G. A. (1987, April). New approaches to identifying rejected children at school. In G. W. Ladd (Chair), *Identification and treatment of socially rejected children in school settings.* Symposium conducted at the annual meeting of the American Educational Research Association, Washington, DC.

Atkinson, J. W. (1966). *A theory of achievement motivation.* Huntington, New York: Krieger.

Austin, B. A. (1983). Factorial structure of the UCLA Loneliness Scale. *Psychological Reports, 53,* 883–889.

Avery, A. W. (1982). Escaping loneliness in adolescence: The case for androgyny. *Journal of Youth and Adolescence, 11,* 451–459.

Bakwin, H. (1942). Loneliness in infants. *American Journal of Diseases of Children, 63,* 30–40.

Baldwin, M. W. (1992). Relational schemas and the processing of social information. *Psychological Bulletin, 112,* 461–484.

Barnes, H. L., & Olson, D. H. (1985). Parent–adolescent communication and the circumplex model. *Child Development, 56,* 438–447.

Baron, R. M., & Kenny, D. A. (1986). The moderator–mediator variable distinction in social psychological research: Conceptual, strategic, and statistical considerations. *Journal of Personality and Social Psychology, 51,* 1173–1182.

Barrett, K. C., & Campos, J. J. (1987). Perspectives on emotional development: Vol. 2. A functionalist approach to emotions. In J. D. Osofsky (Ed.), *Handbook of infant development* (2nd ed.). New York: Wiley.

Baumeister, R. F., & Leary, M. R. (1995). The need to belong: Desire for interpersonal attachments as a fundamental human motivation. *Psychological Bulletin, 3,* 497–529.

Baumrind, D. (1967). Child care practices anteceding three patterns of preschool behavior. *Genetic Psychology Monographs, 75,* 43–88.

Baumrind, D. (1979). The development of instrumental competence through socialization. In A. D. Pick (Ed.), *Minnesota Symposium on Child Psychology* (Vol. 7). Minneapolis: University of Minnesota Press.

Baumrind, D. (1991). Effective parenting during the early adolescent transition. In P. A. Cowan, & E. M. Hetherington (Eds.), *Family transitions* (pp. 11–163). Hillsdale, NJ: Erlbaum.

Beck, A. T. (1967). *Depression: Clinical, experimental, and theoretical aspects.* New York: Harper & Row.

Beck, A. T. (1983). Cognitive therapy of depression: New perspectives. In P. J. Clayton & J. E. Barrett (Eds.), *Treatment of depression: Old controversies and new approaches* (pp. 265–290). New York: Raven Press.

Beck, A. T., Epstein, N., Brown, G., & Steer, R. A. (1988). An inventory for measuring clinical anxiety: Psychometric properties. *Journal of Consulting and Clinical Psychology, 56,* 893–897.

Beck, A. T., Steer, R. A., & Garbin, M. G. (1988). Psychometric properties of the Beck Depression Inventory: Twenty-five years of evaluation. *Clinical Psychology Review, 8,* 77–100.

Beck, A. T., Ward, C. H., Mendelson, M., Mock, J., & Erbaugh, J. (1961). An inventory for measuring depression. *Archives of General Psychiatry, 4,* 561–571.

Beck, A. T., & Young, J. E. (1978, September). College blues. *Psychology Today.*

Behar, L. B., & Stringfield, S. (1974). A behavior rating scale for the preschool child. *Developmental Psychology, 10,* 601–610.

Belcher, M. (1973). *The measure of loneliness: A validation study of the Belcher Extended Loneliness Scale (BELS).* Unpublished doctoral dissertation, Illinois Institute of Technology.

Bell, R. Q. (1968). A reinterpretation of the direction of effects in studies of socialization. *Psychological Review, 75,* 81–85.

Bellah, R. N., Madsen, R., Sullivan, W. M., Swidler, A., & Tipton, S. M. (1985). *Habits of the heart.* New York: Harper & Row.

Belsky, J. (1981). Early human experience: A family perspective. *Developmental Psychology, 17,* 3–33.

Belsky, J., Gilstrap, B., & Rovine, M. R. (1984). Stability and change in mother–infant/father–infant interaction in a family setting. *Child Development, 55,* 692–705.

Belsky, J., & Rovine, M. (1987). Temperament and attachment security in the strange situation: An empirical rapprochement. *Child Development, 58,* 787–795.

Belsky, J., Rovine, M. R., & Fish, M. (1989). The developing family system. In M. Gunnar (Ed.), *Systems and development: Minnesota Symposia on Child Psychology* (Vol. 22, pp. 119–166). Hillsdale, NJ: Erlbaum.

Belsky, J., Youngblade, L. M., Rovine, M. R., & Volling, B. L. (1991). Patterns of marital change and parent–child interaction. *Journal of Marriage and the Family, 53,* 487–498.

Benoit, D., & Parker, K. (1994). Stability and transmission of attachment across three generations. *Child Development, 65,* 1444–1456.

Benenson, J. F. (1994). Ages four to six years: Changes in the structures of play networks of girls and boys. *Merrill-Palmer Quarterly, 40,* 478–487.

Bennett, M. (1989). Children's self-attribution of embarrassment. *British Journal of Developmental Psychology, 7*(3), 207–217.

Berg, J. H., & Peplau, L. A. (1982). Loneliness: The relationship of self-disclosure and androgyny. *Personality and Social Psychology Bulletin, 8,* 624–630.

Berger, J. (1973). *About looking.* New York: Vintage Press.

Berlin, L. J. (1990). *Infant–mother attachment, loneliness, and the ability to be alone in early childhood.* Unpublished masters thesis, Pennsylvania State University.

Berlin, L. J., Cassidy, J., & Belsky, J. (1990, April). *Infant–mother attachment and the ability to be alone in early childhood.* Paper presented at the International Conference on Infant Studies, Montreal, Quebec, Canada.

Berlin, L. J., Cassidy, J., & Belsky, J. (1995). Loneliness in young children and infant mother attachment: A longitudinal study. *Merrill-Palmer Quarterly, 41,* 91–103.

Berlin, L. J., Youngblade, L. M., & Belsky, J. (1991, April). *Antecedents of loneliness and the ability to be alone in young children.* Paper presented at the biennial meeting of the Society for Research in Child Development, Seattle, WA.

Berndt, T. J. (1981). Effects of friendship on prosocial intentions and behavior. *Child Development, 52,* 636–643.

Berndt, T. J. (1982). The features and effects of friendship in early adolescence. *Child Development, 53,* 1447–1460.

Berndt, T. J. (1989). Contributions of peer relationships to children's development. In T. J. Berndt & G. W. Ladd (Eds.), *Peer relationships in child development* (pp. 407–416). New York: Wiley.

Berndt, T. J. (1996). Exploring the effects of friendship quality on social development. In W. M. Bukowski, A. F. Newcomb, & W. W. Hartup (Eds.), *The company they keep: Friendship in childhood and adolescence* (pp. 346–365). New York: Cambridge University Press.

Berndt, T. J., Hawkins, J. A., & Hoyle, S. G. (1986). Changes in friendship during a school year: Effects on children's and adolescents' impressions of friendships and sharing with friends. *Child Development, 57,* 1284–1297.

Berndt, T. J., & Ladd, G. W. (1989). *Peer relationships in child development.* New York: Wiley.

Berndt, T. J., & Miller, K. E. (1992). *Relations of adolescents' self esteem and school adjustment to their friends' characteristics.* Unpublished manuscript, Purdue University.

Berndt, T. J., & Perry, T. B. (1986). Children's perceptions of friendship as supportive relationships. *Developmental Psychology, 22,* 640–648.

Bhana, A. (1995). *Experiences and perceptions of danger among urban adolescents.* Unpublished doctoral dissertation, University of Illinois at Urbana.

Bigelow, B. J., & LaGaipa, J. J. (1980). The development of friendship values and choice. In H. C. Foot, A. J. Chapman, & J. R. Smith (Eds.), *Friendship and social relations in children* (pp. 15–44). New York: Wiley.

Bigelow, B. J., Tesson, G., & Lewko, J. H. (1996). *Learning the Rules.* New York: Guilford Press.

Billings, A. G., & Moos, R. H. (1983). Comparison of children of depressed and nondepressed parents: A social environmental perspective. *Journal of Abnormal Child Psychology, 11,* 463–485.

Birch, S. H., & Ladd, G. W. (1994, April). *The relative contributions of peer and teacher–child relationships to children's early school adjustment.* Paper presented at the 13th Biennial Conference on Human Development, Pittsburgh, PA.

Birch, S. H., & Ladd, G. W. (1996). Continuity and change in the quality of teacher–child relationships: Links with children's early school adjustment. In S. H. Birch (Chair), *Children's relationships with teachers: Assessment, continuity, and linkages with school adjustment.* Symposium presented at the annual meeting of the American Educational Research Association, New York City.

Birch, S. H., & Ladd, G. W. (1997). The teacher–child relationship and children's early school adjustment. *Journal of School Psychology, 35,* 61–79.

Block, J. H. (1983). Differential premised an-sin, from differential socialization of the sexes: Some conjecture. *Child Development, 54,* 1335–1354.

Blos, P. (1962). *On adolescence.* New York: Free Press.

Blos, P. (1967). The second individuation process of adolescence. In A. Freud (Ed.), *The psychoanalytic study of the child* (Vol. 22). New York: International Universities Press.

Boivin, M., & Hymel, S. (1995, May). *Peer experiences and social self-perceptions: A two-stage mediational model.* Paper presented at the biennial meeting of the Society for Research in Child Development, Indianapolis, IN.

Boivin, M., & Hymel, S. (1996, August). *Loneliness among rejected children: Individual differences and peer group processes.* Paper presented at the XIVth Biennial Meeting of the International Society for the Study of Behavior Development, Quebec City, Quebec, Canada.

Boivin, M., & Hymel, S. (1997). Peer experiences and social self-perceptions: A sequential model. *Developmental Psychology, 33,* 135–145.

Boivin, M., Hymel, S., & Bukowski, W. M. (1995). The roles of social withdrawal, peer rejection and victimization by peers in predicting loneliness and depressed mood in childhood. *Development and Psychopathology, 7,* 765–785.

Boivin, M., Poulin, F., & Vitaro, F. (1994). Depressed mood and peer rejection in childhood. *Development and Psychopathology, 6,* 483–498.

Boivin, M., Thomassin, L., & Alain, M. (1989). Peer rejection and self-perceptions among early elementary school children: Aggressive rejectees versus withdrawn rejectees. In B. H. Schneider, G. Attili, J. Nadel, & R. P. Weissberg (Eds.), *Social competence in developmental perspective* (pp. 392–393). Boston: Kluwer Academic Publishing.

Booth, R. (1983). An examination of college GPA, composite ACT scores, IQs, and gender in relation to loneliness of college students. *Psychological Reports, 53,* 347–352.

Borys, S., & Perlman, D. (1985). Gender differences in loneliness. *Personality and Social Psychology Bulletin, 11,* 63–74.

Bosma, H. A. (1992). Identity in adolescence: Managing commitments. In G. R. Adams, T. P. Gullotta, & R. Montemayor (Eds.), *Adolescent identity formation* (pp. 91–121). Newbury Park, CA: Sage.

Boulton, M. J., & Underwood, K. (1992). Bully/victim problems among middle school children. *British Journal of Educational Psychology, 62,* 73–87.

Bowlby, J. (1958). The nature of the child's tie to his mother. *International Journal of Psycho-Analysis, 39,* 350–373.

Bowlby, J. (1982). *Attachment and loss. Vol. 1: Attachment.* New York: Basic Books. (Original work published 1969).

Bowlby, J. (1973). *Attachment and loss. Vol. 2: Separation: Anxiety and anger.* New York: Basic Books.

Bowlby, J. (1977). The making and breaking of affectional bonds: Aetiology and psychopathology in the light of attachment theory. *British Journal of Psychiatry, 130,* 201–210.

Bowlby, J. (1979). *The making and breaking of affectional bonds.* London: Tavistock Press.

Bowlby, J. (1980). *Attachment and loss. Vol. 3: Loss.* New York: Basic Books.

Bowlby, J. (1982). *Attachment.* New York: Harper Collins.

Bowlby, J. (1988). *A secure base.* New York: Basic Books.

Brage, D., Meredith, W., & Woodward, J. (1993). Correlates of loneliness among midwestern adolescents. *Adolescence, 28,* 685–693.

Brennan, T. (1982). Loneliness at adolescence. In L. A. Peplau & D. Perlman (Eds.), *Loneliness: A sourcebook of current theory, research, and therapy* (pp. 269–290). New York: Wiley-Interscience.

Brennan, T., & Auslander, N. (1979). *Adolescent loneliness: An exploratory study of social and psychological predisposition and theory.* Unpublished manuscript, Behavioral Research Institute, Boulder, CO.

Bretherton, I. (1978). Making friends with one-year-olds: An experimental study of infant–stranger interaction. *Merrill-Palmer Quarterly, 24,* 29–52.

Bretherton, I. (1990). Open communication and internal working models: Their role in the development of attachment relationships. In R. A. Thompson (Ed.), *Nebraska Symposium on Motivation: Socio-emotional development.* Lincoln: University of Nebraska Press.

Bretherton, I., & Ainsworth, M. D. S. (1974). Responses of one-year-olds to a stranger in a strange situation. In M. Lewis & L. A. Rosenblum (Eds.), *The origins of fear* (pp. 131–164). New York: Wiley.

Bretherton, I., Biringen, Z., & Ridgeway, D. (1991). The parental side of attachment. In K. Pillemer & K. McCartney (Eds.), *Parent–child relations throughout life* (pp. 1–24). Hillsdale, NJ: Erlbaum.

Bretherton, I., Ridgeway, D., & Cassidy, J. (1990). The role of internal working models in the attachment relationship: Theoretical, empirical, and developmental considerations. In M. Greenberg, D. Cicchetti, & E. M. Cummings (Eds.), *Attachment in the preschool years: Theory, research, and intervention* (pp. 273–310). Chicago: University of Chicago Press.

Bretherton, I., Stolberg, U., & Kreye, M. (1981). Engaging strangers in proximal interaction: Infants' social initiative. *Developmental Psychology, 17,* 746–755.

Bretherton, I., & Waters, E. (Eds.). (1985). Growing points of attachment theory and research. *Monographs of the Society for Research in Child Development, 50* (1 & 2 Serial No. 209).

Bronson, G. (1972). Infants reactions to unfamiliar persons and novel objects. *Monographs of the Society for Research in Child Development, 37* (Serial No. 148).

Brooke, J. (Feb. 28, 1996, late edition). To be young, gay, and going to high school in Utah. *New York Times* Sect. B, p. 8, col. 1.

Broughton, J. M. (1981). The divided-self in adolescence. *Human Development, 24,* 13–32.

Brown, B. (1989). The role of peer groups in adolescents adjustment to secondary school. In T. J. Berndt & G. W. Ladd (Eds.), *Peer relationships in child development* (pp. 188–216). New York: Wiley.

Brown, P., & Levinson, S. (1978). Universals in language usage: Politeness phenomena. In E. N. Goody (Ed.), *Questions and politeness: Strategies in social interaction.* New York: Cambridge University Press.

Bruch, M. A., & Heimberg, R. G. (1994). Differences in perceptions of parental and personal characteristics between generalized and nongeneralized social phobics. *Journal of Anxiety Disorders, 8*(2), 155–168.

Bruch, M. A., Kaflowitz, N. G., & Pearl, L. (1988). Mediated and non-mediated relationships of personality components to loneliness. *Journal of Social and Clinical Psychology, 6,* 346–355.

Bryant, B. K. (1985). The neighborhood walk: Sources of support in middle childhood. *Monographs of the Society for Research in Child Development, 50*(3).

Buhrmester, D. (1992). The developmental courses of sibling and peer relationships. In F. Boer & J. Dunn (Eds.), *Children's sibling relationships: Developmental and clinical issues* (pp. 19–40). Hillsdale, NJ: Erlbaum.

Buhrmester, D. (1996). Need fulfillment, interpersonal competence, and the developmental contexts of early adolescent friendship. In W. M. Bukowski, A. F. Newcomb, & W. W. Hartup (Eds.), *The company they keep: Friendship in childhood and adolescence* (pp. 158–185). New York: Cambridge University Press.

Buhrmester, D., & Furman, W. (1987). The development of companionship and intimacy. *Child Development, 58*(4), 1101–1113.

Bukowski, W. M., & Ferber, J. S. (1987, April). *A study of peer relations, attributional style, and loneliness during adolescence.* Paper presented at the biennial meeting of the Society for Research in Child Development, Baltimore, MD.

Bukowski, W. M., & Hoza, B. (1989). Popularity and friendship: Issues in theory, measurement, and outcome. In T. J. Berndt & G. W. Ladd (Eds.), *Peer relations in child development* (pp. 15–45). New York: Wiley.

Bukowski, W. M. & Hoza, B. (1990, April). *Peer relations and loneliness during early adolescence.* Paper presented at the biennial meetings of the Society for Research in Adolescence, Atlanta, GA.

Bukowski, W. M., Hoza, B., & Boivin, M. (1993). Popularity, friendships, and emotional adjustment during early adolescence. In B. Laursen (Ed.), *Close friendships in adolescence* (pp. 23–37). San Francisco: Jossey-Bass.

Bukowski, W. M., Hoza, B., & Boivin, M. (1994). Measuring friendship quality during pre- and early adolescence: The development and psychometric properties of the Friendship Qualities Scale. *Journal of Social and Personal Relationships, 11,* 471–484.

Bukowski, W. M., Newcomb, A. F., & Hartup, W. W. (1996). *The company they keep: Friendship in childhood and adolescence.* New York: Cambridge University Press.

Burckhardt, J. (1960). *The civilization of the renaissance in Italy.* New York: New American Library.

Burgess, K. B., & Younger, A. (1996, August). *Self-perceptions among passive withdrawn, average, and aggressive preadolescents.* Paper Presented at the 105th

Annual Convention of the American Psychological Association, Toronto, Ontario, Canada.

Burleson, B. R. (1982). The development of communication skills in childhood and adolescence. *Child Development, 53*, 1578–1588.

Butcher, J. (1986). Longitudinal analysis of adolescent girls' aspirations at school and perceptions of popularity. *Adolescence, 21*(81), 133–143.

Cairns, R. B., Cairns, B. D., Neckerman, H. J., Ferguson, L. L., & Gariepy, J. L. (1989). Growth and aggression: 1. Childhood to early adolescence. *Developmental Psychology, 25*, 320–330.

Cairns, R. B., Leung, M., & Cairns, B. D. (1995). Social networks over time and space in adolescence. In L. J. Crockett & A. C. Crouter (Eds.), *Pathways through adolescence: Individual development in relation to social contexts: The Penn State series on child and adolescent development* (pp. 35–56). Hillsdale, NJ: Erlbaum.

Cash, T. F. (1995). Developmental teasing about physical appearance: Retrospective descriptions and relationships with body image. *Social Behavior and Personality, 23*(2), 123–129.

Cassidy, J. (1988). Child–mother attachment and the self in six-year-olds. *Child Development, 59*, 121–134.

Cassidy, J., & Asher, S. R. (1992). Loneliness and peer relations in young children. *Child Development, 63*, 350–365.

Cassidy, J., & Asher, S. R. (1993). *Young children's thinking about loneliness.* Unpublished manuscript, Pennsylvania State University.

Cassidy, J., & Berlin, L. J. (1994). The insecure/ambivalent pattern of attachment: Theory and research. *Child Development, 65*, 971–991.

Cassidy, J., Kirsh, S. J., Scolton, K., & Parke, R. D. (1996). Attachment and representations of peer relationships. *Developmental Psychology, 32*, 892–904.

Cassidy, J., & Kobak, R. R. (1988). Avoidance and its relation to other defensive processes. In J. Belsky & T. Nezworski (Eds.), *Clinical implications of attachment.* Hillsdale, NJ: Erlbaum.

Cauce, A. M., Felner, R. D., & Primavera, J. (1982). Social support in high risk adolescents: Structural components and adaptive impact. *American Journal of Community Psychology, 10*, 417–428.

Chandler, M. J. (1975). Relativism and the problem of epistemological loneliness. *Human Development, 18*, 171–180.

Check, J. V. P., Perlman, D., & Malamuth, N. M. (1985). Loneliness and aggressive behavior. *Journal of Social and Personal Relationships, 2*, 243–252.

Chelune, G. J., Sultan, F. G., & Williams, C. L. (1980). Loneliness, self-disclosure, and interpersonal effectiveness. *Journal of Counseling Psychology, 27*, 462–468.

Cicchetti, D., & Tucker, D. (1994). Development and self-regulatory structures of the mind. *Development and Psychopathology, 6*, 533–549.

Cohn, D. A. (1990). Child–mother attachment of six-year-olds and social competence at school. *Child Development, 61*, 152–162.

Cohen, D., & Nisbett, R. E. (1994). Self-protection and the culture of honor: Explaining southern violence. *Personality and Social Psychology Bulletin, 20*(5), 551–567.

Cohen, S., & Wills, T. A. (1985). Stress, social support, and the buffering hypothesis. *Psychological Bulletin, 98*, 310–357.

Coie, J. D., Dodge, K. A., & Coppotelli, H. (1982). Dimensions and types of social status: A cross-age perspective. *Developmental Psychology, 18*, 557–570.

Coie, J. D., & Koeppl, G. K. (1990). Adapting intervention to the problems of aggressive and disruptive rejected children. In S. R. Asher & J. D. Coie (Eds.), *Peer rejection in childhood* (pp. 309–337). New York: Cambridge University Press.

Coie, J. D., & Kupersmidt, J. B. (1983). A behavioral analysis of emerging social status in boys' groups. *Child Development, 54*, 1400–1416.

Coleman, C. C. (1993). *Relative contributions of classroom friendship and peer status to children's early school adjustment.* Unpublished master's thesis, University of Illinois at Urbana – Champaign.

Coleman, J. C. (1974). *Relationships in adolescence.* London: Routledge & Kegan Paul.

Conger, R. (1977). *Adolescence and youth* (2nd ed.). New York: Harper & Row.

Connell, J. P., & Wellborn, J. G. (1991). Competence, autonomy, and relatedness: A motivational analysis of self-system process. In M. R. Gunnar & L. A. Sroufe (Eds.), *Self processes and development: The Minnesota Symposia on Child Psychology* (Vol. 23, pp. 43–77). Hillsdale, NJ: Erlbaum.

Conrad, M., & Hammen, C. (1989). Role of maternal depression in perceptions of child maladjustment. *Journal of Consulting and Clinical Psychology, 57*, 663–667.

Cooper, C. R., Baker, H., Polichar, D., & Welsh, M. (1993). Values and communication of Chinese, Filipino, European, Mexican, and Vietnamese American adolescents with their families and friends. In S. Shulman & W. Andrew Collins (Eds.), *Father–adolescent relationships* (pp. 73–89). San Francisco: Jossey-Bass.

Cooper, C. R., & Grotevant, H. D. (1987). *Journal of Youth and Adolescence, 16*, 247–264.

Corsaro, W. (1981). Friendship in the nursery school: Social organization in a peer environment. In S. R. Asher & J. M. Gottman (Eds.), *The development of children's friendships* (pp. 207–241). New York: Cambridge University Press.

Costanzo, P. (1970). Conformity development as a function of self-blame. *Journal of Personality and Social Psychology, 14*, 366–374.

Coyne, J. C. (1976). Toward an interactional description of depression. *Psychiatry, 39*, 28–40.

Craig-Bray, L., & Adams, G. R. (1986). Different methodologies in the assessment of identity: Congruence between self-report and interview techniques? *Journal of Youth and Adolescence, 15*, 191–204.

Crick, N. R. (1995). Relational aggression: The role of intent attributions, feelings of distress, and provocation type. *Development and Psychopathology, 7*, 313–322.

Crick, N. R. (1997). Engagement in gender normative vs. gender non-normative forms of aggression: Links to social-psychological adjustment, *Developmental Psychology, 67*, 2317–2327.

Crick, N. R., & Bigbee, M. A. (1998). Relational and overt forms of peer victimization: A multi-informant approach. *Journal of Consulting and Clinical Psychology, 66*, 337–347.

Crick, N. R., Bigbee, M. A., & Howes, C. (1996). Children's normative beliefs about aggression: How do I hurt thee? Let me count the ways. *Child Development, 67,* 1003–1014.

Crick, N. R., Casas, J. F., & Ku, H. C. (in press). Physical and relational peer victimization in preschool, *Developmental Psychology.*

Crick, N. R., & Dodge, K. A. (1994). A review and reformulation of social information-processing mechanisms in children's social adjustment. *Psychological Bulletin, 115,* 74–101.

Crick, N. R., & Dodge, K. A. (1996). Social information-processing mechanisms in reactive and proactive agression. *Child Development, 67,* 993–1002.

Crick, N. R., & Grotpeter, J. K. (1995). Relational aggression, gender, and social–psychological adjustment. *Child Development, 66,* 710–722.

Crick, N. R., & Grotpeter, J. K. (1996). Children's treatment by peers: Victims of relational and overt aggression. *Development and Psychopathology, 8,* 367–380.

Crick, N. R., Grotpeter, J. K., & Bigbee, M. A. (1999). *Relationally and physically aggressive children's intent attributions and feelings of distress for relational and instrumental peer provocation.* Manuscript submitted for publication.

Crick, N. R., Grotpeter, J. K., & Rockhill, C. (1996, August). *A social information-processing approach to children's loneliness.* Paper presented at the XIVth Biennial Meeting of the International Society for the Study of Behavior Development, Quebec City, Quebec, Canada.

Crick, N. R., & Ladd, Ĝ. W. (1993). Children's perceptions of their peer experiences: Attributions, loneliness, social anxiety, and social avoidance. *Developmental Psychology, 29,* 244–254.

Crick, N. A., & Werner, N. E. (1998). Response decision processes in relational and overt aggression, *Child Development, 69,* 1630–1639.

Crnic, K., & Greenberg, M. T. (1990). Minor parenting stresses with young children. *Child Development, 61,* 1628–1637.

Crockenberg, S. B. (1981). Infant irritability, mother responsiveness, and social support influences on the security of infant–mother attachment. *Child Development, 52,* 857–865.

Crowell, J. A., & Feldman, S. S. (1988). Mothers' internal models of relationship and children's behavioral and developmental status: A study of mother–child interaction. *Child Development 59,* 1273–1285.

Crowell, J. A., & Feldman, S. S. (1991). Mothers' working models of attachment relationships and mother and child behavior during separation and reunion. *Developmental Psychology, 27,* 597–605.

Crozier, W. R., & Russel, P. (1992). Blushing, embarrassability, and self-consciousness. *British Journal of Social Psychology 31*(4), 343–349.

Crutchfield, R. S., & Krech, D. (1962). Some guides to the understanding of the history of psychology. In L. Postman (Ed.), *Psychology in the making* (pp. 1–27). New York: Knopf.

Csikszentmihalyi, M., & Larson, R. (1987). Validity and reliability of the Experience Sampling Method. *Journal of Nervous and Mental Disease, 175,* 526–536.

Curtis, R. (1975). Adolescent orientations towards parents and peers: Variations by, sex, age, and socioeconomic status. *Adolescence, 10,* 483–494.

Cutrona, C. E. (1982). Transition to college: Loneliness and the process of social adjustment. In L. A. Peplau & D. Perlman (Eds.), *Loneliness: A sourcebook of current theory, research, and therapy* (pp. 291–309). New York: Wiley-Interscience.

Cutrona, C., Russell, D., & Wallace, R. B. (1997). Loneliness and nursing home admissions among rural older adults. *Psychology and Aging, 12,* 574–589.

Damon, W. (1979). *The social world of the child.* San Francisco: Jossey-Bass.

Damon, W., & Hart, D. (1986). Stability and change in children's self-understanding. *Social Cognition, 4,* 102–118.

Damon, W., & Hart, D. (1988). *Self-understanding in childhood and adolescence.* New York: Cambridge University Press.

Darling, N., & Steinberg, L. (1993). Parenting style as context: An integrative model. *Psychological Bulletin, 113,* 487–496.

Davis, M. H., & Franzoi, S. L. (1986). Adolescent loneliness, self-disclosure and private self-consciousness: A longitudinal investigation. *Journal of Personality and Social Psychology, 51,* 595–608.

Davis, S. S., & Davis, D. A. (1989). *Adolescence in a Moroccan town.* New Brunswick, NJ: Rutgers University Press.

Deci, E. L., & Ryan, R. M. (1991). A motivational approach to self: Integration in personality. In R. Dienstbier (Ed.), *Nebraska Symposium on Motivation: Perspectives in motivation* (Vol. 38, pp. 237–288). Lincoln: University of Nebraska Press.

de Jong-Gierveld, J. (1978). The construct of loneliness: Components and measurement. *Essence, 2,* 221–237.

de Jong-Gierveld, J., & Dykstra, P. (1994, July). *Changes in loneliness: Assessing the impact of changes in the social network and changes in health.* Paper presented at the seventh International Conference on Personal Relationships, Groningen, the Netherlands.

de Tocqueville, A. (1969). *Democracy in America.* (G. Lawrence, Trans. and J. P. Mayer, Ed.). New York: Doubleday/Anchor Books.

Depue, R. A., Krauss, S., Spoont, M. R., & Arbisi, P. (1989). General Behavior Inventory: Identification of unipolar and bipolar affective conditions in a nonclinical university population. *Journal of Abnormal Psychology, 98,* 117–126.

Diamant, L., & Windholz, G. (1981). Loneliness in college students: Some theoretical, empirical, and therapeutic considerations. *Journal of College Student Personnel, 22,* 515–522.

DiTommaso, E., & Spinner, B. (1997). Social and emotional loneliness: A reexamination of Weiss' typology of loneliness. *Personality and Individual Differences, 22,* 417–427.

Dodge, K. A. (1983). Behavioral antecedents of peer social status. *Child Development, 54,* 1386–1399.

Dodge, K. A. (1990). Developmental psychopathology in children of depressed mothers. *Developmental Psychology 26,* 3–6.

Dodge, K. A., & Feldman, E. (1990). Issues in social cognition and sociometric status. In S. R. Asher & J. D. Coic (Eds.), *Peer rejection in childhood.* New York: Cambridge University Press.

Dodge, K. A., & Frame, C. L. (1982). Social cognitive biases and deficits in aggressive boys. *Child Development 53*, 620–635.

Dodge, K. A., McClaskey, C., & Feldman, E. (1985). A situational approach to the assessment of social competence in children. *Journal of Consulting and Clinical Psychology, 53*, 344–353.

Dodge, K. A., Murphy, R. R., & Buchsbaum, K. (1984). The assessment of attention–cue detection skills in children: Implications for developmental psychopathology. *Child Development, 55*, 163–173.

Dodge, K. A., Pettit, G. S., McClaskey, C. L., & Brown, M. (1986). Social competence in children. *Monographs of the Society for Research in Child Development, 51*(2, Serial No. 213). New York: Wiley.

Douvan, E., & Adelson, J. (1996). *The adolescent experience*. New York: Wiley.

Downey, G., & Coyne, J. C. (1990). Children of depressed parents: An integrative review. *Psychological Bulletin, 109*, 50–76.

Dozier, M., & Kobak, R. R. (1992). Psychophysiology in adolescent attachment interviews: Converging evidence for repressing strategies. *Child Development, 63*, 1473–1480.

Dubow, E. F., & Tisak, J. (1989). The relation between stressful life events and adjustment in elementary school children: The role of social support and social problem solving skills. *Child Development, 60*, 1412–1423.

Dunn, J. (1985). *Brothers and sisters*. Cambridge, MA: Harvard University Press.

Dunphy, D. C. (1963). The social structure of urban adolescent peer groups. *Sociometry, 26*, 230–246.

Durkheim, E. (1951). *Suicide*. New York: Free Press.

Edelman, G. M. (1987). *Neural Darwinism*. New York: Basic Books.

Edelmann, R. (1990). Chronic blushing, self-consciousness, and social anxiety. *Journal of Psychopathology and Behavioral Assessment, 1–2*(2), 119–127.

Eder, D. (1985). The cycle of popularity: Interpersonal relations among female adolescents. *Sociology of Education, 58*(3), 154–165.

Eder, D. (1987, June). *The role of teasing in adolescent peer group culture*. Paper presented at the Conference on Ethnographic Approaches to Children's Worlds and Peer Culture, Trondheim, Norway.

Eder, D., & Kinney, D. A. (1995). The effect of middle school extracurricular activities on adolescents' popularity and peer status. *Youth and Society, 26*(3), 298–324.

Eisenberg, J. F. (1966). The social organization of mammals. *Handbuch Zoologie, 8*, 1–92.

Eisenberg, N., & Mussen, P. (1989). *The roots of prosocial behavior in children*. New York: Cambridge University Press.

Elicker, J., Englund, M., & Sroufe, L. A. (1992). Predicting competence and peer relationships in childhood from early parent–child relationships. In R. D. Parke & G. W. Ladd (Eds.), *Family–peer relationships: Modes of linkage* (pp. 77–106). Hillsdale, NJ: Erlbaum.

Elkind, D. (1967). Egocentrism in adolescence. *Child Development, 38*, 1025–1034.

Elkind, D., & Bowen, R. (1979). Imaginary audience behavior in children and adolescents. *Developmental Psychology, 15*, 38–44.

Ellison, C. (1978). Loneliness: A social–developmental analysis. *Journal of Psychology and Theology, 6*, 3–17.

Epstein, S. (1980). The stability of behavior: Implications for psychological research. *American Psychologist, 35*(9), 790–806.

Erdley, C. A., & Asher, S. R. (1996). Children's social goals and self-efficacy perceptions as influences on their responses to ambiguous provocation. *Child Development, 67*, 1329–1344.

Erickson, M. F., Sroufe, L. A., & Egeland, B. (1985). The relationship between quality of attachment and behavior problems in a high risk sample. In I. Bretherton & E. Waters (Eds.), Growing points in attachment theory and research. *Monographs of the Society for Research in Child Development, 50*(1–2, Serial No. 209), 147–166.

Erikson, E. (1950). *Childhood and society.* New York: Norton.

Erikson, E. H. (1968). *Identity: Youth and crisis.* New York: Norton.

Fagot, B. I., & Kavanagh, K. (1990). The prediction of antisocial behavior from avoidant attachment classifications. *Child Development, 61*, 864–873.

Feiring, C., & Lewis, M. (1991). The transition from middle childhood to early adolescence: Sex differences in the social network and perceived self-competence. *Sex Roles, 24*, 489–509.

Feldman, E., & Dodge, K. A. (1987). Social information processing and sociometric status: Sex, age, and situational effects. *Journal of Abnormal Child Psychology, 15*, 211–227.

Feldman, S. S., & Quatman, T. (1988). Factors influencing age expectations for adolescent autonomy: A study of early adolescents and parents. *Journal of Early Adolescence, 8*(4), 325–343.

Fenigstein, A., Scheier, M. F., & Buss, A. H. (1975). Public and private self-consciousness: Assessment and theory. *Journal of Consulting and Clinical Psychology, 43*, 522–527.

Ferreira, A. J. (1962). Loneliness and psychopathology. *American Journal of Psychoanalysis, 22*, 201–207.

Fine, G. A. (1981). Friends, impression management, and preadolescent behavior. In S. R. Asher & J. M. Gottman (Eds.), *The development of children's friendships* (pp. 29–52). New York: Cambridge University Press.

Fischer, K. W. (1980). A theory of cognitive development: The control and construction of hierarchies of skills. *Psychological Review, 87*, 477–531.

Fiske, S., & Taylor, S. (1991). *Social cognition.* New York: McGraw-Hill.

Fitzgerald, P., & Asher, S. R. (1987, August). *Aggressive – rejected children's attributional biases about liked and disliked peers.* Paper presented at the annual meeting of the American Psychological Association, New York.

Flanders, J. P. (1982). A general systems approach to loneliness. In L. A. Peplau & D. Perlman (Eds.), *Loneliness: Current theory, research, and therapy* (pp. 166–179), New York: Wiley.

Flavell, J. H. (1963). *The developmental psychology of Jean Piaget.* New York: Van Nostrand.

Fonagy, P., Steele, H., & Steele, M. (1991). Maternal representations of attachment during pregnancy predict the organization of infant–mother attachment at one year of age. *Child Development, 62*, 891–905.

Frankel, S., & Sherick, L. (1977). Observations on the development of normal envy. *Psychoanalytic Study of the Child, 32,* 287–281.

Frankl, V. (1962). *Man's search for meaning* (I. Lasch, Trans.). Boston: Beacon Press.

Franzoi, S. L., & Davis, M. H. (1985). Adolescent self-disclosure and loneliness: Private self-consciousness and parental influences. *Journal of Personality and Social Psychology, 48,* 768–780.

Freeman, M., Csikszentmihalyi, M., & Larson, R. (1986). Adolescence and its recollection: Towards an interpretative model of development. *Merrill-Palmer Quarterly, 32,* 167–185.

Freud, A. (1946). *The ego and the mechanisms of defence.* New York: International Universities Press.

Freud, A. (1958). Adolescence. *Psychoanalytic Study of the Child, 13,* 255–278.

Freud, S. (1930). *Civilization and its discontents* (J. Riviere, Trans.). London: Hogarth Press.

Fromm-Reichmann, F. (1959). Loneliness. *Psychiatry, 22,* 1–15.

Fromm-Reichmann, F. (1980). Loneliness. In J. Hartog, J. R. Audy, & Y. A. Cohen (Eds.), *The anatomy of loneliness* (pp. 338–361). New York: International Universities Press.

Fuligni, A. J., & Stevenson, H. W. (1995). Time use and mathematics achievement among American, Chinese, and Japanese high school students. *Child Development, 66,* 830–842.

Furman, W. (1996). The measurement of friendship perceptions: Conceptual and methodological issues. In W. M. Bukowski, A. F. Newcomb, & W. W. Hartup (Eds.), *The company they keep: Friendship in childhood and adolescence* (pp. 41–65). New York: Cambridge University Press.

Furman, W., & Bierman, K. L. (1983). Developmental changes in young children's conceptions of friendship. *Child Development, 54,* 549–556.

Furman, W., & Bierman, K. L. (1984). Children's conceptions of friendship: A multimethod study of developmental changes. *Developmental Psychology, 20,* 925–931.

Furman, W., & Buhrmester, D. (1985). Children's perceptions of the personal relationships in their social networks. *Developmental Psychology, 21,* 1016–1024.

Furman, W., & Buhrmester, D. (1992). Age and sex differences in perceptions of networks of personal relationships. *Child Development, 63,* 103–115.

Furman, W., & Robbins, P. (1985). What's the point? Issues in the selection of treatment objectives. In B. H. Schneider, K. H. Rubin, & J. Ledingham (Eds.), *Children's peer relations: Issues in assessment and intervention* (pp. 41–54). New York: Springer-Verlag.

Gadamer, H. G. (1989). *Truth and method* (2nd ed., J. Weinsheimer & G. Marshall, Trans.). New York: Continuum Press. (Original work published 1960).

Garmezy, N., Masten, A. S., & Tellegen, A. (1984). The study of stress and competence in children: A building block for developmental psychopathology. *Child Development, 55,* 97–111.

Gelfand, T. M., & Teti, D. M. (1990). The effects of maternal depression on children. *Clinical Psychology Review, 10,* 329–353.

George, C., & Solomon, J. (1996). Representational models of relationships: Links between caregiving and attachment. *Infant Mental Health Journal, 17,* 198–216.

George, T. P., & Hartmann, D. P. (1996). Friendship networks of unpopular, average, and popular children. *Child Development, 67,* 2301–2316.

Gerson, A. C., & Perlman, D. (1979). Loneliness and expressive communication. *Journal of Abnormal Psychology, 88,* 258–261.

Gerson, R. P., & Damon, W. (1978). Moral understanding and children's conduct. *New Directions in Child Development, 2,* 41–60.

Giddens, A. (1991). *Modernity and self-identity.* Stanford, CA: Stanford University Press.

Ginsberg, D., Gottman, J. M., & Parker, J. G. (1986). The importance of friendship. In J. M. Gottman & J. G. Parker (Eds.), *Conversations of friends: Speculations on affective development.* New York: Cambridge University Press.

Gladstone, T. R., & Koenig, L. K. (1994). Sex differences in depression across the high school to college transition. *Journal of Youth and Adolescence, 23,* 643–669.

Gnepp, J., Klayman, J., & Trabasso, T. (1982). A hierarchy of information sources for inferring emotional reaction. *Journal of Experimental Child Psychology, 33,* 111–123.

Goosen, F. A., & van IJzendoorn, M. (1990). Quality of infants' attachments to professional caregivers: Relations to infant–parent attachment and daycare characteristics. *Child Development, 61,* 832–837.

Goossens, L. (1984). Imaginary audience behavior as a function of age, sex and formal operational thinking. *International Journal of Behavioral Development, 7,* 77–93.

Goossens, L. (1994, February). *Personality predictors of adolescent loneliness: Social anxiety, self-consciousness and introspectiveness.* Poster presented at the 5th Biennial Meeting of the Society for Research on Adolescence, San Diego, CA.

Goossens, L. (1995a). Identity status development and students' perception of the university environment: A cohort-sequential study. In A. Oosterwegel & R. A. Wicklund (Eds.), *The self in European and North American culture: Development and processes* (pp. 19–32). Dordrecht, The Netherlands: Kluwer Academic Publishers.

Goossens, L. (1995b, August). *Loneliness and identity formation in adolescence: Statuses, styles, and behavioral characteristics.* Poster presented at the 7th European Conference on Developmental Psychology, Krakow, Poland.

Goossens, L. (1996a). *Loneliness in early adolescence: Associations with depression and anxiety.* Poster presented at the 14th Biennial Meeting of the International Society for the Study of Behavioral Development, Quebec City, Quebec, Canada.

Goossens, L. (1996b). Loneliness and social dissatisfaction as related to the developmental tasks of adolescence. In L. Goossens (Chair), *Social development in adolescence.* Symposium conducted at the 26th International Congress of Psychology, Montreal, Quebec, Canada.

Goossens, L., Seiffge-Krenke, I., & Marcoen, A. (1992). The many faces of adolescent egocentrism: Two European replications. *Journal of Adolescent Research, 7,* 43–58.

Goswick, R. A., & Jones, W. H. (1981). Loneliness, self-concept, and adjustment. *Journal of Psychology, 107,* 237–240.

Goswick, R. A., & Jones, W. H. (1982). Components of loneliness during adolescence. *Journal of Youth and Adolescence, 11,* 373–383.

Gottman, J. M. (1983). How children become friends. *Monographs of the Society for Research in Child Development, 48*(3 Serial No. 201).

Gottman, J. M., Gonso, J., & Rasmussen, B. (1975). Social interaction, social competence, and friendship in children. *Child Development, 46,* 709–718.

Gottman, J. M., & Parker, J. (1986). *The conversations of friends: Speculations on affective development.* New York: Cambridge University Press.

Gottman, J. M., & Parkhurst, J. T. (1981). A developmental theory of friendship and acquaintanceship processes. In W. A. Collins (Ed.), *The Minnesota Symposia on Child Psychology* (Vol. 13, pp. 197–253). Hillsdale, NJ: Erlbaum.

Green, V. A., & Wildermuth, N. L. (1993). Self-focus, other-focus, and interpersonal needs as correlates of loneliness. *Psychological Reports, 73,* 843–850.

Greenberg, M., & Marvin, R. S. (1982). Reactions of preschool children to an adult stranger: A behavioral systems approach. *Child Development, 53,* 481–490.

Greene, A. L., & Larson, R. W. (1991). Variation in stress reactivity during adolescence. In E. Cummings, A. L. Greene, & K. H. Karraker (Eds.), *Life-span developmental psychology: Perspectives on stress and coping* (pp. 195–209). Hillsdale, NJ: Erlbaum.

Greener, S., & Crick, N. R. (in press). Children's normative beliefs about prosocial behavior: What does it mean to be nice? *Social Development.*

Greenfield, P. M. (1994). Independence and interdependence as developmental scripts: Implications for theory, research, and practice. In P. M. Greenfield & R. R. Cocking (Eds.), *Cross-cultural roots of minority child development* (pp. 1–37). Hillsdale, NJ: Erlbaum.

Grotevant, H. D. (1998). Adolescent development in context. In W. Damon (Ed.), *Handbook of child psychology. Vol. 3: Social, emotional, and personality development* (5th ed.). New York: Wiley.

Grotevant, H. D., & Cooper, C. R. (1986). Individuation in family relationships: A perspective on individual differences in the development of identity and role-taking skill in adolescence. *Human Development, 29,* 82–100.

Hall, G. S. (1904). *Adolescence: Its psychology and its relation to physiology, anthropology, sociology, sex, crime, religion, and education.* New York: D. Appleton.

Hallinan, M. T. (1981). Recent advances in sociometry. In S. R. Asher & J. M. Gottman (Eds.), *The development of children's friendships* (pp. 91–115). New York: Cambridge University Press.

Hamer, R. J., & Bruch, M. A. (1994). The role of shyness and private self-consciousness in identity development. *Journal of Research in Personality, 28,* 436–452.

Hammen, C., Gordon, G., Burge, D., Adrian, C., Jaenicke, C., & Hiroto, G. (1987). Maternal affective disorders, illness, and stress: Risk for children's psychopathology. *American Journal of Psychiatry, 144,* 736–741.

Hanley-Dunn, P., Maxwell, S. E., & Santos, J. F. (1985). Interpretation of interpersonal interactions: The influence of loneliness. *Personality and Social Psychology Bulletin, 11,* 445–456.

Hansell, S., Mechanic, D., & Brondolo, E. (1986). Introspectiveness and adolescent development. *Journal of Youth and Adolescence, 15,* 115–132.

Harlow, H. F. (1969). Age-mate or affectional system. In D. S. Lehrman, R. A. Hinde, & E. Shaw (Eds.), *Advances in the study of behavior* (Vol. 2). New York: Academic Press.

Harlow, H. F., & Harlow, M. K. (1965). The affectional systems. In A. M. Schrier, H. F. Harlow, & F. Stollnitz (Eds.), *Behavior of non-human primates* (Vol. 2, pp. 287–334). New York: Academic Press.

Harris, P. L. (1989). *Children and emotion: The development of psychological understanding.* Oxford, England: Basil Blackwell.

Hart, C. H. (Ed.). (1993). *Children on playgrounds: Research perspectives and applications.* Albany: State University of New York Press.

Hart, D., Maloney, J., & Damon, W. (1987). The meaning and development of identity. In T. Honess & K. Yardley (Eds.), *Self and identity: Perspectives across the lifespan.* London: Routledge & Kegan Paul.

Harter, S. (1983). Developmental perspectives on the self-system. In P. H. Mussen (Ed.) and E. Mavis Hetherington (Vol. Ed.), *Handbook of child psychology. (Vol. 4): Socialization personality, and social development,* New York: Wiley.

Harter, S. (1990). Adolescent self and identity development. In S. S. Feldman & G. R. Elliot (Eds.), *At the threshold: The developing adolescent* (pp. 352–387). Cambridge, MA: Harvard University Press.

Harter, S., Marold, D. B., & Whitesell, N. R. (April, 1993). *A model of conditional parent support and adolescent false self behavior.* Paper presented at the biennial meeting of the Society for Research in Child Development, New Orleans, LA.

Harter, S., & Pike, R. (1984). The pictorial scale of perceived competence and social acceptance in young children. *Child Development, 55,* 1969–1982.

Hartshorne, T. S. (1993). Psychometric properties and confirmatory factor analysis of the UCLA Loneliness Scale. *Journal of Personality Assessment, 61,* 182–195.

Hartup, W. W. (1980). Peer relations and family relations: Two social worlds. In M. Rutter (Ed.), *Scientific foundations of developmental psychiatry.* London: Heinemann.

Hartup, W. W. (1996). The company they keep: Friendships and their developmental significance. *Child Development, 67,* 1–13.

Hartup, W. W., & Sancilio, M. F. (1986). Children's friendships. In E. Schopler & G. B. Mesibov (Eds.), *Social behavior in autism* (pp. 61–80). New York: Plenum.

Hayden, L. K. (1989). *Children's loneliness.* Unpublished doctoral dissertation, University of Waterloo, Waterloo, Ontario, Canada.

Hayden, L., Taruili, D., & Hymel, S. (1988). *Children talk about loneliness.* Paper presented at the biennial University of Waterloo Conference on Child Development, Waterloo, Ontario, Canada.

Hazan, C., & Shaver, P. R. (1987). Romantic love as conceptualized as an attachment process. *Journal of Personality and Social Psychology, 52,* 511–524.

Hazan, C., & Shaver, P. R. (1990). Love and work: An attachment-theoretical perspective. *Journal of Personality and Social Psychology, 59,* 270–280.

Hazan, C., & Zeifman, D. (1994). Sex and the psychological tether. *Advances in Personal Relationships, 5,* 151–177.

Hebdige, D. (1979). *Subculture the meaning of style.* London: Methuen.

Hecht, D. T., & Baum, S. K. (1984). Loneliness and attachment patterns in young adults. *Journal of Clinical Psychology, 40,* 193–197.

Heller, K. (1979). The effects of social support: Prevention and treatment implications. In A. P. Goldstein & F. H. Kanfer (Eds.), *Maximizing treatment gains: Transfer enhancement in psychotherapy* (pp. 353–382). New York: Academic Press.

Heller, K. A., & Berndt, T. J. (1981). Developmental changes in the formation and organization of personality attributions. *Child Development, 52,* 683–691.

Hembry, S., Vandell, D., & Levin, J. (1995). *Reciprocity in rejection: The role of mutual antipathies in predicting children's adjustment.* Unpublished manuscript, University of Wisconsin – Madison.

Henwood, P. G., & Solano, C. H. (1994). Loneliness in young children and their parents. *Journal of Genetic Psychology, 155,* 35–45.

Higgins, E. T. (1987). Self-discrepancy theory: A theory relating self and affect. *Psychological Review, 94,* 319–340.

Higgins, E. T. (1990). Personality, social psychology, and person–situation relations: Standards and knowledge activation as a common language. In L. A. Pervin (Ed.), *Handbook of personality: Theory and research* (pp. 301–338). New York: Guilford Press.

Higgins, E. T., Bond, R. N., Klein, R., & Strauman, T. (1986). Self-discrepancies and emotional vulnerability: How magnitude, accessibility, and type of discrepancy influence affect. *Journal of Personality and Social Psychology, 51,* 5–15.

Higgins, E. T., Klein, R., & Strauman, T. (1985). Self-concept discrepancy theory: A psychological model for distinguishing among different aspects of depression and anxiety. *Social Cognition, 3,* 51–76.

Higgins, E. T., Loeb, I., & Moretti, M. (1995). Self-discrepancies and developmental shifts in vulnerability: Life transitions in the regulatory significance of others. In D. Cicchetti & S. L. Toth (Eds.), *Emotion, cognition, and representation: Rochester Symposium on Developmental Psychopathology* (Vol. 6, pp. 191–230). Rochester: University of Rochester Press.

Hinde, R. A. (1974). *Biological bases of human social behavior.* New York: McGraw-Hill.

Hinde, R. A. (1979). *Towards understanding relationships.* London: Academic Press.

Hinde, R. A. (1987). Interpersonal relationships and child development. *Developmental Review, 7,* 1–21.

Hobson, R. F. (1974). Loneliness. *Journal of Analytical Psychology, 19,* 71–78.

Hojat, M. (1982). Loneliness as a function of parent–child and peer relations. *The Journal of Psychology, 112,* 129–133.

Hojat, M. (1983). Comparison of transitory and chronic loners on selected personality variables. *British Journal of Psychology, 74,* 199–202.

Hojat, M. (1987). A psychodynamic view of loneliness and mother–child relationships: A review of theoretical perspectives and empirical findings. In M. Hojat & R. Crandall (Eds.), Loneliness: Theory, research and applications [Special issue]. *Journal of Social Behavior and Personality, 89–104.*

Hollingshead, A. B., & Redlich, F. C. (1958). *Social class and mental illness.* New York: Wiley.

Holmes, T., & Rahe, R. (1967). The social readjustment rating scale. *Journal of Psychosomatic Research, 11,* 213–218.

Hoover, J., & Hazler, R. J. (1991). Bullies and victims. *Elementary School Guidance and Counseling, 25,* 212–219.

Hopmeyer, A., & Asher, S. R. (1997). Children's responses to peer conflict involving a rights infraction, *Merrill-Palmer Quarterly, 43,* 235–254.

Hopmeyer, A., Parkhurst, J. T., & Asher, S. R. (1995, August). *Vulnerability to negative self-evaluative emotions and loneliness in early adolescence.* Poster presented at the 104th Annual Convention of the American Psychological Association, New York.

Horowitz, L. M., French, R., & Anderson, C. A. (1982). The prototype of a lonely person. In L. A. Peplau & D. Perlman (Eds.), *Loneliness: A sourcebook of current theory, research, and therapy* (pp. 183–205). New York: Wiley.

Howe, I. (1967a). Culture of modernism. *Commentary, 44*(5), 48–59.

Howe, I. (1967b). *The idea of the modern in literature and the arts.* New York: Horizon.

Howes, C., Hamilton, C., & Matheson, C. C. (1994). Children's relationships with peers: Differential associations with aspects of the teacher–child relationship. *Child Development, 65,* 253–263.

Howes, C., Matheson, C. C., & Hamilton, C. (1994). Maternal, teacher, and child care correlates of children's relationships with peers. *Child Development, 65,* 264–273.

Howes, C., & Phillipsen, L. (1996, April). The consistency and predictability of teacher–child relationships during the transition to kindergarten. In S. H. Birch (Chair), *Children's relationships with teachers: Assessment, continuity, and linkages with school adjustment.* Symposium conducted at the annual meeting of the American Educational Research Association, New York.

Humphreys, A. P., & Smith, P. K. (1987). Rough and tumble, friendship, and dominance in school children: Evidence for continuity and change with age. *Child Development, 2*(1), 201–212.

Hunter, F., & Youniss, J. (1982). Changes in functions of three relations during adolescence. *Developmental Psychology, 18,* 806–811.

Huntingford, F. (1984). *The study of animal behavior.* London: Chapman & Hall.

Hymel, S., Bowker, A., & Woody, E. (1993). Aggressive versus withdrawn unpopular children: Variations in peer and self-perceptions in multiple domains. *Child Development, 64,* 879–896.

Hymel, S., & Franke, S. (1985). Children's peer relations: Assessing self-perceptions. In B. H. Schneider, K. H. Rubin, & J. E. Ledingham (Eds.), *Children's peer relations: Issues in assessment and intervention* (pp. 78–91). New York: Springer-Verlag.

Hymel, S., Franke, S., & Freigang, R. (1985). Peer relationships and their dysfunction: Considering the child's perspective. *Journal of Social and Clinical Psychology, 3*, 405–415.

Hymel, S., Freigang, R., Franke, S., Both, L., Bream, L., & Borys, S. (June, 1983). *Children's attributions for social situations: Variations as a function of social status and self-perception variables.* Paper presented at the annual meeting of the Canadian Psychological Association, Winnipeg, Manitoba, Canada.

Hymel, S., Rubin, K. H., Rowden, L., & LeMare, L. (1990). Children's peer relationships: Longitudinal prediction of internalizing and externalizing problems from middle to late childhood. *Child Development, 61*, 2004–2021.

Hymel, S., Woody, E., & Bowker, A. (1993). Social withdrawal in childhood: Considering the child's perspective. In K. H. Rubin & J. B. Asendorpf (Eds.), *Social withdrawal, inhibition, and shyness in childhood* (pp. 237–262). Hillsdale, NJ: Erlbaum.

Hymel, S., Woody, E., Ditner, E., & LeMare, L. (1988, May). *Children's self-perceptions in different domains: Are children consistent across measures, and do they see what others see?* Paper presented at the Biennial University of Waterloo Conference on Child Development, Waterloo, Ontario, Canada.

Illingsworth, R. S. (1955, January 8). Crying in infants and children. *British Medical Journal*, 75–78.

Inderbitzen-Pisaruk, H., Clark, M. L., & Solano, C. H. (1992). Correlates of loneliness in mid-adolescence. *Journal of Youth and Adolescence, 21*, 151–167.

Inhelder, B., & Piaget, J. (1958). *The growth of logical thinking from childhood to adolescence.* New York: Basic Books.

Jack, D. C., & Dill, D. (1992). The silencing the self scale. *Psychology of Women Quarterly, 16*, 97–106.

Jackson, J., & Cochran, S. D. (1991). Loneliness and psychological distress. *The Journal of Psychology, 125*, 257–262.

Jacobson, J. L., & Wille, D. E. (1986). The influence of attachment pattern on developmental changes in peer interaction from the toddler to the preschool period. *Child Development, 57*, 338–347.

James, W. (1890). *The principles of psychology.* New York: Holt.

Jarvinen, D. W., & Nicholls, J. G. (1996). Adolescents' social goals, beliefs about the causes of social success, and satisfaction in peer relations. *Developmental Psychology, 32*, 435–441.

Jones, W. (1982). Loneliness and social behavior. In L. A. Peplau & D. Perlman (Eds.), *Loneliness: A sourcebook of current theory, research, and therapy* (pp. 238–252). New York: Wiley-Interscience.

Jones, W. H., & Carver, M. D. (1991). Adjustment and coping implications of loneliness. In C. R. Snyder & D. R. Forsyth (Eds.), *Handbook of social and clinical psychology: The health perspective* (pp. 395–415). New York: Persimmon Press.

Jones, W. H., Freemon, J. E., & Goswick, R. A. (1981). The persistence of loneliness: Self and other determinants. *Journal of Personality, 49*, 27–48.

Jones, W. H., Hobbs, S., & Hockenbury, D. (1982). Loneliness and social skill deficits. *Journal of Personality and Social Psychology, 42*, 682–689.

Jones, W. H., & Moore, T. L. (1987). Loneliness and social support. *Journal of Social Behavior and Personality, 2*(2, Pt. 2), 145–156.

Jylha, M., & Jokela, J. (1990). Individual experiences as cultural: A cross-cultural study on loneliness among the elderly. *Aging and Society, 10,* 295–315.

Kagan, J., Hans, S., Markowitz, A., & Lopez, D. (1982). Validity of children's self-reports of psychological qualities. In B. A. Maher & W. B. Maher (Eds.), *Progress in experimental personality research (Vol. II): Normal personality processes* (pp. 171–211). New York: Academic Press.

Kahlbaugh, P. E., & Haviland, J. M. (1994). Nonverbal communication between parents and adolescents: A study of approach and avoidance behaviors. Special Issue: Development of nonverbal behavior: Vol. 11. Social development and nonverbal behavior. *Journal of Nonverbal Behavior, 18*(1), 91–113.

Karweit, N., & Hansell, S. (1982). Sex differences in adolescent relationships. In J. L. Epstein & N. Karweit (Eds.), *Friends in school* (pp. 115–130). New York: Academic Press.

Kashani, J. H., Beck, N. C., Hoeper, E. W., Fallahi, C., Corcoran, C. M., McAllister, J. A., Rosenberg, T. K., & Reid, J. C. (1987). Psychiatric disorders in a community sample of adolescents. *American Journal of Psychiatry, 144,* 584–589.

Kashani, J. H., & Orvachel, H. (1988). Anxiety disorders in mid-adolescence: A community sample. *American Journal of Psychiatry, 145,* 960–964.

Keating, D. P. (1990). Adolescent thinking. In G. R. Elliot & S. S. Feldman (Eds.), *At the threshold: The developing adolescent.* Cambridge, MA: Harvard University Press.

Kegan, R. (1982). *The evolving self.* Cambridge, MA: Harvard University Press.

Keller, B. B., & Bell, R. Q. (1977). Child effects on adults' method of eliciting altruistic behavior. *Child Development, 50,* 1004–1009.

Kestenbaum, R., Farber, E. A., & Sroufe, L. A. (1989). Individual differences in empathy among preschoolers: Relation to attachment history. In N. Eisenberg (Ed.), *Empathy and related emotional responses* (pp. 51–64). San Francisco: Jossey-Bass.

King, G. A., Specht, J. A., Schultz, I., Warr-Leeper, G., Redekop, W., & Risebrough, N. (1997). Social skills training for withdrawn unpopular children with physical disabilities: A preliminary evaluation. *Rehabilitation Psychology, 42,* 47–60.

Klein, D. C. (1991). The humiliation dynamic: An overview. *The Journal of Primary Prevention, 12*(2), 93–121.

Klinger, E. (1977). *Meaning and void: Inner experience and the incentives in people's lives.* Minneapolis: University of Minnesota Press.

Knight, R. G., & Chisholm, B. J. (1988). Some normative, reliability, and factor analytic data for the revised UCLA Loneliness Scale. *Journal of Clinical Psychology, 44,* 203–206.

Kobak, R. R., & Sceery, A. (1988). Attachment in late adolescence: Working models, affect regulation, and representations of self and others. *Child Development, 59,* 135–146.

Kochenderfer, B. J., & Ladd, G. W. (1996a). Peer victimization: Cause or consequence of school maladjustment? *Child Development, 67,* 1293–1305.

Kochenderfer, B. J., & Ladd, G. W. (1996b). Peer victimization: Manifestations and relations to school adjustment in kindergarten. *Journal of School Psychology, 34,* 267–283.

Koenig, L. J., & Embry, L. (1993, March). *Teenage optimism: Meaning and measurement.* Paper presented at the annual meeting of the Southeastern Psychological Association, Atlanta, GA.

Koenig, L. J., Isaacs, A. M., & Schwartz, J. A. J. (1994). Sex differences in adolescent depression and loneliness: Why are boys lonelier if girls are more depressed? *Journal of Research in Personality, 28,* 27–43.

Kovacs, M. (1985). The Children's Depression Inventory (CDI). *Psychopharmacology Bulletin, 21,* 995–998.

Kovacs, M. (1986). A developmental perspective on methods and measures in the assessment of depressive disorders: The clinical interview. In M. Rutter, C. Izard, & P. Read (Eds.), *Depression in young people: Developmental and clinical perspectives* (pp. 435–465). New York: Guilford Press.

Kroger, J. (1985). Relationships during adolescence: A cross-national comparison of New Zealand and United States teenagers. *Journal of Adolescence, 8,* 47–56.

Kupersmidt, J. B., Buchele, K. S., Voegler, M. E., & Sedikides, C. (1996). Social self-discrepancy: A theory relating peer relations problems and school maladjustment (pp. 66–97). In J. Juvonen & K. R. Wentzel (Eds.), *Social motivation: Understanding children's school adjustment* (pp. 66–97). Cambridge, England: Cambridge University Press.

Kupersmidt, J. B., Voegler, M. E., Sigda, K. B., & Sedikides, C. (1996). *The Social Selves Questionnaire.* Unpublished manuscript, University of North Carolina at Chapel Hill.

Ladd, G. W. (1983). Social networks of popular, average, and rejected children in school settings. *Merrill-Palmer Quarterly, 9,* 283–307.

Ladd, G. W. (1988). Friendship patterns and peer status during early and middle childhood. *Journal of Developmental and Behavioral Pediatrics, 9,* 229–238.

Ladd, G. W. (1990). Having friends, keeping friends, making friends, and being liked by peers in the classroom: Predictors of children's early school adjustment? *Child Development, 61,* 1081–1100.

Ladd, G. W. (1991). Family–peer relations during childhood: Pathways to competence and pathology? *Journal of Social and Personal Relationships 8,* 307–314.

Ladd, G. W. (1992). Themes and theories: Perspectives on processes in family–peer relationships. In R. D. Parke & G. W. Ladd (Eds.), *Family–peer relationships: Modes of linkage* (pp. 1–34). Hillsdale, NJ: Erlbaum.

Ladd, G. W. (1996). Shifting ecologies during the 5 to 7 year period: Predicting children's adjustment during the transition to grade school. In A. Sameroff & M. Haith (Eds.), *The five to seven year shift* (pp. 363–386). Chicago: University of Chicago Press.

Ladd, G. W., & Burgess, K. B. (in press). Charting the relationship trajectories of aggressive, withdrawn, and aggressive/withdrawn children during early grade school child development. *Child Development.*

Ladd, G. W., & Coleman, C. C. (1997). Children's classroom peer relationships and early school attitudes: Concurrent and longitudinal associations. *Early Education and Development, 8,* 51–66.

Ladd, G. W., & Golter, B. S. (1988). Parents' management of preschooler's peer relations: Is it related to children's social competence? *Developmental Psychology, 24,* 109–117.

Ladd, G. W., & Kochenderfer, B. J. (1996). Linkages between friendship and adjustment during early school transitions. In W. M. Bukowski, A. F. Newcomb, & W. W. Hartup (Eds.), *The company they keep: Friendship in childhood and adolescence* (pp. 322–345). New York: Cambridge University Press.

Ladd, G. W., Kochenderfer, B. J., & Coleman, C. C. (1996). Friendship quality as a predictor of young children's early school adjustment. *Child Development, 67,* 1103–1118.

Ladd, G. W., Kochenderfer, B. J., & Coleman, C. C. (1997). Classroom peer acceptance, friendship, and victimization: Distinct relational systems that contribute uniquely to children's school adjustment? *Child Development, 68,* 1181–1197.

Ladd, G. W., Price, J. M., & Hart, C. H. (1990). Preschoolers' behavioral orientations and patterns of peer contact: Predictive of social status? In S. R. Asher & J. D. Coie (Eds.), *Peer rejection in childhood* (pp. 90–118). New York: Cambridge University Press.

LaFreniere, P. J., & Sroufe, L. A. (1985). Profiles of peer competence in the preschool: Interrelations between measures, influence of social ecology, and relation to attachment history. *Developmental Psychology, 21,* 56–66.

Lambert, S. F. (1997). *Familial factors and child reported loneliness in kindergarten.* Paper presented at the Biennial Meeting of Society for Research in Child Development, Washington, DC.

Lamborn, S. D., Fischer, K. W., & Pipp, S. (1994). Constructive criticism and social lies: A developmental sequence for understanding honesty and kindness in social interactions. *Developmental Psychology, 10*(4), 495–508.

Larson, R. W. (1983). Adolescents' daily experience with family and friends: Contrasting opportunity systems. *Journal of Marriage and the Family, 45,* 739–750.

Larson, R. W. (1990). The solitary side of life: An examination of the time people spend alone from childhood to old age. *Developmental Review, 10,* 155–183.

Larson, R. W. (1995). Secrets in the bedroom: Adolescents' private use of media. *Journal of Youth and Adolescence, 24,* 535–550.

Larson, R. W. (1997). The emergence of solitude as a constructive domain of experience in early adolescence. *Child Development, 68,* 80–93.

Larson, R. W., & Csikszentmihalyi, M. (1978). Experiential correlates of time alone in adolescence. *Journal of Personality, 46,* 677–693.

Larson, R. W., & Csikszentmihalyi, M. (1980). The significance of time alone in adolescent development. *Journal of Current Adolescent Medicine, 2,* 33–40.

Larson, R. W., Csikszentmihalyi, M., & Graef, R. (1982). Time alone in daily experience: Loneliness or renewal? In L. A. Peplau & D. Perlman (Eds.), *Loneliness: A sourcebook of current theory, research, and therapy* (pp. 40–53). New York: Wiley-Interscience.

Larson, R. W., & Lampman-Petraitis, C. (1989). Daily emotional states as reported by children and adolescents. *Child Development, 60,* 1250–1260.

Larson, R. W., & Lee, M. (1996). The capacity to be alone as a stress buffer. *Journal of Social Psychology, 136,* 5–16.

Larson, R. W., Rafaelli, M., Richards, M. H., Ham, M., & Jewel, L. (1990). Ecology of depression in late childhood and early adolescence: A profile of daily states and activities. *Journal of Abnormal Psychology, 99,* 92–102.

Larson, R. W., & Richards, M. H. (Eds.). (1989). The changing life space of early adolescence [Special issue]. *Journal of Youth and Adolescence, 18,* 501–626.

Larson, R. W., & Richards, M. H. (1991). Daily companionship in late childhood and early adolescence: Changing developmental contexts. *Child Development, 62,* 284–300.

Larson, R. W., & Richards, M. H. (in press). Waiting for the weekend: The development of Friday and Saturday nights as the emotional climax of the week. In R. W. Larson & A. C. Crouter (Eds.), *Temporal rhythms in the lives of adolescents: Themes and variations.* San Francisco: Jossey-Bass.

Larson, R. W., Richards, M. H., Moneta, G., Holmbeck, G., & Duckett, E. (1996). Changes in adolescents' daily interactions with their families from ages 10 to 18: Disengagement and transformation. *Developmental Psychology, 32,* 744–754.

Laursen, B. (Ed.) (1993). *Close friendships in adolescence.* In W. Damon (Series Ed.), *New directions for child development.* San Francisco: Jossey-Bass.

Lazarus, R. S. (1991). *Emotion and adaptation.* New York: Oxford University Press.

Leary, M. R. (1983). Social anxiousness: The construct and its measurement. *Journal of Personality Assessment, 47,* 66–75.

Lee, C., & Gotlib, L. (1989). Clinical status and emotional adjustment of children of depressed mothers. *American Journal of Psychiatry, 146,* 478–483.

Lee, M. (1994). *Cultural differences in the daily manifestation of adolescent depression: A comparative study of American and Korean high school seniors.* Unpublished doctoral dissertation, University of Illinois, Urbana – Champaign.

LeVine, R. A. (1990). Infant environments in psychoanalysis: A cross-cultural view. In J. W. Stigler, R. A. Shweder, & G. Herdt (Eds.), *Cultural psychology: Essays on comparative human development* (pp. 454–474). New York: Cambridge University Press.

Lewinsohn, P. M., Hops, H., Roberts, R. E., Seeley, J. R., & Andrews, J. A. (1993). Adolescent psychopathology: Vol. 1. Prevalence and incidence of depression and other *DSM – III-R* disorders in high school students. *Journal of Abnormal Psychology, 102,* 133–144.

Lewis, M. (1992). *The exposed self.* New York: Free Press.

Lewis, M., Alessandri, S. M., & Sullivan, M. W. (1992). Differences in shame and pride as a function of children's gender and task difficulty. *Child Development, 63,* 630–638.

Lewis, M., & Feiring, C. (1989). Early predictors of childhood friendship. In T. J. Berndt & G. W. Ladd (Eds.), *Peer relationships in child development* (pp. 246–273). New York: Wiley.

Lewis, M., & Rosenblum, L. A. (1975). *Friendship and peer relations.* New York: Wiley.

Lewis, M., Young, G., Brooks, & Michalson, L. (1975). The beginning of friendship. In M. Lewis & R. A. Rosenblum (Eds.), *Friendship and peer relations.* New York: Wiley.

Lieberman, A. F. (1977). Preschoolers' competence with a peer: Relations with attachment and peer experience. *Child Development, 48,* 1277–1287.

Lobdell, J., & Perlman, D. (1986). The intergenerational transmission of loneliness: A study of college females and their parents. *Journal of Marriage and the Family, 48,* 589–595.

Lonigan, C. J., Kistner, J. A., Risi, S., & Balthazor, M. (1994, November). *Paradox lost: Are loneliness and depression really measures of similar constructs?* Paper presented at the annual meeting of the Association for the Advancement of Behavior Therapy, San Diego, CA.

Lynch, J. J. (1977). *The broken heart: The medical consequences of loneliness.* New York: Basic Books.

Lyons-Ruth, K. (1995). Broadening our conceptual frameworks: Can we reintroduce relational strategies and implicit representational systems to the study of psychopathology? *Developmental Psychology, 31,* 432–436.

Maccoby, E. E. (1988). Gender as a social category. *Developmental Psychology, 24,* 755–765.

Maccoby, E. E., & Martin, J. (1983). Socialization in the context of the family: Parent–child interaction. In P. H. Mussen (Series Ed.) & E. M. Hetherington (Vol. Ed.), *Handbook of child psychology (Vol. 4): Socialization, personality, and social development* (4th ed., pp. 1–101). New York: Wiley.

MacDonald, K., & Parke, R. D. (1984). Bridging the gap: Parent–child play interaction and peer interactive competence. *Child Development, 55,* 1265–1277.

Mahler, M. S., Pine, F., & Bergman, A. (1975). *The psychological birth of the infant.* New York: Basic Books.

Main, M. (1981). Avoidance in the service of attachment: A working paper. In K. Immelman, G. Barlow, M. Main, & L. Petrinovich (Eds.), *The Bielefeld interdisciplinary project* (pp. 651–693). New York: Cambridge University Press.

Main, M. (1990). Cross-cultural studies of attachment organization: Recent studies, changing methodologies, and the concept of conditional strategies. *Human Development, 33,* 48–61.

Main, M., Kaplan, N., & Cassidy, J. (1985). Security in infancy, childhood, and adulthood: A move to the level of representation. In I. Bretherton & E. Waters (Eds.), Growing points of attachment theory and research. *Monographs of the Society for Research in Child Development, 50* (1–2, Serial No. 209), 66–104.

Main, M., & Weston, D. (1981). The quality of the toddler's relationship to mother and to father: Related to conflict behavior and the readiness to establish new relationships. *Child Development, 52,* 932–940.

Malik, S. (1981) *Psychological modernity: A comparative study of some African and American graduate students.* Unpublished doctoral dissertation, University of Chicago.

Mandler, J. M. (1990). A new perspective on cognitive development in infancy. *American Scientist, 78,* 236–243.

Marangoni, C., & Ickes, W. (1989). Loneliness: A theoretical review with implications for measurement. *Journal of Social and Personal Relationships, 6,* 93–128.

Marcia, J. E. (1966). Development and validation of ego-identity status. *Journal of Personality and Social Psychology, 3,* 551–558.

Marcia, J. E. (1980). Identity in adolescence. In J. Adelson (Ed.), *Handbook of adolescent psychology* (pp. 159–187). New York: Wiley.

Marcoen, A., & Brumagne, M. (1985). Loneliness among children and young adolescents. *Developmental Psychology, 21*(6), 1025–1031.

Marcoen, A., & Goossens, L. (1989, July). *Adolescents' feelings of loneliness and aloneness: Relationships with ideological identity, interpersonal identity, and intimacy.* Paper presented at the 10th Biennial Meeting of the International Society for the Study of Behavioral Development, Jyvaskyla, Finland.

Marcoen, A., & Goossens, L. (1993). Loneliness, attitude towards aloneness, and solitude: Age differences and developmental significance during adolescence. In S. Jackson & H. Rodriguez-Tome (Eds.), *Adolescence and its social worlds* (pp. 197–227). Hillsdale, NJ: Erlbaum.

Marcoen, A., & Goossens, L. (1995, November). *Loneliness and depression in mid-adolescence: A multi-dimensional approach.* Poster presented at the International Conference on Conflict and Development in Adolescence, Ghent, Belgium.

Marcoen, A., Goossens, L., & Caes, P. (1987). Loneliness in pre- through late adolescence: Exploring the contributions of a multidimensional approach. *Journal of Youth and Adolescence, 16,* 561–577.

Margalit, M. (1994). *Loneliness among children with special needs: Theory, research, coping, and intervention.* New York: Springer.

Margalit, M., & Ben-Dov, I. (in press). Kibbutz versus city comparisons of social competence among students with and without learning disabilities. *International Journal of Behavioral Development.*

Maroldo, G. (1981). Shyness and loneliness among college men and women. *Psychological Reports, 48,* 885–886.

Marsh, H. W., Smith, I. D., & Barnes, J. (1983). Multitrait–multimethod analyses of the Self-Description Questionnaire: Student–teacher agreement on multidimensional ratings of student self-concept. *American Educational Research Journal, 20*(3), 333–357.

Marsh, H. W., Smith, I. D., & Barnes, J. (1985). Multidimensional self-concepts: Relations with sex and academic achievement. *Journal of Educational Psychology, 77*(5), 518–596.

Maslow, A. H. (1968). *Toward a psychology of being.* New York: Van Nostrand.

Masters, J. C., & Furman, W. (1981). Popularity, individual friendship selection, and specific peer interaction among children. *Developmental Psychology, 17,* 344–350.

Mathes, E. W., Adams, H. E., & Davies, R. M. (1985). Jealousy: Loss of relationship rewards, loss of self-esteem, depression, anxiety, and anger. *Journal of Personality and Social Psychology, 48,* 1552–1561.

Matteson, D. R. (1977). Exploration and commitment: Sex differences and methodological problems in the use of identity status categories. *Journal of Youth and Adolescence, 6,* 353–374.

Maybury-Lewis, D. (1992). *Millennium: Tribal wisdom and the modern world.* New York: Viking Press.

McClelland, D. C. (1985). *Human motivation.* Glenview, IL: Scott, Foresman, & Co.

McCormack, J. (1984). *Interpersonal influences and the channeling of goals in adolescence.* Unpublished doctoral dissertation, University of Chicago.

McGee, R., Feehan, M., Williams, S., Partridge, F., Silva, P., & Kelly, J. (1990). DSM–III disorders in a large sample of adolescents. *Journal of the American Academy of Child and Adolescent Psychiatry, 29,* 611–619.

McNally, S., Eisenberg, N., & Harris, J. D. (1991). Consistency and change in maternal child-rearing practices and values: A longitudinal study. *Child Development, 62,* 190–198.

McWhirter, B. T. (1990a). Factor analysis of the revised UCLA Loneliness Scale. *Current Psychology: Research and Reviews, 9,* 56–68.

McWhirter, B. T. (1990b). Loneliness: A review of current literature, with implications for counseling and research. *Journal of Counseling and Development, 68,* 417–422.

Medora, N., Woodward, J., & Larson, J. (1987). Adolescent loneliness: A cross-cultural comparison of Americans and Asian Indians. *International Journal of Comparative Sociology, 28,* 3–4.

Mijuskovic, B. L. (1985). *Loneliness.* New York: Associated Faculty Press.

Miller, L. C., Murphy, R., & Buss, A. H. (1981). Consciousness of body: Private and public. *Journal of Personality and Social Psychology, 41,* 397–406.

Miller, R., Caul, W., & Mirsky, I. (1967). Communication of affect between feral and socially isolated monkeys. *Journal of Personality and Social Psychology, 7,* 231–239.

Miller, R. S. (1992). The nature and severity of self-reported embarrassing circumstances. *Personality and Social Psychology Bulletin, 18*(2), 190–198.

Miller, S. B. (1988). Humiliation and shame: Comparing two affect states as indicators of narcissistic stress. *Bulletin of the Menninger Foundation, 52,* 40–51.

Montemayor, R. (1982). The relationship between parent–adolescent conflict and the amount of time adolescents spend alone and with parents and peers. *Child Development, 53,* 1512–1519.

Moore, D., & Schultz, N. R. (1983). Loneliness at adolescence: Correlates, attributions, and coping. *Journal of Youth and Adolescence, 12,* 95–100.

Morelli, G. A., Rogoff, B., Oppenheim, D., & Goldsmith, D. (1992). Cultural variation in infants' sleeping arrangements: Questions of independence. *Developmental Psychology, 28,* 604–613.

Moustakas, C. E. (1961). *Loneliness.* New York: Prentice-Hall.

Murray, H. (1938). *Explorations in personality.* New York: Oxford University Press.

Nathanson, D. L. (1992). *Shame and pride: Affect, sex. and the birth of the self,* New York: W. W. Norton.

Newcomb, M. D., & Bentler, P. M. (1986). Loneliness and social support: A confirmatory hierarchical analysis. *Personality and Social Psychology Bulletin, 12,* 520–535.

Nicholls, J. G., Licht, B. G., & Pearl, R. A. (1982). Some dangers of using personality questionnaires to study personality. *Psychological Bulletin, 92*(3), 572–580.

Niemi, T. (1979). Effect of loneliness on mortality after retirement. *Scandinavian Journal of Social Medicine, 7*(2), 63–65.

Nolen-Hoeksema, S. (1987). Sex differences in unipolar depression: Evidence and theory. *Psychological Bulletin, 101*, 259–282.

Nolen-Hoeksema, S., & Girgus, J. S. (1994). The emergence of gender differences in depression during adolescence. *Psychological Bulletin, 115*, 424–443.

Offer, D., Ostrov, E., & Howard, K. (1981). *The adolescent: A psychological self-portrait.* New York: Basic Books.

Offord, D. R., Boyle, M. H., Szatmari, P., Rae-Grant, N. I., Links, P. S., Cadman, D. T., Byles, J. A., Crawford, J. W., Blum, H. M., Byrne, C., Thomas, H., & Woodward, C. A. (1987). Ontario Child Health Study. II: Six-month prevalence of disorder and rates of service utilization. *Archives of General Psychiatry, 44*, 832–836.

Olmstead, R. E., Guy, S. M., O'Malley, P. M., & Bentler, P. (1991). Longitudinal assessment of the relationship between self-esteem, fatalism, loneliness, and substance use. *Journal of Social Behavior and Personality, 6*, 749–770.

Olweus, D. (1993a). *Bullying at school: What we know and what we can do.* Oxford, England: Blackwell Publishers.

Olweus, D. (1993b). Victimization by peers: Antecedents and long-term outcomes. In K. H. Rubin & J. B. Asendorpf (Eds.), *Social withdrawal, inhibition, and shyness in childhood* (pp. 315–341). Hillsdale, NJ: Erlbaum.

Oppenheim, D., Sagi, A., & Lamb, M. (1988). Infant–adult attachments on the kibbutz and their relation to socioemotional development 4 years later. *Developmental Psychology, 24*, 427–433.

Ostrov, E., & Offer, D. (1978). Loneliness and the adolescent. *Adolescent Psychiatry, 6*, 34–50.

Ostrov, E., & Offer, D. (1980). Loneliness and the adolescent. In J. Hartog, J. R. Audy, & Y. A. Cohen (Eds.), *The anatomy of loneliness.* New York: International Universities Press.

Page, R. M. (1990). High school size as a factor in adolescent loneliness. *High School Journal,* Feb./March, 150–153.

Page, R. M., Frey, J., Talbert, R., & Falk, C. (1992). Children's feelings of loneliness and social dissatisfaction: Relationship to measures of physical fitness and activity. *Journal of Teaching in Physical Education, 11*, 211–219.

Paloutzian, R. F., & Janigian, A. S. (1987). Models and methods in loneliness research: Their status and direction. In M. Hojat & R. Crandall (Eds.), Loneliness: Theory, research, and applications [Special issue]. *Journal of Social Behavior and Personality, 2*, 31–36.

Paloutzian, R. F., & Ellison, C. W. (1979). *Emotional, behavioral, and physical correlates of loneliness.* Paper presented at Research Conference on Loneliness, University of California, Los Angeles.

Paloutzian, R. F., & Ellison, C. W. (1982). Loneliness, spiritual well-being, and the quality of life. In L. A. Peplau & D. Perlman (Eds.), *Loneliness: Current theory, research, and therapy* (pp. 224–237). New York: Wiley.

Park, K. A., & Waters, E. (1989). Security of attachment and preschool friendships. *Child Development, 60,* 1076–1081.

Parke, R. D. (1992). Epilogue: Remaining issues and future trends in the study of family–peer relationships. In R. D. Parke & G. W. Ladd (Eds.), *Family–peer relationships: Modes of linkage* (pp. 425–438). Hillsdale, NJ: Erlbaum.

Parke, R. D., & Bhavnagri, N. P. (1989). Parents as managers of children's peer relationships. In D. Belle (Ed.), *Children's social networks and social supports* (pp. 241–259). New York: Wiley.

Parke, R. D., & Ladd, G. W. (1992). *Family–peer relationships: Modes of linkage.* Hillsdale, NJ: Erlbaum.

Parke, R. D., MacDonald, K. B., Burks, V. M., Carson, J., Bhavnagri, N., Barth, J. M., & Beitel, A. (1989). Family and peer systems: In search of linkages. In K. Kreppner & R. M. Lerner (Eds.), *Family systems and life-span development* (pp. 65–104). Hillsdale, NJ: Erlbaum.

Parke, R. D., & Sawin, D. B. (1979). Children's privacy in the home: Developmental, ecological, and child-rearing determinants. *Environment and Behavior, 11,* 87–104.

Parker, J. G., & Asher, S. R. (1987). Peer relations and later personal adjustment: Are low accepted children at risk? *Psychological Bulletin, 102,* 357–389.

Parker, J. G., & Asher, S. R. (1993a). Beyond group acceptance: Friendship adjustment and friendship quality as distinct dimensions of children's peer adjustment. In D. Perlman & W. H. Jones (Eds.), *Advances in personal relationships* (Vol. 4, pp. 261–294). London: Kingsley.

Parker, J. G., & Asher, S. R. (1993b). Friendship and friendship quality in middle childhood: Links with peer group acceptance and feelings of loneliness and social dissatisfaction. *Developmental Psychology, 29,* 611–621.

Parker, J. G., & Gottman, J. M. (1989). Social and emotional development in a relational context: Friendship interaction from early childhood to adolescence. In T. J. Berndt & G. W. Ladd (Eds.), *Peer relationships in child development* (pp. 95–131). New York: Wiley.

Parker, J. G., Saxon, J. L., Houlihan, K., & Casas, J. (1997, April). Assessing children's best friendships: Conceptual issues and the development and evaluation of a new q-sort instrument. In C. Leaper & J. G. Parker (Chairs), *Gender dynamics in the features and organization of children's friendships.* Symposium conducted at the Biennial meeting of the Society for Research in Child Development, Washington, DC.

Parker, J. G., Rubin, K. H., Price, J. M., & DeRosier, M. E. (1995). Peer relationships, child development, and adjustment: A developmental psychopathology perspective. In D. Cicchetti & D. J. Cohen (Eds.), *Developmental psychopathology. Vol. 2: Risk, disorder, and adaptation* (pp. 96–161). New York: Wiley.

Parker, J. G., & Seal, J. (1996). Forming, losing, renewing, and replacing friendships: Applying temporal parameters to the assessment of children's friendship experiences. *Child Development, 67,* 2248–2268.

Parkhurst, J. T., & Asher, S. R. (1985). Goals and concerns: Implications for the study of children's social competence. In B. B. Lahey & A. E. Kazdin (Eds.), *Advances in clinical child psychology* (Vol. 8, pp. 199–228). New York: Plenum.

Parkhurst, J. T., & Asher, S. R. (1992). Peer rejection in middle school: Subgroup differences in behavior, loneliness, and interpersonal concerns. *Developmental Psychology, 28,* 231–241.

Parkhurst, J. T., & Cain, K. (1999). *A model of the self, its functioning, and several emotions.* Manuscript in preparation.

Parkhurst, J. T., & Gottman, J. M. (1986). How young children get what they want. In J. M. Gottman & J. G. Parker (Eds.), *Conversations of friends: Speculations on affective development.* New York: Cambridge University Press.

Parkhurst, J. T., Roedel, T. D., Bendixen, L. D., & Potenza, M. T. (1991, April). Subgroups of rejected middle school students: Their behavioral characteristics, friendships, and social concerns. In J. T. Parkhurst & D. L. Rabiner (Co-Chairs), *The behavioral characteristics and the subjective experience of aggressive and withdrawn/submissive rejected children.* Symposium conducted at the biennial meeting of the Society for Research in Child Development, Seattle, WA.

Parkhurst, J. T., & Troop, W. (1999). *Distinctions among guilt, shame, humiliation, and embarrassment.* Manuscript in preparation.

Parrott, W. G., & Smith, R. H. (1993). Distinguishing the experiences of envy and jealousy. *Journal of Personality and Social Psychology, 64*(6), 906–920.

Parten, M. B. (1932). Social participation among preschool children. *Journal of Abnormal Psychology, 27,* 243–269.

Pastor, D. (1981). The quality of mother–infant attachment and its relationship to toddlers' initial sociability with peers. *Developmental Psychology, 17,* 326–335.

Patterson, C., Cohn, D., & Kao, B. (1989). Maternal warmth as a protective factor against risks associated with peer rejection among children. *Development and Psychopathology, 1,* 21–38.

Patterson, C. J., Kupersmidt, J. B., & Griesler, P. C. (1990). Children's perceptions of self and of relationships with others as a function of sociometric status. *Child Development, 61,* 1335–1349.

Patterson, C. J., Vaden, N. A., & Kupersmidt, J. B. (1991). Family background, recent life events, and peer rejection during childhood. *Journal of Social and Personal Relationships, 8,* 347–361.

Peplau, L. A., & Perlman, D. (1979). Blueprint for a social psychological theory of loneliness. In M. Cook & G. Wilson (Eds.), *Love and attraction: An interpersonal conference* (pp. 101–110). New York: Pergamon.

Peplau, L. A., & Perlman, D. (1982a). *Loneliness: A sourcebook of current theory, research, and therapy.* New York: Wiley-Interscience.

Peplau, L. A., & Perlman, D. (1982b). Perspectives on loneliness. In L. A. Peplau & D. Perlman (Eds.), *Loneliness: A sourcebook of current theory, research, and therapy* (pp. 1–18). New York: Wiley-Interscience.

Peplau, L. A., & Miceli, M., & Morasch, B. (1982). Loneliness and self-evaluation. In L. A. Peplau & D. Perlman (Eds.), *Loneliness: A sourcebook of current theory, research, and therapy* (pp. 135–151). New York: Wiley-Interscience.

Perlman, D. (1988). Loneliness: A life span, developmental perspective. In R. M. Milardo (Ed.), *Families and social networks* (pp. 190–220). Newbury Park, CA: Sage.

Perlman, D. (1991). *Age differences in loneliness: A meta analysis.* Vancouver, Canada: University of British Columbia (ERIC Document Reproduction Service No. ED 326767).

Perlman, D., & Peplau, L. A. (1981). Toward a social psychology of loneliness. In R. Gilmour & S. Duck (Eds.), *Personal relationships. Vol. 3: Personal relationships in disorder* (pp. 31–44). London: Academic Press.

Perlman, D., & Peplau, L. A. (1982). Theoretical approaches to loneliness. In L. A. Peplau & D. Perlman (Eds.), *Loneliness: Current theory, research, and therapy* (pp. 123–134). New York: Wiley.

Perlman, D., & Peplau, L. A. (1984). Loneliness research: A survey of empirical findings. In L. A. Peplau & S. E. Goldston (Eds.), *Preventing the harmful consequences of severe and persistent loneliness* (pp. 13–46) (DHHS Publication No. ADM 84-1312). Washington, DC: U.S. Government Printing Office.

Perry, D. G. (1995). *Uses and abuses of the peer rejection construct.* Unpublished manuscript.

Perry, D. G., Kusel, S. J., & Perry, L. C. (1988). Victims of peer aggression. *Developmental Psychology, 24,* 807–814.

Peterson, C., Semmel, A., Von Baeyer, C., Abramson, L. Y., Metalsky, G. I., & Seligman, M. E. P. (1982). The attributional style questionnaire. *Cognitive Therapy and Research, 6,* 287–300.

Piaget, J. (1926). *The language and thought of the child.* London: Routledge & Kegan Paul.

Piaget, J. (1954). *The construction of reality in the child.* New York: Basic Books. (Original work published 1937)

Piaget, J. (1965). *The moral-judgment of the child.* New York: Free Press.

Pierce, G. R., Sarason, L. G., & Sarason, B. R. (1991). General and relationship-based perceptions of social support: Are two constructs better than one? *Journal of Personality and Social Psychology, 61,* 1028–1039.

Piliavin, J. A., & Charng, H. (1988). What *is* the factorial structure of the private and public self-consciousness scales? *Personality and Social Psychology Bulletin, 14,* 587–595.

Pierrehumbert, B., Iannotti, R. J., Cummings, E. M., & Zahn-Waxler, C. (1989). Social functioning with mother and peers at 2 and 5 years: The influence of attachment. *International Journal of Behavioral Development, 12,* 85–100.

Putallaz, M. (1987). Maternal behavior and children's sociometric status. *Child Development, 58,* 324–340.

Putallaz, M., & Gottman, J. M. (1981). Social skills and group acceptance. In S. R. Asher & J. M. Gottman (Eds.), *The development of children's friendships* (pp. 116–149). New York: Cambridge University Press.

Putallaz, M., & Heflin, A. H. (1990). Parent–child interaction. In S. R. Asher & J. D. Coie (Eds.), *Peer rejection in childhood* (pp. 189–216). New York: Cambridge University Press.

Quay, H. C., & Werry, J. S. (1986). *Psychopathological disorders of childhood.* New York: Wiley.

Quay, L. C. (1992). Personal and family effects on loneliness. *Journal of Applied Developmental Psychology, 13,* 97–110.

Rabiner, D. L., & Coie, J. D. (1989). The effect of expectancy inductions on rejected children's acceptance by unfamiliar peers. *Developmental Psychology* 25, 450–457.

Radloff, L. S. (1977). The CES-D Scale: A self-report depression scale for research in the general population. *Applied Psychological Measurement, 1,* 385–401.

Rafaelli, M., & Duckett, E. (1989). "We were just talking...": Conversations in early adolescence. *Journal of Youth and Adolescence, 18,* 567–582.

Rauste-Von Wright, M., & Von Wright, J. (1992). Habitual somatic discomfort in a representative sample of adolescents. *Journal of Psychosomatic Research, 36,* 383–390.

Rawlins, W. K. (1992). *Friendship matters.* New York: Aldine de Gruyter.

Renken, B., Egeland, B., Marvinney, D., Mangelsdorf, S., & Sroufe, L. A. (1989). Early childhood antecedents of aggression and passive–withdrawal in early elementary school. *Journal of Personality, 57,* 257–282.

Renshaw, P. D., & Asher S. R. (1983). Children's social goals and strategies for social interaction. *Merrill-Palmer Quarterly, 29,* 353–374.

Renshaw, P. D., & Brown, P. J. (1992). Loneliness in middle childhood. *Journal of Social Psychology, 132,* 545–547.

Renshaw, P. D., & Brown, P. J. (1993). Loneliness in middle childhood: Concurrent and longitudinal predictors. *Child Development, 64,* 1271–1284.

Reynolds, C. R., & Richmond, B. O. (1978). What I think and feel: A revised measure of children's manifest anxiety. *Journal of Abnormal Child Psychology, 6,* 271–280.

Richards, M., Crowe, P., Larson, R., & Swarr, A. (1998). Developmental patterns and gender differences in the experience of peer companionship during adolescence. *Child Development, 69,* 154–163.

Richards, M. H., Crowe, P. A., Larson, R. W., & Swarr, A. (1998). Developmental patterns in the experience of heterosocial companionship during adolescence. *Child Development, 69,* 154–163.

Richards, M. H., & Larson, R. (1989). The life space and socialization of the self: Sex differences in the young adolescent. *Journal of Youth and Adolescence, 18,* 617–626.

Roberts, G. C., Block, J. H., & Block, J. (1984). Continuity and change in parents' child rearing practices. *Child Development, 55,* 586–597.

Rockhill, C., & Asher, S. R. (1992, April). *Peer assessment of the behavioral characteristics of poorly accepted boys and girls.* Paper presented at the meeting of the American Educational Research Association, San Francisco, CA.

Rogers, C. (1961). *On becoming a person.* Boston: Houghton Mifflin.

Rook, K. S. (1984). Promoting social bonding: Strategies for helping the lonely and socially isolated. *American Psychologist, 39,* 1389–1407.

Rook, K. S. (1988). Toward a more differentiated view of loneliness. In S. W. Duck (Ed.), *Handbook of personal relationships* (pp. 571–589). New York: Wiley.

Rose, T. (1994). *Black noise: Rap music and black culture in contemporary America.* Hanover, NH: Wesleyan/University Press of New England.

Roseman, I. J., Wiest, C., & Swartz, T. S. (1994). Phenomenology, behaviors, and goals differentiate discrete emotions. *Journal of Personality and Social Psychology, 67*(2), 206–221.

Rosenberg, M. (1965). *Society and the adolescent self-image.* Princeton, NJ: Princeton University Press.

Rotenberg, K. J. (1994). Loneliness and interpersonal trust. *Journal of Social and Clinical Psychology, 13,* 152–173.

Rotenberg, K. J. (1995). The socialisation of trust: Parents' and children's interpersonal trust. *International Journal of Behavioral Development, 18,* 713–726.

Rotenberg, K. J., & Chase, N. (1992). Development of the reciprocity of self-disclosure. *Journal of Genetic Psychology, 153,* 75–86.

Rotenberg, K. J., & Holowatuik, M. (1995). Lonely preadolescents' disclosure to familiar peers and related social problems. In K. Rotenberg (Ed.), *Disclosure processses in children and adolescents.* (pp. 100–110) Cambridge University Press.

Rotenberg, K. J., & Morrison, J. (1993). Loneliness and college achievement: Do loneliness scale scores predict college drop-out? *Psychological Reports, 73,* 1283–1288.

Rotenberg, K. J., & Whitney, P. (1992). Loneliness and disclosure processes in preadolescence. *Merrill-Palmer Quarterly, 38,* 401–416.

Rubenstein, C., & Shaver, P. (1982). The experience of loneliness. In L. A. Peplau & D. Perlman (Eds.), *Loneliness: A sourcebook of current theory, research, and therapy* (pp. 255–268). New York: Wiley-Interscience.

Rubin, E. C., Cohen, R., Houston, D. A., & Cockrel, J. (1996). Children's self-discrepancies and peer relationships. *Social Cognition, 14,* 93–112.

Rubin, K. H. (1985). Socially withdrawn children: An "at risk" population? In B. H. Schneider, K. H. Rubin, & J. E. Ledingham (Eds.), *Children's peer relations: Issues in assessment and intervention* (pp. 125–139). New York: Springer-Verlag.

Rubin, K. H. (1993). The Waterloo longitudinal project: Correlates and consequences of social withdrawal from childhood to adolescence. In K. H. Rubin & J. B. Asendorpf (Eds.), *Social withdrawal, inhibition, and shyness in childhood.* (pp. 291–314) Hillsdale, NJ: Erlbaum.

Rubin, K. H., & Asendorpf, J. B. (1993). Social withdrawal, inhibition, and shyness in childhood: Conceptual and definitional issues. In K. H. Rubin & J. B. Asendorpf (Eds.), *Social withdrawal, inhibition, and shyness in childhood* (pp. 3–17). Hillsdale, NJ: Erlbaum.

Rubin, K. H., & Clark, M. L. (1983). Preschool teachers' ratings of behavioral problems: Observational, sociometric, and social–cognitive correlates. *Journal of Abnormal Child Psychology, 11,* 273–285.

Rubin, K. H., Bukowski, W., & Parker, J. G. (1997). Peer interactions, relationships, and groups. In W. Damon (Ed.), *Handbook of child psychology.* Vol. 3: *Social, emotional, and personality development* (5th ed., pp. 619–700). New York: Wiley.

Rubin, K. H., Chen, X., & Hymel, S. (1993). Socioemotional characteristics of withdrawn and aggressive children. *Merrill-Palmer Quarterly, 39,* 518–534.

Rubin, K. H., Fein, G. G., & Vandenberg, B. (1983). Play. In E. M. Hetherington (Ed.), *Handbook of child psychology. Vol. 4: Socialization, personality, and social development* (pp. 693–774). New York: Wiley.

Rubin, K. H., Hymel, S., & Mills, R. S. L. (1989). Sociability and social withdrawal in childhood: Stability and outcomes. *Journal of Personality, 57*, 237–255.

Rubin, K. H., LeMare, L., & Lollis, S. (1990). Social withdrawal in children: Developmental pathways to peer rejection. In S. R. Asher & J. D. Coie (Eds.), *Peer rejection in childhood* (pp. 217–252). New York: Cambridge University Press.

Rubin, K. H., & Lollis, S. (1988). Peer relationships, social skills, and infant attachment: A continuity model. In J. Belsky & T. Nezworski (Eds.), *Clinical implications of attachment* (pp. 219–252). Hillsdale, NJ: Erlbaum.

Rubin, K. H., & Mills, R. S. L. (1988). The many faces of social isolation in childhood. *Journal of Consulting and Clinical Psychology, 56*, 916–924.

Rubin, K. H., & Mills, R. S. L. (1991). Conceptualizing developmental pathways to internalizing disorders in childhood. *Canadian Journal of Behavioural Science, 23*(3), 300–317.

Rubin, Z. (1980). *Children's friendships*. Cambridge, MA: Harvard University Press.

Rubin, Z. (1982). Children without friends. In L. A. Peplau & D. Perlman (Eds.), *Loneliness: A sourcebook of current theory, research, and therapy* (pp. 206–223). New York: Wiley-Interscience.

Rubinstein, C., & Shaver, P. (1980). Loneliness in two northeastern cities. In J. Hartog, J. R. Audy, & Y. A. Cohen (Eds.), *The anatomy of loneliness* (pp. 319–337). New York: International Universities Press.

Rushton, J. P., Brainerd, C., & Pressley, M. (1983). Behavioral development and construct validity: The principle of aggregation. *Psychological Bulletin, 94*, 18–38.

Russell, A., & Finnie, V. (1990). Preschool children's social status and maternal instructions to assist group entry. *Developmental Psychology, 26*, 603–611.

Russell, D. (1982). The measurement of loneliness. In L. A. Peplau & D. Perlman (Eds.), *Loneliness: A sourcebook of current theory, research and therapy* (pp. 81–104). New York: Wiley.

Russell, D. (1996). The UCLA Loneliness Scale (Version 3): Reliability, validity and factorial structure. *Journal of Personality Assessment, 66*, 20–40.

Russell, D., & Cutrona, C. (1985, August). *Loneliness and physical health among the rural elderly*. Paper presented at the Iowa Conference on Personal Relationships, Iowa City.

Russell, D., Cutrona, C., Rose, J., & Yurko, K. (1984). Social and emotional loneliness: An examination of Weiss's typology of loneliness. *Journal of Personality and Social Psychology, 46*, 1313–1321.

Russell, D., Peplau, L. A., & Cutrona, C. E. (1980). The revised UCLA Loneliness Scale: Concurrent and discriminant validity evidence. *Journal of Personality and Social Psychology, 39*, 472–480.

Russell, D., Peplau, L. A., & Ferguson, M. (1978). Developing a measure of loneliness. *Journal of Personality Assessment, 42*, 290–293.

Rutter, M. (1979). Protective factors in children's responses to stress and disadvantage. In M. W. Kent & J. E. Rolf (Eds.), *Primary intervention of psychopathology: Social competence in children* (Vol. 3, pp. 49–74). Hanover, NH: University Press of New England.

Rutter, M. (1986). The developmental psychopathology of depression: Issues and perspectives. In M. Rutter, C. Izard, & P. Read (Eds.), *Depression in young people* (pp. 3–30). New York: Guilford Press.

Rutter, M. (1990). Commentary: Some focus and process considerations regarding effects of parental depression on children. *Developmental Psychology, 26,* 60–67.

Saarni, C. (1988). Children's understanding of the interpersonal consequences of dissemblance of non-verbal emotional–expressive behavior: Deception [Special issue]. *Journal of Nonverbal Behavior, 12*(4), 275–294.

Saarni, C. (1989). Children's understanding of strategic control of emotional expression in social transactions. In C. Saarni & P. L. Harris (Eds.), *Children's understanding of emotion* (pp. 3–26). New York: Cambridge University Press.

Sadava, S. W., & Thompson, M. M. (1986). Loneliness, social drinking, and vulnerability to alcohol problems. *Canadian Journal of Behavioural Science, 18,* 133–139.

Salovey, P. (1991). *The psychology of envy and jealousy.* New York: Guilford Press.

Sameroff, A., & Chandler, M. (1975). Reproductive risk and the continuum of caretaking casualty. In F. D. Horowitz (Ed.), *Review of child development research* (Vol. 4, pp. 187–244). Chicago: University of Chicago Press.

Sameroff, A. J., & Seilfer, R. (1983). Familial risk and child competence. *Child Development, 54,* 1254–1268.

Sampson, E. E. (1977). Psychology and the American ideal. *Journal of Personality and Social Psychology, 35,* 767–782.

Sampson, E. E. (1988). The debate on individualism: Indigenous psychologies of the individual and their role in personal and societal functioning. *American Psychologist, 43,* 15–22.

Sanderson, J. A., & Siegal, M. (1995). Loneliness and stable friendship in rejected and nonrejected preschoolers. *Journal of Applied Developmental Psychology, 16,* 555–567.

Sarason, I. G., Sarason, B. R., & Shearin, E. N. (1986). Social support as an individual difference variable: Its stability, origins, and relational aspects. *Journal of Personality and Social Psychology, 50,* 845–855.

Saraswathi, T. S., & Dutta, R. (1988). *Invisible boundaries: Grooming for adult roles.* New Delhi, India: Northern Book Centre.

Saxon, J. L. (1996). *Distinguishing between the behavioral and affective features of children's friendships.* Unpublished master's thesis, University of Illinois at Urbana – Champaign.

Saxon, J. L., & Asher, S. R. (1998). *Distinguishing between the behavioral and affective features of children's friendships: Implications for the Understanding of loneliness.* Manuscript in preparation.

Scalise, J. J., Gintner, E. J., & Gerstein, L. H. (1984). A multi-dimensional loneliness measure: The loneliness rating scale (LRS). *Journal of Personality Assessment, 48,* 485–496.

Schaefer, E. (1965a). Children's reports of parental behavior: An inventory. *Child Development, 36,* 413–424.

Schaefer, E. (1965b). A configurational analysis of children's reports of parent behavior. *Journal of Consulting Psychology, 29*, 552–557.

Schaefer, E. S., Edgarton, M., & Aaronson, M. (1978). *Classroom behavior inventory: A teacher behavior checklist (Research version)*. Chapel Hill, NC: Frank Porter Graham Child Development Center.

Schaefer, E., & Bayley, N. (1963). Maternal, child behavior, and their inter-correlations from infancy through adolescence. *Monographs of the Society for Research in Child Development, 28* (3, Serial No. 87).

Schmidt, N. (1976). *The construction of a scale for the measurement of loneliness*. Unpublished master's thesis, York University, Toronto, Ontario, Canada.

Schmidt, N., & Sermat, V. (1983). Measuring loneliness in different relationships. *Journal of Personality and Social Psychology, 44*, 1038–1047.

Schmitt, J. P., & Kurdek, L. A. (1985). Age and gender differences in and personality correlates of loneliness in different relationships. *Journal of Personality Assessment, 49*, 485–496.

Schneider, C. D. (1977). *Shame, exposure, and privacy*. Boston: Beacon Press.

Schonert-Reichl, K. A., & Offer, D. (1992). Gender differences in adolescent symptoms. In B. B. Lahey & A. E. Kazdin (Eds.), *Advances in clinical child psychology* (Vol. 14, pp. 27–60). New York: Plenum Press.

Schore, A. (1994). *Affect regulation and the origin of the self: The neurobiology of emotional development*. Hillsdale, NJ: Erlbaum.

Schultz, N. R., Jr., & Moore, D. (1986). The loneliness experience of college students: Sex differences. *Personality and Social Psychology Bulletin, 12*, 111–119.

Schultz, N. R., Jr., & Moore, D. (1988). Loneliness: Differences across three age levels. *Journal of Social and Personal Relationships, 5*, 275–284.

Schultz, N. R., Jr., & Moore D. (1989). Further reflections on loneliness research: Commentary on Weiss's assessment of loneliness research. In M. Hojat & R. Crandall (Eds.), *Loneliness: Theory, research, and applications* (pp. 37–40). Newbury Park, CA: Sage.

Schumaker, J. F., Krejci, R. C., Small, L., & Sargent, R. G. (1985). Experience of loneliness by obese individuals. *Psychological Reports, 57*, 1147–1154.

Schwartz, J. A. J., & Koenig, L. J. (1996). Response styles and negative affect among adolescents. *Cognitive Therapy and Research, 20*, 13–36.

Schwartz, J. C., Barton-Henry, M. L., & Pruzinsky, T. (1985). Assessing childrea-ring behaviors: A comparison of ratings made by mother, father, child and sibling on the CRPBI. *Child Development, 56*, 462–479.

Schwartz, W. (1979). Degradation, accreditation, and rites of passage. *Psychiatry, 42*, 138–146.

Sedikides, C., & Skowronski, J. J. (1990). Toward reconciling personality and social psychology: A construct accessibility approach. *Journal of Social Behavior and Personality, 5*, 531–546.

Sedikides, C., & Skowronski, J. J. (1991). The law of cognitive structure activation. *Psychological Inquiry, 2*, 169–184.

Segrin, C. (1993). Social skills deficits and psychosocial problems: Antecedent, concomitant, or consequent? *Journal of Social and Clinical Psychology, 12*, 336–353.

Selman, R. L. (1980). *The growth of interpersonal understanding: developmental and clinical analyses*. New York: Academic Press.

Shaffer, D. R. (1994). *Social and personality development* (3rd ed.). Pacific Grove, CA: Brooks/Cole.

Shain, L., & Farber, B. A. (1989). Female identity development and self-reflection in late adolescence. *Adolescence, 24*, 381–392.

Shanahan, D. (1992). *Toward a genealogy of individualism*. Amherst: University of Massachusetts Press.

Shaver, P. (1982). Loneliness and loneliness prevention. In L. A. Peplau & S. E. Goldston (Eds.), *Preventing the harmful consequences of severe and persistent loneliness: Proceedings of a research planning workship*. (DHHS Publication No. ADM 84-1312). Rockville, MD: National Institute of Mental Health.

Shaver, P., Furman, W., & Buhrmester, D. (1985). Transition to college: Network changes, social skills and loneliness. In S. Duck & D. Perlman (Eds.), *Understanding Personal relationships: An interdisciplinary approach* (pp. 193–219). London: Sage.

Shaver, P., & Hazen, C. (1985). Incompatibility, loneliness, and "limerance." In W. Ickles (Ed.), *Compatible and incompatible relationships* (pp. 163–184). New York: Springer-Verlag.

Shaver, P., & Rubenstein, C. (1980). Childhood attachment experience and adult loneliness. In L. Wheeler (Ed.), *Review of personality and social psychology* (Vol. 1, pp. 42–73). Beverly Hills, CA: Sage.

Shields, S. A., Mallory, M. E., & Simon, A. (1990). The experience and symptoms of blushing as a function of age and reported frequency of blushing. *Journal of Nonverbal Behavior, 14*(3), 171–187.

Shute, R., & Howitt, D. (1990). Unravelling the paradoxes of loneliness: Research and elements of a social theory of loneliness. *Social Behaviour, 5*, 169–184.

Slavin, L. A. (1991). Validation studies of the PEPSS: A measure of perceived emotional support for use with adolescents. *Journal of Adolescent Research, 6*, 316–335.

Slavin, L. A., & Rainer, K. L. (1990). Gender differences in emotional support and depressive symptoms among adolescents: A prospective analysis. *American Journal of Community Psychology, 18*, 407–421.

Slee, P. T. (1993). Bullying: A preliminary investigation of its nature and the effects of social cognition. *Early Child Development and Care, 87*, 47–57.

Sletta, O., Valas, H., Skaalvik, E., & Sobstad, F. (1996). Peer relations, loneliness, and self-perceptions in school-aged children. *British Journal of Educational Psychology, 66*, 431–445.

Slough, N. M., & Greenberg, M. T. (1990). Attachment and mental representations of self and other in five-year-olds. In I. Bretherton & M. Waston (Eds.), *New Directions Child Development*, (Vol. XX) San Francisco: Jossey-Bass.

Smetana, J. G. (1988a). Adolescents' and parents' conceptions of parental authority. *Child Development, 59*, 321–335.

Smetana, J. G. (1988b). Concepts of self and social convention: Adolescents' and parents' reasoning about hypothetical and actual family conflicts. In M. Gunnar & W. A. Collins (Eds.), *Development during the transition to adolescence:*

Minnesota Symposium on Child Psychology (Vol. 21, pp. 79–122). Hillsdale, NJ: Erlbaum.

Smith, T. W., & Greenberg, J. (1981). Depression and self-focused attention. *Motivation and Emotion, 5*(4), 323–331.

Snyder, C. R., Harris, C., Anderson, J. R., Holleran, S. A., Irving, L. M., Sigmon, S. T., Yoshinobu, L., Gibb, J., Lagnelle, C., & Harney, P. (1991). The will and the ways: Development and validation of an individual-difference measure of hope. *Journal of Personality and Social Psychology, 60*, 570–588.

Solano, C. H. (1980). Two measures of loneliness: A comparison. *Psychological Reports, 46*, 23–28.

Solano, C. H., Batten, P. G., & Parish, E. A. (1982). Loneliness and patterns of self-disclosure. *Journal of Personality and Social Psychology, 43*, 524–531.

Spetter, D. S., La Greca, A. M., Hogan, A., & Vaughn, S. (1992). Subgroups of rejected boys: Aggressive responses to peer conflict situations. *Journal of Clinical Child Psychology, 21*, 20–26.

Spielberger, C. D., Jacobs, G. A., Russell, S., & Crane, R. S. (1983). Assessment of anger: The State–Trait Anger Scale. In J. N. Butcher & C. D. Spielberger (Eds.), *Advances in personality assessment* (Vol. 2, pp. 161–189). Hillsdale, NJ: Erlbaum.

Spitzberg, B. H., & Hurt, H. T. (1987). The relationship of interpersonal competence and skills to reported loneliness across time. *Journal of Social Behavior and Personality, 2*(2, Pt. 2), 157–172.

Spitzer, R. L., Williams, J. B. W., Gibbon, M., & First, M. B. (1990). *Structured clinical interview for DSM–III–R – Non-patient edition* (SCID-NP, Version 1.0). Washington, DC: American Psychiatric Press.

Spores, J. M. (1994, October). *Developmental and behavioral correlates of loneliness in children and adolescents.* Paper presented at the New England Psychological Association, Hamden, CT.

Spores, J. M. (1995). *Developmental changes in understanding loneliness among children and adolescents.* Unpublished manuscript, Purdue University North Central.

Sroufe, L. A. (1990). An organizational perspective on the self. In D. Cicchetti & M. Beeghly (Eds.), *The self in transition: Infancy to childhood.* Chicago: University of Chicago Press.

Sroufe, L. A., & Fleeson, J. (1986). Attachment and the construction of relationships. In W. W. Hartup & Z. Rubin (Eds.), *The nature of relationships* (pp. 51–71). Hillsdale, NJ: Erlbaum.

Steele, J. R., & Brown, J. D. (1995). Adolescent room culture: Studying media in the context of everyday life. *Journal of Youth and Adolescence, 24*, 551–576.

Steinberg, L. (1987). Impact of puberty on family relations: Effects of pubertal status and pubertal timing. *Developmental Psychology, 23*, 451–460.

Steinberg, L. (1989). Pubertal maturation and parent–adolescent distance: An evolutionary perspective. In G. R. Adams, R. Montemayor, & T. P. Gullotta (Eds.), *Biology of adolescent behavior and development* (pp. 71–97). Newbury Park, CA: Sage.

Steinberg, L. (1990). Autonomy, conflict, and harmony in the family relationship. In S. Feldman & G. Elliot (Eds.), *At the threshold: The developing adolescent* (pp. 255–276). Cambridge, MA: Harvard University Press.

Steinberg, L., & Silverberg, S. (1986). The vicissitudes of autonomy in early adolescence. *Child Development, 57*, 473–476.

Stevenson, H. W., Parker, T., Wilkinson, A., Hegion, A., & Fish, E. (1976). Predictive value of teachers' ratings of young children. *Journal of Educational Psychology, 5*, 507–517.

Stocker, C. M. (1994). Children's perceptions of relationships with siblings, friends, and mothers: Compensatory processes and links with adjustment. *Journal of Child Psychology and Psychiatry, 35*, 1447–1459.

Stoddard, T. L. (1932). *Lonely America*. Garden City, NY: Doubleday/Doran.

Stokes, J. P. (1985). The relation of social network and individual difference variables to loneliness. *Journal of Personality and Social Psycholoay, 48*, 981–990.

Strauman, T. J., & Higgins, E. T. (1987). Automatic activation of self-discrepancies and emotional syndromes: When cognitive structures influence affect. *Journal of Personality and Social Psychology, 53*, 1004–1014.

Strauss, A. L. (1987). *Qualitative analyses for social scientists*. New York: Cambridge University Press.

Suedfeld, P. (1989). Past the reflection and through the looking-glass: Extending loneliness research. In M. Hojat & R. Crandall (Eds.), *Loneliness: Theory, research, and applications* (pp. 51–56). Newbury Park, CA: Sage.

Suess, G. J., Grossmann, K. E., & Sroufe, L. A. (1992). Effects of infant attachment to mother and father on quality of adaptation in preschool: From dyadic to individual organization of self. *International Journal of Behavioral Development, 15*, 43–65.

Sullivan, H. S. (1953). *The interpersonal theory of psychiatry*. New York: Norton.

Super, C., & Harkness, S. (1986). The developmental niche: A conceptualization at the interface of child and culture. *International Journal of Behavioral Development, 9*, 545–569.

Tangney, J. P., Burgraf, S. A., & Wagner, P. E. (1995). Shame-proneness, guilt-proneness, and psychological symptoms. In J. P. Tangney & K. W. Fischer (Eds.), *Self-conscious emotions: The psychology of shame, guilt, embarrassment, and pride* (pp. 174–197). New York: Guilford Press.

Tannen, D. (1990). *You just don't understand: Women and men in conversation*. New York: Morrow.

Tenbrink, S. S. (1990, March). *Management of time alone in early adolescence*. Paper presented at Biennial Meeting of the Society for Research on Adolescence, Atlanta, GA.

Terrell-Deutsch, B. (1991). *Loneliness in popular, average status and unpopular children*. Unpublished doctoral dissertation, University of Toronto, Toronto, Ontario, Canada.

Terrell-Deutsch, B. (1993). Loneliness in popular, average status and unpopular children. *Dissertation Abstracts International, 54*(05), 2778A (University Microfilms No. DANN78725).

Teyber, E. C., Messe, L. A., & Stollak, G. E. (1977). Adult responses to child communications. *Child Development, 48*, 1577–1582.

Thompson, J. K., & Heinberg, L. (1993). Preliminary test of two hypotheses of body image disturbance. *International Journal of Eating Disorders, 14*(1), 59–63.

Thompson, R. A., Connell, J. P., & Bridges, L. J. (1988). Temperament, emotion, and social interactive behavior in the strange situation: An analysis of attachment system functioning. *Child Development, 59,* 1102–1110.

Tischer, M., Lang-Takac, E., & Lang, M. (1992). The Children's Depression Scale: Review of Australian and overseas experience. *Australian Journal of Psychology, 44,* 27–35.

Townsend, P. (1968). Isolation, desolation and loneliness. In E. Shanas, P. Townsend, D. Wedderbum, H. Friis, P. Milhoj, & J. Stehouwer (Eds.), *Old people in three industrial societies* (pp. 258–287). New York: Atherton Press.

Townsend, P. (1973). Isolation and loneliness in the aged. In R. S. Weiss (Ed.), *Loneliness: The experience of emotional and social isolation* (pp. 175–188). Cambridge, MA: MIT Press.

Triandis, H. C. (1990). Cross-cultural studies of individualism and collectivism. *Nebraska Symposium on Motivation* Vol. 37, 41–133. Lincoln: University of Nebraska Press.

Troy, M., & Sroufe, L. A. (1987). Victimization among preschoolers: Role of attachment relationship history. *Journal of the American Academy of Child and Adolescent Psychiatry, 26,* 166–172.

Trueba, H. T., & Delgado-Gaitan, C. (1985). Socialization of Mexican children for cooperation and competition: Sharing and copying. *Journal of Educational Equity and Leadership, 5,* 189–204.

Turner, P. J. (1991). Relations between attachment, gender, and behavior with peers in preschool. *Child Development, 62,* 1475–1488.

van Buskirk, A. M., & Duke, M. P. (1991). The relationship between coping style and loneliness in adolescents: Can "sad passivity" be adaptive? *The Journal of Genetic Psychology, 152,* 145–157.

van den Boom, D. C. (1995). Do first-year intervention effects endure? Follow-up during toddlerhood of a sample of Dutch irritable infants. *Child Development, 66,* 1798–1816.

van IJzendoorn, M. H., & Kroonenberg, P. M. (1988). Cross-cultural patterns of attachment: A meta-analysis of the strange situation. *Child Development, 59,* 147–156.

van IJzendoorn, M. H., Kranenburg, M. J., Zwart-Woudstre, H. A., van Bussehback, A. M., & Lambermon, M. W. E. (1991). Parental attachment and children's socio-emotional development: Some findings on the validity of the Adult Attachment Interview in the Netherlands. *International Journal of Behavioral Development, 14,* 375–394.

Vandell, D. L. (1980). Sociability with peer and mother during the first year. *Developmental Psychology, 16,* 355–361.

Vandell, D. L., & Hembree, S. E. (1994). Peer social status and friendship: Independent contributors to children's social and academic adjustment. *Merrill-Palmer Quarterly, 40,* 461–477.

Vitkus, J., & Horowitz, L. M. (1987). Poor social performance of lonely people: Lacking a skill or adopting a role. *Journal of Personality and Social Psychology, 52,* 1266–1273.

Waas, G. A. (1988). Social attributional biases of peer-rejected and aggressive children. *Child Development, 59,* 969–992.

Wartner, U. G., Grossmann, K., Fremmer-Bombik, E., & Suess, G. (1994). Attachment patterns at age six in South Germany: Predictability from infancy and implications for preschool behavior. *Child Development, 65,* 1014–1027.

Waterman, A. S. (1984). *The psychology of individualism.* New York: Praeger.

Waters, E., & Sroufe, L. A. (1983). Social competence as a developmental construct. *Developmental Review, 3,* 79–97.

Weiss, R. (1973). *Loneliness: The experience of emotional and social isolation.* Cambridge, MA: MIT Press.

Waters, E., Vaughn, B. E., Posada, G., & Kondo-Ikemura, K. (Eds). (1995). Caregiving, cultural, and cognitive perspectives on security-based behavior and working models. *Monographs of the Society for Research in Child Development, 60* (2–3, Serial No. 244).

Waters, E., Wippman, J., & Sroufe, L. A. (1979). Attachment, positive affect and competence in the peer group: Two studies in construct validation. *Child Development, 50,* 821–829.

Weeks, D. G., Michela, J. L., Peplau, L. A., & Bragg, M. E. (1980). Relation between loneliness and depression: A structural equation analysis. *Journal of Personality and Social Psychology, 39,* 1238–1244.

Weiner, B. (1985). An attributional theory of achievement motivation and emotion. *Psychological Review, 92,* 548–573.

Weintraub, K. J. (1978). *The value of the individual.* Chicago: University of Chicago Press.

Weisfeld, G. E., Bloch, S. A., & Ivers, J. W. (1983). A factor analytic study of peer-perceived dominance in adolescent boys. *Adolescence, 18*(70), 229–243.

Weiss, R. S. (1973). *Loneliness: The experience of emotional and social isolation.* Cambridge, MA: MIT Press.

Weiss, R. S. (1974). The provisions of social relationships. In Z. Rubin (Ed.), *Doing unto others: Joining, molding, conforming, helping, loving* (pp. 17–26). Englewood Cliffs, NJ: Prentice Hall.

Weiss, R. S. (1982a). Attachment in adults. In C. M. Parkes & J. Stevenson-Hinde (Eds.), *The place of attachment in human behavior* (pp. 171–184). New York: Basic Books.

Weiss, R. S. (1982b). Issues in the study of loneliness. In L. A. Peplau & D. Perlman (Eds.), *Loneliness: Current theory research and therapy* (pp. 71–80). New York: Wiley.

Weiss, R. S. (1987). Reflections on the present state of loneliness research. *Journal of Social Behavior and Personality, 2,* 1–16.

Wentworth, W. M., & Yardley, D. (1994). Deep sociality: A bioevolutionary perspective on the sociology of emotions. In D. D. Franks, W. M. Wentworth, & J. Ryan (Eds.), *Perspectives on emotion* (pp. 21–56). Greenwich, CT: JAI Press.

Wenz, F. V. (1977). Seasonal suicide attempts and forms of loneliness. *Psychological Reports, 40,* 807–810.

Whitaker, A., Johnson, J., Shaffer, D., Rapoport, J. L., Kalikow, K., Walsh, B. T., Davies, M., Brairnan, S., & Dolinsky, A. (1990). Uncommon troubles in young people. *Archives of General Psychiatry, 47,* 487–496.

Wicker, R. W., Payne, G. C., & Morgan, R. D. (1983). Participant descriptions of guilt and shame. *Motivation and Emotion, 7*(1), 25–39.

Williams, G. A., & Asher, S. R. (1987, April). *Peer and self-perceptions of peer rejected children: Issues in classification and subgrouping.* Paper presented at the biennial meeting of the Society for Research in Child Development, Baltimore, MD.

Williams, G. A., & Asher, S. R. (1992). Assessment of loneliness at school among children with mild mental retardation. *American Journal of Mental Retardation, 96*, 376–385.

Williams, G. A., Ladd, G. W., & Asher, S. R. (1996, August). *Peer relationship provisions, victimization, and children's loneliness at school.* Paper presented at the XIVth Biennial Meeting of the International Society for the Study of Behavioral Development, Quebec City, Quebec, Canada.

Williams, J. G., & Solano, C. H. (1983). The social reality of feeling lonely: Friendship and reciprocation. *Personality and Social Psychology Bulletin, 9*, 237–242.

Wilson, D., Sibanda, J., Sibanda, P., & Wilson, C. (1989). Personality concomitants of loneliness among black and white male Zimbabwean adolescents. *The Journal of Social Psychology, 129*, 577–578.

Winnicott, D. (1958). The capacity to be alone. *International Journal of Psychoanalysis, 39*, 416–420.

Winnicott, D. W. (1965). *The maturational processes and the facilitating environment: Studies in the theory of emotional development.* New York: International Universities Press.

Wittenberg, M. T., & Reis, H. T. (1986). Loneliness, social skills, and social perception. *Personality and Social Psychology Bulletin, 12*, 121–130.

Wolfe, M. (1978). Childhood and privacy. In I. Altman & J. Wohlhill (Eds.), *Children and the environment* (pp. 175–222). New York: Plenum.

Wolfe, M., & Laufer, R. (1974). The concept of privacy in childhood and adolescence. In D. Carson (Ed.), *Man–environment interactions* (Part II). Stroudsburg, PA: Dowden, Hutchinson & Ross.

Wolfe, V. V., Finch, A. J., Jr., Saylor, C. F., Blount, R. L., Pallmeyer, T. P., & Carek, D. J. (1987). Negative affectivity in children: A multitrait–multimethod investigation. *Journal of Consulting and Clinical Psychology, 55*, 245–250.

Wood, L. A. (1986). Loneliness. In R. Harre (Ed.), *The social construction of emotions* (pp. 184–209). New York: Basil Blackwell.

Woodward, J. (1988). *The solitude of loneliness.* Lexington, MA: Lexington Books.

Woodward, J. C., & Kalyan-Masih, V. (1990). Loneliness, coping strategies and cognitive styles of the gifted rural adolescent. *Adolescence, 100*, 977–988.

Wright, J. C., Zakriski, A. L., & Fisher, P. (1996). Age differences in the correlates of perceived dominance. *Social Development, 5*(1), 25–39.

Yeates, K. O., & Selman, R. L. (1989). Social competence in the schools: Toward an interactive developmental model for intervention. *Developmental Review, 9*, 64–100.

Young, J. E. (1982). Loneliness, depression and cognitive therapy: Theory and application. In L. A. Peplau & D. Perlman (Eds.), *Loneliness: A sourcebook of current theory, research, and therapy* (pp. 379–405). New York: Wiley-Interscience.

Youngblade, L. M. (1990). *From family to friend: Links between the parent–child relationship and the child's relationship with a close friend.* Unpublished doctoral dissertation, Pennsylvania State University.

Youngblade, L. M., & Belsky, J. (1992). Parent–child antecedents of 5-year-olds' close friendships: A longitudinal analysis. *Developmental Psychology, 28,* 700–713.

Younger, A. J., & Boyko, K. A. (1987). Aggression and withdrawal as social schemas underlying children's peer perceptions. *Child Development, 58,* 1094–1100.

Younger, A. J., & Daniels, T. M. (1992). Children's reasons for nominating their peers as withdrawn: Passive withdrawal versus active isolation. *Developmental Psychology, 28,* 955–960.

Younger, A. J., Gentile, C., & Burgess, K. B. (1993). Children's perceptions of social withdrawal: Changes across age. In K. Rubin & J. Asendorpf (Eds.), *Social withdrawal, inhibition, and shyness in childhood* (pp. 215–235). Hillsdale, NJ: Erlbaum.

Youngren, M. A., & Lewinsohn, P. M. (1980). The functional relation between depression and problematic interpersonal behavior. *Journal of Abnormal Psychology, 89,* 333–341.

Youniss, J. (1980). *Parents and peers in social development.* Chicago: University of Chicago Press.

Youniss, J., & Smollar, J. (1985). *Adolescents relations with mothers, fathers, and friends.* Chicago: University of Chicago Press.

Zahn-Waxler, C., Denham, S., Iannotti, R. J., & Cummings, E. M. (1992). Peer relations in children with a depressed caregiver. In R. D. Parke & G. W. Ladd (Eds.), *Family–peer relationships: Modes of linkage* (pp. 317–344). Hillsdale, NJ: Erlbaum.

Zeanah, C., Benoit, D., Hirschberg, L., Barton, M., & Regan, C. (1995). Mothers' representations of their infants are concordant with infant attachment classifications. *Developmental Issues in Psychiatry and Psychology, 1,* 1–14.

Zilboorg, G. (1938, January). Loneliness. *The Atlantic Monthly,* 45–54.

Zukier, H. (1994). The twisted road to genocide: On the psychological development of evil during the holocaust. *Social Research, 61,* 423–455.

Author Index

Subject Index

Future Outlook by Bill Hoopes, 1997.